Yamaha
YFZ450 & YFZ450R ATVs
Service and Repair Manual

by Alan Ahlstrand

Models covered
YFZ450 and YFZ450R, 2004 through 2010

ABCDE
FGHIJ
KLMNO
PQRST

All rights reserved. No part of this book may be reproduced or transmitted in any form or by any means, electronic or mechanical, including photocopying, recording or by any information storage or retrieval system, without permission in writing from the copyright holder.

ISBN-13: **978-1-56392-899-4**
ISBN-10: **1-56392-899-X**

Library of Congress Control Number 2011921564
Printed in the USA

Haynes Publishing
Sparkford, Nr Yeovil, Somerset BA22 7JJ, England

© **Haynes North America, Inc. 2011**
With permission from J.H. Haynes & Co. Ltd.

Haynes North America, Inc
861 Lawrence Drive, Newbury Park, California 91320, USA

A book in the **Haynes Service and Repair Manual Series**

Contents

LIVING WITH YOUR YAMAHA ATV

Introduction

Yamaha - Musical Instruments to Motorcycles	Page	0•4
Acknowledgements	Page	0•7
About this manual	Page	0•7
Identification numbers	Page	0•8
Buying spare parts	Page	0•9
Safety first!	Page	0•10

Daily (pre-ride) checks

Engine/transmission oil level check	Page	0•11
Coolant level check	Page	0•12
Brake fluid level check	Page	0•13
Tire checks	Page	0•14

MAINTENANCE

Routine maintenance and servicing

Specifications	Page	1•1
Recommended lubricants and fluids	Page	1•2
Maintenance schedule	Page	1•3
Component locations	Page	1•4
Maintenance procedures	Page	1•6

Contents

REPAIRS AND OVERHAUL

Engine, transmission and associated systems

Engine, clutch and transmission	Page	2•1
Cooling system	Page	3•1
Fuel and exhaust systems (YFZ450)	Page	4A•1
Fuel and exhaust systems (YFZ450R)	Page	4B•1
Ignition and electrical systems	Page	5•1

Chassis and bodywork components

Steering, suspension and final drive	Page	6•1
Brakes, wheels and tires	Page	7•1
Bodywork and frame	Page	8•1

Wiring diagrams

Page 9•1

REFERENCE

Dimensions and Weights	Page	REF•1
Tools and Workshop Tips	Page	REF•4
Conversion Factors	Page	REF•22
Storage	Page	REF•24
Troubleshooting	Page	REF•27
Troubleshooting equipment	Page	REF•38
ATV chemicals and lubricants	Page	REF•42
Technical terms explained	Page	REF•43
Trail rules	Page	REF•50

Index

Page REF•51

Introduction

Yamaha
Musical instruments to Motorcycles

The Yamaha Motor Company

The Yamaha name can be traced back to 1889, when Torakusu Yamaha founded the Yamaha Organ Manufacturing Company. Such was the success of the company, that in 1897 it became Nippon Gakki Limited and manufactured a wide range of reed organs and pianos.

During World War II, Nippon Gakki's manufacturing base was utilised by the Japanese authorities to produce propellers and fuel tanks for their aviation industry. The end of the war brought about a huge public demand for low cost transport and many firms decided to utilise their obsolete aircraft tooling for the production of motorcycles. Nippon Gakki's first motorcycle went on sale in February 1955 and was named the 125 YA-1 Red Dragonfly. This machine was a copy of the German DKW RT125 motorcycle, featuring a single cylinder two-stroke engine with a four-speed gearbox. Due to the outstanding success of this model the motorcycle operation was separated from Nippon Gakki in July 1955 and the Yamaha Motor Company was formed.

The YA-1 also received acclaim by winning two of Japan's biggest road races, the Mt. Fuji Climbing race and the Asama Volcano race. The high level of public demand for the YA-1 led to the development of a whole series of two-stroke singles and twins.

Having made a large impact on their home market, Yamahas were exported to the USA in 1958 and to the UK in 1962. In the UK the signing of an Anglo-Japanese trade agreement during 1962 enabled the sale of Japanese lightweight motorcycles and scooters in Britain. At that time, competition between the many motorcycle producers in Japan had reduced numbers significantly and by the end of the sixties, only the big-four which are familiar with today remained.

Yamaha Europe was founded in 1968 and based in Holland. Although originally set up to market marine products, the Dutch base is now the official European Headquarters and distribution centre. Yamaha motorcycles are built at factories in Holland, Denmark, Norway, Italy, France, Spain and Portugal. Yamahas are imported into the UK by Yamaha Motor UK Ltd, formerly Mitsui Machinery Sales (UK) Ltd. Mitsui and Co. were originally a trading house, handling the shipping, distribution and marketing of Japanese products into western countries. Ultimately Mitsui Machinery Sales was formed to handle Yamaha motorcycles and outboard motors.

The FS1-E - first bike of many sixteen year olds in the UK

Introduction

Based on the technology derived from its motorcycle operation, Yamaha have produced many other products, such as automobile and lightweight aircraft engines, marine engines and boats, generators, pumps, ATVs, snowmobiles, golf cars, industrial robots, lawnmowers, swimming pools and archery equipment.

Two-strokes first

Part of Yamaha's success was a whole string of innovations in the two-stroke world. Autolube engine lubrication, pressed steel monocoque frame, electric starting, torque induction, multi-ported engines, reed valves and power valves kept their two-strokes at the forefront of technology.

In the 1960s and 70s the two-stroke engined YAS3 125, YDS1 to YDS7 250 and YR5 350 formed the core of Yamaha's range. By the mid-70s they had been superseded by the RD (Race-Developed) 125, 250, and 350 range of two-stroke twins, featuring improved 7 port engines with reed valve induction. Braking was improved by the use of an hydraulic brake on the front wheel of DX models, instead of the drum arrangement used previously, and cast alloy wheels were available as an option on later RD models. The RD350 was replaced by the RD400 in 1976.

Running parallel with the RD twins was a range of single-cylinder two-strokes. Used in a variety of chassis types, the engine was used in the popular 50 cc FS1-E moped, the V50 to 90 step-thrus, RS100 and 125, YB100 and the DT trail range.

The air-cooled single and twin cylinder RD models were eventually replaced by the LC series in 1980, featuring liquid-cooled engines, radical new styling, spiral pattern cast wheels and cantilever rear suspension (Yamaha's Monoshock). Of all the LC models, the RD350LC, or RD350R as it was later known, has made the most impact in the market. Later models had YPVS (Yamaha Power Valve System) engines, another first for Yamaha - this was essentially a valve located in the exhaust ports which was electronically operated to alter port timing to achieve maximum power output. The RD500LC was the largest two-stroke made by Yamaha and differed from the other LCs by the use of its vee-four cylinder engine.

With the exception of the RD350R, now manufactured in Brazil, the LC range has been discontinued. Two-stroke engined models have given way to environmental pressure, and thus with a few exceptions, such as the TZR125 and TZR250, are used only in scooters and small capacity bikes.

The distinctive paintwork and trim of the RD models

The Four-strokes

Yamaha concentrated solely on two-stroke models until 1970 when the XS1 was produced, their first four-stroke motorcycle. It was perhaps Yamaha's success with two-strokes that postponed an earlier move into the four-stroke motorcycle market, although their work with Toyota during the 1960s had given them a sound base in four-stroke technology.

The XS1 had a 650 cc twin-cylinder SOHC engine and was later to become known as the XS650, appearing also in the popular SE custom form. Yamaha introduced a three cylinder 750 cc engine in 1976, fitted in a sport-tourer frame and called the XS750, TX750 in the USA. The XS750 established itself well in the sport tourer class and remained in production with very few changes until uprated to 850 cc in 1980.

Other four-strokes followed in 1976, with the introduction of the XS250/360/400 series twins. The XS range was strengthened in 1978

The XS650 led the way for Yamaha's four-stroke range

Introduction

Yamaha's XS750 was produced from 1976 to 1982 and then uprated to 850 cc

by the four-cylinder XS1100.

The 1980s saw a new family of four-strokes, the XJ550, 650, 750 and 900 Fours. Improvements over the XS range amounted to a slimmer DOHC engine unit due to the relocation of the alternator behind the cylinders, electronic ignition and uprated braking and suspension systems. Models were available mainly in standard trim, although custom-styled Maxims were produced especially for the US market. The XJ650T was the first model from Yamaha to have a turbo-charged engine. Although these early XJ models have now been discontinued, their roots live on in the XJ600S and XJ900S Diversion (Seca II) models.

The FZR prefix encompasses the pure sports Yamaha models. With the exception of the 16-valve FZR400 and FZR600 models, the FZ/FZR750 and FZR1000 used 20-valve engines, two exhaust valves and three inlet valves per cylinder. This concept was called Genesis and gave improved gas flow to the combustion chambers. Other features of the new engine were the use of down-draught carburetors and the engine's inclined angle in the frame, plus the change to liquid-cooling. Lightweight Deltabox design aluminium frames and uprated suspension improved the bikes's handling. The Genesis engine lives on in the YZF750 and 1000 models.

The vee-twin engine has been the mainstay of the XV Virago range. Since 1981 XVs have been produced in 535, 700, 750, 920, 1000 and 1100 engine sizes, all using the same basic air-cooled sohc vee-twin engine. Other uses of vee engines have been in the XZ550 of the early 1980s, the XVZ12 Venture and the mighty VMX-12 V-Max.

Anti-lock braking, engine management and catalytic converters are all features found on present-day models, ensuring that Yamaha remains at the forefront of technology.

Yamaha's entry into the field of four-stroke off-road competition came in 1998 with the introduction of the YZ400F motocrosser and its companion, the WR400F enduro bike. The WR was basically the same as the YZ, but with lights and wide-ratio transmission gears (hence the WR designation). Since the introduction, the four-strokes have enjoyed growing success.

Yamaha entered the ATV market in 1980 with the YT125 Tri-Moto three-wheeler. A competitor to Honda's ATC (All-Terrain Cycle) models, the Tri-Moto featured a 123cc air-cooled 2-stroke engine, five-speed transmission with reverse, and chain drive. Several other three-wheel models were added over the next five years. Production of three-wheelers was discontinued by all ATV manufacturers after the 1985 model year.

The company's first four-wheeler was the 1985 YFM200, introduced in 1984. The engine was a 196cc four-stroke single with an overhead cam. Power was transferred to the five-speed transmission by an automatic centrifugal clutch, and from the transmission to the rear wheels by a driveshaft. The transmission included reverse gear.

The first automatic transmission ATV was the Breeze in 1986. A centrifugal clutch transferred engine power to a continuously variable belt-drive transmission. The Breeze also had reverse gear.

The YFZ450, built around the engine/transmission unit from the YZF450 motocross bike, was a significant addition to Yamaha's sport ATV line, beginning in 2004. The YFZ450 continued mostly unchanged for several years. In 2009 the YFZ450R, a motocross

A new family of four-strokes was released in 1980 with the introduction of the XJ range

variant of the YFZ450, was introduced, with fuel injection replacing the carburetor and significant modifications to the chassis.

Yamaha has continued to increase its range of models, adding youth ATV's as small as 60 cc and sport and utility ATVs as large as 686 cc. Carburetors are being replaced by fuel injection, and sophisticated improvements such as power steering have been introduced on larger models.

Acknowledgements

Our thanks to GP Sports of Santa Clara and San Jose, California, for supplying the ATVs used in the photographs throughout this manual; to David Guy, service manager, for arranging the teardowns and fitting them into GP Sports' busy schedule; and to Craig Wardner, service technician, for doing the mechanical work and providing valuable technical information.

About this manual

The aim of this manual is to help you get the best value from your motorcycle. It can do so in several ways. It can help you decide what work must be done, even if you choose to have it done by a dealer; it provides information and procedures for routine maintenance and servicing; and it offers diagnostic and repair procedures to follow when trouble occurs.

We hope you use the manual to tackle the work yourself. For many simpler jobs, doing it yourself may be quicker than arranging an appointment to get the vehicle into a dealer and making the trips to leave it and pick it up. More importantly, a lot of money can be saved by avoiding the expense the shop must pass on to you to cover its labor and overhead costs. An added benefit is the sense of satisfaction and accomplishment that you feel after doing the job yourself.

References to the left or right side of the vehicle assume you are sitting on the seat, facing forward.

We take great pride in the accuracy of information given in this manual, but motorcycle manufacturers make alterations and design changes during the production run of a particular motorcycle of which they do not inform us. No liability can be accepted by the authors or publishers for loss, damage or injury caused by any errors in, or omissions from, the information given.

Identification numbers

Engine and frame numbers

The frame serial number is stamped into the right side of the frame. The engine number is stamped into the crankcase and is visible from the right side of the machine. Both of these numbers should be recorded and kept in a safe place so they can be given to law enforcement officials in the event of a theft.

The frame serial number and engine serial number should also be kept in a handy place (such as with your driver's license) so they are always available when purchasing or ordering parts for your machine.

Year and model	Initial vehicle identification
2004 YFZ450S	JY4AJ11Y74C000026
2005 YFZ450T	JY4AJ11Y75C023898
2006	
YFZ450V	JY4AJ11Y74C000026
YFZ450BBV Bill Ballance Edition	JY4AJ20Y96C003293
YFZ450SPV 50th Anniversary Special Edition	JY4AJ20Y36C010403
2007	
YFZ450W	JY4AJ20Y87C021141
YFZ450BBW Bill Ballance Edition	JY4AJ20Y67C026418
YFZ450SPW Special Edition	JY4AJ20Y67C025740
2008	
YFZ450X	JY4AJ35Y38C000004
YFZ450SPX Special Edition	JY4AJ35Y68C001311
YFZ450SP2X Special Edition II	JY4AJ35Y18C001426
2009	
YFZ450Y	JY4AJ35Y39C012011
YFZ450RY	Not available
2010	
YFZ450RZ	Not available

Identification numbers 0•9

Buying spare parts

Once you have found all the identification numbers, record them for reference when buying parts. Since the manufacturers change specifications, parts and vendors (companies that manufacture various components on the machine), providing the ID numbers is the only way to be reasonably sure that you are buying the correct parts.

Whenever possible, take the worn part to the dealer so direct comparison with the new component can be made. Along the trail from the manufacturer to the parts shelf, there are numerous places that the part can end up with the wrong number or be listed incorrectly.

The two places to purchase new parts for your motorcycle – the accessory store and the franchised dealer – differ in the type of parts they carry. While dealers can obtain virtually every part for your ATV, the accessory dealer is usually limited to normal high wear items such as shock absorbers, tune-up parts, various engine gaskets, cables, chains, brake parts, etc. Rarely will an accessory outlet have major suspension components, cylinders, transmission gears, or cases.

Used parts can be obtained for considerably less than new ones, but you can't always be sure of what you're getting. Once again, take your worn part to the salvage yard for direct comparison.

Whether buying new, used or rebuilt parts, the best course is to deal directly with someone who specializes in parts for your particular make.

The engine number is stamped into the right side of the crankcase

The frame serial number is stamped into the left frame rail forward of the footrest

Safety first!

Professional mechanics are trained in safe working procedures. However enthusiastic you may be about getting on with the job at hand, take the time to ensure that your safety is not put at risk. A moment's lack of attention can result in an accident, as can failure to observe simple precautions.

There will always be new ways of having accidents, and the following is not a comprehensive list of all dangers; it is intended rather to make you aware of the risks and to encourage a safe approach to all work you carry out on your bike.

Asbestos

● Certain friction, insulating, sealing and other products - such as brake pads, clutch linings, gaskets, etc. - contain asbestos. Extreme care must be taken to avoid inhalation of dust from such products since it is hazardous to health. If in doubt, assume that they do contain asbestos.

Fire

● Remember at all times that gasoline is highly flammable. Never smoke or have any kind of naked flame around, when working on the vehicle. But the risk does not end there - a spark caused by an electrical short-circuit, by two metal surfaces contacting each other, by careless use of tools, or even by static electricity built up in your body under certain conditions, can ignite gasoline vapor, which in a confined space is highly explosive. Never use gasoline as a cleaning solvent. Use an approved safety solvent.

● Always disconnect the battery ground terminal before working on any part of the fuel or electrical system, and never risk spilling fuel on to a hot engine or exhaust.

● It is recommended that a fire extinguisher of a type suitable for fuel and electrical fires is kept handy in the garage or workplace at all times. Never try to extinguish a fuel or electrical fire with water.

Fumes

● Certain fumes are highly toxic and can quickly cause unconsciousness and even death if inhaled to any extent. Gasoline vapor comes into this category, as do the vapors from certain solvents such as trichloro-ethylene. Any draining or pouring of such volatile fluids should be done in a well ventilated area.

● When using cleaning fluids and solvents, read the instructions carefully. Never use materials from unmarked containers - they may give off poisonous vapors.

● Never run the engine of a motor vehicle in an enclosed space such as a garage. Exhaust fumes contain carbon monoxide which is extremely poisonous; if you need to run the engine, always do so in the open air or at least have the rear of the vehicle outside the workplace.

The battery

● Never cause a spark, or allow a naked light near the vehicle's battery. It will normally be giving off a certain amount of hydrogen gas, which is highly explosive.

● Always disconnect the battery ground terminal before working on the fuel or electrical systems (except where noted).

● If possible, loosen the filler plugs or cover when charging the battery from an external source. Do not charge at an excessive rate or the battery may burst.

● Take care when topping up, cleaning or carrying the battery. The acid electrolyte, even when diluted, is very corrosive and should not be allowed to contact the eyes or skin. Always wear rubber gloves and goggles or a face shield. If you ever need to prepare electrolyte yourself, always add the acid slowly to the water; never add the water to the acid.

Electricity

● When using an electric power tool, inspection light etc., always ensure that the appliance is correctly connected to its plug and that, where necessary, it is properly grounded. Do not use such appliances in damp conditions and, again, beware of creating a spark or applying excessive heat in the vicinity of fuel or fuel vapor. Also ensure that the appliances meet national safety standards.

● A severe electric shock can result from touching certain parts of the electrical system, such as the spark plug wires (HT leads), when the engine is running or being cranked, particularly if components are damp or the insulation is defective. Where an electronic ignition system is used, the secondary (HT) voltage is much higher and could prove fatal.

Remember...

✗ **Don't** start the engine without first ascertaining that the transmission is in neutral.

✗ **Don't** suddenly remove the pressure cap from a hot cooling system - cover it with a cloth and release the pressure gradually first, or you may get scalded by escaping coolant.

✗ **Don't** attempt to drain oil until you are sure it has cooled sufficiently to avoid scalding you.

✗ **Don't** grasp any part of the engine or exhaust system without first ascertaining that it is cool enough not to burn you.

✗ **Don't** allow brake fluid or antifreeze to contact the machine's paintwork or plastic components.

✗ **Don't** siphon toxic liquids such as fuel, hydraulic fluid or antifreeze by mouth, or allow them to remain on your skin.

✗ **Don't** inhale dust - it may be injurious to health (see Asbestos heading).

✗ **Don't** allow any spilled oil or grease to remain on the floor - wipe it up right away, before someone slips on it.

✗ **Don't** use ill-fitting wrenches or other tools which may slip and cause injury.

✗ **Don't** lift a heavy component which may be beyond your capability - get assistance.

✗ **Don't** rush to finish a job or take unverified short cuts.

✗ **Don't** allow children or animals in or around an unattended vehicle.

✗ **Don't** inflate a tire above the recommended pressure. Apart from overstressing the carcass, in extreme cases the tire may blow off forcibly.

✔ **Do** ensure that the machine is supported securely at all times. This is especially important when the machine is blocked up to aid wheel or fork removal.

✔ **Do** take care when attempting to loosen a stubborn nut or bolt. It is generally better to pull on a wrench, rather than push, so that if you slip, you fall away from the machine rather than onto it.

✔ **Do** wear eye protection when using power tools such as drill, sander, bench grinder etc.

✔ **Do** use a barrier cream on your hands prior to undertaking dirty jobs - it will protect your skin from infection as well as making the dirt easier to remove afterwards; but make sure your hands aren't left slippery. Note that long-term contact with used engine oil can be a health hazard.

✔ **Do** keep loose clothing (cuffs, ties etc. and long hair) well out of the way of moving mechanical parts.

✔ **Do** remove rings, wristwatch etc., before working on the vehicle - especially the electrical system.

✔ **Do** keep your work area tidy - it is only too easy to fall over articles left lying around.

✔ **Do** exercise caution when compressing springs for removal or installation. Ensure that the tension is applied and released in a controlled manner, using suitable tools which preclude the possibility of the spring escaping violently.

✔ **Do** ensure that any lifting tackle used has a safe working load rating adequate for the job.

✔ **Do** get someone to check periodically that all is well, when working alone on the vehicle.

✔ **Do** carry out work in a logical sequence and check that everything is correctly assembled and tightened afterwards.

✔ **Do** remember that your vehicle's safety affects that of yourself and others. If in doubt on any point, get professional advice.

● If in spite of following these precautions, you are unfortunate enough to injure yourself, seek medical attention as soon as possible.

Daily (pre-ride) checks 0•11

1 Engine/transmission case oil level check

Warning: *On models with an oil level dipstick, never remove the dipstick to check oil level immediately after hard or high-speed riding. Hot oil could spurt out and cause burns. Let the engine cool to approximately 70-degrees C (150-degrees F) before removing the dipstick.*

Before you start:
✔ The engine and transmission share a common oil supply, which is checked through the oil tank filler plug/dipstick.
✔ Park the vehicle in a level position, then start the engine and allow it to reach normal operating temperature. **Caution:** *Do not run the engine in an enclosed space such as a garage or shop.*
✔ Stop the engine and allow the machine to sit undisturbed in a level position for about five minutes.

Vehicle care:
● If you have to add oil frequently, you should check whether you have any oil leaks. If there is no sign of oil leakage from the joints and gaskets the engine could be burning oil (see *Troubleshooting*).

The correct oil
● Modern, high-revving engines place great demands on their oil. It is very important that the correct oil for your bike is used.
● Always top up with a good quality oil of the specified type and viscosity and do not overfill the engine.

Oil type
API grade SG or higher meeting JASO standard MA - the MA standard is required to prevent clutch slippage. See Chapter 1 for viscosity ratings.

1 Warm the engine to normal operating temperature, let it idle for 10 seconds, shut it off and let the oil settle for several minutes. Remove the dipstick from the oil tank (this is a YFZ450) . . .

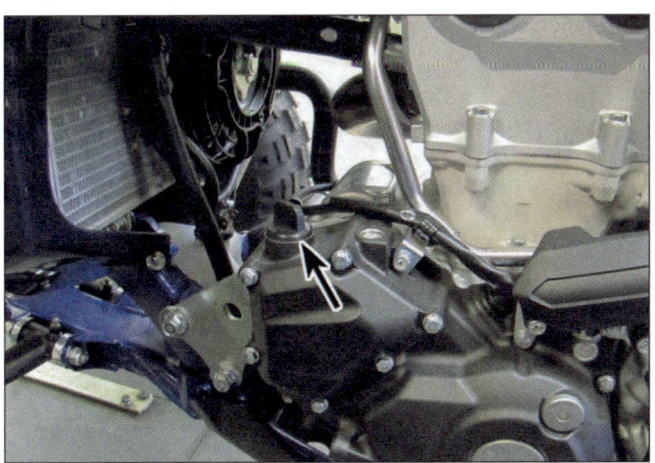

2 . . . and this is a YFZ450R. Wipe the dipstick with a clean rag and put it back in the tank (don't screw it in - just let it rest on the threads). Pull the dipstick out and check the oil level on the dipstick scale.

3 If the oil level is low on a YFZ450, unscrew the oil filler cap (arrow). On YFZ450R models, oil is added through the dipstick hole. Add enough oil of the specified grade and type to bring the level on the dipstick up to the upper mark. Do not overfill.

0•12 Daily (pre-ride) checks

2 Coolant level check

 Warning: DO NOT remove the radiator cap while the engine is warm or scalding coolant will spray out. Let the engine cool down before removing the cap.

Before you start:
✔ Make sure you have a supply of coolant available (a mixture of 50% distilled water and 50% corrosion inhibited ethylene glycol antifreeze is needed).
✔ Always check the coolant level when the engine is cold.

 Warning: Antifreeze is poisonous. Do not leave open containers of coolant about.

 Warning: Do not run the engine in an enclosed space such as a garage or workshop.

✔ Make sure the motorcycle is on level ground while checking the coolant level.

Bike care:
● Use only the specified coolant mixture. It is important that anti-freeze is used in the system all year round, and not just in the winter. Do not top the system up using only water, as the system will become too diluted.
● Do not overfill the reservoir tank. If the coolant is significantly above the F (full) level line at any time, the surplus should be siphoned or drained off to prevent the possibility of it being expelled out of the overflow hose.
● If the coolant level falls steadily, check the system for leaks (see Chapter 1). If no leaks are found and the level continues to fall, it is recommended that the machine is taken to a Yamaha dealer for a pressure test.

1 Check coolant level in the reservoir under the left rear fender (YFZ450) . . .

2 . . . or at the left front of the vehicle (YFZ450R). It should be between the Low and Full marks with the engine warmed up. If it's low, top off the reservoir with a 50/50 mixture of ethylene glycol-based antifreeze and distilled water, then reinstall the cap.

Daily (pre-ride) checks

3 Brake fluid level check

> **Warning:** Brake fluid can harm your eyes and damage painted or some plastic surfaces, so use extreme caution when handling and pouring it and cover surrounding surfaces with rag. Do not use fluid that has been standing open for some time, as it absorbs moisture from the air which can cause a dangerous loss of braking effectiveness.

Before you start:
✔ Make sure the vehicle is on level ground.
✔ Make sure you have the correct brake fluid. DOT 4 is recommended. Never reuse old fluid.

✔ Wrap a rag around the reservoir to ensure that any spillage does not come into contact with painted surfaces.

Vehicle care:
● The fluid in the front or rear master cylinder reservoir will drop slightly as the brake pads wear down.

● If the fluid reservoir requires repeated topping-up this is an indication of a hydraulic leak somewhere in the system, which should be investigated immediately.

● Check for signs of fluid leakage from the hydraulic hoses and components – if found, rectify immediately.

● Check the operation of the front and rear brakes before taking the machine on the road; if there is evidence of air in the system (spongy feel to lever), it must be bled as described in Chapter 7.

1 With the front brake reservoir as level as possible, check that the fluid level is above the LOWER line next to the inspection window. If the level is below the LOWER line, remove the cover screws (arrows) and lift off the cover and diaphragm. Top up fluid to the upper level line; don't overfill the reservoir, and take care to avoid spills (see WARNING above). Compress the diaphragm, reinstall the diaphragm and cover, and tighten the cover screws securely.

2 Check rear brake fluid level through the translucent reservoir. It should be between the upper and lower lines. If it's low, remove the seat (all models) and right side cover (YFZ450) for access to the reservoir cap. Unscrew the cap and lift it off. Add the specified brake fluid until the level is up to the upper line on the reservoir, then install the cap and tighten it securely.

Daily (pre-ride) checks

3 Tire checks

The correct pressures:
- The tires must be checked when **cold**, not immediately after riding. Note that low tire pressures may cause the tire to slip on the rim or come off. High tire pressures will cause abnormal tread wear and unsafe handling.
- Use an accurate pressure gauge.
- Proper air pressure will increase tire life and provide maximum stability and ride comfort.

Tire care:
- Check the tires carefully for cuts, tears, embedded nails or other sharp objects and excessive wear. Operation of the motorcycle with excessively worn tires is extremely hazardous, as traction and handling are directly affected.
- Check the condition of the tire valve and ensure the dust cap is in place.
- Pick out any stones or nails which may have become embedded in the tire tread. If left, they will eventually penetrate through the casing and cause a puncture.
- If tire damage is apparent, or unexplained loss of pressure is experienced, seek the advice of a tire fitting specialist without delay.

Tire tread depth:
The minimum tread depth for these vehicles is 3 mm (1/8 inch) for all others. To maintain good performance and handling, check the profile of the knobs on the tires as well as the tread depth. When the knobs begin to get excessively rounded on their edges, the tire should be replaced.

Tire pressures

2004 and 2005
- Front   4.4 psi (30 kPa)
- Rear   5.0 psi (35 kPa)

2006 and later
- Front   4.0 psi (27.5 kPa)
- Rear   4.4 psi (30 kPa)

1 Unscrew the cap from the tire valve and measure air pressure with a gauge designed for the low pressures used in ATV tires

2 Measure tread depth with a depth gauge or tape measure

Service record

Date　　　Mileage　　　　　Work performed

Service record

Date *Mileage* *Work performed*

Chapter 1
Tune-up and routine maintenance

Contents

Air filter element and drain tube - cleaning	14
Battery - check	23
Brake levers and pedal - check and adjustment	5
Brake system - general check	4
Carburetor adjustment	26
Choke (carbureted models) - operation check	22
Clutch lever freeplay - check and adjustment	19
Compression check	See Chapter 2
Cooling system - inspection and coolant change	18
Drive chain and sprockets - check, adjustment and lubrication	8
Engine oil and filter - change	17
Exhaust system - inspection	25
Fasteners - check	12
Fluid levels - check	3
Front wheel bearings - check	10
Fuel system - inspection	15
Idle speed - check and adjustment	20
Introduction to tune-up and routine maintenance	2
Lubrication - general	11
Routine maintenance intervals	1
Skid plates - check	13
Spark plug - inspection, cleaning and gapping	16
Steering system - inspection and toe-in adjustment	6
Suspension - check	7
Throttle cable and speed limiter - check and adjustment	21
Tires/wheels - general check	9
Valve clearance - check and adjustment	24

Degrees of difficulty

| Easy, suitable for novice with little experience | Fairly easy, suitable for beginner with some experience | Fairly difficult, suitable for competent DIY mechanic | Difficult, suitable for experienced DIY mechanic  | Very difficult, suitable for expert DIY or professional  |

Specifications

Engine
Spark plug
   Type NGKCR8E
   Gap .... 0.7 to 0.8 mm (0.028 to 0.031 inch)
Valve clearance
   Intake .... 0.10 to 0.15 mm (0.004 to 0.006 inch)
   Exhaust .... 0.20 to 0.25 mm (0.008 to 0.010 inch)
Engine idle speed
   YFZ450 .... 1750 to 1850 rpm
   YFZ450R .... 1950 to 2050 rpm

Chassis

Brake pad thickness (limit)	1.0 mm (0.03 inch)
Front brake lever freeplay	
YFZ450	Zero
YFZ450R	Not specified
Rear brake pedal height	11.7 mm (0.46 inch) below footpeg
Brake pedal adjusting bolt limit	2.2 to 3.2 mm (0.09 to 0.13 inch)
Throttle lever freeplay	2 to 4 mm (0.08 to 0.16 inch)
Clutch lever freeplay	8 to 13 mm (0.31 to 0.51 inch)
Drive chain slack	25 to 35 mm (1.0 to 1.38 inches)
Speed limiter screw setting	Do not back out more than 12 mm (0.47 inch)
Minimum tire tread depth	See *Daily (pre-ride) checks*
Tire pressures (cold)	See *Daily (pre-ride) checks*
Front wheel toe-in	0 to 10 mm (0 to 0.4 inch)

Torque specifications

Coolant drain bolt	10 Nm (84 in-lbs)
Oil drain bolt	20 Nm (168 in-lbs)
Oil filter cover bolts	10 Nm (84 in-lbs)
Spark plugs	13 Nm (113 in-lbs)
Tie rod locknuts	
YFZ450	15 Nm (132 in-lbs)
YFZ450R	18 Nm (156 in-lbs)

Recommended lubricants and fluids

Engine oil	
Type	Yamalube 4-CW or Yamalube 4 or equivalent API Service SG or higher, meeting JASO Standard MA*
	To avoid clutch slippage, do not use oils rated diesel CD or Energy Conserving II.
Viscosity	
50-degrees F (10-degrees C) or above	20W-50
10-degrees to 110-degrees F (-10 to 40-degrees C)	10W-40
30-degrees F (0-degrees C) or below	5W-30
Capacity (YFZ450)	
At oil change (without filter replacement)	1.75 liters (1.85 quarts)
At oil change (with filter replacement)	1.85 liters (1.96 quarts)
After engine overhaul	1.95 liters (2.06 quarts)
Capacity (YFZ450R)	
At oil change (without filter replacement)	1.4 liters (1.48 quarts)
At oil change (with filter replacement)	1.45 liters (1.53 quarts)
After engine overhaul	1.65 liters (1.74 quarts)
Air filter oil	Yamaha foam air filter oil, or 10W-30 engine oil
Cooling system	
System capacity	
YFZ450	1.3 liters (1.37 quarts)
YFZ450R	1.25 liters (1.32 quarts)
Reservoir tank capacity	
YFZ450	0.29 liter (0.31 quart)
YFZ450R	0.25 liter (0.26 quart)
Miscellaneous	
Wheel bearings	Medium weight, lithium-based multi-purpose grease
Swingarm pivot bearings	Medium weight, lithium-based multi-purpose grease
Steering shaft bushings	Medium weight, lithium-based multi-purpose grease
Cables and lever pivots	Medium weight, lithium-based multi-purpose grease
Brake pedal/shift lever/throttle lever pivots	Medium weight, lithium-based multi-purpose grease

1 Yamaha YFZ450/X/R Routine maintenance intervals

Note: *The pre-ride inspection outlined in the owner's manual covers checks and maintenance that should be carried out on a daily basis. It's condensed and included here to remind you of its importance. Always perform the pre-ride inspection at every maintenance interval (in addition to the procedures listed). The intervals listed below are the shortest intervals recommended by the manufacturer for each particular operation during the model years covered in this manual. Your owner's manual may have different intervals for your model.*

Daily or before riding
- [ ] Check the operation of both brakes - check the brake lever and pedal for correct freeplay
- [ ] Check the throttle for smooth operation and correct freeplay
- [ ] Make sure the engine kill switch works correctly
- [ ] Check the tires for damage, the presence of foreign objects and correct air pressure
- [ ] Check the engine oil level
- [ ] Check the fuel level and inspect for leaks
- [ ] Check the air cleaner drain tube and clean it if necessary
- [ ] If the drain tube is clogged, clean the air filter element
- [ ] Inspect the drive chain
- [ ] Make sure the steering operates smoothly
- [ ] Verify that the headlight and taillight are operating satisfactorily
- [ ] Check all fasteners, including wheel nuts and axle nuts, for tightness
- [ ] Check the underbody for mud or debris that could start a fire or interfere with vehicle operation

Every 20 to 40 hours
- [ ] Clean the air filter element and replace it if necessary*

More often in dusty or wet conditions.

Every six months (1600 miles, 2500 kilometers)
- [ ] Change the engine oil
- [ ] Clean and gap and, if necessary, replace the spark plug(s)
- [ ] Inspect the fuel tap (carbureted models) and fuel line (all models)
- [ ] Check the throttle for smooth operation and correct freeplay
- [ ] Check choke operation (carbureted models)
- [ ] Check idle speed (all models) and adjust it if necessary (carbureted models)
- [ ] Inspect the front and rear brake discs
- [ ] Check brake operation and brake lever and pedal freeplay
- [ ] Check the clutch for smooth operation and correct lever freeplay
- [ ] Lubricate the steering shaft and front suspension
- [ ] Lubricate and inspect the drive chain, sprockets and rollers
- [ ] Check steering system operation and freeplay
- [ ] Inspect the wheels and tires
- [ ] Check the wheel bearings for looseness or damage
- [ ] Inspect the front and rear suspension
- [ ] Check all chassis fasteners for tightness
- [ ] Check the skid plates for looseness or damage
- [ ] Check the exhaust system for leaks and check fastener tightness

1•4 Tune-up and routine maintenance

Maintenance points - left side

1. Air filter (under seat)
2. Battery (under seat)
3. Drive chain
4. Valve clearances
5. Engine oil dipstick (YFZ450R shown; YFZ450 similar)
6. YFZ450R coolant reservoir
7. Headlight adjuster
8. Clutch and parking brake levers

Tune-up and routine maintenance 1•5

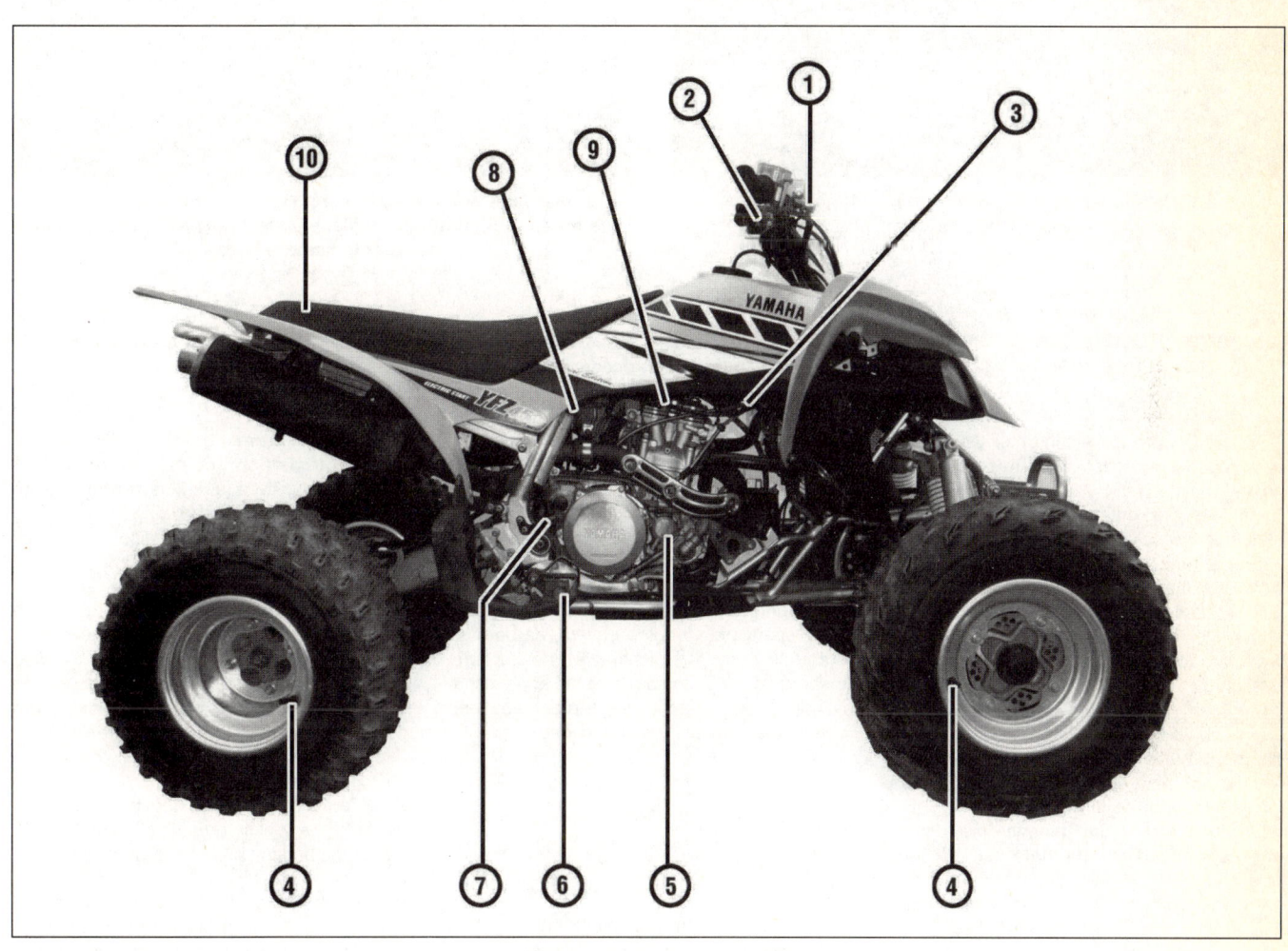

Maintenance points - right side

1. Front brake fluid reservoir
2. Throttle lever
3. Clutch and parking brake cable mid-line adjusters
4. Tire pressures
5. Oil filter
6. Brake pedal
7. Rear brake light switch
8. Rear brake fluid reservoir
9. Spark plug
10. YFZ450 coolant reservoir (under left rear fender)

2.1 Decals on the vehicle include maintenance and safety information

4.5 Press the brake pedal to bring the pads out where you can see the friction material - replace pads if they're worn to or near the wear indicators (arrow)

2 Introduction to tune-up and routine maintenance

This Chapter covers in detail the checks and procedures necessary for the tune-up and routine maintenance of your vehicle. Section 1 includes the routine maintenance schedule, which is designed to keep the machine in proper running condition and prevent possible problems. The remaining Sections contain detailed procedures for carrying out the items listed on the maintenance schedule, as well as additional maintenance information designed to increase reliability. Maintenance information is also printed on decals, which are mounted in various locations on the vehicle **(see illustration)**. Where information on the decals differs from that presented in this Chapter, use the decal information.

Since routine maintenance plays such an important role in the safe and efficient operation of your vehicle, it is presented here as a comprehensive check list. These lists outline the procedures and checks that should be done on a routine basis.

Deciding where to start or plug into the routine maintenance schedule depends on several factors. If you have a vehicle whose warranty has recently expired, and if it has been maintained according to the warranty standards, you may want to pick up routine maintenance as it coincides with the next mileage or calendar interval. If you have owned the machine for some time but have never performed any maintenance on it, then you may want to start at the nearest interval and include some additional procedures to ensure that nothing important is overlooked. If you have just had a major engine overhaul, then you may want to start the maintenance routine from the beginning. If you have a used machine and have no knowledge of its history or maintenance record, you may desire to combine all the checks into one large service initially and then settle into the maintenance schedule prescribed.

The Sections that describe the inspection and maintenance procedures are written as step-by-step comprehensive guides to the actual performance of the work. They explain in detail each of the routine inspections and maintenance procedures on the check list. References to additional information in applicable Chapters is also included and should not be overlooked.

Before beginning any actual maintenance or repair, the machine should be cleaned thoroughly, especially around the oil filler plug, spark plug, engine covers, carburetor or throttle body, etc. Cleaning will help ensure that dirt does not contaminate the engine and will allow you to detect wear and damage that could otherwise easily go unnoticed.

3 Fluid levels - check

Check, and if necessary, top up, the front brake fluid, rear brake fluid, engine oil and coolant as described in *Daily (Pre-ride) checks* at the front of this manual.

4 Brake system - general check

1 Always inspect the brakes before riding! A routine pre-ride general check will ensure that problems are discovered and remedied before they become dangerous.
2 Inspect the brake lever and pedal for loose pivots, excessive play, bending, cracking and other damage. Replace any damaged parts (see Chapter 7).
3 Make sure all brake fasteners are tight.
4 Squeeze the front brake lever so that the brake pads protrude from the calipers and look at the wear indicators. If the pad material has been worn down so that the wear indicators touch the disc - or are getting close to the disc - it's time for new pads (see Chapter 7).
5 Depress the rear brake pedal so that the pads protrude from the caliper and look at the wear indicators **(see illustration)**. Again, if the pad material is worn down so that the indicators are at or near the disc, install new pads (see Chapter 7).
6 If you have difficulty determining whether the pads are excessively worn because the wear indicator is hard to see (or you have aftermarket pads that don't have any kind of indicator), remove the pads (see Chapter 7), measure the thickness of the pads and compare your measurements to the pad thickness limits listed in this Chapter's Specifications.
7 Verify that the parking brake system will hold the vehicle on an incline. If it won't, adjust the parking brake (see Chapter 7).
8 These vehicles are equipped with a brake light which is activated by a brake light switch **(see illustration)** at the rear brake pedal. Make sure that the brake light works when the rear brake pedal is applied (it should come on just before the brake light begins to work). If it doesn't, hold the body of the brake light switch so that it doesn't turn, and rotate the switch adjusting nut as necessary.

5 Brake levers and pedal - check and adjustment

Front brake lever freeplay

1 Operate the brake lever and measure freeplay at the tip of the lever **(see illustration)**. There shouldn't be any (zero freeplay). If there is freeplay, bleed the front brakes (see Chapter 7). If this doesn't work, check

Tune-up and routine maintenance

4.8 The brake light switch is adjusted by turning the adjusting nut (arrow)

5.1 Measure brake lever freeplay at the lever tip - loosen the locknut (left arrow) and turn the adjuster (right arrow) to change lever position

5.3 Measure brake pedal height from the top of the footpeg to the top of the pedal (arrows)

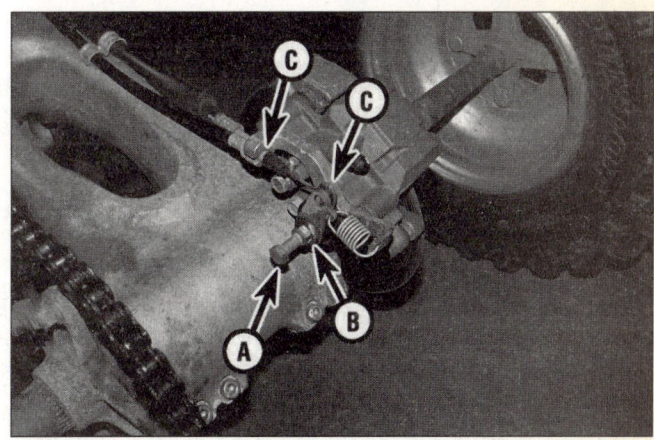

5.6 Parking brake cable details

A Adjusting bolt
B Locknut
C Cable length measurement points

the master cylinder and calipers for wear and check the brake lines for leaks (see Chapter 7). Front brake freeplay is not adjustable.

2   The position of the front brake lever can be adjusted to suit rider preference. To make the adjustment, loosen the adjuster locknut **(see illustration 5.1)** while pushing the brake lever toward the front of the vehicle. While holding pressure on the lever, turn the adjusting bolt until the lever is where you want it to be. Tighten the adjuster locknut securely and recheck the lever position.

Rear brake pedal height

3   The upper side of the rear brake pedal should be the specified distance (listed in this Chapter's Specifications) below the top of the footpeg **(see illustration)**.
4   If the pedal height is incorrect, loosen the locknut on the adjusting bolt **(see illustration 4.8)**. Turn the adjusting bolt to obtain the correct pedal height, then tighten the locknut.

Caution: The distance between the locknut and the hex on the adjusting bolt must not exceed the value listed in this Chapter's Specifications. If it does, check the master cylinder and pedal for wear.

5   After making the adjustment, jack up the rear of the vehicle, spin the rear wheels and check for brake drag. If the brake drags, repeat the height adjustment.

Parking brake lever

6   Loosen the locknut and adjuster bolt at the parking brake lever on the rear caliper **(see illustration)**.
7   Locate the mid-line adjuster in the parking brake cable on the right side of the vehicle **(see illustration)**. Pull the cover toward the front of the vehicle to expose the adjuster. Loosen the adjuster locknut, turn the adjuster to obtain the specified cable length at the caliper **(see illustration 5.6)**, then tighten the locknut.
8   At the caliper, turn the adjusting bolt in

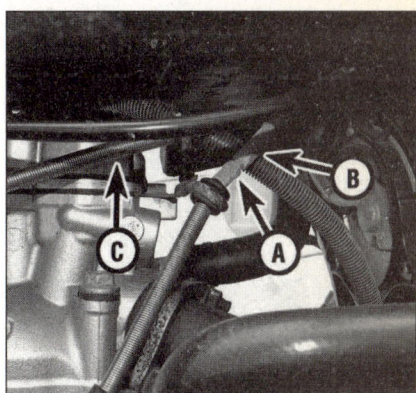

5.7 The parking brake cable adjuster is on the right side of the vehicle; don't confuse it with the clutch cable, which is close by

A Parking brake cable locknut
B Parking brake cable adjuster
C Clutch cable

6.11a Loosen the locknut (arrow) at each tie rod inner end . . .

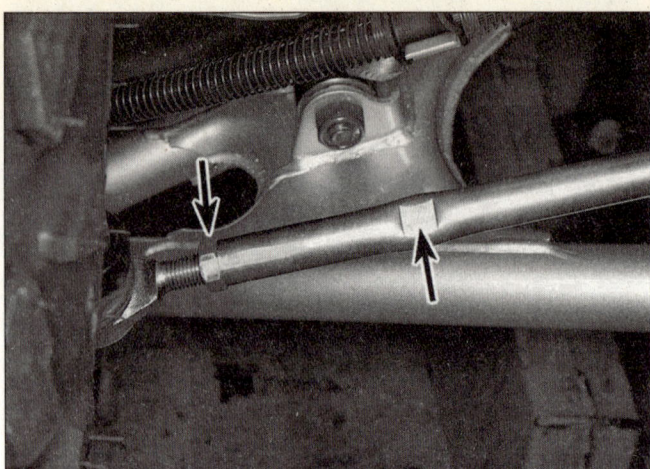

6.11b . . . and at the outer ends (left arrow); use a wrench on the flat (right arrow) to hold and turn the tie rod

until it feels tight, then back it out 1/8 turn and tighten the locknut.
9   At the mid-line cable adjuster, slide the cover back over the adjuster.

6 Steering system - inspection and toe-in adjustment

Inspection

1   These vehicles are equipped with bearings at the upper and lower ends of the steering shaft. These can become dented, rough or loose during normal use of the machine. In extreme cases, worn or loose parts can cause steering wobble that is potentially dangerous.
2   To check, block the rear wheels so the vehicle can't roll, jack up the front end and support it securely on jackstands.
3   Point the wheels straight ahead and slowly move the handlebar from side-to-side. Dents or roughness in the bearing will be felt and the bars will not move smoothly. **Note:** *Make sure any hesitation in movement is not being caused by the cables and wiring harnesses that run to the handlebar.*
4   If the handlebar doesn't move smoothly, or if it has excessive lateral play, remove and inspect the steering shaft bushings (see Chapter 6).
5   Look at the tie-rod ends (inner and outer) while slowly turning the handlebar from side-to-side. If there's any vertical movement in the tie-rod balljoints, replace them (see Chapter 6).

Toe-in adjustment

6   Roll the vehicle forward onto a level surface and stop it with the front wheels pointing straight ahead.
7   Make a mark at the front and center of each tire, even with the centerline of the front hub.
8   Measure the distance between the marks with a toe-in gauge or steel tape measure.
9   Have an assistant push the vehicle backward while you watch the marks on the tires. Stop pushing when the tires have rotated exactly one-half turn, so the marks are at the backs of the tires.
10 Again, measure the distance between the marks. Subtract the front measurement from the rear measurement to get toe-in.
11 If toe-in is not as specified in this Chapter's Specifications, hold each tie-rod with a wrench on the flats and loosen the locknuts **(see illustrations)**. Turn the tie-rods an equal amount to change toe-in. When toe-in is set correctly, tighten the locknuts to the torque listed in this Chapter's Specifications.

7 Suspension - check

1   The suspension components must be maintained in top operating condition to ensure rider safety. Loose, worn or damaged suspension parts decrease the vehicle's stability and control.
2   Lock the front brake and push on the handlebars to compress the front shock absorbers several times. See if they move up-and-down smoothly without binding. If binding is felt, the shocks should be inspected as described in Chapter 6.
3   Check the tightness of all front suspension nuts and bolts to be sure none have worked loose.
4   Inspect the rear shock absorber for fluid leakage and tightness of the mounting nuts and bolts. If leakage is found, the shock should be replaced.
5   Raise the rear of the vehicle and support it securely on jackstands. Grab the swingarm on each side, just ahead of the axle. Rock the swingarm from side to side - there should be no discernible movement at the rear. If there's a little movement or a slight clicking can be heard, make sure the swingarm pivot shaft is tight. If the pivot shaft is tight but movement is still noticeable, the swingarm will have to be removed and the bearings replaced as described in Chapter 6.
6   Inspect the tightness of the rear suspension nuts and bolts.

8 Drive chain and sprockets - check, adjustment and lubrication

1   A neglected drive chain won't last long and can quickly damage the sprockets. Routine chain adjustment isn't difficult and will ensure maximum chain and sprocket life.

Check

2   To check the chain, support the vehicle securely on jackstands with the rear wheels off the ground. Place the transmission in neutral.
3   Push down and pull up on the top run of the chain and measure the slack midway between the two sprockets **(see illustration)**, then compare the measurements to the value listed in this Chapter's Specifications. As wear occurs, the chain will actually stretch, which means adjustment is necessary to remove some slack from the chain. In some cases where lubrication has been neglected, corrosion and galling may cause the links to bind and kink, which effectively shortens the chain's length. If the chain is tight between the sprockets, rusty or kinked, it's time to replace it with a new one. **Note:** *Repeat the chain slack measurement along the length of the chain - ideally, every inch or so. If you find a tight area, mark it with felt pen or paint and repeat the measurement after the machine has been ridden. If the chain's still tight in the same areas, it may be damaged or worn. Because a tight or kinked chain can damage the transmission counter-*

Tune-up and routine maintenance 1•9

8.3 Measure drive chain slack along the upper chain run (arrow)

8.5 Inspect the front sprocket teeth for excessive wear; make sure there's no play in the sprocket

shaft bearing, it's a good idea to replace it.
4   Check the entire length of the chain for damaged rollers or O-rings, loose links and loose pins.
5   Look through the slots in the engine sprocket cover and inspect the engine sprocket **(see illustration)**. Check the teeth on the engine sprocket and the rear sprocket for wear (see Chapter 7). Refer to Chapter 6 for the sprocket replacement procedure if the sprockets appear to be worn excessively. **Note:** *Never install a new chain on old sprockets and never use the old chain if you install new sprockets - replace the chain and sprockets as a set.*
6   Check the chain roller and slider **(see illustration)**. If a roller or slider is worn, replace it.

Adjustment

7   Rotate the rear wheels until the chain is positioned with the least amount of slack present.
8   On 2004 and 2005 models, loosen the upper and lower rear hub bolts **(see illus-**

8.6 Check the chain roller and slider (arrows)

trations). Loosen the adjuster locknuts and turn the adjuster on each side of the swingarm evenly until the proper chain tension is obtained. Be sure to turn the adjusters evenly

8.8a Loosen the upper hub nut and bolt . . .

to keep the wheel in alignment **(see illustration)**. If the adjusters reach the end of their travel, the chain is excessively worn and should be replaced with a new one (see Chapter 6).

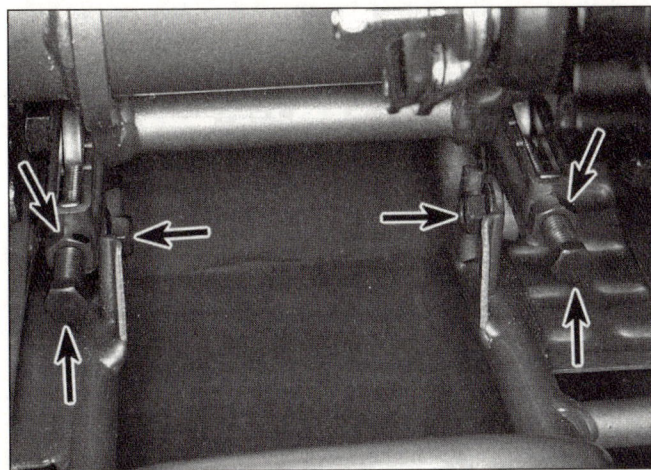

8.8b . . . the lower hub bolt, chain adjuster locknuts and adjusters (arrows)

8.8c Use the chain adjuster marks (arrows) to set the adjusters evenly

1•10 Tune-up and routine maintenance

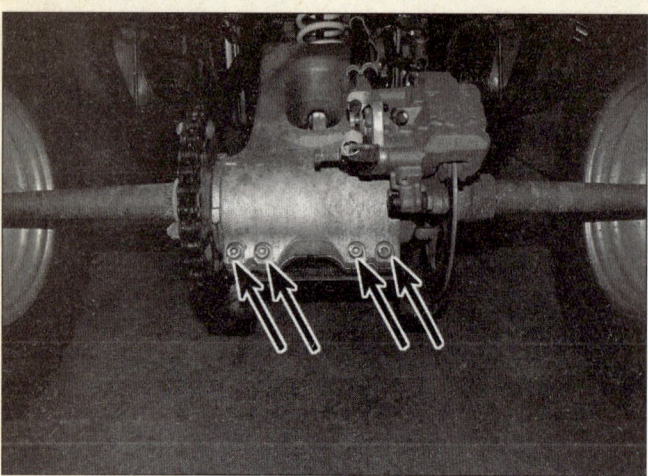

8.9a Loosen the hub pinch bolts (arrows) (outer two bolts first, then the inner two) . . .

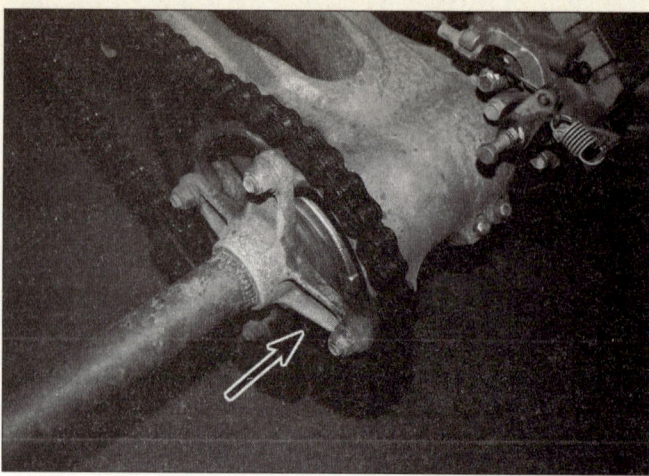

8.9b . . . and insert a rod (a Phillips screwdriver will work) into one of the three adjusting holes (hidden behind the sprocket) and turn the hub inside the swingarm to adjust chain slack

9   On 2006 and later models, loosen the pinch bolts at the rear edge of the swingarm **(see illustration)**. Loosen the outer two bolts first, then loosen the inner two. Insert a rod into one of the holes in the hub from the left side, through the sprocket (there are three holes) **(see illustration)**. Pull or push the rod to rotate the hub inside the swingarm (the hub is an eccentric shape, so rotating it will change the drive chain slack). Once the slack is adjusted correctly, remove the rod and tighten the pinch bolts. Tighten the inner two bolts first, then the outer two.

Lubrication

Note: *If the chain is dirty, it should be removed and cleaned before it's lubricated (see Chapter 6).*

10   The best time to lubricate the chain is after the vehicle has been ridden. When the chain is warm, the lubricant will penetrate the joints between the side plates to provide lubrication. Yamaha specifies SAE 30 to 50 engine oil only; do not use chain lube, which may contain solvents that can damage the chain's rubber O-rings. Apply the oil to the area where the side plates overlap - not to the middle of the rollers.

11   Apply the lubricant along the top of the lower chain run, so that when the machine is ridden centrifugal force will move the lubricant into the chain, rather than throwing it off.

12   After applying the lubricant, let it soak in a few minutes before wiping off any excess.

9 Tires/wheels - general check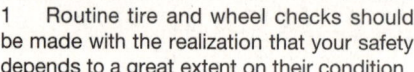

1   Routine tire and wheel checks should be made with the realization that your safety depends to a great extent on their condition.

2   Check the tires carefully for cuts, tears, embedded nails or other sharp objects and excessive wear. Operation of the vehicle with excessively worn tires is extremely hazardous, as traction and handling are directly affected. Measure the tread depth at the center of the tire and replace worn tires with new ones when the tread depth is less than that listed in this Chapter's Specifications.

3   Repair or replace punctured tires as soon as damage is noted. Do not try to patch a torn tire, as wheel balance and tire reliability may be impaired.

4   Check the tire pressures when the tires are cold and keep them properly inflated (see *Daily (Pre-ride) checks* at the front of this manual). Proper air pressure will increase tire life and provide maximum stability and ride comfort. Keep in mind that low tire pressures may cause the tire to slip on the rim or come off, while high tire pressures will cause abnormal tread wear and unsafe handling.

Caution: ATV tires operate at very low pressures. Over-inflation may rupture them.

5   Make sure the tires are installed on the correct side of the vehicle. ATV tires are directional; that is, they are designed to rotate in only one forward direction. The direction of forward rotation is indicated by an arrow molded into the tire sidewall **(see illustration)**.

6   The steel wheels used on this machine are virtually maintenance free, but they should be kept clean and checked periodically for cracks, bending and rust. Never attempt to repair damaged wheels; they must be replaced with new ones.

7   Check the valve stem locknuts to make sure they're tight. Also, make sure the valve stem cap is in place and tight. If it is missing, install a new one made of metal or hard plastic.

10 Front wheel bearings - check

1   Raise the front of the vehicle and support it securely on jackstands.

2   Spin the front wheels by hand. Listen for noise, which indicates dry or worn wheel bearings.

3   Grasp the top and bottom of the tire and try to rock it back-and-forth **(see illustration)**. If there's more than a very small amount of play, the wheel bearings are in need of adjustment or replacement. Refer to Chapter 7 for service procedures.

11 Lubrication - general

1   Since the controls, cables and various other components of an ATV are exposed to the elements, they should be lubricated periodically to ensure safe and trouble-free operation.

9.5 Be sure the directional arrow points in the forward rotating direction of the tire

Tune-up and routine maintenance 1•11

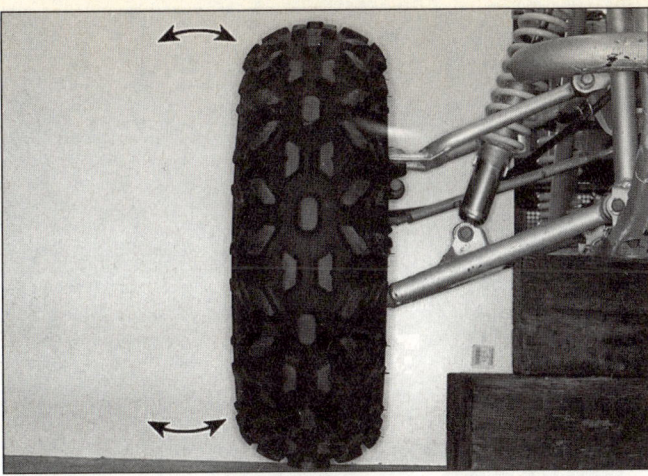

10.3 Rock the wheel and tire from side-to-side to check wheel bearing play

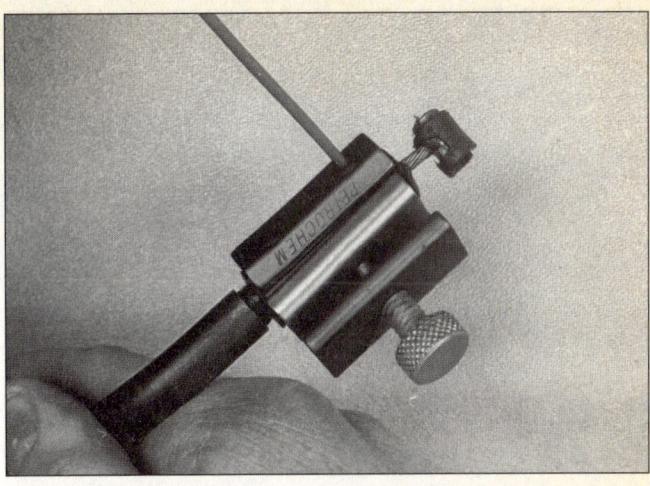

11.3 Lubricating a cable with a pressure lube adapter (make sure the tool seats around the inner cable)

2 The throttle lever, brake levers and brake pedal should be lubricated frequently. Yamaha recommends 10W-30 motor oil inside cables and for the pivot points of levers and pedals. Multi-purpose lithium grease is recommended for cable ends and other lubrication points, such as suspension and steering bushings. In order for the lubricant to be applied where it will do the most good, the component should be disassembled. However, if chain and cable lubricant is being used, it can be applied to the pivot joint gaps and will usually work its way into the areas where friction occurs. If motor oil or light grease is being used, apply it sparingly as it may attract dirt (which could cause the controls to bind or wear at an accelerated rate). **Note:** *One of the best lubricants for the control lever pivots is a dry-film lubricant (available from many sources by different names).*

3 The throttle and clutch cables should be removed and treated with a commercially available cable lubricant which is specially formulated for use on ATV control cables. Small adapters for pressure lubricating the cables with spray can lubricants are available and ensure that the cable is lubricated along its entire length **(see illustration)**. When attaching a cable to its handlebar lever, be sure to lubricate the barrel-shaped fitting at the end with multi-purpose grease.

4 To lubricate the cables, disconnect one end, then lubricate the cable with a pressure lube adapter **(see illustration 11.3)** (clutch cable, see Chapter 2; throttle cable, see Chapter 4).

5 Refer to Chapter 6 for the following lubrication procedures:
  a) Steering shaft bushings
  b) Swingarm bearings and dust seals

6 Refer to Chapter 7 for the following lubrication procedures:
  a) Rear brake pedal pivot
  b) Front wheel bearings

7 Using a grease gun, lubricate the front suspension bushings through the grease nipples **(see illustration)**.

12 Fasteners - check

1 Since vibration of the machine tends to loosen fasteners, all nuts, bolts, screws, etc. should be periodically checked for proper tightness. Also make sure all cotter pins or other safety fasteners are correctly installed.
2 Pay particular attention to the following:
  Spark plug(s)
  Engine oil drain plug
  Gearshift pedal
  Brake pedal
  Footpegs
  Engine mount bolts
  Shock absorber mount bolts
  Front axle nuts
  Rear axle nuts
  Skid plate bolts

3 If a torque wrench is available, use it along with the torque specifications at the beginning of this, or other, Chapters.

13 Skid plates - check

1 Check the skid plates under the vehicle for damage (see Chapter 8). Have damaged plates repaired, or else replace them.
2 Make sure the skid plate fasteners are all in position and tightly secured.

14 Air filter element and drain tube - cleaning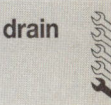

Element cleaning

1 Remove the seat (see Chapter 8).
2 Remove the cover from the air filter

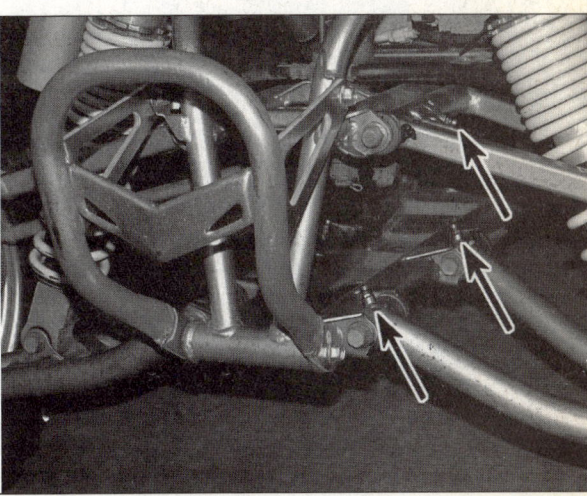

11.7 There are three grease fittings (arrows) on each pair of front suspension arms

1•12 Tune-up and routine maintenance

14.2 To remove the air cleaner cover, release these clips (arrows) and pull the cover rearward to disengage the two tabs at the front

14.3a Remove the wing nut (arrow) and lift the air filter out of the air cleaner housing

housing. The cover is secured by three clips at the back and two tabs at the front **(see illustration)**.

3 Remove the air filter element **(see illustration)** and separate the element from the element guide **(see illustration)**.

4 Clean the element and guide in a high flash point solvent, squeeze the solvent out of the foam and let the guide and element dry completely.

5 Soak the foam element in the foam filter oil listed in this Chapter's Specifications, then squeeze it firmly to remove the excess oil. Don't wring it out or the foam may be damaged. The element should be thoroughly oil-soaked, but not dripping.

6 Reassemble the element and guide.

7 Installation is the reverse of removal.

Drain tube cleaning

8 Check the air cleaner housing drain tube for accumulated water and oil **(see illustration)**. If oil or water has built up in the tube,

squeeze its clamp, remove the tube from the air cleaner housing and clean it out. Install the drain tube on the housing and secure it with the clamp. **Note:** *A drain tube that's full indicates the need to clean the filter element and the inside of the case.*

15 Fuel system - inspection

⚠ **Warning:** *Gasoline is extremely flammable, so take extra precautions when you work on any part of the fuel system. Don't smoke or allow open flames or bare light bulbs near the work area, and don't work in a garage where a gas-type appliance (such as a water heater or clothes dryer) is present. Since gasoline is carcinogenic, wear latex gloves when there's a possibility of being exposed to fuel, and if you spill any fuel on your skin, rinse it off immediately with soap and water. Mop up any fuel spills immediately and do not store fuel-soaked rags where they could ignite. When you perform any kind of work on the fuel system, wear safety glasses and have a fire extinguisher suitable for class B type fires (flammable liquids) on hand.*

Carbureted models

1 Check the fuel tank, the fuel tap, the fuel line and the carburetor for leaks and evidence of damage **(see illustration)**.

2 If carburetor gaskets are leaking, the carburetor should be disassembled and rebuilt (see Chapter 4).

3 If the fuel tap is leaking, tightening the screws may help. If leakage persists, the tap should be disassembled and repaired or replaced with a new one.

4 If the fuel line is cracked or otherwise deteriorated, replace it with a new one.

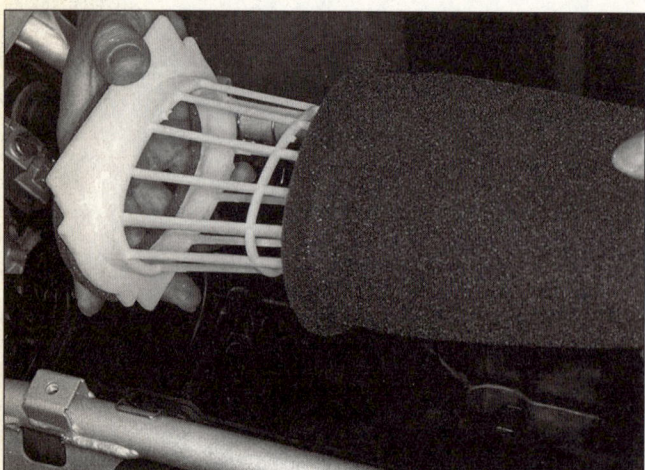

14.3b Separate the filter element from the guide

14.8 Check the drain tube (arrow) for accumulated water and oil

Tune-up and routine maintenance 1•13

15.1 Inspect the fuel tap (hidden, at the upper end of the fuel line), fuel line and float chamber seam for leaks (arrows)

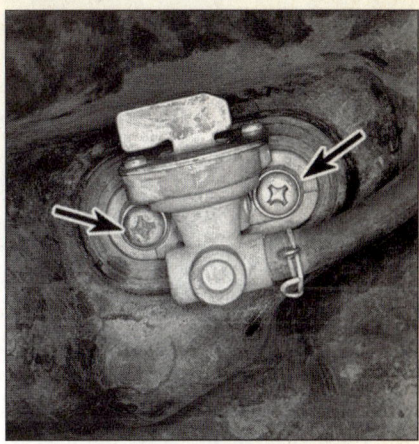

15.5a Remove the fuel tap screws (arrows) . . .

5 Place the fuel tap lever in the Off position. Remove and drain the fuel tank. Remove the screws and detach the tap from the tank **(see illustrations)**.
6 Clean the strainer with solvent and let it dry.
7 Installation is the reverse of removal. Be sure to use a new O-ring. Hand-tighten the screws firmly, but don't overtighten them. If you do, the O-ring will be distorted, which will result in fuel leaks.
8 After installation, run the engine and check for fuel leaks.
9 Any time the vehicle is going to be stored for a month or more, remove and drain the fuel tank. Also remove the float chamber drain plug (in the bottom of the carburetor on the left-hand side) and drain the fuel from the carburetor.

Fuel injected models

10 Remove the fuel tank cover (see Chapter 8).
11 Check the fuel line from the tank to the throttle body for leaks and evidence of damage. If problems are visible, refer to Chapter 4 and replace the line.

 Warning: Refer to the precautions in Chapter 4 regarding disconnecting of fuel injection system lines before disconnecting the fuel line.

12 Check the fuel tank breather hose that runs from the fuel filler cap to the handlebar. Replace it if it's cracked or deteriorated.

All models

13 Inspect the condition of the crankcase breather hose. Replace it if it's cracked, torn or deteriorated.

16 Spark plug - inspection, cleaning and gapping

1 Remove the fuel tank (see Chapter 4).
2 On YFZ450 models, the ignition coil is built into the spark plug boot **(see illustration)**. Disconnect the electrical connector and twist the ignition coil to break it free from the spark plug, then pull it off.
Caution: Don't use pliers or a screwdriver to remove the coil - it's easily damaged.

3 On YFZ450R models, the spark plug cap is a conventional type. Twist it to break the seal, then pull it off the spark plug.
4 If available, use compressed air to blow any accumulated debris from around the spark plug. Remove the plug with a spark plug socket.
5 Inspect the electrodes for wear. Both the center and side electrodes should have square edges and the side electrode should be of uniform thickness. Look for excessive deposits and evidence of a cracked or chipped insulator around the center electrode. Compare your spark plugs to the color spark plug reading chart on the inside back cover. Check the threads, the washer and the ceramic insulator body for cracks and other damage.
6 If the electrodes are not excessively worn, and if the deposits can be easily removed with a wire brush, the plug can be regapped and reused (if no cracks or chips are visible in the insulator). If in doubt concerning the condition of the plug, replace it with a new one, as the expense is minimal.

15.5b . . . and separate the tap and strainer from the tank

16.2 The ignition coil is built into the spark plug boot (arrow) - twist and pull to free it from the cylinder head, but don't use pliers or a screwdriver

1•14 Tune-up and routine maintenance

16.8a Spark plug manufacturers recommend using a wire type gauge when checking the gap - if the wire doesn't slide between the electrodes with a slight drag, adjustment is required

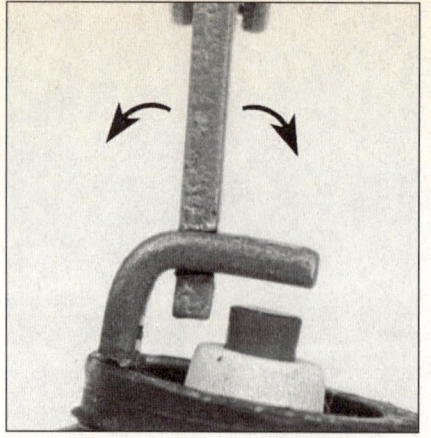

16.8b To change the gap, bend the side electrode only, as indicated by the arrows, and be very careful not to crack or chip the ceramic insulator surrounding the center electrode

16.11 Lubricate the spark plug seal with silicone spray (YFZ450)

7 Cleaning the spark plug by sandblasting is permitted, provided you clean the plug with a high flash-point solvent afterwards.

8 Before installing a new plug, make sure it is the correct type and heat range. Check the gap between the electrodes, as it is not preset. For best results, use a wire-type gauge rather than a flat gauge to check the gap **(see illustration)**. If the gap must be adjusted, bend the side electrode only and be very careful not to chip or crack the insulator nose **(see illustration)**. Make sure the washer is in place before installing the plug.

9 Since the cylinder head is made of aluminum, which is soft and easily damaged, thread the plug into the head by hand. Slip a short length of hose over the end of the plug to use as a tool to thread it into place. The hose will grip the plug well enough to turn it, but will start to slip if the plug begins to cross-thread in the hole - this will prevent damaged threads and the accompanying repair costs.

10 Once the plug is finger tight, the job can be finished with a socket. If a torque wrench is available, tighten the spark plug to the torque listed in this Chapter's Specifications. If you do not have a torque wrench, tighten the plug finger tight (until the washer bottoms on the cylinder head) then use a spark plug socket to tighten it an additional 1/4 turn. Regardless of the method used, do not over-tighten it.

11 If you're working on a YFZ450, lubricate the seal on the ignition coil with silicone lubricant **(see illustration)**. Push the ignition coil down onto the plug and connect its electrical connector.

17 Engine oil and filter - change

1 Consistent routine oil and filter changes are the single most important maintenance procedure you can perform on a vehicle. The oil not only lubricates the internal parts of the engine, transmission and clutch, but it also acts as a coolant, a cleaner, a sealant and a protectant. Because of these demands, the oil takes a terrific amount of abuse and should be replaced often with new oil of the recommended grade and type.

2 Before changing the oil and filter, warm up the engine by running it for several minutes so the oil will drain easily. Be careful when draining the oil, as the exhaust pipe, the engine and the oil itself can cause severe burns.

3 Place a clean drain pan under the vehicle, positioned underneath the two drain plugs **(see illustrations)**.

4 Remove the dipstick from the oil tank (and the oil filler cap from the crankcase on YFZ450 models) to vent the crankcase and act as a reminder that there is no oil in the engine **(see illustrations 17.3a, YFZ450, or 17.3b, YFZ450R)**.

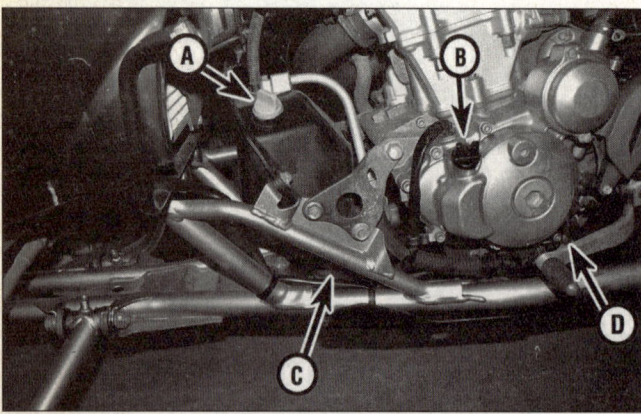

17.3a YFZ450 oil drain and fill details

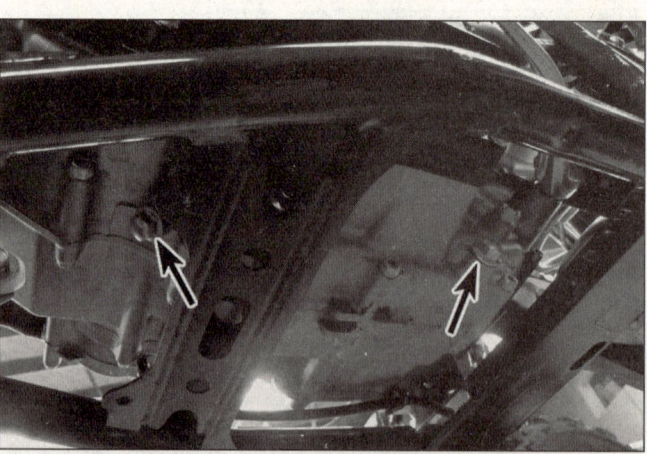

17.3b Engine oil drain plug locations - YFZ450R

A Dipstick
B Oil filler cap
C Front drain plug (hidden)
D Rear drain plug

Tune-up and routine maintenance 1•15

17.6 Remove the lower bolt to drain the oil from the filter housing, then remove the upper bolts

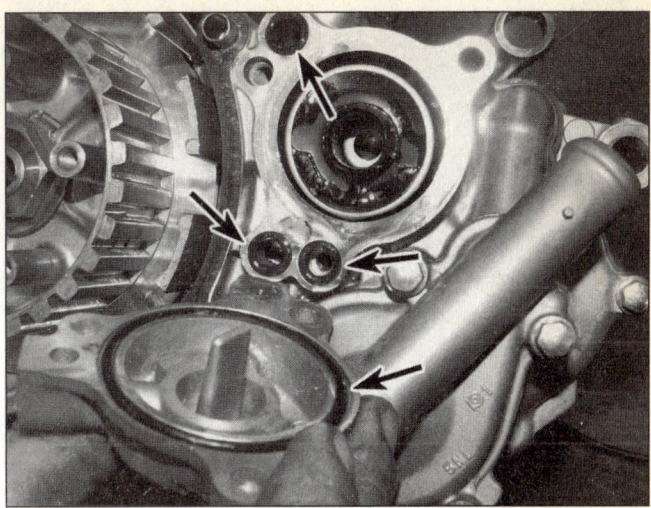

17.7a Take off the cover, noting the locations of the O-rings (arrows) . . .

5   Remove the drain plugs from the engine (see illustration 17.3a, YFZ450, or 17.3b, YFZ450R) and allow the oil to drain into the pan.

6   Remove the lower bolt from the oil filter cover and let the oil filter drain (see illustration).

7   Remove the remaining cover bolts, take the cover off and remove the filter element (see illustrations). If additional maintenance is planned for this time period, check or service another component while the oil is allowed to drain completely.

8   Wipe any remaining oil out of the filter housing area of the crankcase and make sure the oil passage is clear.

9   Check the condition of the drain plug threads and the O-rings.

10 Install the filter element with its closed end facing into the engine (see illustration).

Caution: The filter must be installed facing the correct direction or oil starvation may cause severe engine damage.

11 Install the cover with a new O-ring and tighten the bolts to the torque listed in this Chapter's Specifications.

12 Install the oil strainer, spring and engine drain plug, using a new O-ring if the old one is worn or damaged. Tighten the plug to the torque listed in this Chapter's Specifications. Avoid overtightening, as damage to the engine case will result.

13 Before refilling the engine, check the old oil carefully. If the oil was drained into a clean pan, small pieces of metal or other material can be easily detected. If the oil is very metallic colored, then the engine is experiencing wear from break-in (new engine) or from insufficient lubrication. If there are flakes or chips of metal in the oil, then something is drastically wrong internally and the engine will have to be disassembled for inspection and repair.

14 If there are pieces of fiber-like material in the oil, the clutch is experiencing excessive wear and should be checked.

15 If the inspection of the oil turns up nothing unusual, refill the crankcase to the proper level with the recommended oil and install the dipstick/filler cap.

16 Start the engine and let it run for two or three minutes. Shut it off, wait a few minutes, then check the oil level. If necessary, add more oil to bring the level up to the upper level mark on the dipstick. Check around the drain plug and filter cover for leaks.

17 If the vehicle has an external oil tube, loosen the oil check bolt or upper union bolt

17.7b . . . then remove the filter element, noting how the post (arrow) fits inside the open end of the filter element

17.10 The closed end of the filter element goes into the engine first

1•16 Tune-up and routine maintenance

17.17a On models with an external oil pipe, loosen the oil pressure check plug (right arrow) if equipped; if not, loosen the upper banjo bolt (left arrow)

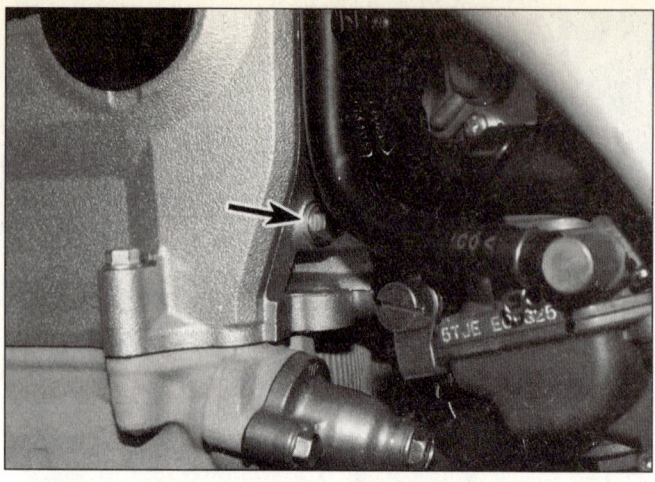

17.17b On models without an external oil pipe, loosen the oil gallery plug (arrow) slightly; if oil doesn't seep from the plug within one minute of idling, stop the engine and find out why

slightly **(see illustration)**. If it doesn't have an external oil tube, loosen the oil gallery plug on the cylinder head slightly **(see illustration)**. Start the engine and let it idle. Oil should seep from the plug within one minute. If not, oil is not flowing properly. Shut the engine off and find the problem before running it further. Make sure the oil filter is installed in the proper direction.

18 The old oil drained from the engine cannot be reused in its present state and should be disposed of. Check with your local refuse disposal company, disposal facility or environmental agency to see if they will accept the oil for recycling. Don't pour used oil into drains or onto the ground. After the oil has cooled, it can be drained into a suitable container (capped plastic jugs, topped bottles, milk cartons, etc.) for transport to one of these disposal sites.

18 Cooling system - inspection and coolant change

Inspection

1 The cooling system should be carefully inspected at the recommended intervals. Look for evidence of leaks, check the condition of the coolant, check the radiator for clogged fins and damage and make sure the fan operates when required.
2 Examine each of the rubber coolant hoses along its entire length. Look for swelling, cracks, abrasions and other damage. Squeeze each hose at various points. They should feel firm, yet pliable, and return to their original shape when released. If they are dried out or hard, replace them.
3 Look for leaks at each cooling system joint. Tighten the hose clamps carefully to halt minor leaks. If a hose is seriously cracked or torn at a hose clamp, tightening the clamp won't stop the leak; it might even accelerate it. If a hose leaks after tightening the hose clamp, drain the coolant (see Steps 13 through 17), loosen the clamp, pull off the hose and inspect it closely. If the damage is close to the end of the hose, cut off the damaged end and reattach the hose. If the damage is too far from the end of the hose, cutting off the end of the hose is not an option; replace the hose.
4 Check for leaks at the water pump weep hole **(see illustration)** and water pump gaskets. Also check for leaks at the coolant drain plug(s). Replace water pump or drain plug gaskets if they've been leaking. If coolant has been leaking from the weep hole, it's time for a new water pump seal (see Chapter 3).
5 Inspect the radiator for evidence of leaks and other damage. Radiator leaks usually produce tell-tale deposits or stains on the surface of the core below the leak. If the radiator is leaking, remove it (see Chapter 3) and have it repaired by a radiator shop or replace it.

Caution: Do NOT use a liquid leak-stopping compound to try to repair leaks.

6 Inspect the radiator cooling fins for mud, dirt and insects. Debris stuck in the fins can impede the flow of air through the radiator. If the fins are dirty, force water or low-pressure compressed air through the fins from the backside of the radiator. If any of the fins are bent or distorted, straighten them carefully with a screwdriver.
7 Remove the radiator cover.
8 Remove the radiator cap as follows: Turn it counterclockwise until it reaches the first detent. If you hear a hissing sound (indicating there is still pressure in the system), wait until it stops. Then press down on the cap and continue turning it counterclockwise until it's free.
9 Inspect the condition of the coolant in the radiator. If it's rust-colored, or if accumulations of scale are visible in the radiator, drain, flush and refill the system with new coolant. Inspect the cap gaskets for cracks and other damage. Have the cap tested by a dealer service department or replace it with a new one. Install the cap by turning it clockwise until it reaches the first detent, then push down on the cap and continue turning it until it stops.
10 Analyze the condition of the antifreeze in the coolant with an antifreeze hydrometer. Sometimes coolant may look like it's in good condition, but might be too weak to offer adequate protection. If the hydrometer indicates a weak mixture, flush and refill the cooling system (see later in this Section).
11 Start the engine and let it reach normal operating temperature, then check for leaks again. As the coolant temperature increases, the fan should come on automatically and the temperature should begin to drop. If it doesn't, check the fan and fan circuit (see Chapter 3).

18.4 If coolant has been leaking from the water pump weep hole (arrow), the water pump should be removed and inspected

Tune-up and routine maintenance 1•17

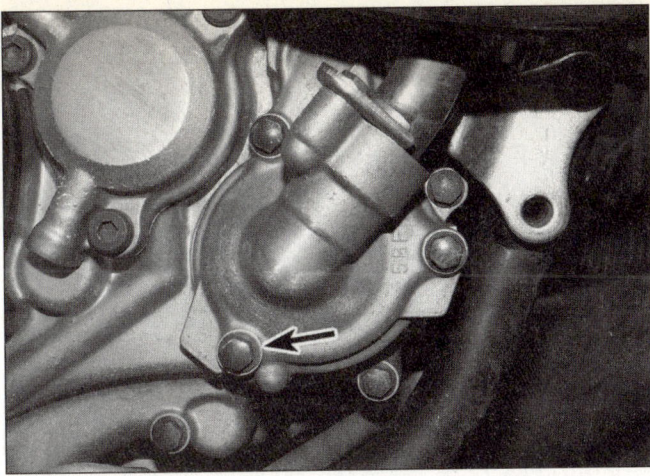

18.15a Remove the drain bolt and sealing washer (arrow) to drain the coolant

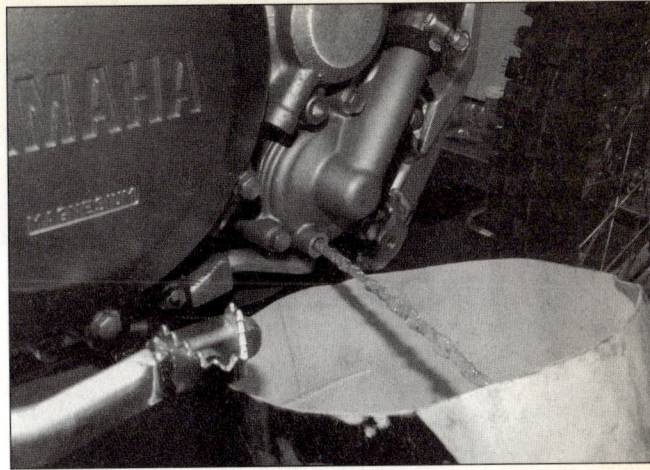

18.15b Coolant will spurt out once the radiator cap is removed, so have a container ready

12 If the coolant level is constantly low, but there is no evidence of leaks, have the system pressure checked by a Yamaha dealer service department, motorcycle repair shop or service station.

Coolant change

 Warning: *Don't allow antifreeze to come into contact with your skin or with painted surfaces of the vehicle. Rinse off spills immediately with plenty of water. Antifreeze is highly toxic if ingested. Never leave antifreeze in an open container or in puddles on the floor; children and pets are attracted by its sweet odor and may drink it. Check with local authorities regarding the proper disposal of used antifreeze. Many communities have collection centers that can dispose of antifreeze safely. Finally, antifreeze is combustible, so don't store it or put it near open flames.*

 Warning: *Let the engine cool completely before performing this Step. Opening the radiator cap while the engine is hot will allow scalding coolant to spray out.*

Draining

13 Remove the seats, fuel tank cover and right side cover. If you're working on a YFZ450R, also remove the left side cover, radiator side cover and front fender (see Chapter 8).
14 Put a shop rag over the radiator cap. Slowly rotate the cap counterclockwise to the first detent and allow any residual pressure to escape. When the hissing sound ceases, push down on the cap, turn it counterclockwise again and remove it.
15 Place a large, clean drain pan under the engine, remove the drain plug **(see illustrations)** and drain the coolant into the container.

 *The coolant will rush out with considerable force, so be prepared to quickly readjust the position of the drain pan.*

16 Remove the coolant reservoir (see Chapter 3) and drain it. Wash out the reservoir with clean water. Install the reservoir.
17 If you're working on a YFZ450R, remove the radiator (see Chapter 3). Pour the coolant from the radiator into the drain pan.

Flushing

18 If you're working on a YFZ450R, install the radiator (see Chapter 3).
19 Flush the system with clean tap water by inserting a garden hose into the radiator filler neck. Allow the water to run through the system until it is clear when it exits the drain bolt holes. If the radiator is extremely corroded, remove it (see Chapter 3) and have it cleaned by a radiator shop.
20 Using new gaskets, install the drain bolts and tighten them to the torque listed in this Chapter's Specifications.
21 Fill the cooling system with clean water mixed with a flushing compound. Make sure the flushing compound is compatible with aluminum, and follow the manufacturer's instructions carefully.
22 Start the engine and allow it to reach normal operating temperature. Let it run for about ten minutes.
23 Stop the engine. Let the machine cool for awhile, then cover the radiator cap with a heavy rag and turn it counterclockwise to the first stop, releasing any pressure that may be present in the system. Once the hissing stops, push down on the cap and remove it completely.
24 Drain the system.
25 Fill the system with clean water, then repeat Steps 22, 23 and 24.

Refilling

26 Fill the system with the correct coolant mixture (listed in this Chapter's Specifications). Fill the system to the top of the radia-

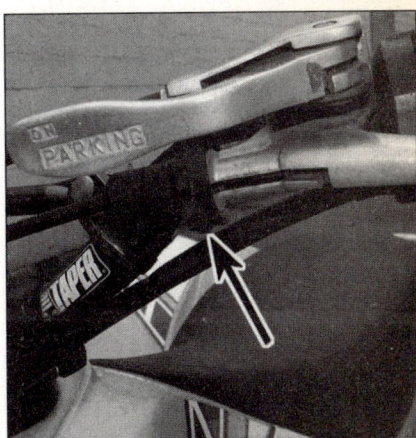

19.2 Measure clutch lever freeplay at the lever tip - to adjust, turn the adjuster (arrow)

tor cap filler neck and install the radiator cap. Fill the reservoir to the FULL mark and install the reservoir cap.
27 Run the engine for several minutes, checking for leaks. Shut it off, let the coolant level settle for several minutes, then recheck the level in the reservoir. Top up as needed.

19 Clutch lever freeplay - check and adjustment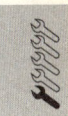

1 The clutch cable is adjusted at the clutch lever. Clutch freeplay can also be adjusted at the crankcase end of the clutch cable if adjustment at the handlebar doesn't bring freeplay within the specified range.

Adjusting clutch lever freeplay at the handlebar

2 Operate the clutch lever and check freeplay at the lever tip **(see illustration)**.

1•18 Tune-up and routine maintenance

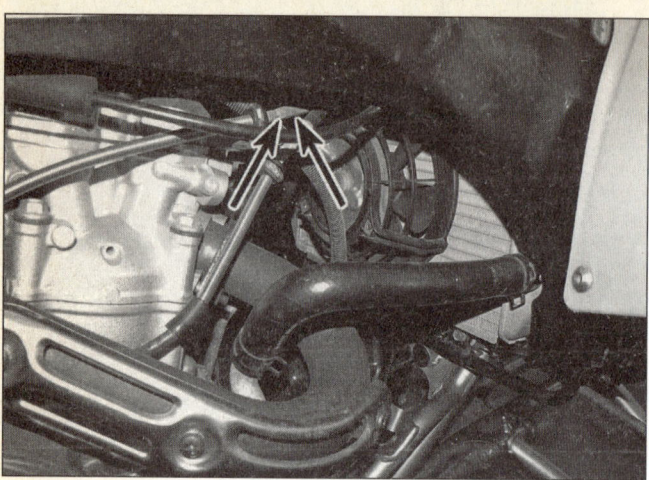

19.4 To adjust clutch freeplay at the crankcase, pull back the rubber dust cover (right arrow) to expose the adjuster, then loosen the locknut (left arrow) and turn the adjuster as needed

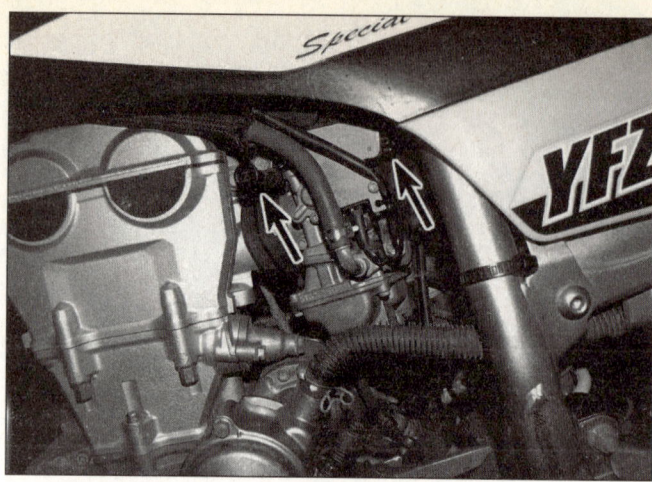

20.3 Here are the idle speed screw (right arrow) and choke knob (left arrow)

3 If freeplay isn't within the range listed in this Chapter's Specifications, turn the adjuster to set freeplay **(see illustration 19.2)** and tighten the locknut.

Adjusting clutch freeplay at the crankcase

4 Pull the cover back from the adjuster **(see illustration)**.
5 Loosen the adjuster locknut, turn the adjuster in or out until clutch freeplay is within the limits listed in this Chapter's Specifications.
6 Tighten the locknut securely and slide the cover back over it.

20 Idle speed - check and adjustment

Carbureted models

1 Before adjusting the idle speed, make sure the spark plug gap is correct (see Section 16). Also, turn the handlebars back-and-forth and note whether the idle speed changes. If it does, the throttle cable may be incorrectly routed. Be sure to correct this problem before proceeding.
2 Start the engine and warm it up to its normal operating temperature. Make sure the transmission is in Neutral, then hook up an inductive-type tachometer.
3 Turn the idle speed adjustment screw **(see illustration)** to bring the idle speed within the range listed in this Chapter's Specifications. Turning the screw in increases the idle speed; backing it out decreases the idle speed.
4 Snap the throttle open and shut a few times, then recheck the idle speed. If neces-

21.3 Check throttle lever freeplay at the lever tip

sary, repeat the adjustment procedure.
5 If a smooth, steady idle can't be achieved, the fuel/air mixture may be incorrect. Refer to Section 26 for pilot screw adjustment and Chapter 4 for additional carburetor information.

Fuel injected models

6 Periodic checking of the idle speed is not required, and adjustment is not possible (it's controlled by the engine control unit).
7 If the idle speed seems to be too high or too low, remove the seat, fuel tank cover and right side cover (see Chapter 8).
8 Start the engine and warm it up to its normal operating temperature. Make sure the transmission is in Neutral, then hook up an inductive-type tachometer.
9 Compare the idle speed to the value listed in this Chapter's Specifications. If it's not within the specified range, refer to Chapter 4 and check the throttle body.

21 Throttle cable and speed limiter - check and adjustment

Throttle cable

1 Before proceeding, check and, if necessary, adjust the idle speed (see Section 20).
2 Make sure the throttle lever moves easily from fully closed to fully open with the front wheel turned at various angles. The lever should return automatically from fully open to fully closed when released. If the throttle sticks, check the throttle cable for cracks or kinks in the housing. Also, make sure the inner cable is clean and well-lubricated.
3 Measure freeplay at the throttle lever **(see illustration)**. If it's within the range listed in this Chapter's Specifications, no adjustment is necessary. If not, adjust it as follows.
4 Pull the rubber boot to expose the

Tune-up and routine maintenance 1•19

21.4 Slide the rubber boot (arrow) off the adjuster, loosen the locknut and turn the adjuster

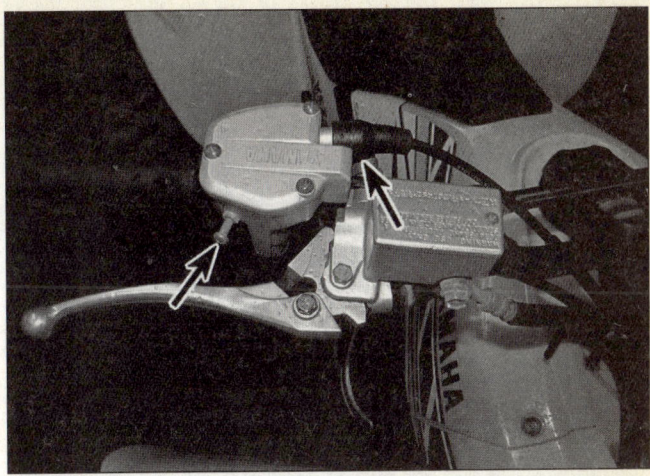

21.5 If necessary, pull back the rubber cover (right arrow) to expose the handlebar adjuster; measure limiter screw length from the throttle housing to the underside of the screw head (left arrow)

adjuster at the carburetor end of the throttle cable **(see illustration)**. Loosen the adjuster locknut. Turn the adjuster to set freeplay, then tighten the locknut.

5 If freeplay can't be brought within the specified range by adjusting it at the carburetor, pull back the rubber boot from the adjuster at the handlebar end of the throttle cable **(see illustration)**. Loosen the adjuster locknut. Turn the adjuster to set freeplay, then tighten the locknut.

6 Reposition the rubber boot(s) over the adjuster(s).

Speed limiter

7 The speed limiter **(see illustration 21.5)** can be used to restrict maximum throttle opening. Turning the screw in reduces the maximum throttle opening; backing it out increases maximum throttle opening.

8 To change the speed limiter screw setting, loosen the locknut, turn the screw in or out as necessary and tighten the locknut. Screw length is measured from the underside of the screw head to the throttle housing.

 Warning: Do NOT back out the speed limiter screw farther than the maximum setting listed in this Chapter's Specifications; doing so will affect throttle lever operation.

22 Choke (carbureted models) - operation check

1 Operate the choke knob **(see illustration 20.3)** and note whether it operates smoothly.

2 If the choke knob doesn't operate smoothly, inspect the choke system (see Chapter 4).

23 Battery - check

1 All models use a sealed, maintenance-free battery. Periodic checking of the electrolyte specific gravity is not possible. Inspect the battery as described in Chapter 5.

2 If the vehicle will be stored for an extended time, fully charge the battery, then remove it. Disconnect the negative cable and remove the battery retainer strap. Disconnect the positive cable and vent tube and lift the battery out.

 **Warning: Always disconnect the negative cable first and reconnect it last to avoid sparks which could cause a battery explosion.**

3 Store the battery in a cool dark place. Check open circuit voltage (see Chapter 9) at least once a month and recharge the battery if it's low.

24 Valve clearance - check and adjustment

Check

1 The engine must be cool to the touch for this maintenance procedure, so if possible let the machine sit overnight before beginning.

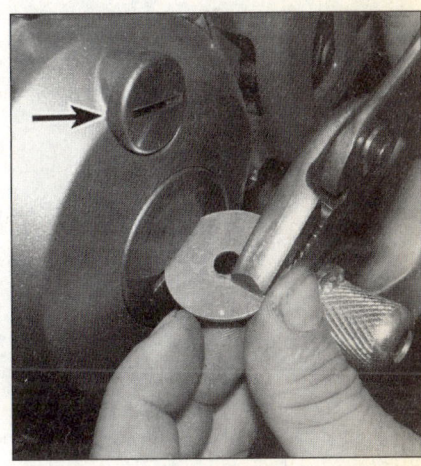

24.8 On YFZ450 models, use a coin or large washer and a pair of pliers to unscrew the crankshaft bolt cover and the timing hole cover directly above it (arrow). On YFZ450R models, use a 14 mm Allen wrench or a bolt with a 14 mm head turned with vise grips

2 Remove the seat, fuel tank cover and both sides covers (see Chapter 8).

3 If you're working on a YFZ450, remove the ignition coil (see Chapter 5).

4 Remove the fuel tank (see Chapter 4).

5 Disconnect the crankcase breather hose (all models) and oil tank breather hose (YFZ450).

6 Remove the spark plug (see Section 16). This will make it easier to turn the crankshaft.

7 Remove the valve cover (see Chapter 2).

8 Unscrew the crankshaft end plug and timing hole access plug **(see illustration)**.

1•20 Tune-up and routine maintenance

24.9a Align the timing mark with the notch (arrow) - if the piston is on the compression stroke . . .

24.9b . . . the camshaft punch marks will align with the valve cover gasket surface on the cylinder head (arrows) . . .

24.9c . . . and the cam lobes on the right-hand side of the engine will point away from each other like this

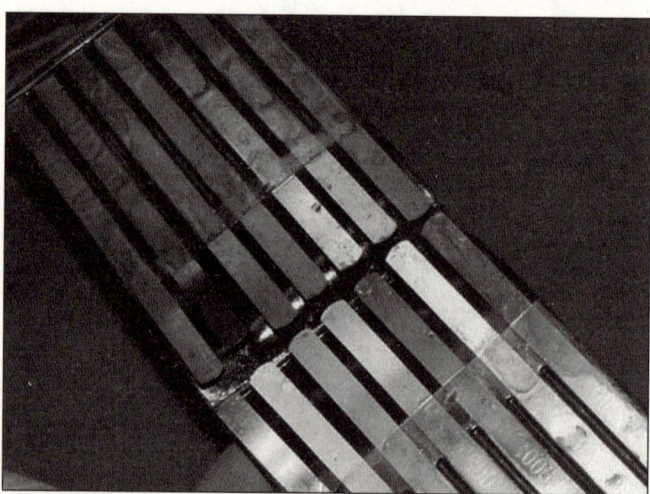

24.11a You'll need narrow feeler gauges to check the valve clearances - they can be bought in sets like this

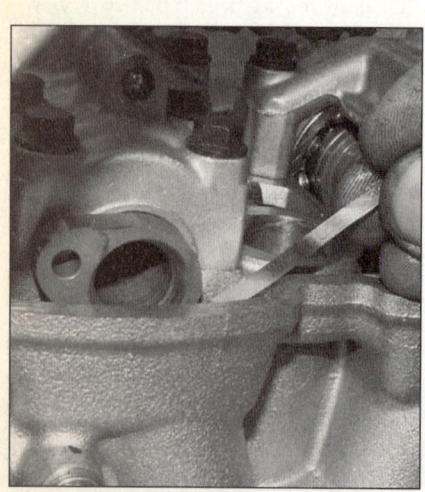

24.11b Slip the feeler gauge between the cam lobe and lifter to measure the clearance

HAYNES HINT On YFZ450 models, use a coin gripped with pliers if you don't have a screwdriver big enough to fit the slots. On YFZ450R models, use a 14 mm Allen wrench or a bolt with a 14 mm head, turned with vise grips.

9 Make sure the transmission is in Neutral. Using a socket on the crankshaft rotation bolt, turn the engine to position the piston at Top Dead Center on the compression stroke. **Note:** *Rotate the crankshaft counterclockwise.* When this occurs, the timing mark on the rotor will align with the notch in the crankcase cover **(see illustration)**. To make sure the piston is on the compression stroke, not the exhaust stroke, check the camshaft position. The punch marks on the camshaft should be 180-degrees away from each other and aligned with the gasket surface on top of the cylinder head **(see illustration)**. In addition, the camshaft lobes should point away from each pother **(see illustration)**. If the camshaft lobes and marks are out of position, rotate the crankshaft one full turn, so the crankshaft timing mark again aligns with the notch.

10 With the engine in this position, all five valve clearances can be checked. There are five valves, three intakes and two exhausts.

11 Insert a feeler gauge of the same thickness as the valve clearance listed in this Chapter's Specifications between each of the cam lobes and the lifter beneath it **(see illustrations)**.

TOOL TIP *You'll need narrow feeler gauges to check the valve clearances.*

12 Pull the feeler gauge out slowly - you should feel a light drag. If there's no drag, the clearance is too loose. If there's a heavy drag, the clearance is too tight.

Tune-up and routine maintenance 1•21

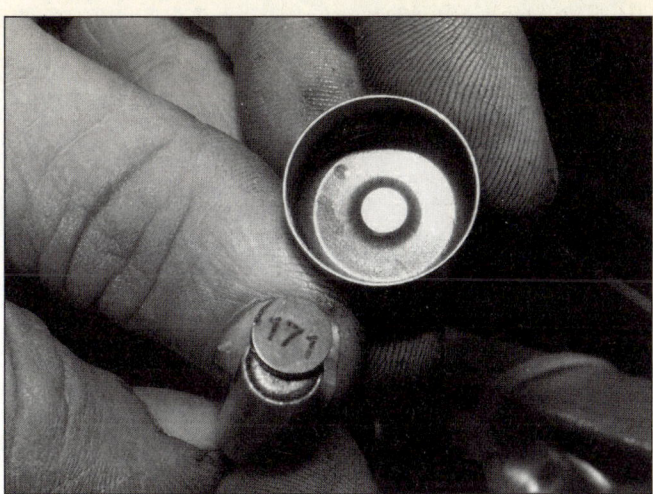

24.16a The shim thickness is marked on the shim . . .

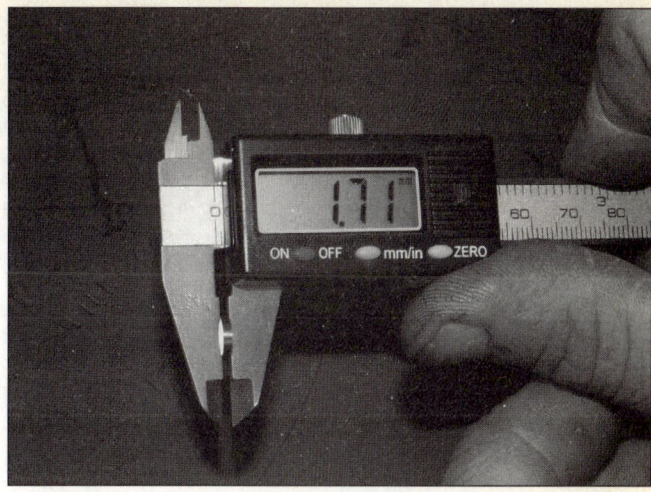

24.16b . . . but it should also be checked with a vernier caliper or micrometer

13 Write down the locations of any valves with incorrect clearances. Recheck the clearances of these valves, trying different feeler gauges until you find the thickness that fits correctly (a light drag). Once you do, write this thickness down - you'll need this information later to select a new valve adjusting shim.

14 If any of the clearances need to be adjusted, go to Step 15. If all of the clearances are within the Specifications, go to Step 21.

Adjustment

15 Remove the camshaft (see Chapter 2). Remove the lifter and shim for each of the valves that need to be adjusted.

16 Determine the thickness of the shim that was removed. It should be marked on the bottom of the shim **(see illustration)**, but the ideal way is to measure it with a micrometer or vernier caliper **(see illustration)**. **Note:** *If the number on the shim does not end with zero or 5, round it off to the nearest zero or 5. For example, if the number on the shim is 228, round it off to 230. If it's 224, round it off to 225.*

17 If the clearance (measured in Steps 11 and 12 and written down in Step 13) was too large, you need a thicker shim. If it was too small, you need a thinner shim.

18 If the measured valve clearance in Steps 11 and 12 was too great, subtract the mid-range specified clearance from the measured clearance. Write this number down, then add it to the thickness of the adjusting shim you removed. This will give you the thickness of the needed new shim. For example:
Measured clearance: 0.20 mm
Specified clearance: 0.10 to 0.15 mm
Mid-range (desired) clearance: 0.12 mm
Measured clearance minus desired clearance: 0.08 mm

So if the existing shim is numbered 180 (1.80 mm thick), the new shim should be 1.88 mm thick. The closest to this is a 200 (2.0 mm thick). This is the thickness of the new shim that you will need for that valve.

19 Select new shims for any remaining valves that are not within the Specifications.

20 Install the new shims and their lifters (see Chapter 2).

21 The remainder of installation is the reverse of the removal steps. After the camshafts are reinstalled, recheck the valve clearances to make sure they're within the Specifications.

25 Exhaust system - inspection

1 Periodically, inspect the exhaust system for leaks and loose fasteners.

2 The exhaust pipe flange nuts at the cylinder head are especially prone to loosening, which could cause damage to the head (see Chapter 4). Check them frequently and keep them tight. If tightening the flange nuts fails to stop the leak, replace the gasket (see Chapter 4).

3 The spark arrester should be removed and cleaned at the specified intervals.

 Warning: *To avoid burns, be sure the exhaust system has cooled down before you start this procedure.*

 Warning: *To avoid carbon monoxide poisoning, run the engine in a well-ventilated area.*

4 Unbolt the spark arrester. If you're working on a YFZ450, remove three bolts from the rear end of the tailpipe **(see illustration)**.

25.4 The YFZ450 tailpipe/spark arrester is secured by three bolts (arrows)

If you're working on a YFZ450R, remove the single bolt from the underside of the spark arrester, located just inside the tailpipe (not the purging bolt, located on the outside of the muffler on the underside).

5 Pull the spark arrester out of the muffler. Tap it lightly with a soft-faced mallet to loosen any deposits, then clean the deposits off with a wire brush. Also clean any deposits from the inside of the muffler, again using a wire brush.

6 Reinstall the spark arrester and tighten the bolt(s) to the torque listed in this Chapter's Specifications.

7 Remove the purging bolt from the underside of the muffler. Start the engine and rev it 20 or more times to blow out any remaining deposits. Shut the engine off, let it cool down again, and reinstall the purging bolt.

26.3 The pilot screw is in the underside of the carburetor at the front of the float bowl (carburetor removed for clarity)

26 Carburetor pilot screw adjustment

Note: *The manufacturer doesn't specify an initial pilot screw setting, but a good starting point would be 1-1/2 turns out (from the seated position).*

1 Warm-up the engine to normal operating temperature.
2 Adjust the idle speed (see Section 20).
3 Turn the pilot screw **(see illustration)** clockwise until the idle speed slows or starts to run rough, then back out the screw 1-1/4 turns.
4 Readjust the idle speed.
5 Ride the quad to check its performance. If it runs lean ("bogs") exiting a corner, turn the screw out an additional 1/4 turn and test it again. If it runs rich ("blubbers") exiting a corner, turn the screw in 1/4-turn and test it again).
6 Once performance is satisfactory, readjust the idle speed.

Chapter 2
Engine, clutch and transmission

Contents

Cam chain tensioner - removal, inspection and installation	9
Camshaft chain and guides - removal, inspection and installation..............	20
Camshafts and lifters - removal, inspection and installation	10
Clutch and release mechanism - removal, inspection and installation	19
Crankcase - disassembly and reassembly..........	24
Crankcase components - inspection and servicing........	25
Crankcase covers - removal and installation	18
Crankshaft and connecting rod - removal, inspection and installation...........	27
Cylinder - removal, inspection and installation	14
Cylinder compression - check	5
Cylinder head - removal, inspection and installation	11
Cylinder head and valves - disassembly, inspection and reassembly...........	13
Engine - removal and installation	6
Engine disassembly and reassembly - general information........	7
External oil tank and lines (YFZ450) - removal and installation....	17
External shift mechanism - removal, inspection and installation............	23
General information..........	1
Initial start-up after overhaul	28
Major engine repair - general note.............	4
Oil pump - removal, inspection and installation	22
Operations possible with the engine in the frame.............	2
Operations requiring engine removal	3
Piston - removal, inspection and installation	15
Piston rings - installation	16
Primary drive gear and balancer - removal, Inspection and installation...........	21
Recommended break-in procedure	29
Transmission shafts and shift drum - removal, inspection and installation...........	26
Valve cover - removal and installation...........	8
Valves/valve seats/valve guides - servicing	12

Degrees of difficulty

| **Easy,** suitable for novice with little experience  | **Fairly easy,** suitable for beginner with some experience | **Fairly difficult,** suitable for competent DIY mechanic | **Difficult,** suitable for experienced DIY mechanic  | **Very difficult,** suitable for expert DIY or professional |

Specifications

YFZ450

General
Bore............	95 mm (3.74 inches)
Stroke............	62 mm (2.44 inches)
Displacement............	439 cc

2•2 Engine, clutch and transmission

Camshaft
Lobe height (intake)
   Standard .... 31.2 to 31.3 mm (1.2283 to 1.2323 inches)
   Limit .... 31.1 mm (1.2244 inches)
Lobe height (exhaust)
   Standard .... 30.950 to 31.050 mm (1.2185 to 1.2224 inches)
   Limit .... 30.850 mm (1.2146 inches)
Camshaft runout limit .... 0.03 mm (0.0012 inch)
Bearing oil clearance
   Standard
      2004 and 2005.. 0.020 to 0.054 mm (0.0008 to 0.0021 inch)
      2006 and later... 0.028 to 0.062 mm (0.0011 to 0.0024 inch)
   Limit .... 0.08 mm (0.0031 inch)

Cylinder head, valves and valve springs
Cylinder head warpage limit.. 0.05 mm (0.002 inch)
Valve stem runout... 0.01 mm (0.0004 inch)
Valve stem diameter
   Intake
      Standard .... 4.475 to 4.490 mm (0.1762 to 0.1768 inch)
      Limit .... 4.445 mm (0.175 inch)
   Exhaust
      Standard .... 4.965 to 4.980 mm (0.1955 to 0.1961 inch)
      Limit .... 4.935 mm (0.194 inch)
Valve guide inside diameter
   Intake
      Standard .... 4.500 to 4.512 mm (0.1772 to 0.176 inch)
      Limit .... 4.550 mm (0.1594 inch)
   Exhaust
      Standard .... 5.000 to 5.012 mm (0.1969 to 0.1973 inch)
      Limit .... 5.050 mm (0.199 inch)
Stem-to-guide clearance
   Intake
      Standard .... 0.010 to 0.037 mm (0.0004 to 0.0015 inch)
      Limit .... 0.08 mm (0.0031 inch)
   Exhaust
      Standard .... 0.020 to 0.047 mm (0.0008 to 0.0019 inch)
      Limit .... 0.1 mm (0.004 inch)
Valve seat width (intake and exhaust)
   Standard .... 0.9 to 1.1 mm (0.0354 to 0.0433 inch)
   Limit .... 1.6 mm (0.063 inch)
Valve margin thickness (intake and exhaust) .... 1.0 mm (0.394 inch)
Valve spring free length (intake)
   Standard .... 37.03 mm (1.46 inches)
   Limit .... 35.17 mm (1.38 inches)
Valve spring free length (exhaust)
   Standard .... 37.68 mm (1.48 inches)
   Limit .... 35.79 mm (1.41 inches)
Valve spring bend limit .... Not specified

Cylinder
Bore diameter
   Standard .... 95.00 to 95.01 mm (3.7402 to 3.7406 inches)
   Limit .... Not specified
Out-of-round limit... 0.05 mm (0.002 inch)
Taper limit.. 0.05 mm (0.002 inch)
Measuring point... Top, center and bottom of bore

Piston
Diameter.. 94.945 to 94.960 mm (3.7380 to 3.7386 inches)
Measuring point... 10.0 mm (0.394 inch) from bottom of skirt
Piston-to-cylinder clearance
   Standard .... 0.040 to 0.065 mm (0.0016 to 0.0026 inch)
   Limit .... 0.1 mm (0.004 inch)
Piston pin bore
   Standard .... 20.004 to 20.015 mm (0.7876 to 0.7880 inch)
   Limit .... 20.045 mm (0.789 inch)
Piston pin outer diameter
   Standard .... 19.991 to 20.000 mm (0.7870 to 0.7874 inch)
   Limit .... 19.971 mm (0.7863 inch)

Engine, clutch and transmission 2•3

Piston pin-to-piston clearance	0.004 to 0.024 mm (0.0002 to 0.0009 inch)
Ring side clearance	
Top ring	
Standard	0.030 to 0.065 mm (0.0012 to 0.0026 inch)
Limit	0.12 mm (0.0047 inch)
Second ring	
Standard	0.035 to 0.050 mm (0.0014 to 0.0020 inch)
Limit	0.12 mm (0.0047 inch)
Oil ring	
2004 and 2005	Not specified
2006 and later	0.04 to 0.14 mm (0.0016 to 0.0055 inch)
Ring end gap	
Top ring	
Standard	0.20 to 0.30 mm (0.008 to 0.012 inch)
Limit	0.55 mm (0.22 inch)
Second ring	
Standard	0.35 to 0.50 mm (0.014 to 0.020 inch)
Limit	0.85 mm (0.34 inch)
Oil ring	
Standard	0.20 to 0.50 mm (0.008 to 0.020 inch)
Limit	Not specified

Clutch

Spring free length	
2006 and earlier	
Standard	51.8 mm (2.04 inches)
Limit	50.0 mm (1.97 inches)
2007 and later	
Standard	47.8 mm (1.88 inches)
Limit	46.0 mm (1.81 inches)
Metal plate thickness	1.5 to 1.7 mm (0.059 to 0.067 inch)
Friction plate thickness	
Standard	2.92 to 3.08 mm (0.115 to 0.121 inch)
Limit	2.8 mm (0.110 inch)
Friction and metal plate warpage limit	0.2 mm (0.008 inch)

Oil pump

Outer rotor-to-body clearance	0.09 to 0.17 mm (0.0012 to 0.0039 inch)
Inner-to-outer rotor clearance	
Standard	0.12 mm (0.005 inch) or less
Limit	0.20 mm (0.008 inch)

Transmission

Shift fork shaft bend limit	0.05 mm (0.002 inch)
Main axle and driveaxle runout limit	0.08 mm (0.003 inch)

Crankshaft and connecting rod

Runout limit	0.05 mm (0.002 inch)
Assembly width	61.95 to 62.00 mm (2.439 to 2.441 inches)
Connecting rod big-end side clearance	
Standard	0.15 to 0.45 mm (0.006 to 0.018 inch)
Limit	0.50 mm (0.020 inch)
Connecting rod big-end freeplay	
Standard	0.010 to 0.025 mm (0.0004 to 0.0010 inch)
Limit	Not specified

Torque specifications

Valve cover bolts	10 Nm (86 inch-lbs)
Cylinder head underside nuts	10 Nm (86 inch-lbs)
Cylinder head main bolts (1)	
Step 1	30 Nm (22 ft-lbs)
Step 2	Loosen all the way
Step 3	20 Nm (168 inch-lbs)
Step 4	An additional 90-degrees
Step 5	90-degrees past Step 4

Torque specifications (continued)

Oil check bolt	See Chapter 1
Oil line union bolts (three-fitting metal line)	
M10 thread	20 Nm (168 inch-lbs)
M8 thread	18 Nm (156 inch-lbs)
Oil hose mounting bolts	8 Nm (70 inch-lbs)
Oil tube (outside of right crankcase)	10 Nm (86 inch-lbs)
Camshaft bearing cap bolts	10 Nm (86 inch-lbs) (4)
Cam chain guide bolts	10 Nm (86 inch-lbs) (2)
Cam chain tensioner body bolts	10 Nm (86 inch-lbs)
Cam chain tensioner cap bolt	7 Nm (61 inch-lbs)
Cylinder base bolt	10 Nm (86 inch-lbs)
Crankcase bolts	10 Nm (86 inch-lbs)
Crankcase cover bolts	10 Nm (86 inch-lbs)
Oil pump mounting bolts	10 Nm (86 inch-lbs)
Oil pump assembly screw	2 Nm (17 inch-lbs)
Clutch boss nut	75 Nm (54 ft-lbs) (3)
Clutch spring bolts	8 Nm (70 inch-lbs)
Shift drum segment retaining pin	30 Nm (22 ft-lbs)
External shift linkage stopper lever bolt	10 Nm (86 inch-lbs) (2)
External shift linkage shift guide bolts	10 Nm (86 inch-lbs) (2)
Shift pedal pinch bolt	12 Nm (104 inch-lbs)
Primary drive gear nut	75 Nm (54 ft-lbs) (3)
Balancer nut	50 Nm (36 ft-lbs) (3)
Engine mounting bolts/nuts	
Upper rear bracket center to frame	33 Nm (24 ft-lbs)
Upper rear bracket sides to center	26 Nm (19 ft-lbs)
Upper rear bracket to engine	55 Nm (40 ft-lbs)
Front bracket to frame	38 Nm (27 ft-lbs)
Front bracket to engine	66 Nm (48 ft-lbs)
Rear through-bolt and nut	100 Nm (72 ft-lbs)

1 Apply molybdenum disulfide oil to the threads, bolt seating surfaces and upper and lower sides of the washers.
2 Apply non-permanent thread locking agent to the threads.
3 Use a new lockwasher.
4 Apply engine oil to the bolt threads and the undersides of the bolt heads.

YFZ450R

General

Bore	95 mm (3.74 inches)
Stroke	63.4 mm (2.50 inches)
Displacement	449 cc

Camshaft

Lobe height (intake)	
Standard	31.2 to 31.3 mm (1.2283 to 1.2323 inches)
Limit	31.1 mm (1.2244 inch)
Lobe height (exhaust)	
Standard	30.100 to 30.200 mm (1.1850 to 1.1890 inches)
Limit	30.850 mm (1.2146 inches)
Camshaft runout limit	0.03 mm (0.0012 inch)
Bearing oil clearance	
Standard	0.028 to 0.062 mm (0.0011 to 0.0024 inch)
Limit	0.08 mm (0.0031 inch)

Cylinder head, valves and valve springs

Cylinder head warpage limit	0.05 mm (0.002 inch)
Valve stem runout	0.01 mm (0.0004 inch)
Valve stem diameter	
Intake	
Standard	4.475 to 4.490 mm (0.1762 to 0.1768 inch)
Limit	4.445 mm (0.175 inch)
Exhaust	
Standard	4.965 to 4.980 mm (0.1955 to 0.1961 inch)
Limit	4.935 mm (0.194 inch)

Valve guide inside diameter
  Intake
    Standard .... 4.500 to 4.512 mm (0.1772 to 0.176 inch)
    Limit .... 4.550 mm (0.1594 inch)
  Exhaust
    Standard .... 5.000 to 5.012 mm (0.1969 to 0.1973 inch)
    Limit .... 5.050 mm (0.199 inch)
Stem-to-guide clearance
  Intake
    Standard .... 0.010 to 0.037 mm (0.0004 to 0.0015 inch)
    Limit .... 0.08 mm (0.0031 inch)
  Exhaust
    Standard .... 0.020 to 0.047 mm (0.0008 to 0.0019 inch)
    Limit .... 0.1 mm (0.004 inch)
Valve seat width (intake and exhaust)
  Standard .... 0.9 to 1.1 mm (0.0354 to 0.0433 inch)
  Limit .... 1.6 mm (0.063 inch)
Valve margin thickness (intake and exhaust)
  Standard .... 1.0 mm (0.394 inch)
  Limit .... 0.85 mm (0.033 inch)
Valve spring free length (intake)
  Standard .... 39.46 mm (1.55 inches)
  Limit .... 38.46 mm (1.51 inches)
Valve spring free length (exhaust)
  Standard .... 37.68 mm (1.48 inches)
  Limit .... 36.68 mm (1.44 inches)
Valve spring bend limit .... Not specified

Cylinder

Bore diameter
  Standard .... 95.00 to 95.01 mm (3.7402 to 3.7406 inches)
  Limit .... Not specified
Out-of-round limit .... 0.05 mm (0.002 inch)
Taper limit .... 0.05 mm (0.002 inch)
Measuring point .... Top, center and bottom of bore

Piston

Diameter .... 94.945 to 94.960 mm (3.7380 to 3.7386 inches)
Measuring point .... 10.0 mm (0.394 inch) from bottom of skirt
Piston-to-cylinder clearance
  Standard .... 0.040 to 0.065 mm (0.0016 to 0.0026 inch)
  Limit .... 0.15 mm (0.006 inch)
Piston pin bore
  Standard .... 20.004 to 20.015 mm (0.7876 to 0.7880 inch)
  Limit .... 20.045 mm (0.789 inch)
Piston pin outer diameter
  Standard .... 19.991 to 20.000 mm (0.7870 to 0.7874 inch)
  Limit .... 19.971 mm (0.7863 inch)
Piston pin-to-piston clearance
  Standard .... 0.004 to 0.024 mm (0.0002 to 0.0009 inch)
  Limit .... 0.074 mm (0.003 inch)
Ring side clearance
  Top ring
    Standard .... 0.030 to 0.070 mm (0.0012 to 0.0028 inch)
    Limit .... 0.12 mm (0.0047 inch)
  Second ring
    Standard .... 0.020 to 0.055 mm (0.0008 to 0.0022 inch)
    Limit .... 0.12 mm (0.0047 inch)
  Oil ring .... 0.04 to 0.14 mm (0.0016 to 0.0055 inch)
Ring end gap
  Top ring
    Standard .... 0.20 to 0.30 mm (0.008 to 0.012 inch)
    Limit .... 0.55 mm (0.22 inch)
  Second ring
    Standard .... 0.35 to 0.50 mm (0.014 to 0.020 inch)
    Limit .... 0.85 mm (0.34 inch)
  Oil ring
    Standard .... 0.20 to 0.50 mm (0.008 to 0.020 inch)
    Limit .... Not specified

Clutch

Spring free length	
Standard	47.8 mm (1.88 inches)
Limit	46.0 mm (1.81 inches)
Metal plate thickness	1.5 to 1.7 mm (0.059 to 0.067 inch)
Friction plate thickness	
Standard	2.92 to 3.08 mm (0.115 to 0.121 inch)
Limit	2.8 mm (0.110 inch)
Friction and metal plate warpage limit	0.2 mm (0.008 inch)

Oil pump

Outer rotor-to-body clearance	0.09 to 0.17 mm (0.0012 to 0.0039 inch)
Inner-to-outer rotor clearance	
Standard	0.12 mm (0.005 inch) or less
Limit	0.20 mm (0.008 inch)
Oil pump to housing clearance	
Feed pump	
Standard	0.050 to 0.100 mm (0.002 to 0.004 inch)
Limit	0.170 mm (0.007 inch)
Scavenging pump	
Standard	0.030 to 0.100 mm (0.001 to 0.004 inch)
Limit	0.170 mm (0.007 inch)

Transmission

Shift fork shaft bend limit	Not specified
Main axle and driveaxle runout limit	0.08 mm (0.003 inch)

Crankshaft and connecting rod

Runout limit	0.03 mm (0.001 inch)
Assembly width	63.95 to 64.00 mm (2.518 to 2.520 inches)
Connecting rod big-end side clearance	0.15 to 0.45 mm (0.006 to 0.018 inch)

Torque specifications

Valve cover bolts	10 Nm (86 inch-lbs)
Cylinder head small bolts	Not specified
Cylinder head main bolts (1)	
Step 1	Finger-tight
Step 2	30 Nm (22 ft-lbs)
Step 3	Loosen all the way and re-lubricate
Step 3	20 Nm (168 inch-lbs)
Step 5	An additional 90-degrees
Step 6	90-degrees past Step 4
Oil check bolt	See Chapter 1
Camshaft bearing cap bolts	10 Nm (86 inch-lbs) (4)
Cam chain guide bolts	10 Nm (86 inch-lbs) (2)
Cam chain tensioner body bolts	10 Nm (86 inch-lbs)
Cam chain tensioner cap bolt	7 Nm (61 inch-lbs)
Cylinder base bolt	10 Nm (86 inch-lbs)
Crankcase bolts	12 Nm (104 inch-lbs)
Crankcase cover bolts	10 Nm (86 inch-lbs)
Oil pump mounting bolts	10 Nm (86 inch-lbs)
Clutch boss nut	75 Nm (54 ft-lbs) (3)
Clutch spring bolts	10 Nm (86 inch-lbs)
Shift drum segment retaining pin	30 Nm (22 ft-lbs)
External shift linkage stopper lever bolt	10 Nm (86 inch-lbs) (2)
External shift linkage shift guide bolts	10 Nm (86 inch-lbs) (2)
Shift pedal pinch bolt	12 Nm (104 inch-lbs)
Primary drive gear nut	110 Nm (80 ft-lbs) (3)
Balancer nut	50 Nm (36 ft-lbs) (3)
Engine mounting bolts/nuts	
Upper rear bracket center to frame	33 Nm (24 ft-lbs)
Upper rear bracket to engine	40 Nm (29 ft-lbs)
Front bracket to frame	48 Nm (35 ft-lbs)
Front bracket to engine	66 Nm (48 ft-lbs)
Rear through-bolt (swingarm bolt) and nut	100 Nm (72 ft-lbs)

1   Apply molybdenum disulfide oil to the threads, bolt seating surfaces and upper and lower sides of the washers.
2   Apply non-permanent thread locking agent to the threads.
3   Use a new lockwasher.
4   Apply engine oil to the bolt threads and the undersides of the bolt heads.

Engine, clutch and transmission 2•7

1 General information

The engine/transmission unit is of the liquid-cooled, single-cylinder four-stroke design.

All models have five valves (three intake and two exhaust). The valves are operated by dual overhead camshafts, which are chain driven off the crankshaft.

The engine/transmission assembly is constructed from aluminum alloy. The crankcase is divided vertically.

The crankcase incorporates a dry sump, pressure-fed lubrication system which uses a gear-driven rotor-type oil pump and an oil filter. YFZ450 models have an external oil tank, mounted in front of the engine. The oil tank on YFZ450R models is integral with the crankcase.

On all models, a wet, multi-plate clutch connects the crankshaft to the transmission. Engagement and disengagement of the clutch is controlled by a lever on the left handlebar through a cable.

The transmission has five forward gears and one reverse gear.

2 Operations possible with the engine in the frame

The components and assemblies listed below can be removed without having to remove the engine from the frame. If, however, a number of areas require attention at the same time, removal of the engine is recommended.

Starter motor (if equipped)
Starter reduction gears
Starter clutch
Alternator rotor and stator
Clutch
External shift mechanism
Cam chain tensioner
Camshafts and lifters
Cylinder head
Cylinder and piston
Oil pump
Balancer gears

3 Operations requiring engine removal

It is necessary to remove the engine/transmission assembly from the frame and separate the crankcase halves to gain access to the following components:

Crankshaft and connecting rod
Transmission shafts
Shift drum and forks

4 Major engine repair - general note

1 It is not always easy to determine when or if an engine should be completely overhauled, as a number of factors must be considered.
2 High mileage is not necessarily an indication that an overhaul is needed, while low mileage, on the other hand, does not preclude the need for an overhaul. Frequency of servicing is probably the single most important consideration. An engine that has regular and frequent oil and filter changes, as well as other required maintenance, will most likely give many miles of reliable service. Conversely, a neglected engine, or one which has not been broken in properly, may require an overhaul very early in its life.
3 Exhaust smoke and excessive oil consumption are both indications that piston rings and/or valve guides are in need of attention. Make sure oil leaks are not responsible before deciding that the rings and guides are bad. Refer to Chapter 1 and perform a cylinder compression check to determine for certain the nature and extent of the work required.
4 If the engine is making obvious knocking or rumbling noises, the connecting rod and/or main bearings are probably at fault.
5 Loss of power, rough running, excessive valve train noise and high fuel consumption rates may also point to the need for an overhaul, especially if they are all present at the same time. If a complete tune-up does not remedy the situation, major mechanical work is the only solution.
6 An engine overhaul generally involves restoring the internal parts to the specifications of a new engine. During an overhaul the piston rings are replaced and the cylinder walls are bored and/or honed. If a rebore is done, then a new piston is also required. Generally the valves are serviced as well, since they are usually in less than perfect condition at this point. While the engine is being overhauled, other components such as the carburetor and the starter motor (if equipped) can be rebuilt also. The end result should be a like-new engine that will give as many trouble-free miles as the original.
7 Before beginning the engine overhaul, read through all of the related procedures to familiarize yourself with the scope and requirements of the job. Overhauling an engine is not all that difficult, but it is time consuming. Plan on the vehicle being tied up for a minimum of two weeks. Check on the availability of parts and make sure that any necessary special tools, equipment and supplies are obtained in advance.
8 Most work can be done with typical shop hand tools, although a number of precision measuring tools are required for inspecting parts to determine if they must be replaced. Often a dealer service department

5.5 A compression gauge with a threaded fitting for the spark plug hole is preferable to the type that requires hand pressure to maintain the seal

or repair shop will handle the inspection of parts and offer advice concerning reconditioning and replacement. As a general rule, time is the primary cost of an overhaul so it doesn't pay to install worn or substandard parts.
9 As a final note, to ensure maximum life and minimum trouble from a rebuilt engine, everything must be assembled with care in a spotlessly clean environment.

5 Cylinder compression - check

1 Among other things, poor engine performance may be caused by leaking valves, incorrect valve clearances, a leaking head gasket, or worn piston, rings and/or cylinder wall. A cylinder compression check will help pinpoint these conditions and can also indicate the presence of excessive carbon deposits in the cylinder head.
2 The only tools required are a compression gauge and a spark plug wrench. Depending on the outcome of the initial test, a squirt-type oil can may also be needed.
3 Check valve clearances and adjust if necessary (see Chapter 1). Start the engine and allow it to reach normal operating temperature, then remove the spark plug (see Chapter 1). Work carefully - don't strip the spark plug hole threads and don't burn your hands.
4 If you're working on a YFZ450R, disable the ignition by disconnecting the primary (low tension) wires from the coil (see Chapter 5). Be sure to mark the locations of the wires before detaching them. (On YFZ450 models, the coil is removed in the process of removing the spark plug).
5 Install the compression gauge in the spark plug hole (see illustration). Hold or block the throttle wide open.
6 Crank the engine over a minimum of

2•8 Engine, clutch and transmission

6.12 Slide back the clip and disconnect the breather hose (right arrow) from the top of the engine - some models also have an oil tank vent hose (left arrow)

four or five revolutions (or until the gauge reading stops increasing) and observe the initial movement of the compression gauge needle as well as the final total gauge reading. Compare the results to the value listed in this Chapter's Specifications.

7 If the compression built up quickly and evenly to the specified amount, you can assume the engine upper end is in reasonably good mechanical condition. Worn or sticking piston rings and a worn cylinder will produce very little initial movement of the gauge needle, but compression will tend to build up gradually as the engine spins over. Valve and valve seat leakage, or head gasket leakage, is indicated by low initial compression which does not tend to build up.

8 To further confirm your findings, add a small amount of engine oil to the cylinder by inserting the nozzle of a squirt-type oil can through the spark plug hole. The oil will tend to seal the piston rings if they are leaking.

9 If the compression increases significantly after the addition of the oil, the piston rings and/or cylinder are definitely worn. If the compression does not increase, the pressure is leaking past the valves or the head gasket. Leakage past the valves may be due to insufficient valve clearances, burned, warped or cracked valves or valve seats or valves that are hanging up in the guides.

10 If compression readings are considerably higher than specified, the combustion chamber is probably coated with excessive carbon deposits. It is possible (but not very likely) for carbon deposits to raise the compression enough to compensate for the effects of leakage past rings or valves. Refer to Section 11, remove the cylinder head and carefully decarbonize the combustion chamber.

6 Engine - removal and installation

Warning: Engine removal and installation should be done with the aid of an assistant to avoid damage or injury that could occur if the engine is dropped.

Removal

1 Remove the seat, both side covers, right footrest, engine skid plate and fuel tank cover (see Chapter 8).
2 Disconnect the negative cable from the battery (see Chapter 9).
3 Remove the fuel tank (YFZ450) and exhaust system (all models) (see Chapter 4).
4 Drain the engine oil and coolant (see Chapter 1).
5 Disconnect the radiator hoses (all models). If you're working on a YFZ450R, remove the radiator (see Chapter 3).
6 Remove the carburetor (YFZ450) or throttle body (YFZ450R) (see Chapter 4).
7 Disconnect the clutch cable from the engine (see Section 19).
8 If you're working on a YFZ450, remove the ignition coil from the spark plug (see Chapter 1).
9 If you're working on a YFZ450R, disconnect the spark plug wire (see Chapter 1) and remove the ignition coil (see Chapter 5).
10 Disconnect the starter motor cable (see Chapter 5).
11 Remove the drive sprocket from the engine (see Chapter 6).
12 Disconnect the breather hose(s) from the valve cover **(see illustration)**.
13 If you're working on a YFZ450R, disconnect the external oil hoses from the engine (see Section 17).
14 Label and disconnect the following wires (see Chapter 5 for component locations if necessary):
   CDI magneto and alternator
   Neutral switch
15 If you're working on a YFZ450R, label and disconnect the following wires (see Chapter 4 for component locations if necessary):
   Speed sensor
   Crankshaft position sensor
16 If you're working on a YFZ450R, remove the parking brake cable bracket. On all models, disconnect the parking brake cable (see Chapter 7).
17 Support the engine securely from below.
18 Remove the engine mounting bolts, nuts and brackets at the lower front and upper rear **(see illustrations)**.
19 Remove the swingarm pivot bolt partway (see Chapter 6).

 **HAYNES HiNT** *The swingarm pivot bolt acts as an engine mounting bolt. Pull out the bolt just far enough to free the engine, but leave it in far enough to support one side of the swingarm.*

20 Have an assistant help you support the engine. Remove it from the right side.
21 Slowly lower the engine to a suitable work surface.

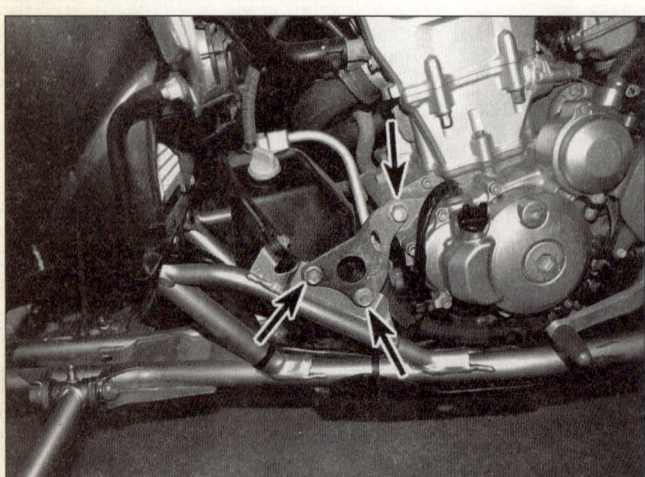

6.18a With the engine supported, remove the left front mount bolts (arrows) . . .

6.18b . . . and the right front mount bolts (arrows)

Engine, clutch and transmission 2•9

6.18c Unbolt the upper bracket from the engine (lower arrow) and frame (upper bolts) (YFZ450 shown) . . .

6.18d . . . and remove the lower through-bolt and nut (arrow)

Installation

22 Check the engine supports for wear or damage and replace them if necessary before installing the engine.

23 Make sure the motorcycle is securely supported so it can't be knocked over during the remainder of this procedure.

24 With the help of an assistant, lift the engine up into the frame. Install the mounting nuts and bolts at the rear, front and top. Be sure the mount brackets are installed on the correct sides of the bike (refer to their L and R marks). Finger-tighten the mounting bolts, but don't tighten them to the specified torque yet.

25 Tighten the engine mounting bolts and nuts evenly to the torques listed in this Chapter's Specifications.

26 The remainder of installation is the reverse of the removal steps, with the following additions:

a) Use new gaskets at all exhaust pipe connections.

b) Adjust the throttle cable, clutch cable and parking brake cable following the procedures in Chapter 1.

c) Fill the engine with oil and coolant, also following the procedures in Chapter 1. Run the engine and check for oil, coolant and exhaust leaks.

7 Engine disassembly and reassembly - general information

1 Before disassembling the engine, clean the exterior with a degreaser and rinse it with water. A clean engine will make the job easier and prevent the possibility of getting dirt into the internal areas of the engine.

2 In addition to the precision measuring tools mentioned earlier, you will need a torque wrench, a valve spring compressor, oil gallery brushes (see illustration), a piston ring removal and installation tool, a piston ring compressor. Some new, clean engine oil of the correct grade and type, some engine assembly lube (or moly-based grease) and a tube of RTV (silicone) sealant will also be required.

3 An engine support stand made from short lengths of 2 x 4s bolted together will facilitate the disassembly and reassembly procedures (see illustration). If you have an automotive-type engine stand, an adapter plate can be made from a piece of plate, some angle iron and some nuts and bolts.

4 When disassembling the engine, keep "mated" parts together (including gears, rocker arms and shafts, etc.) that have been in contact with each other during engine operation. These "mated" parts must be reused or replaced as an assembly.

5 Engine/transmission disassembly should be done in the following general order with reference to the appropriate Sections.

Remove the cam chain tensioner
Remove the camshafts and lifters
Remove the cylinder head
Remove the cylinder

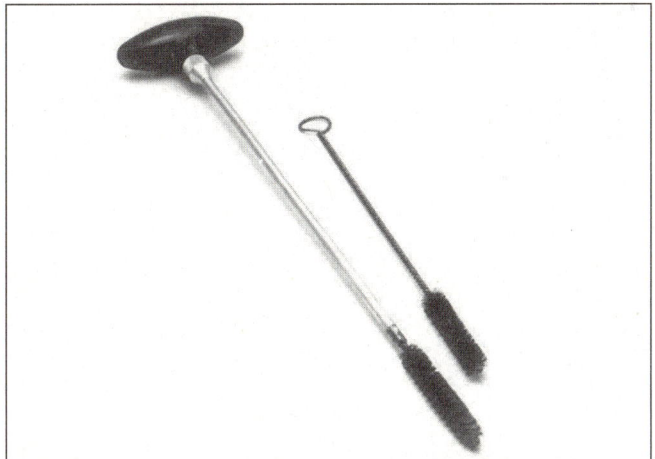

7.2 A selection of brushes is required for cleaning holes and passages in the engine components

7.3 An engine stand can be made from short lengths of lumber and lag bolts or nails

2•10 Engine, clutch and transmission

8.5 Remove the valve cover Allen bolts

8.6a Tilt the valve cover sharply to the left and remove it from the left side

8.6b Remove the sealing washers, noting the direction they face

Remove the piston
Remove the clutch
Remove the balancer gears
Remove the oil pump
Remove the external shift mechanism
Remove the alternator rotor
Remove the starter reduction gears
Separate the crankcase halves
Remove the shift drum and forks
Remove the transmission gears and shafts
Remove the crankshaft and
connecting rod

6 Reassembly is accomplished by reversing the general disassembly sequence.

8 Valve cover - removal and installation

1 Remove the seat, fuel tank cover and both side covers (see Chapter 8).
2 Remove the spark plug (see Chapter 1).
3 If you're working on a YFZ450, remove the upper engine mount (see illustration 6.18c).
4 Disconnect the cylinder head breather hose (all models) and oil tank breather hose (YFZ450) (see illustration 6.12).
5 Unscrew the valve cover mounting bolts (see illustration).
6 Lift the valve cover off the cylinder head (see illustration). If it's stuck, don't attempt to pry it off - tap around the sides of it with a plastic hammer to dislodge it. Remove the sealing washers (see illustration).
7 Work the gasket free of the cylinder head and remove it (see illustration).
8 Check the valve cover gasket for damage or deterioration and replace it as needed. It's a good idea to replace the bolt sealing washers whenever they're removed.
9 Installation is the reverse of the removal steps, with the following additions:

a) Coat the area of the valve cover gasket that fits into the cylinder head cutouts with non-hardening sealer (see illustration 8.7).

b) Install new sealing washers and tighten the valve cover bolts evenly to the torque listed in this Chapter's Specifications.

9 Cam chain tensioner - removal, inspection and installation

Removal

Caution: *Once you start to remove the tensioner bolts, you must remove the tensioner all the way and reset it before tightening the bolts. The tensioner extends and locks in place, so if you loosen the bolts partway and then tighten them, the tensioner or cam chain will be damaged.*

1 Unscrew the tensioner cap bolt and remove the sealing washer (see illustration).
2 Turn the tensioner piston clockwise with

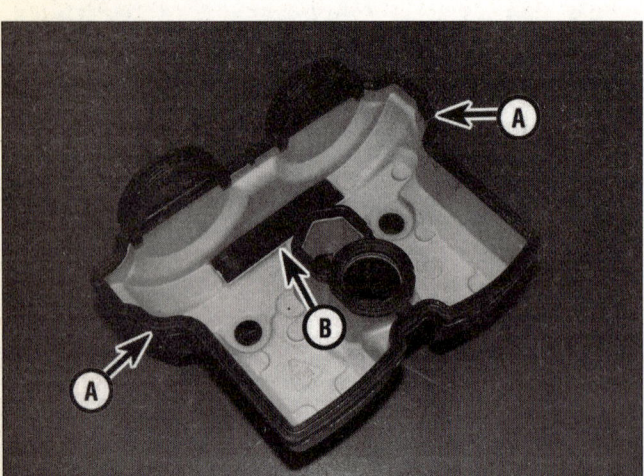

8.7 Apply non-hardening sealant to the lower side of the gasket, in the area between the arrows (A) (including the semi-circular cutouts) - check the cam chain guide (B) for wear

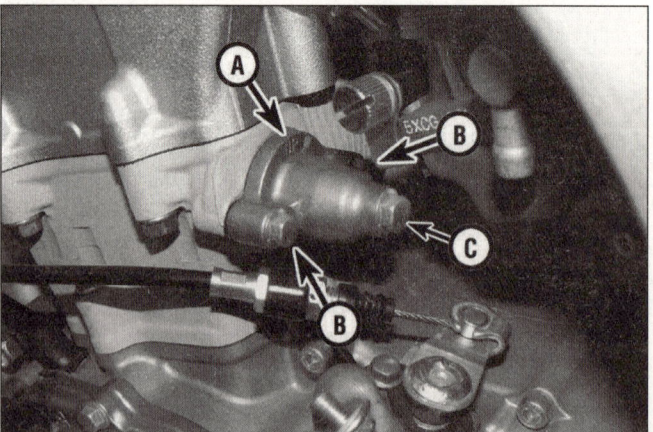

9.1 Remove the tensioner cap bolt and copper washer

A UP mark
B Tensioner bolts (inner bolt has a sealing washer)
C Tensioner cap bolt

Engine, clutch and transmission 2•11

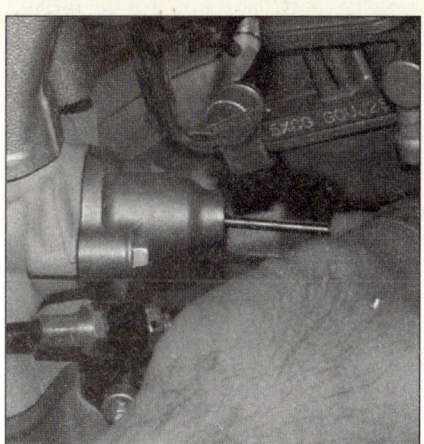

9.2a Insert a thin screwdriver into the tensioner and turn it clockwise to retract the piston - it will lock when fully retracted

9.2b As the tensioner piston retracts, the top run of the cam chain will develop slack (arrow)

9.2c Here's an easily fabricated tool that will allow access to retract the tensioner piston

a small screwdriver to retract it **(see illustration)**. When the piston is fully retracted, there will be slack in the upper run of the cam chain **(see illustration)**.

TOOL TiP *If you don't have a small enough screwdriver, you can make one by bending a piece of coat hanger into an L shape and grinding the tip of the long end into a screwdriver shape (see illustration).*

3 Remove the tensioner mounting bolts and detach the tensioner from the cylinder **(see illustration 9.1)**.

Installation

4 Clean all old gasket material from the tensioner body and engine.
5 Place a new gasket on the tensioner body **(see illustration)**.
6 Insert a narrow-bladed screwdriver into the tensioner and rotate it clockwise to retract the tensioner piston **(see illustrations)**. The tensioner piston should lock in the retracted position if you turn it far enough. If not, hold the screwdriver in position while installing the tensioner on the cylinder.
7 Position the tensioner body on the cylinder, making sure the UP mark is upward **(see illustration 9.1)**. Install the bolts, tightening them to the torque listed in this Chapter's Specifications.
8 Remove the screwdriver so the tensioner piston can extend. When this happens, the slack will disappear from the top run of the cam chain **(see illustration 9.2b)**.
9 Install the cap bolt with a new sealing washer and tighten it to the torque listed in this Chapter's Specifications.

10 Camshafts and lifters - removal, inspection and installation

Removal

Camshafts

1 Remove the valve cover (see Section 8).
2 Refer to *Valve clearances - check*

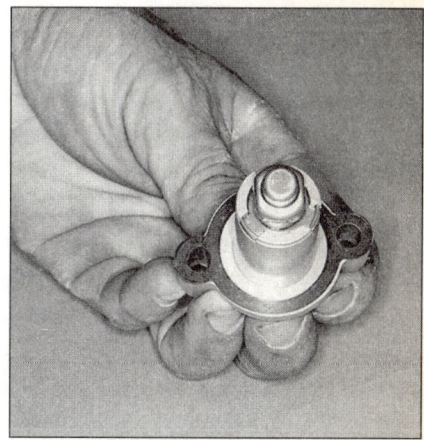

9.5 Place a new gasket on the tensioner body

and *adjustment* in Chapter 1 and place the engine at top dead center on the compression stroke.

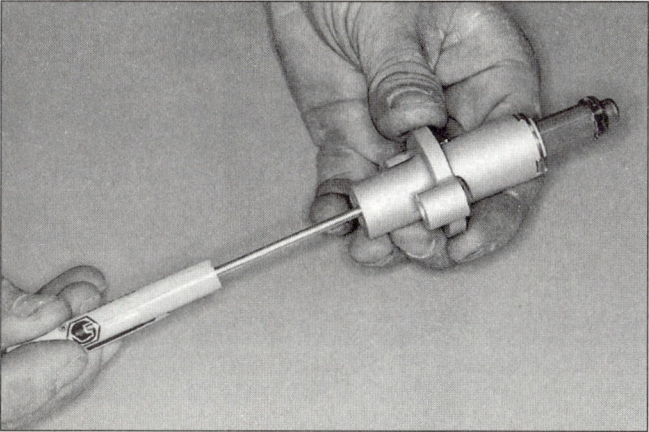

9.6a Turn the screwdriver clockwise to retract the piston . . .

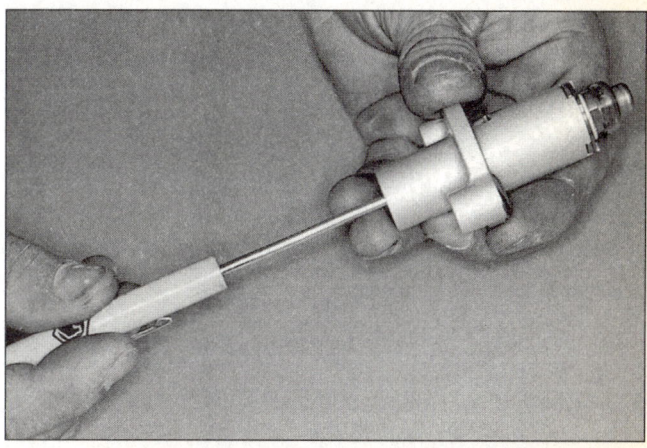

9.6b . . . until it's in this position; it should lock and stay by itself, but if not, then hold the screwdriver

2•12 Engine, clutch and transmission

10.5a Camshaft bolt TIGHTENING sequence

10.5b Lift up two of the bearing cap bolts and rock them to free the cap from the cylinder head

10.5c Lift off the bearing caps and remove the retaining ring (arrow); there's one for each cap

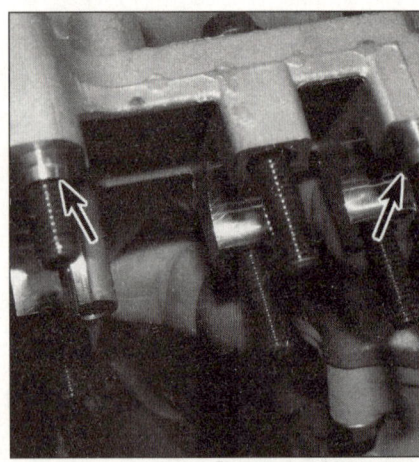

10.5d Here are the intake cap dowels (arrows) . . .

3 Remove the cam chain tensioner (see Section 9).
4 Tie the cam chain up with wire so it can't fall into the chain cavity.
5 Loosen the camshaft cap bolts in several stages, in the reverse of the tightening sequence **(see illustration)**. On the intake cap, work from the inner bolts to the outer bolts. On the exhaust cap, loosen the bolts in a criss-cross pattern. Take off the caps and dowels **(see illustrations)**.
6 Lift the intake camshaft out of its saddles and disengage the sprocket from the chain **(see illustrations)**. Remove the exhaust camshaft in the same way.

 *If you're removing the camshafts to adjust the valves, don't remove them all the way - you can just roll them out of their saddles (one at a time), leaving them attached to the chain as*

10.5e . . . and the exhaust cap dowels (arrows)

10.6a If you're removing the camshafts for valve adjustment, you can roll them out of position while leaving them engaged with the chain

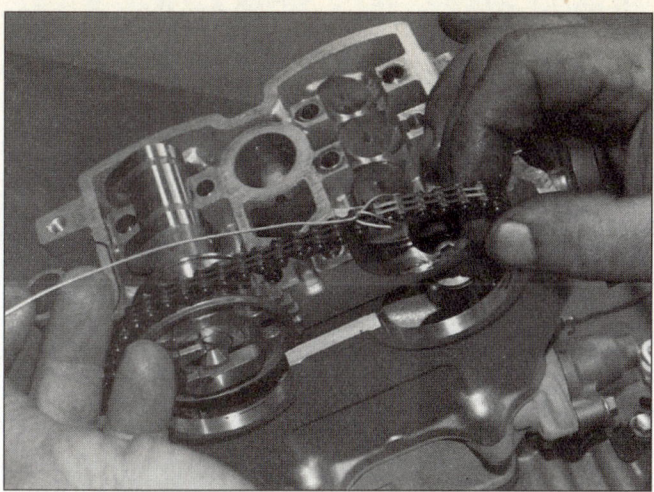

10.6b To remove the camshafts completely, disengage the intake sprocket and support the chain . . .

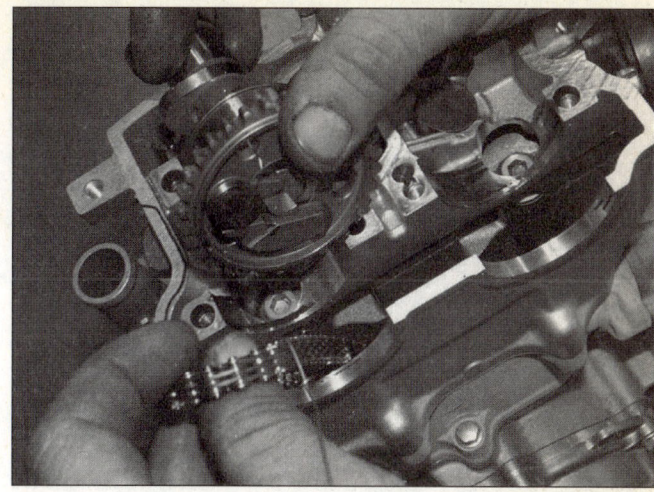

10.6c . . . then disengage the exhaust cam sprocket from the chain and remove the camshaft

shown in illustration 10.6a. That way, you won't need to realign the timing marks when you install the camshafts.

Lifters

7 Stuff a clean shop rag into the cam chain cavity so the valve adjusting shims can't fall into it when they're removed.

8 Remove the camshafts following the procedure given above. Be sure to keep tension on the cam chain.

9 Make a holder for each lifter and its adjusting shim (an egg carton or box will work). Label the sections according to whether the lifter belongs with the intake or exhaust camshaft, and left or right valve (or center valve on the intake camshaft). The lifters form a wear pattern with their bores and must be returned to their original locations if reused.

10 Label each lifter and pull each lifter out of the bore, using a magnet or suction cup **(see illustrations)**. Make sure the shims stay with their lifters. The shims are inside the lifters, so be careful not to let them fall as you lift the lifters out **(see illustration)**.

Cam chain and guides

11 The front (exhaust) cam chain guide is held in position by the cylinder head. If inspection procedures below indicate a problem, you'll need to remove the head to lift the guide out of the cylinder (see Sections 11 and 20). The rear (intake) guide is bolted at the bottom, so the left crankcase cover and alternator rotor will have to be removed for access if the guide or the cam chain need to be removed (see Section 20 and Chapter 5).

12 Stuff clean rags into the cam chain opening so dirt, small parts or tools can't fall into it.

Inspection

Camshaft, chain and guides

Note: *Before replacing camshafts or the cylinder head because of damage, check*

10.10a Before removing the lifters, label them (intake or exhaust, left, center and right) - these are the intake lifters

10.10b Pull the lifters out of their bores with a magnet . . .

10.10c . . . the valve adjusting shim should come up with the lifter, but it may stick in the valve spring retainer

10.10d Make sure each valve adjusting shim stays with its lifter

2•14 Engine, clutch and transmission

10.13a Check the cam lobes for wear - here's a good example of damage which will require replacement (or repair) of the camshaft

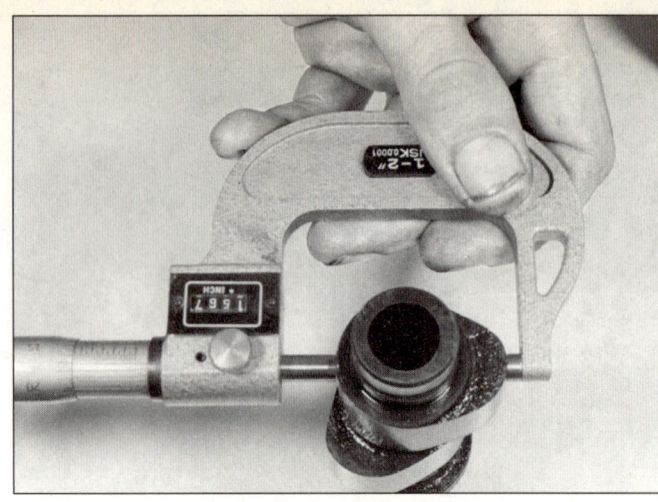

10.13b Measure the height of the cam lobes with a micrometer

with local machine shops specializing in motorcycle engine work. In the case of the camshaft, it may be possible for cam lobes to be welded, reground and hardened, at a cost far lower than that of a new camshaft. If the bearing surfaces in the cylinder head are damaged, it may be possible for them to be bored out to accept bearing inserts. Due to the cost of a new cylinder head it is recommended that all options be explored before condemning it as trash!

13 Check the camshaft lobes for heat discoloration (blue appearance), score marks, chipped areas, flat spots and spalling **(see illustration)**. Measure the height of each lobe with a micrometer **(see illustration)** and compare the results to the minimum lobe height listed in this Chapter's Specifications. If damage is noted or wear is excessive, the camshaft must be replaced. Check the bearing surfaces for scoring or wear. Also, be sure to check the condition of the lifters, as described below.

14 Except in cases of oil starvation, the camshaft chain wears very little. If the chain has stretched excessively, which makes it difficult to maintain proper tension, replace it with a new one. To remove the chain from the crankshaft sprocket, remove the alternator rotor (see Chapter 5).

15 Check the sprockets for wear, cracks and other damage, replacing it if necessary. If a sprocket is worn, the chain is also worn, and possibly the sprocket on the crankshaft. If wear this severe is apparent, the entire engine should be disassembled for inspection. The sprockets are permanently attached to the camshaft, so if the sprockets must be replaced, the camshafts must be replaced as well.

16 Check the chain guides for wear or damage, especially along the friction surfaces **(see illustration)**. Use a flashlight to look down the cam chain tunnel. If they are worn or damaged, replace them (see Section 20).

17 Check the camshaft bearing oil clearances with Plastigage, referring to "Tools and Workshop Tips" at the end of this manual.

18 Compare the results to this Chapter's Specifications.

19 If oil clearance is greater than specified, measure the diameter of the cam bearing journal with a micrometer. If the journal diameter is less than the specified limit, replace the camshaft with a new one and recheck the clearance.

20 If the clearance is still too great, replace the cylinder head and bearing caps with new parts (see the **Note** that precedes Step 13).

21 Check the automatic compression release in the left camshaft **(see illustration 10.6c)**. Operate the lever on the sprocket end of the camshaft by hand. It should move smoothly, causing the plunger in the camshaft to extend. When released, it should return by itself. If the compression release doesn't work properly, replace the camshaft.

Lifters

22 Check the lifters and their bores for wear, scuff marks, scratches and other damage. Check the camshaft contact surface, as well as the outer surface that rides in the bore. Replace the lifters if they're visibly worn or damaged.

Installation

23 Make sure the piston is still at Top Dead Center on the compression stroke (refer to the valve adjustment procedure in Chapter 1 if necessary).

24 Coat the lifters and their bores with clean engine oil. Apply a small amount of moly-based grease to the shims and stick them to their respective valve stems with the thickness number upward.

25 Slide the lifters into their bores, taking care not to knock the valve shims out of position. When the lifters are correctly installed, it should be possible to rotate them with a finger.

26 Coat the camshaft contact surfaces of the lifters and the bearing surfaces of the camshafts with moly-based grease.

27 Install the exhaust camshaft, then the intake camshaft in the cylinder head, engaging the sprocket with the chain as you do so, and make sure the sprockets are in the correct positions (see Chapter 1). Install the cap dowels in their holes (if they were removed).

28 Install the camshaft bearing caps **(see illustrations)**. Tighten the cap bolts in stages to the torque listed in this Chapter's Specifications, following the tightening sequence **(see illustration 10.5a)**.

Caution: The caps must be tightened in the proper sequence with an accurate torque wrench, or the camshafts may seize.

29 Install the cam chain tensioner (see Section 9). Release the tensioner so its piston presses against the chain.

30 Recheck the crankshaft timing mark in the timing hole cover and the match marks on both camshafts. If they are not still aligned, stop and find out why before continuing.

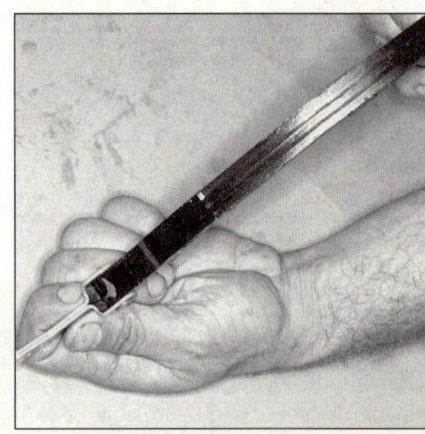

10.16 Check the chain guides for wear, especially on the friction surface

Engine, clutch and transmission 2•15

10.28a The camshaft caps should press on easily and make even contact with the cylinder head (arrows) - if not, the bearing retaining clip may have slipped out of position

10.28b Be sure to tighten the camshaft caps in the correct sequence with an accurate torque wrench

Caution: Don't run the engine with the marks misaligned or the valves may strike the pistons, bending the valves.

31 Rotate the crankshaft two full turns and make sure the timing marks still line up correctly.
32 Check the valve clearances (see Chapter 1). This is necessary to make sure none of the shims has slipped out of position.
33 Change the engine oil (see Chapter 1).
34 The remainder of installation is the reverse of removal.

11 Cylinder head - removal, inspection and installation

Removal

1 Drain the cooling system (see Chapter 1).
2 Remove the seat, side covers and fuel tank cover (see Chapter 8).
3 Remove the fuel tank, carburetor or throttle body and exhaust system (see Chapter 4).
4 Remove the valve cover and camshafts (see Sections 8 and 10).
5 Remove the two nuts (YFZ450) or bolts (YFZ450R) that secure the left-hand side of the cylinder head **(see illustration)**.
6 Loosen the four main head bolts in several stages, in a criss-cross pattern, until they're completely loose **(see illustration)**. Lift out the bolts and their washers.
7 Lift the cylinder head off the cylinder **(see illustration)**. If it's stuck, don't attempt to pry it off - tap around the sides of it with a plastic hammer to dislodge it.
8 Locate the dowels **(see illustration 11.7)**. There are two of them, one in each of the head bolt holes nearest the cam chain. The dowels may be in the cylinder or they may have come off with the head.
9 Remove the old head gasket from the cylinder or head.

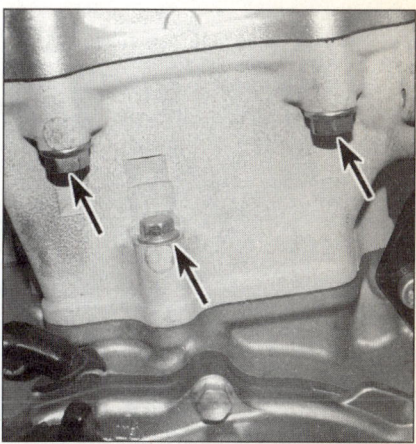

11.5 Remove the two small bolts or nuts that secure the underside of the cylinder head (upper arrows) - the single bolt (lower arrow) secures the cylinder to the crankcase

11.6 Loosen the four main bolts evenly in a criss-cross pattern

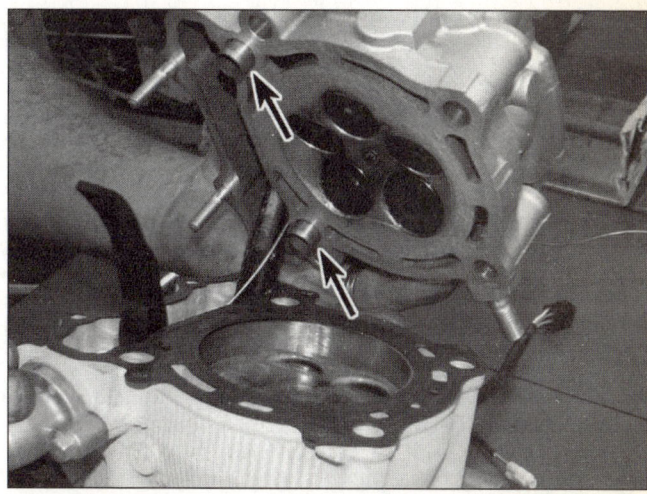

11.7 Lift the head off the cylinder and locate the dowels (arrows)

2•16 Engine, clutch and transmission

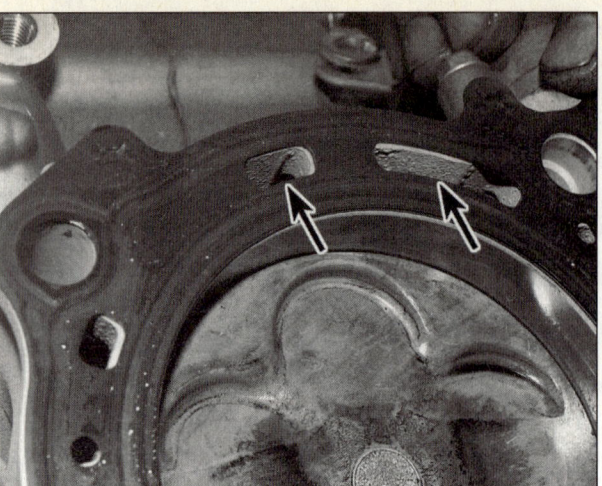

11.13 Make sure these coolant passages in the gasket and head line up correctly - if they don't, the gasket is on upside down

Inspection

10 Check the cylinder head gasket and the mating surfaces on the cylinder head and cylinder for leakage, which could indicate warpage.
11 Refer to Section 13 and check the flatness of the cylinder head.
12 Clean all traces of old gasket material from the cylinder head and cylinder. Be careful not to let any of the gasket material fall into the crankcase, the cylinder bore or the bolt holes.

Installation

13 Install the two dowel pins, then place the new head gasket on the cylinder (see illustration). Never reuse the old gasket and don't use any type of gasket sealant.

 **The head gasket will line up almost exactly with the coolant passages and bolt holes if it's installed upside down. Make sure the coolant passages and bolt holes line up exactly.**

14 Install the exhaust side cam chain guide, fitting the lower end and the middle guide into their notches (see illustrations 20.2a and 20.2b).

 **Don't forget to install the chain guide at this point. It won't be possible to install it once the cylinder head is installed.**

15 Carefully lower the cylinder head over the dowels, guiding the cam chain through the slot in the cylinder head. It's helpful to have an assistant support the cam chain with a piece of wire so it doesn't fall and become kinked or detached from the crankshaft. When the head is resting on the cylinder, wire the cam chain to another component to keep tension on it.
16 Lubricate the threads and seating surfaces of the four main cylinder head bolts with molybdenum disulfide grease. Lubricate the upper and lower sides of the head bolt washers with the same grease.
17 Install the washers on the four main head bolts and install the bolts finger-tight. Tighten the four bolts in a criss-cross pattern, in several stages, to the initial torque listed in this Chapter's Specifications.
18 Loosen the bolts all the way, again in a criss-cross pattern. Retighten them to the second-step torque setting listed in this Chapter's Specifications, then tighten them exactly 1/2 turn further.
19 After the main nuts or bolts are tightened, tighten the two Allen bolts to the torque listed in this Chapter's Specifications.
20 The remainder of installation is the reverse of removal.

12 Valves/valve seats/valve guides - servicing

1 Because of the complex nature of this job and the special tools and equipment required, servicing of the valves, the valve seats and the valve guides (commonly known as a valve job) is best left to a professional.
2 The home mechanic can, however, remove and disassemble the head, do the initial cleaning and inspection, then reassemble and deliver the head to a dealer service department or properly equipped vehicle repair shop for the actual valve servicing. Refer to Section 13 for those procedures.
3 The dealer service department will remove the valves and springs, recondition or replace the valves and valve seats, replace the valve guides, check and replace the valve springs, spring retainers and keepers (as necessary), replace the valve seals with new ones and reassemble the valve components.
4 After the valve job has been performed, the head will be in like-new condition. When the head is returned, be sure to clean it again very thoroughly before installation on the engine to remove any metal particles or abrasive grit that may still be present from the valve service operations. Use compressed air, if available, to blow out all the holes and passages.

13 Cylinder head and valves - disassembly, inspection and reassembly

1 As mentioned in the previous Section, valve servicing and valve guide replacement should be left to a dealer service department or other repair shop. However, disassembly, cleaning and inspection of the valves and related components can be done (if the necessary special tools are available) by the home mechanic. This way no expense is incurred if the inspection reveals that service work is not required at this time.
2 To properly disassemble the valve components without the risk of damaging them, a valve spring compressor is absolutely necessary. If the special tool is not available, have a dealer service department or vehicle repair shop handle the entire process of disassembly, inspection, service or repair (if required) and reassembly of the valves.

Disassembly

3 Before the valves are removed, scrape away any traces of gasket material from the head gasket sealing surface. Work slowly and do not nick or gouge the soft aluminum of the head. Gasket removing solvents, which work very well, are available at most motorcycle shops and auto parts stores.
4 Carefully scrape all carbon deposits out of the combustion chamber area. A hand held wire brush or a piece of fine emery cloth can be used once most of the deposits have been scraped away. Do not use a wire brush mounted in a drill motor, or one with extremely stiff bristles, as the head material is soft and may be eroded away or scratched by the wire brush.
5 Before proceeding, arrange to label and store the valves along with their related components so they can be kept separate and reinstalled in the same valve guides they are removed from (plastic bags work well for this).
6 Compress the valve spring(s) on the first valve with a spring compressor, then remove the keepers and the retainer from the valve assembly (see illustration). Do not compress the spring(s) any more than is absolutely necessary. Carefully release the valve spring compressor and remove the spring(s), spring seat and valve from the head. If the valve binds in the guide (won't pull through), push it back into the head and deburr the area around the keeper groove with a very fine file or whetstone (see illustration).
7 Repeat the procedure for the remaining valve. Remember to keep the parts for each valve together so they can be reinstalled in the same location.
8 Once the valves have been removed and labeled, pull off the valve stem seals with pliers and discard them (the old seals should never be reused).
9 Next, clean the cylinder head with solvent and dry it thoroughly. Compressed air

Engine, clutch and transmission 2•17

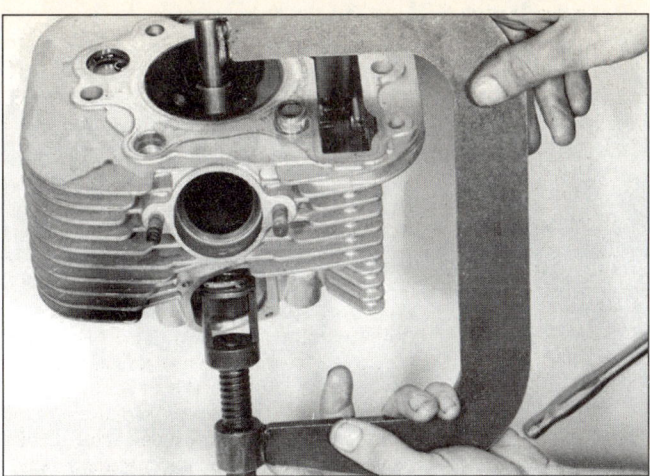

13.6a Compress the valve springs with a valve spring compressor

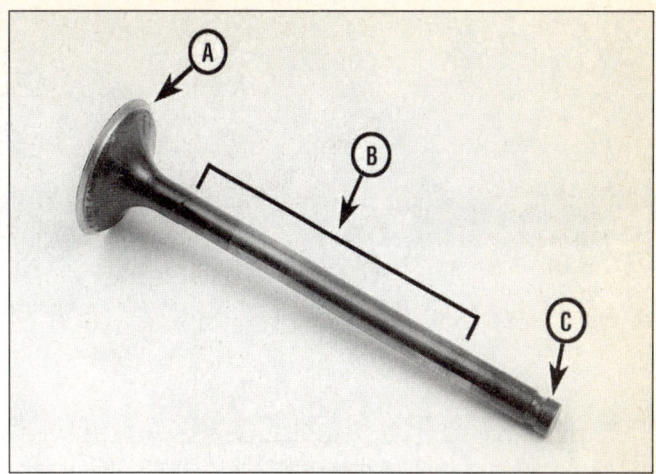

13.6b Check the valve face (A), stem (B) and keeper groove (C) for wear and damage

will speed the drying process and ensure that all holes and recessed areas are clean.

10 Clean all of the valve springs, keepers, retainers and spring seats with solvent and dry them thoroughly. Do the parts from one valve at a time so that no mixing of parts between valves occurs.

11 Scrape off any deposits that may have formed on the valve, then use a motorized wire brush to remove deposits from the valve heads and stems. Again, make sure the valves do not get mixed up.

Inspection

12 Inspect the head very carefully for cracks and other damage. If cracks are found, a new head will be required. Check the cam bearing surfaces for wear and evidence of seizure. Check the camshaft for wear as well (see Section 10).

13 Using a precision straightedge and a feeler gauge, check the head gasket mating surface for warpage as described in "Tools and Workshop Tips" at the end of this manual. If the head is warped it must either be machined or, if warpage is excessive, replaced with a new one.

14 Examine the valve seats in each of the combustion chambers. If they are pitted, cracked or burned, the head will require valve service that is beyond the scope of the home mechanic. Measure the valve seat width and compare it to this Chapter's Specifications. If it is not within the specified range, or if it varies around its circumference, valve service work is required.

15 Clean the valve guides to remove any carbon buildup, then measure the inside diameters of the guides (at both ends and the center of the guide) as described in "Tools and Workshop Tips" at the end of this manual. Record the measurements for future reference. The guides are measured at the ends and at the center to determine if they are worn in a bell-mouth pattern (more wear at the ends). If they are, guide replacement is an absolute must.

16 Carefully inspect each valve face for cracks, pits and burned spots. Check the valve stem and the keeper groove area for cracks **(see illustration 13.6b)**. Rotate the valve and check for any obvious indication that it is bent. Check the end of the stem for pitting and excessive wear and make sure the bevel is the specified width. The presence of any of the above conditions indicates the need for valve servicing.

17 Measure the valve stem diameter with a micrometer. If the diameter is less than listed in this Chapter's Specifications, the valves will have to be replaced with new ones. Also check the valve stem for bending. Set the valve in a V-block with a dial indicator touching the middle of the stem. Rotate the valve and look for a reading on the gauge (which indicates a bent stem). If the stem is bent, replace the valve.

18 Check the end of each valve spring for wear and pitting. Measure the free length **(see illustration)** and compare it to this Chapter's Specifications. Any springs that are shorter than specified have sagged and should not be reused. Stand the spring on a flat surface and check it for squareness **(see illustration)**.

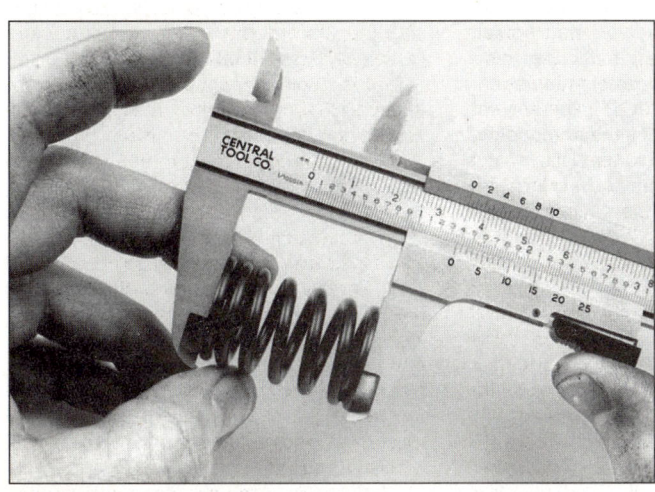

13.18a Measuring the free length of the valve springs

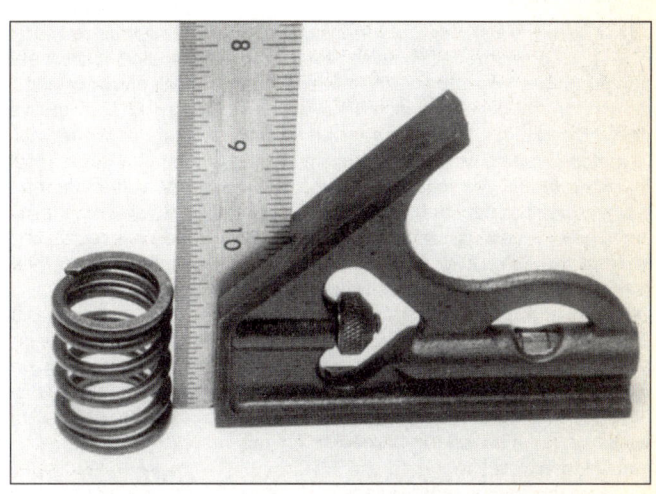

13.18b Checking the valve springs for squareness

2•18 Engine, clutch and transmission

13.22 Apply the lapping compound very sparingly, in small dabs, to the valve face only

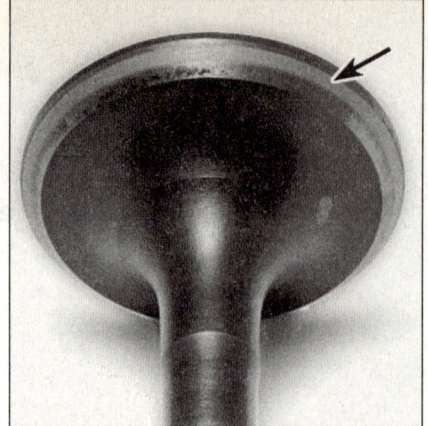

13.23 After lapping, the valve face should exhibit a uniform, unbroken contact pattern (arrow)

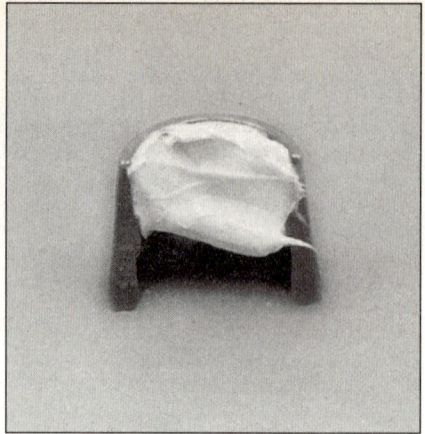

13.26 A small dab of grease will help hold the keepers in place on the valve while the spring compressor is released

19 Check the spring retainers and keepers for obvious wear and cracks. Any questionable parts should not be reused, as extensive damage will occur in the event of failure during engine operation.
20 If the inspection indicates that no service work is required, the valve components can be reinstalled in the head.

Reassembly

21 If the valve seats have been ground, the valves and seats should be lapped before installing the valves in the head to ensure a positive seal between the valves and seats. This procedure requires coarse and fine valve lapping compound (available at auto parts stores) and a valve lapping tool. If a lapping tool is not available, a piece of rubber or plastic hose can be slipped over the valve stem (after the valve has been installed in the guide) and used to turn the valve.
22 Apply a small amount of coarse lapping compound to the valve face **(see illustration)**, then slip the valve into the guide. **Note:** *Make sure the valve is installed in the correct guide and be careful not to get any lapping compound on the valve stem.*
23 Attach the lapping tool (or hose) to the valve and rotate the tool between the palms of your hands. Use a back-and-forth motion rather than a circular motion. Lift the valve off the seat and turn it at regular intervals to distribute the lapping compound properly. Continue the lapping procedure until the valve face and seat contact area is of uniform width and unbroken around the entire circumference of the valve face and seat **(see illustration)**. Once this is accomplished, lap the valves again with fine lapping compound.
24 Carefully remove the valve from the guide and wipe off all traces of lapping compound. Use solvent to clean the valve and wipe the seat area thoroughly with a solvent soaked cloth. Repeat the procedure for the remaining valves.
25 Lay the spring seat in place in the cylinder head, then install new valve stem seals on both of the guides **(see illustration)**. Use an appropriate size deep socket to push the seals into place until they are properly seated. Don't twist or cock them, or they will not seal properly against the valve stems. Also, don't remove them again or they will be damaged.
26 Coat the valve stems with assembly lube or moly-based grease, then install one of them into its guide. Next, install the spring seat, springs and retainers, compress the springs and install the keepers. **Note:** *Install the springs with the tightly wound coils at the bottom (next to the spring seat).* When compressing the springs with the valve spring compressor, depress them only as far as is absolutely necessary to slip the keepers into place. Apply a small amount of grease to the keepers **(see illustration)** to help hold them in place as the pressure is released from the springs. Make certain that the keepers are securely locked in their retaining grooves.
27 Support the cylinder head on blocks so the valves can't contact the workbench top, then very gently tap each of the valve stems with a soft-faced hammer. This will help seat the keepers in their grooves.
28 Once all of the valves have been installed in the head, check for proper valve sealing by pouring a small amount of solvent into each of the valve ports. If the solvent leaks past the valve(s) into the combustion chamber area, disassemble the valve(s) and repeat the lapping procedure, then reinstall the valve(s) and repeat the check. Repeat the procedure until a satisfactory seal is obtained.

14 Cylinder - removal, inspection and installation

Removal

1 Remove the cylinder head (see Section 11). Make sure the crankshaft is positioned at Top Dead Center (TDC).
2 Lift out the cam chain front guide **(see illustration 20.2a)**.
3 Remove the bolt securing the base of the cylinder to the crankcase **(see illustration 11.5)**.
4 Lift the cylinder straight up to remove it **(see illustration)**. If it's stuck, tap around its perimeter with a soft-faced hammer. Don't attempt to pry between the cylinder and the crankcase, as you'll ruin the sealing surfaces.
5 Locate the dowel pins (they may have come off with the cylinder or still be in the crankcase) **(see illustrations)**. YFZ450 models have three dowels, two next to the cam chain cavity and one near the front; the front dowel, which is larger, has an O-ring. YFZ450R models have two dowels, located opposite the cam chain cavity. Be careful not to let these drop into the engine. Stuff rags around the piston and remove the gasket and all traces of old gasket material from the surfaces of the cylinder and the crankcase.

14.4 Lift the cylinder straight off and locate the dowels - they may stay in the crankcase like this (arrow) . . .

Engine, clutch and transmission 2•19

14.5a ... or come off with the cylinder (arrow) - remove all traces of old base gasket (arrow) and install a new one on assembly

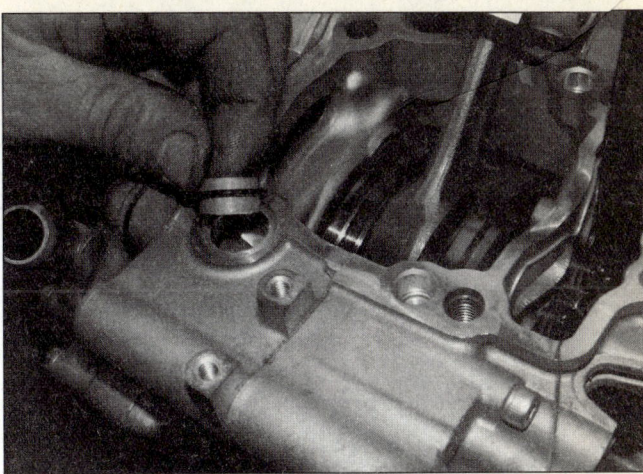

14.5b The large dowel has an O-ring

Inspection

6 Don't attempt to separate the liner from the cylinder.

7 Check the cylinder walls carefully for scratches and score marks.

8 Using the appropriate precision measuring tools, check the cylinder's diameter. Measure parallel to the crankshaft axis and across the crankshaft axis, at the depth from the top of the cylinder listed in this Chapter's Specifications. Average the two measurements and compare the results to this Chapter's Specifications. If the cylinder walls are tapered, out-of-round, worn beyond the specified limits, or badly scuffed or scored, have the cylinder rebored and honed by a dealer service department or a motorcycle repair shop. If a rebore is done, an oversize piston and rings will be required as well. Check with your dealer service department about available oversizes.

9 As an alternative, if the precision measuring tools are not available, a dealer service department or repair shop will make the measurements and offer advice concerning servicing of the cylinder.

10 If it's in reasonably good condition and not worn to the outside of the limits, and if the piston-to-cylinder clearance can be maintained properly, then the cylinder does not have to be rebored; honing is all that is necessary.

11 To perform the honing operation you will need the proper size flexible hone with fine stones as shown in Maintenance techniques, tools and working facilities at the front of this book, or a "bottle brush" type hone, plenty of light oil or honing oil, some shop towels and an electric drill motor. Hold the cylinder block in a vise (cushioned with soft jaws or wood blocks) when performing the honing operation. Mount the hone in the drill motor, compress the stones and slip the hone into the cylinder. Lubricate the cylinder thoroughly, turn on the drill and move the hone up and down in the cylinder at a pace which will produce a fine crosshatch pattern on the cylinder wall with the crosshatch lines intersecting at approximately a 60-degree angle. Be sure to use plenty of lubricant and do not take off any more material than is absolutely necessary to produce the desired effect. Do not withdraw the hone from the cylinder while it is running. Instead, shut off the drill and continue moving the hone up and down in the cylinder until it comes to a complete stop, then compress the stones and withdraw the hone. Wipe the oil out of the cylinder and repeat the procedure on the remaining cylinder. Remember, do not remove too much material from the cylinder wall. If you do not have the tools, or do not desire to perform the honing operation, a dealer service department or vehicle repair shop will generally do it for a reasonable fee.

12 Next, the cylinder must be thoroughly washed with warm soapy water to remove all traces of the abrasive grit produced during the honing operation. Be sure to run a brush through the bolt holes and flush them with running water. After rinsing, dry the cylinder thoroughly and apply a coat of light, rust-preventative oil to all machined surfaces.

Installation

13 Lubricate the cylinder bore with plenty of clean engine oil. Apply a thin film of moly-based grease to the piston skirt.

14 Install the dowel pins (and O-ring on the large dowel), then slip a new cylinder base gasket over them (see illustrations 14.5a and 14.5b).

15 Attach a piston ring compressor to the piston and compress the piston rings. A large hose clamp can be used instead - just make sure it doesn't scratch the piston, and don't tighten it too much.

16 Install the cylinder and carefully lower it down until the piston crown fits into the cylinder liner (see illustration). While doing this, pull the camshaft chain up, using a hooked tool or a piece of stiff wire. Push down on the cylinder, making sure the piston doesn't get cocked sideways, until the bottom of the cyl-

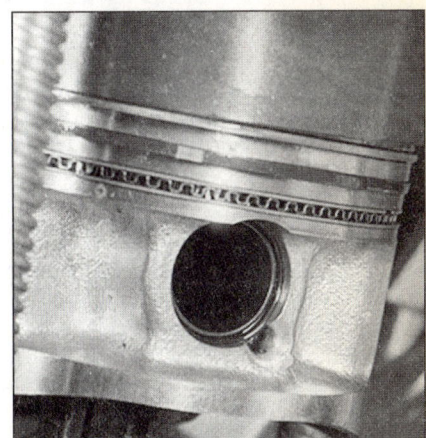

14.16 If you're experienced and very careful, the cylinder can be installed over the rings without a ring compressor, but a compressor is recommended

inder liner slides down past the piston rings. A wood or plastic hammer handle can be used to gently tap the cylinder down, but don't use too much force or the piston will be damaged.

17 Remove the piston ring compressor or hose clamp, being careful not to scratch the piston.

18 The remainder of installation is the reverse of the removal steps.

15 Piston - removal, inspection and installation

1 The piston is attached to the connecting rod with a piston pin that's a slip fit in the piston and rod.

2 Before removing the piston from the rod, stuff a clean shop towel into the crankcase hole, around the connecting rod. This will prevent the snap-rings from falling into the crankcase if they are inadvertently dropped.

2•20 Engine, clutch and transmission

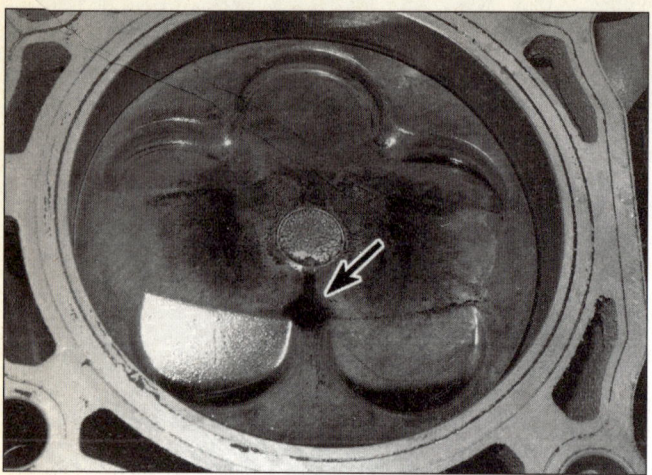

15.3a The arrow mark on top of the piston (arrow) faces the exhaust (front) side of the engine - if you can't see it, install the piston with two valve notches toward the front and three valve notches toward the rear

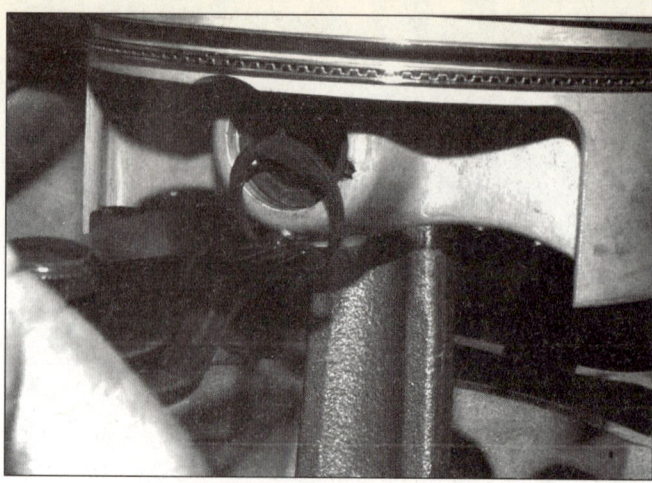

15.3b Wear eye protection and remove the snap-ring from its groove with snap-ring pliers

Removal

3 The piston should have an arrow mark on its crown that points toward the exhaust (front) side of the engine **(see illustration)**. If this mark is not visible due to carbon buildup, you can refer to the valve notches. There are two notches on the exhaust side of the piston and three on the intake side. Support the piston and remove the snap-ring with snap-ring pliers **(see illustration)**.

4 Push the piston pin out from the opposite end to free the piston from the rod **(see illustration)**. You may have to deburr the area around the groove to enable the pin to slide out (use a triangular file for this procedure). If the pin won't come out, you can fabricate a piston pin removal tool from a long bolt, a nut, a piece of tubing and washers **(see illustration)**.

Inspection

5 Before the inspection process can be carried out, the piston must be cleaned and the old piston rings removed.

6 Using a piston ring removal and installation tool, carefully remove the rings from the piston **(see illustration)**. Do not nick or gouge the piston in the process.

7 Scrape all traces of carbon from the top of the piston. A hand-held wire brush or a piece of fine emery cloth can be used once the majority of the deposits have been scraped away. Do not, under any circumstances, use a wire brush mounted in a drill motor to remove deposits from the piston; the piston material is soft and will be eroded away by the wire brush.

8 Use a piston ring groove cleaning tool to remove any carbon deposits from the ring grooves. If a tool is not available, a piece broken off the old ring will do the job. Be very careful to remove only the carbon deposits. Do not remove any metal and do not nick or gouge the sides of the ring grooves.

9 Once the deposits have been removed, clean the piston with solvent and dry them thoroughly. Make sure the oil return holes below the oil ring grooves are clear.

10 If the piston is not damaged or worn excessively and if the cylinder is not rebored, a new piston will not be necessary. Normal piston wear appears as even, vertical wear on the thrust surfaces of the piston and slight looseness of the top ring in its groove. New piston rings, on the other hand, should always be used when an engine is rebuilt.

11 Carefully inspect each piston for cracks around the skirt, at the pin bosses and at the ring lands **(see illustration)**.

12 Look for scoring and scuffing on the thrust faces of the skirt, holes in the piston crown and burned areas at the edge of the crown. If the skirt is scored or scuffed, the engine may have been suffering from overheating and/or abnormal combustion, which caused excessively high operating temperatures. The oil pump should be checked thoroughly. A hole in the piston crown, an extreme to be sure, is an indication that

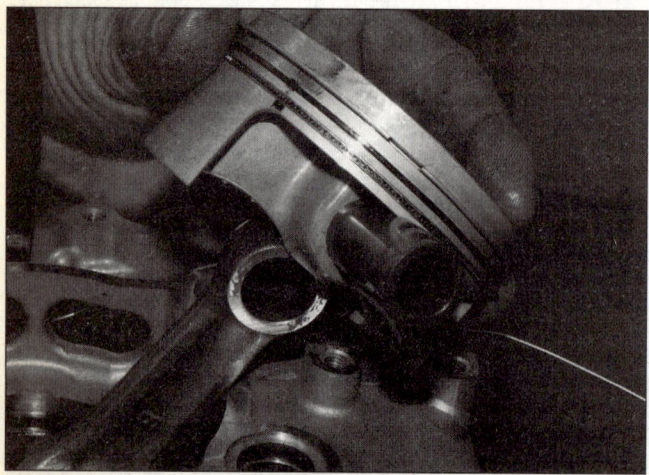

15.4a The piston pin should come out with hand pressure . . .

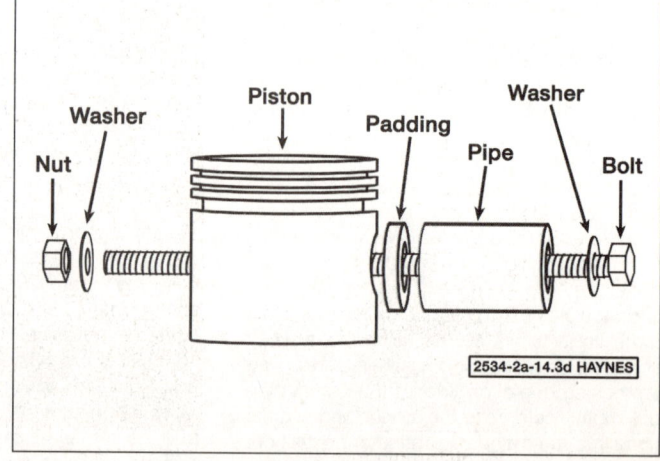

15.4b . . . if it doesn't, this removal tool can be fabricated from readily available parts

Engine, clutch and transmission 2•21

15.6 Remove the piston rings with a ring removal and installation tool

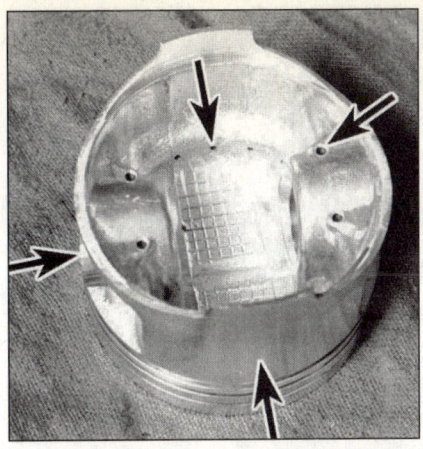

15.11 Check the piston pin bore and the piston skirt for wear, and make sure the internal holes are clear (arrows)

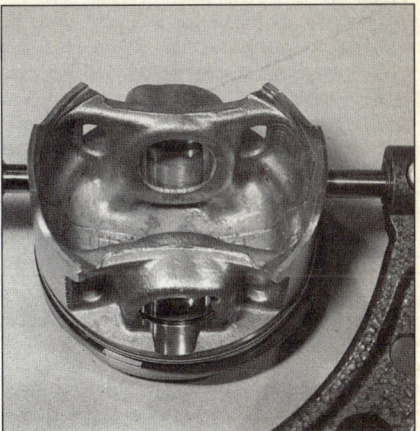

15.14 Measure the piston diameter with a micrometer

abnormal combustion (pre-ignition) was occurring. Burned areas at the edge of the piston crown are usually evidence of spark knock (detonation). If any of the above problems exist, the causes must be corrected or the damage will occur again.

13 Measure the piston ring-to-groove clearance (side clearance) by laying a new piston ring in the ring groove and slipping a feeler gauge in beside it. Check the clearance at three or four locations around the groove. Be sure to use the correct ring for each groove; they are different. If the clearance is greater then specified, a new piston will have to be used when the engine is reassembled.

14 Check the piston-to-bore clearance by measuring the bore (see Section 13) and the piston diameter **(see illustration)**. Measure the piston across the skirt on the thrust faces at a 90-degree angle to the piston pin, at the specified distance up from the bottom of the skirt. Subtract the piston diameter from the bore diameter to obtain the clearance. If it is greater than specified, the cylinder will have to be rebored and a new oversized piston and rings installed. If the appropriate precision measuring tools are not available, the piston-to-cylinder clearance can be obtained, though not quite as accurately, using feeler gauge stock. Feeler gauge stock comes in 12-inch lengths and various thicknesses and is generally available at auto parts stores. To check the clearance, slip a piece of feeler gauge stock of the same thickness as the specified piston clearance into the cylinder along with appropriate piston. The cylinder should be upside down and the piston must be positioned exactly as it normally would be. Place the feeler gauge between the piston and cylinder on one of the thrust faces (90-degrees to the piston pin bore). The piston should slip through the cylinder (with the feeler gauge in place) with moderate pressure. If it falls through, or slides through easily, the clearance is excessive and a new piston will be required. If the piston binds at the lower end of the cylinder and is loose toward the top, the cylinder is tapered, and if tight spots are encountered as the piston/feeler gauge is rotated in the cylinder, the cylinder is out-of-round. Be sure to have the cylinder and piston checked by a dealer service department or a repair shop to confirm your findings before purchasing new parts.

15 Apply clean engine oil to the pin, insert it into the piston and check for freeplay by rocking the pin back-and-forth. If the pin is loose, a new piston and possibly new pin must be installed.

16 Repeat Step 15, this time inserting the piston pin into the connecting rod **(see illustration)**. If the pin is loose, measure the pin diameter and the pin bore in the rod (or have this done by a dealer or repair shop). A worn pin can be replaced separately; if the rod bore is worn, the rod and crankshaft must be replaced as an assembly.

17 Refer to Section 16 and install the rings on the piston.

Installation

18 Install the piston with its arrow mark toward the exhaust side (front) of the engine. Lubricate the pin and the rod bore with moly-based grease. Install a new snap-rings in the groove in one side of the piston (don't reuse the old snap-rings). Push the pin into position from the opposite side and install another new snap-ring. Compress the snap-rings only enough for them to fit in the piston. Make sure the circlips are properly seated in the grooves **(see illustration)**.

16 Piston rings - installation

1 Before installing the new piston rings, the ring end gaps must be checked.

2 Insert the top (No. 1) ring into the bottom of the first cylinder and square it up with the cylinder walls by pushing it in with the top of the piston. The ring should be about one-half inch above the bottom edge of the cylinder.

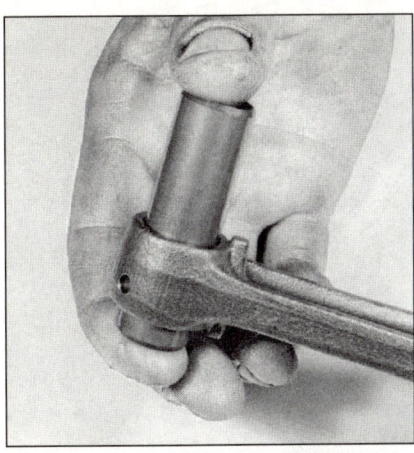

15.16 Slip the piston pin into the connecting rod and check for looseness

15.18 Make sure both piston pin snap-rings are securely seated in the piston grooves

2•22 Engine, clutch and transmission

16.2 Check the piston ring end gap with a feeler gauge at the bottom of the ring travel area

16.4 If the end gap is too small, clamp a file in a vise and file the ring ends (from the outside in only) to enlarge the gap slightly

16.7a Installing the oil ring expander - make sure the ends don't overlap

To measure the end gap, slip a feeler gauge between the ends of the ring (see illustration) and compare the measurement to the Specifications.

3 If the gap is larger or smaller than specified, double check to make sure that you have the correct rings before proceeding.

4 If the gap is too small, it must be enlarged or the ring ends may come in contact with each other during engine operation, which can cause serious damage. The end gap can be increased by filing the ring ends very carefully with a fine file (see illustration). When performing this operation, file only from the outside in.

5 Repeat the procedure for the second compression ring (ring gap is not specified for the oil ring rails or spacer).

6 Once the ring end gaps have been checked/corrected, the rings can be installed on the piston.

7 The oil control ring (lowest on the piston) is installed first. It is composed of three separate components. Slip the spacer into the groove, then install the upper side rail (see illustrations). Do not use a piston ring installation tool on the oil ring side rails as they may be damaged. Instead, place one end of the side rail into the groove between the spacer expander and the ring land. Hold it firmly in place and slide a finger around the piston while pushing the rail into the groove (taking care not to cut your fingers on the sharp edges). Next, install the lower side rail in the same manner.

8 After the three oil ring components have been installed, check to make sure that both the upper and lower side rails can be turned smoothly in the ring groove.

9 Install the no. 2 (middle) ring next with its identification mark facing up (see illustration). Do not mix the top and middle rings;

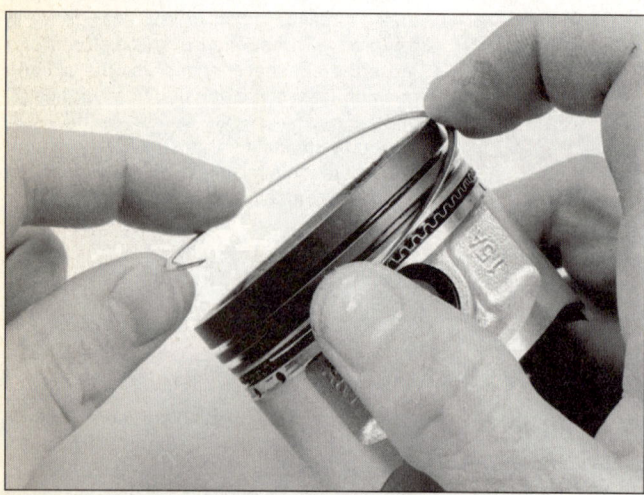

16.7b Installing an oil ring side rail - don't use a ring installation tool to do this

16.9 Install the middle ring with its identification mark up

Engine, clutch and transmission 2•23

16.12 Arrange the ring gaps like this

A Oil ring spacer
B Oil ring upper rail
C Oil ring lower rail
D Second compression ring
E Top compression ring

17.2a Here's the YFZ450 left side oil hose; it's bolted to the oil tank at the front and to the engine at the rear (arrow)

17.2b Here's the right side oil line/hose; it's bolted to the engine and oil tank (arrows)

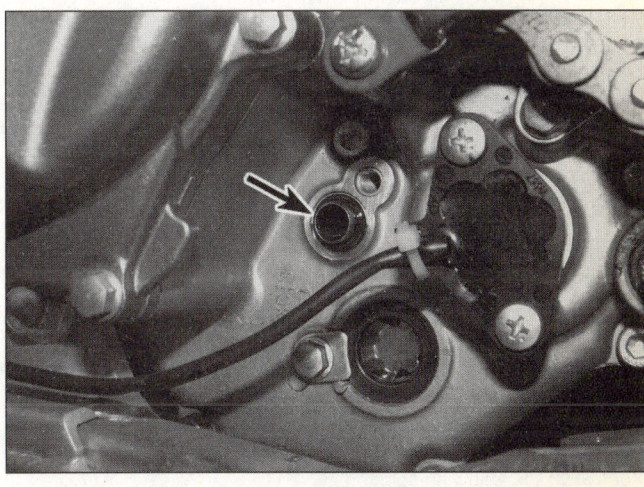

17.2c The bolted connections at the engine use an O-ring and dowel (arrow)

their profiles are slightly different, but the difference can be hard to see. The most important indicator is the ring thickness. The top ring is thicker than the second ring. On a new piston, the top ring will not fit into the second ring's groove. If you're not sure which ring is which, measure their thicknesses with a micrometer.

10 To avoid breaking the ring, use a piston ring installation tool and make sure that the identification mark is facing up. Fit the ring into the middle groove on the piston. Do not expand the ring any more than is necessary to slide it into place.

11 Finally, install the no. 1 (top) ring in the same manner. Make sure the identifying mark is facing up. Be very careful not to confuse the top and second rings.

12 Once the rings have been properly installed, stagger the end gaps, including those of the oil ring side rails **(see illustration)**.

17 External oil tank and lines (YFZ450) - removal and installation

1 YFZ450 models have the following tank and line components:
 a) Combined oil pipe/hose on each side of the engine
 b) Oil tank to the frame forward of the engine
 c) External three-fitting oil tube at right rear corner of engine

Oil lines
Removal

2 To disconnect an oil pipe/hose from the engine, remove its mounting bolt **(see illustrations)**. The connection at the engine has a dowel and O-ring **(see illustration)**. The connection at the oil tank has a bolted fitting

17.2d The YFZ450 external oil tank has a mounting bolt on each side

A Mounting bolt and bushing
B Oil hose
C Vent hose

2•24 Engine, clutch and transmission

17.4 The external oil pipe is attached to the crankcase and cylinder head with union bolts

17.5a Unbolt the oil pipe (arrow) . . . .

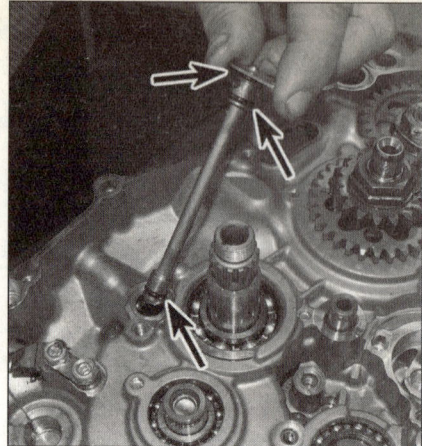

17.5b . . . and pull it out, together with its three O-rings (arrows)

with an O-ring **(see illustration 17.2b and the accompanying illustration)**.

3 To disconnect the oil tank vent hose, loosen its clamps and carefully pry it off the fittings **(see illustration 17.2d)**.

4 To remove the three-branched oil pipe, remove the banjo bolts and sealing washers from each of the three fittings **(see illustration)**. Take the pipe off.

5 All YFZ450 models have an oil tube in the left crankcase half. To remove it, remove the left crankcase cover, alternator rotor and stator (see Section 18 and Chapter 5). Remove the tube retaining bolt and pull it out of the crankcase, together with its O-rings **(see illustrations)**.

Installation

6 Installation is the reverse of the removal steps, with the following additions:

a) Replace the sealing washers whenever the union bolts or hose fittings are loosened. Note that the three-branched pipe's right union bolt is larger than the others **(see illustration)**.

b) Replace O-rings whenever they are removed.

c) Tighten the union bolts and tube retaining bolt to the torques listed in this Chapter's Specifications.

External oil tank

Removal

7 Refer to the oil change procedure in Chapter 1 and drain the oil tank.

8 Disconnect the hoses from the tank as described above.

9 Remove the tank mounting bolts and lift the tank off the frame **(see illustration 17.2d)**.

Installation

10 Check the mounting bushings for damage or deterioration and replace them as needed **(see illustration 17.2d)**.

11 Position the tank on the frame and tighten the mounting bolts. Connect the hoses as described above.

12 Refer to Chapter 1 and change the engine oil.

18 Crankcase covers - removal and installation

Right crankcase cover

Outer cover removal

1 Remove the cover mounting bolts **(see illustration)**.

2 Tap the cover gently with a soft-faced mallet to free it and take it off the engine. Locate the dowels and remove the old gasket **(see illustration)**.

3 Installation is the reverse of the removal steps. Tighten the cover bolts evenly, in a criss-cross pattern, to the torque listed in this Chapter's Specifications.

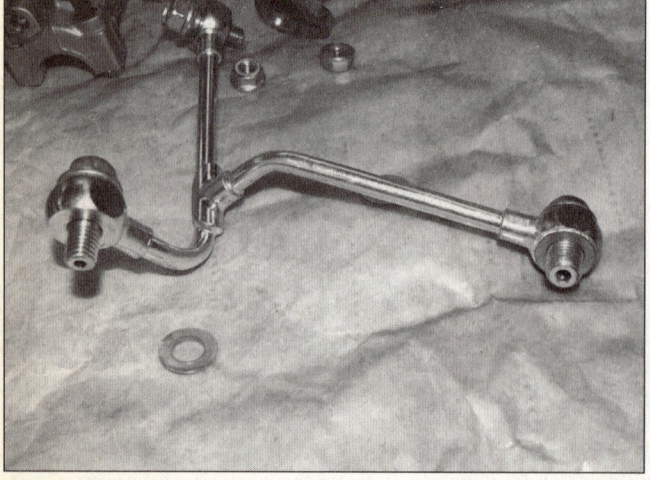

17.6 The oil pipe union bolts are different sizes

18.1 Remove the outer cover mounting bolts (arrows)

Engine, clutch and transmission

18.2 Remove the cover and locate the dowel pins (arrows)

18.8 Remove the inner cover mounting bolts (arrows) (YFZ450 shown, YFZ450R similar)

A) Hidden bolt   B) Allen bolts (some models)

Inner cover removal

4   Remove the oil filter and drain the cooling system (see Chapter 1). Remove the outer cover as described above.

5   Remove the exhaust system and brake pedal (see Chapters 4 and 7).

6   Remove the coolant tube from the cover (see Chapter 3).

7   If you're working on a YFZ450, disconnect the oil hose from the cover (see Section 17).

8   Remove the cover bolts **(see illustration)**. Loosen the bolts evenly in a criss-cross pattern, then remove them.

9   Pull the cover off. Tap it with a rubber mallet if it won't come evenly. Don't pry the cover off or the gasket surfaces will be damaged.

10   Locate the cover dowels and O-rings **(see illustration)**. They may have stayed in the crankcase or come off with the cover.

11   Remove all traces of the old gasket from the cover and crankcase.

Installation

12   Installation is the reverse of the removal steps. When installing the inner cover, use a new gasket, coated on both sides with gasket sealer. Be sure the dowels and O-rings are installed.

13   Tighten the cover bolts evenly to the torque listed in this Chapter's Specifications.

Left crankcase cover

YFZ450

Removal

14   Remove the front fender (see Chapter 8).

15   Drain the engine oil (see Chapter 1).

16   Follow the alternator wiring harness to the electrical connector and disconnect it (see Chapter 5).

17   Disconnect the crankcase breather hose from the top rear of the cover **(see illustration)**.

18   Remove the starter torque limiter (see Chapter 5). One of the crankcase cover bolts is hidden behind the torque limiter **(see illustration 18.17)**.

19   Remove the shift pedal (see Section 23).

20   Remove the cover bolts **(see illustration 18.17)**. Loosen the bolts evenly in a criss-cross pattern, then remove them.

21   Pull the cover off. Tap it with a rubber mallet if it won't come easily. Don't pry the cover off or the gasket surfaces will be damaged.

18.10 Remove the cover and locate the dowel pins (arrows) (YFZ450 shown)

18.17 Remove the cover bolts (arrows) - on YFZ450 models, one bolt is behind the starter slipper clutch (upper right arrow) which you'll need to remove for access to the bolt

2•26 Engine, clutch and transmission

18.22 Locate the cover dowels (arrows)

18.29 Oil tank and left crankcase cover screws (YFZ450R)

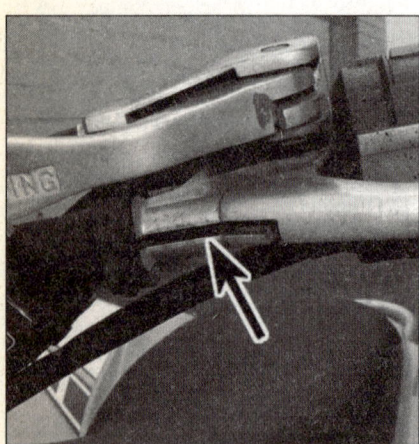

19.1a Slip the cable end out of the gap (arrow) . . .

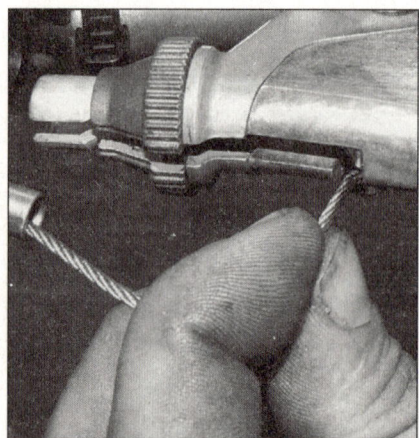

19.1b . . . rotate the cable and lower it away from the lever

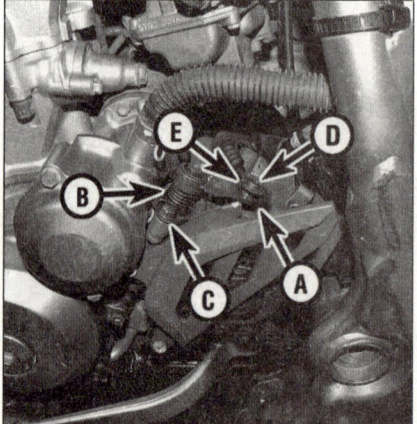

19.2 Clutch release lever details

- A Release lever
- B Spring
- C Retaining bolt (YFZ450 - YFZ450R models use a snap-ring)
- D Cable end
- E Removal slot

22 Locate the cover dowels **(see illustration)**. They may have stayed in the crankcase or come off with the cover.
23 Remove all traces of the old gasket from the cover and crankcase.

Installation
24 Installation is the reverse of the removal steps. Use a new gasket, coated on both sides with gasket sealer. Be sure the dowels are installed. Don't forget to refill the engine oil (see Chapter 1).
25 Tighten the cover bolts evenly to the torque listed in this Chapter's Specifications.

YFZ450R
Removal
26 Drain the engine oil (see Chapter 1). Leave the dipstick out.
27 Remove the shift pedal (see Section 23).
28 Follow the wiring harness from the top of the left side cover to the connector and disconnect it.

29 Unbolt the oil tank cover from the outer cover and pull it off **(see illustration)**. Tap it with a rubber mallet if it won't come easily. Don't pry the cover off or the gasket surfaces will be damaged.
30 Locate the cover dowel. It may have stayed in the crankcase cover or come off with the oil tank cover.
31 Remove the crankcase cover bolts. Take the cover off, together with the alternator stator and crankshaft position sensor.
32 Remove all traces of the old gaskets from the oil tank cover and crankcase cover.
33 If necessary, remove the crankshaft position sensor (see Chapter 4) or stator (see Chapter 5).
34 Installation is the reverse of removal. Use a new gasket, coated on both sides with gasket sealer. Be sure the dowels are installed. Don't forget to refill the engine oil (see Chapter 1).
35 Tighten the cover bolts evenly to the torque listed in this Chapter's Specifications.

19 Clutch and release mechanism - removal, inspection and installation

Cable and lever
Removal
1 Loosen the midline cable adjuster or handlebar cable adjuster all the way to create slack (see Chapter 1). Rotate the cable so the inner cable aligns with the slot in the lever, then slip the cable and fitting out of the lever **(see illustrations)**.
2 Slip the end of the cable through the lever slot on the engine to detach it from the lever **(see illustration)**.
3 Pull the cable partway out of the engine

Engine, clutch and transmission

19.4 This bracket on the engine supports and clutch and parking brake cables

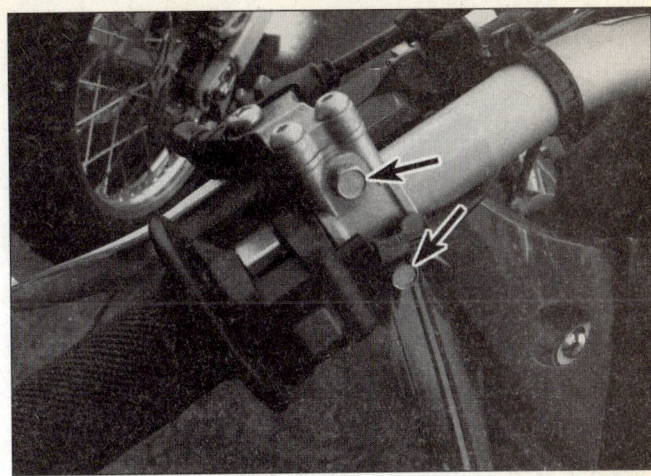

19.5 Remove the clamp screws (arrows) and detach the lever from the handlebar

19.10a Remove the spring bolts, washers and springs

19.10b Remove the pressure plate and push piece

19.10c Slide the plates out of the clutch housing . . .

bracket **(see illustration 19.2)**. Turn the cable to align it with the slot in the lever and lift the cable end out of the lever.

4 Detach the cable bracket from the engine and take it off the bike together with the cable **(see illustration)**. Separate the cable from the bracket.

5 To remove the lever from the handlebar, undo the clamp screws **(see illustration)**.

Inspection

6 Slide the inner cable back and forth in the housing and make sure it moves freely. If it doesn't, try lubricating it as described in Chapter 1. If that doesn't help, replace the cable.

Installation

7 Installation is the reverse of the removal steps. Refer to Chapter 1 and adjust clutch freeplay.

Clutch

Removal

8 If you're just going to remove the clutch plates, remove the outer cover from the right crankcase cover (see Section 18). If you're going to remove the clutch center or housing, remove the right crankcase cover (see Section 18). If you're not sure how much clutch work will be needed, start by removing the outer cover and plates. This will make it possible to inspect the center and housing to see if they need to be removed.

9 Hold the clutch from turning with a holding tool. You can make your own holding tool from steel strap if you don't have one. **Note:** *If you've removed the right crankcase cover, you can wedge a copper washer or penny between the primary drive gear and clutch housing driven gear to keep the clutch housing from turning while you loosen the clutch spring bolts and clutch housing nut.*

10 Refer to the accompanying illustrations to remove the clutch **(see illustrations)**.

19.10d . . . the last friction plate is narrower than the others; a damper spring (arrow) fits within it

2•28 Engine, clutch and transmission

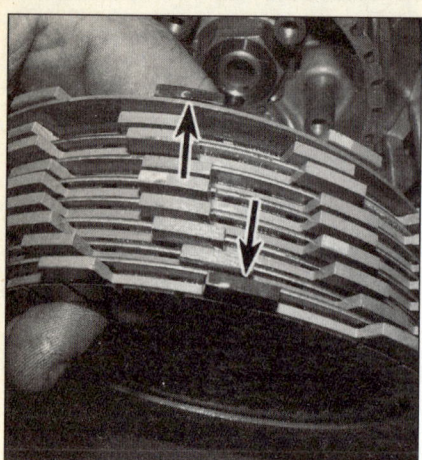

19.10e The metal plates with blue tabs go on first and last

19.10f On YFZ450 models, the damper spring (left arrow) has a spring seat behind it (right arrow) - the concave side of the damper spring faces away from the engine

19.10g The clutch center and housing are secured by a nut and lockwasher (arrow)

19.10h Bend back the lockwasher tabs

19.10i Slip a copper washer between the primary drive gear and the primary driven gear on the back of the clutch housing (arrow) to lock the gears so they won't turn, then unscrew the nut . . .

19.10j . . . remove the lockwasher and pull off the clutch center (arrow) . . .

19.10k . . . remove the thrust washer . . .

19.10l . . . then remove the clutch housing

Engine, clutch and transmission 2•29

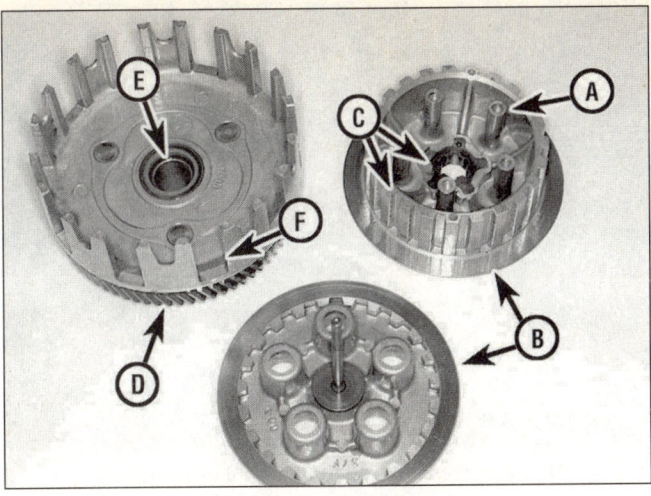

19.12a Clutch inspection points

A Spring posts
B Friction surfaces
C Splines
D Primary driven gear
E Clutch housing bushing
F Clutch housing slots

19.12b Grip the clutch housing and try to rotate the primary gear; if there's any play, replace the housing

Inspection

11 Check the bolt posts and the friction surface on the pressure plate for damaged threads, scoring or wear. Replace the pressure plate if any defects are found.

12 Check the edges of the slots in the clutch housing for indentations made by the friction plate tabs **(see illustration)**. If the indentations are deep they can prevent clutch release, so the housing should be replaced with a new one. If the indentations can be removed easily with a file, the life of the housing can be prolonged to an extent. Check the bushing surface in the center of the clutch housing for score marks, scratches and excessive wear. Also, check the driven gear teeth for cracks, chips and excessive wear. If the bushing or gear is worn or damaged, the clutch housing must be replaced with a new one. Check the primary driven gear for play **(see illustration)**. If there is any, replace the clutch housing.

13 Check the splines of the clutch boss for indentations made by the tabs on the metal plates. Check the clutch boss friction surface for wear or scoring. Replace the clutch boss if problems are found.

14 Measure the free length of the clutch springs **(see illustration)** and compare the results to this Chapter's Specifications. If the springs have sagged, or if cracks are noted, replace them with new ones as a set.

15 If the lining material of the friction plates smells burnt or if it is glazed, new parts are required. If the metal clutch plates are scored or discolored, they must be replaced with new ones. Measure the thickness of the friction plates **(see illustration)** and replace with new parts any friction plates that are worn.

16 Lay the metal plates, one at a time, on a perfectly flat surface (such as a piece of plate glass) and check for warpage by trying to slip a feeler gauge between the flat surface and the plate **(see illustration)**. The feeler gauge should be the same thickness as the maximum warp listed in this Chapter's Specifications. Do this at several places around the

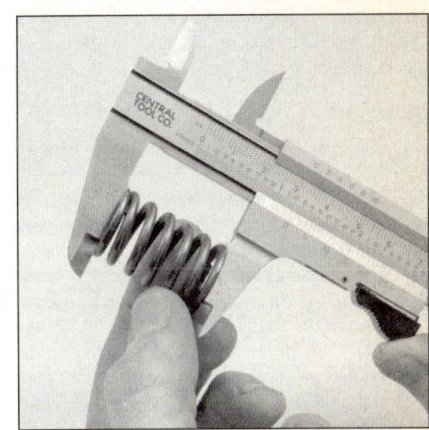

19.14 Measure the clutch spring free length

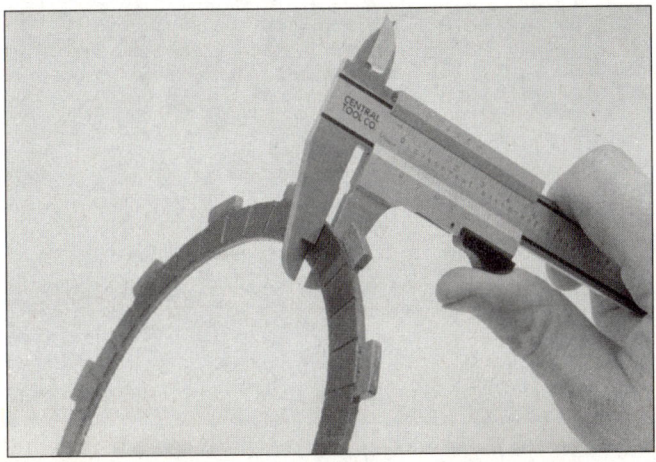

19.15 Measure the thickness of the friction plates

19.16 Check the metal plates for warpage

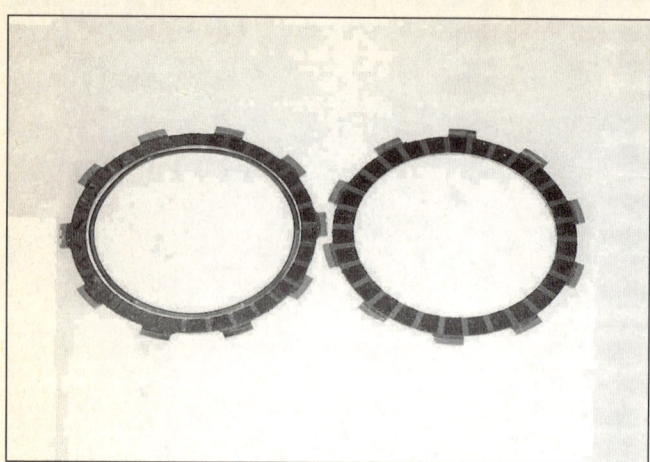

19.19 On YFZ450 models, the narrower friction plate and damper (left) go into the clutch housing first

19.21a Pull the ball out of the transmission shaft with a magnet . . .

plate's circumference. If the feeler gauge can be slipped under the plate, it is warped and should be replaced with a new one.

17 Check the tabs on the friction plates for excessive wear and mushroomed edges. They can be cleaned up with a file if the deformation is not severe. Check the friction plates for warpage as described in Step 13.

18 Check the thrust washer for score marks, heat discoloration and evidence of excessive wear.

Installation

19 Installation is the reverse of the removal steps, with the following additions:

a) Install a new lockwasher and position its tabs between the ribs of the clutch center. Tighten the clutch nut to the torque listed in this Chapter's Specifications, then bend the lockwasher tabs against two of the flats on the nut.

b) Coat the friction plates with clean engine oil before you install them.

c) Install a friction plate, then the remaining metal and friction plates until they're all installed. Friction plates go on first and last, so the friction material contacts the metal surfaces of the clutch center and the pressure plate. On YFZ450 models, note the location of the narrower friction plate and the damper that fits inside it **(see illustration)**.

d) Apply grease to the ends of the clutch pushrod, the steel ball and the end of the adjuster rod.

Lifter lever and pushrod

Removal

20 Remove the right crankcase cover (see Section 18). Remove the clutch pressure plate and push piece as described above.

21 Remove the ball and pushrod **(see illustrations)**.

22 If you're working on a YFZ450, remove the retaining bolt and pull the lifter lever out of the crankcase **(see illustration 19.2)**. If you're working on a YFZ450R, remove the snap-ring and washer and pull the lifter lever out of the crankcase.

23 Check for visible wear or damage at the contact points of the lifter lever and pushrod **(see illustration)**. Replace any parts that show problems.

24 Remove the snap-ring (if you haven't already done so) and pry the lifter shaft seal out of the crankcase. If the needle bearing is worn or damaged, drive it out with a shouldered drift the same diameter as the bearing, then use the same tool to drive in a new one. Pack the needle bearing with grease and press in a new seal.

25 Installation is the reverse of removal. Engage the notch in the lever shaft with the pushrod and hook the spring to the crankcase.

26 Refer to Chapter 1 and adjust clutch freeplay.

20 Camshaft chain and guides - removal, inspection and installation

1 If inspection procedures in Section 10 indicate problems with the chain or guides,

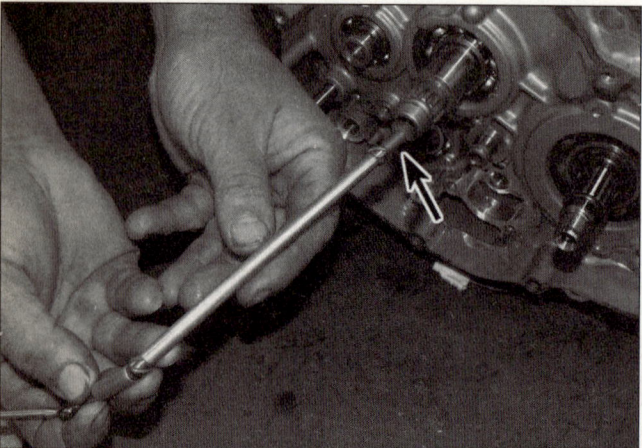

19.21b . . . then pull out the shaft - the long end of the shaft (arrow) goes into the transmission shaft first on installation

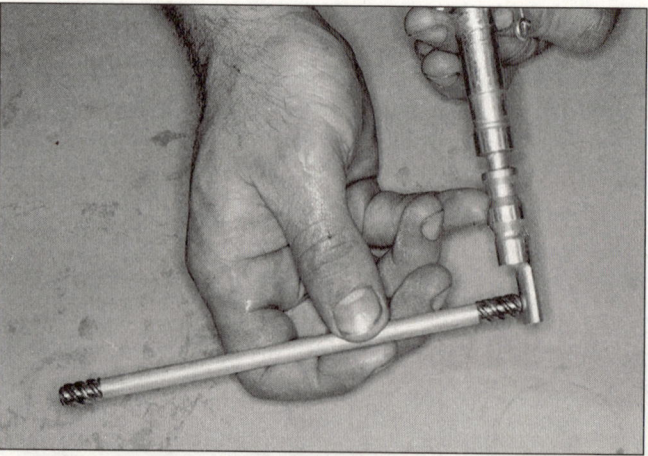

19.23 The pushrod engages the lifter lever like this when they're installed

Engine, clutch and transmission 2•31

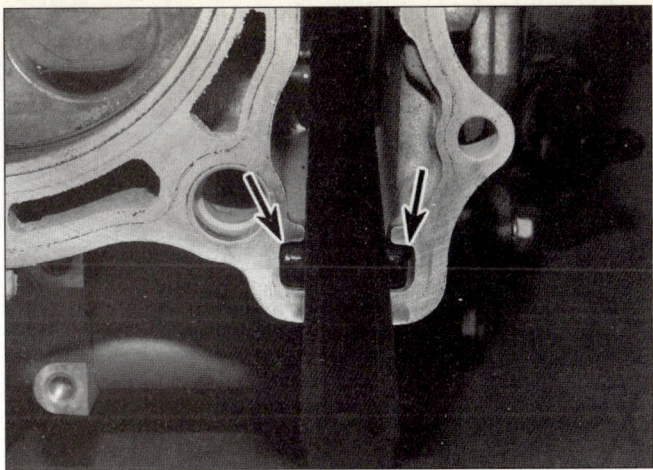

20.2a The upper end of the chain guide fits in these pockets (arrows) - be sure to install the chain guide before installing the cylinder head

20.2b The lower end of the front chain guide fits in this pocket (left arrow) - the lower end of the rear chain guide is bolted to the crankcase (arrows)

remove them for further inspection.

2 To remove the exhaust side chain guide, remove the cylinder head (see Section 11). Lift the guide out of its pockets in the cylinder and crankcase **(see illustrations)**.

3 To remove the intake side guide or the chain, remove the left crankcase cover and alternator rotor (see Section 18 and Chapter 5). Unbolt the guide and slip the chain off the crankshaft sprocket **(see illustration 20.2b)**.

4 Installation is the reverse of removal.

21 Primary drive gear and balancer - removal, inspection and installation

Removal

1 If you're just planning to remove the gears, remove the right crankcase cover and clutch (see Sections 18 and 19). If you're planning to remove the balancer weight or shaft, remove the left crankcase cover (see Section 18).

2 Turn the crankshaft so the match marks on the balancer drive and driven gears align **(see illustration)**.

3 Bend back the tabs on the balancer driven gear lockwasher. The drive gear has a conical lockwasher with no tabs.

4 Wedge a copper washer or penny between the teeth of the balancer drive and driven gears to prevent them from turning. Loosen the driven gear nut. If you plan to remove the primary drive gear or balancer drive gear, wedge the gears from the other side and loosen the primary drive gear nut.

5 Unscrew the nuts and remove the lockwashers **(see illustrations)**.

6 Slide off the primary drive gear. Note the location of the short spline, then remove

21.2 The alignment marks on the balancer gears (arrows) must be aligned on installation

21.5a Unscrew the nuts, noting the direction they face . . .

21.5b . . . and remove the lockwashers - on installation, place the lockwasher tabs in the gear slots (arrow)

2•32 Engine, clutch and transmission

21.6a Remove the primary drive gear - the short spline arrow allows the gear to be installed only one way

21.6b Remove the balancer drive gear - its punch mark aligns with the short spline (arrow)

21.6c The shouldered side of the gear faces the engine

the balancer drive gear (see illustrations).

7 Note the location of the short spline, then remove the balancer driven gear (see illustration).

8 Pull the balancer shaft out of the engine from the left side (see illustrations).

Inspection

9 Check the gears for worn or damaged teeth and replace them as a set if problems are found.

10 Check the ball bearings for wear, looseness or rough movement. If any problems are found, replace the bearings as described in Section 25.

11 Check the remaining components for wear and damage and replace any worn or damaged parts. Replace the lockwasher with a new one whenever it's removed.

12 Inspect the balancer and crankshaft ball bearings to the extent possible without disassembling the crankcase. If wear, looseness or roughness can be detected, the crankcase will have to be disassembled to replace the bearings.

Installation

13 If you removed the balancer shaft, install it.

14 Install the balancer drive and driven gears so their short splines align with the short splines on the shafts and the match marks align with each other (see illustrations 21.7, 21.6b and 21.6a).

15 Install the primary drive gear next to the balancer drive gear.

16 Install the lockwashers and nuts on the balancer shaft and crankshaft. Engage the tab in the driven gear locknut with the hole in the drive gear (see illustration 21.5b).

21.7 Remove the balancer driven gear/ weight - its punch mark aligns with the short spline (arrow)

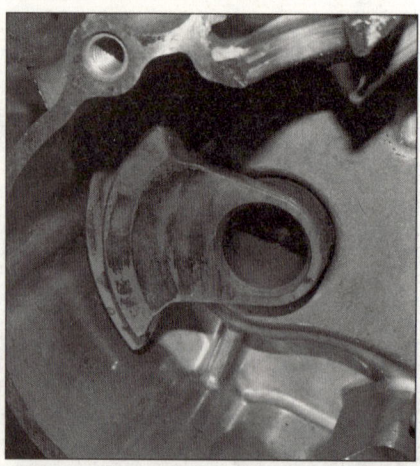

21.8a Turn the balancer shaft so the weight is toward the front of the engine as shown . . .

21.8b . . . this allows the flat on the shaft (arrow) to clear the crankshaft when the balancer shaft is removed

Engine, clutch and transmission 2•33

22.2 Remove the snap-ring and take the oil pump drive gear of its shaft

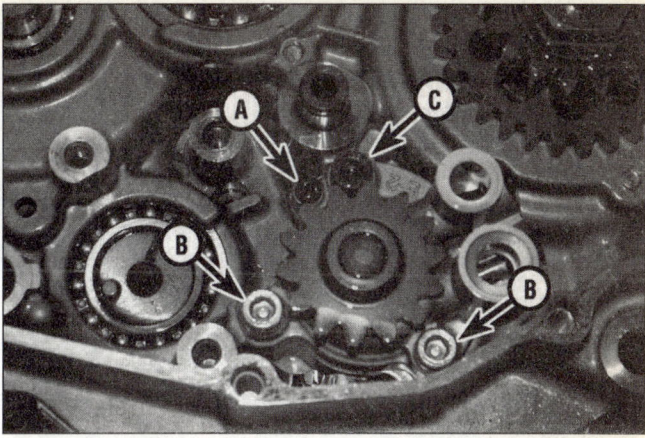

22.3a If you plan to disassemble the pump on a YFZ450, loosen the assembly screw now, while the pump is still bolted to the engine

A Assembly screw (YFZ450 - YFZ450R assembly screw is in cover plate)
B Light colored Allen bolts
C Dark colored Allen bolt (longer)

17 Wedge the gears as described in Step 4 and tighten the nuts to the torque listed in this Chapter's Specifications. On tabbed lockwashers, bend the lockwasher tabs to secure the nut(s).
18 The remainder of installation is the reverse of removal

22 Oil pump - removal, inspection and installation

Removal

1 Remove the right crankcase cover and clutch (see Sections 18 and 19).
2 Remove the snap-ring and washer and take the oil pump drive gear off its shaft (see illustration).
3 Remove the oil pump mounting bolts and take it off the engine (see illustration). The outer rotor of the no. 2 rotor set may remain in the engine (see illustration). If so, remove it.
4 Locate the pump dowel(s) (see illustration 22.3b). They may have come off with the pump or stayed in the engine.

Inspection

5 Remove the snap-ring, no. 2 inner rotor and drive pin from the pump shaft (see illustrations).
6 If you're working on a YFZ450, remove the assembly screw from the oil pump body. If you're working on a YFZ450R, remove the assembly screw from the cover plate. Take

22.3b Lift the pump off the engine and locate the dowel (upper arrow, all models; YFZ450 models have two dowels) - the no. 2 outer rotor may stay in the engine (lower arrow)

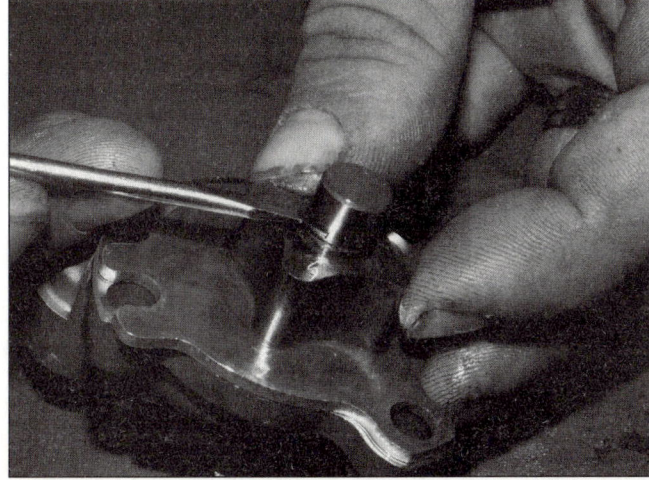

22.5a Remove the circlip from the pump shaft, slide the no. 2 inner rotor off . . .

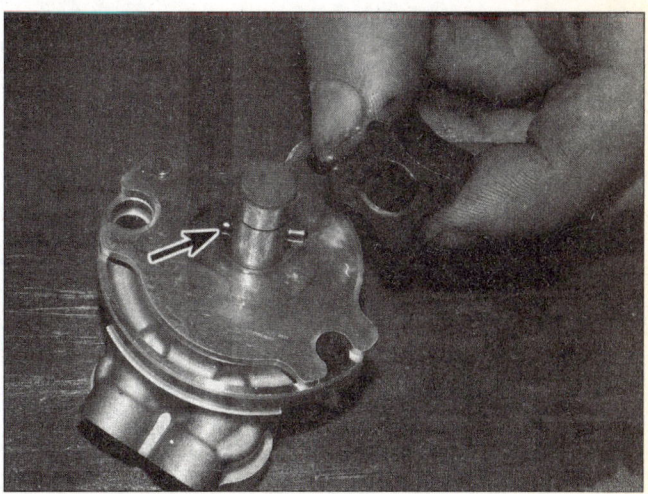

22.5b . . . and remove the drive pin (arrow)

2•34 Engine, clutch and transmission

22.6a Remove the pump cover ...

22.6b ... and the outer rotor (arrow) ...

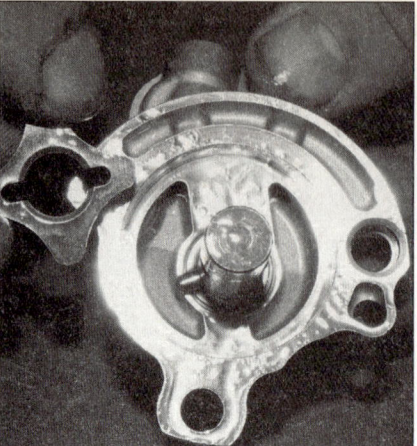

22.6c ... lift the inner rotor off the drive pin and remove it ...

the cover plate off and remove the drive pin, shaft and rotors **(see illustrations)**.

7 Wash all the components in solvent, then dry them off. Check the pump body, the rotors and the cover for scoring and wear. If any damage or uneven or excessive wear is evident, replace the pump. If you are rebuilding the engine, it's a good idea to install a new oil pump.

8 Place the rotors in the pump cover. Measure the clearance between the outer rotor and body, and between the inner and outer rotors, with a feeler gauge **(see illustrations)**. Place a straightedge across the pump body and rotors and measure the gap with a feeler gauge **(see illustration)**. If any of the clearances are beyond the limits listed in this Chapter's Specifications, replace the pump.

9 Reassemble the pump by reversing the disassembly steps, with the following additions:

a) *Before installing the cover, pack the cavities between the rotors with petroleum jelly - this will ensure the pump develops suction quickly and begins oil circulation as soon as the engine is started.*
b) *Make sure the drive pin is in position.*
c) *Tighten the cover screw to the torque listed in this Chapter's Specifications.*

Installation

10 Installation is the reverse of removal, with the following additions:

a) *Make sure the pump dowels are in position.*
b) *Tighten the oil pump mounting screws to the torque listed in this Chapter's Specifications.*

23 External shift mechanism - removal, inspection and installation

Shift pedal

Removal

1 Look for alignment marks on the end of the shift pedal and shift shaft **(see illustration)**. If they aren't visible, make your own marks with a felt pen or sharp punch. Remove the shift pedal pinch bolt completely (it fits in a groove) and slide the pedal off the shaft.

Inspection

2 Check the shift pedal for wear or damage such as bending. Check the splines on the shift pedal and shaft for stripping or step wear. Replace the pedal or shaft if these problems are found.

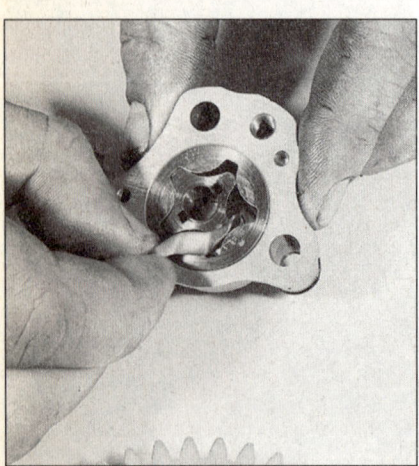

22.6d ... and take the thrust washer out of the case

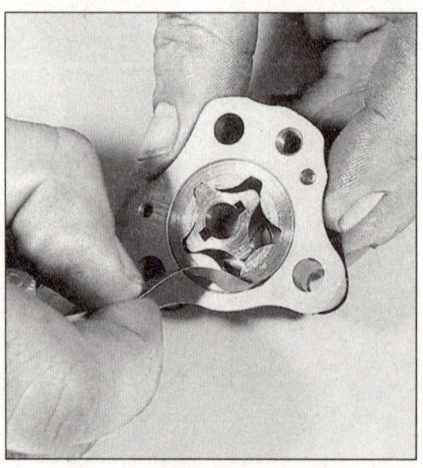

22.8a Measure the gap between the inner and outer rotors ...

22.8b ... between the outer rotor and body ...

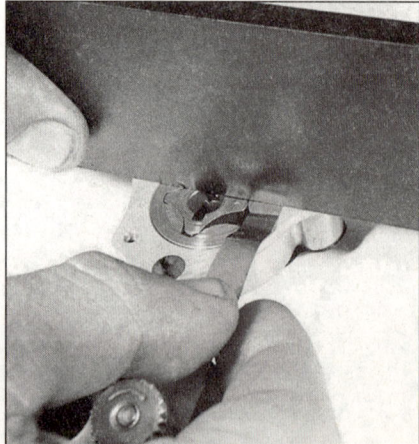

22.8c ... and between the rotors and a straightedge

Engine, clutch and transmission 2•35

23.1 Make an alignment mark on the end of the shift shaft, then remove the pedal bolt all the way

23.7a Pull the shift shaft out of the crankcase, noting how the return spring ends fit over their pin (arrow)

23.7b Take the roller off the pawl holder, noting which direction it faces

3   Check the shift shaft seal in the alternator cover for signs of leakage. If the seal has been leaking, remove the left crankcase cover (see Section 18). Pry the seal out of the cover, then tap in a new one with a seal driver or socket the same diameter as the seal.

Installation

4   Install the shift pedal or shift arm. Line up its punch marks and tighten the pinch bolt to the torque listed in this Chapter's Specifications.

External shift linkage

Removal

5   Remove the shift pedal as described above.
6   Remove the right crankcase cover and the clutch (see Sections 18 and 19).
7   Remove the linkage (see illustrations).

23.7c Remove the shift guide bolts (arrows)

23.7d Take the pawl assembly and shift guide off

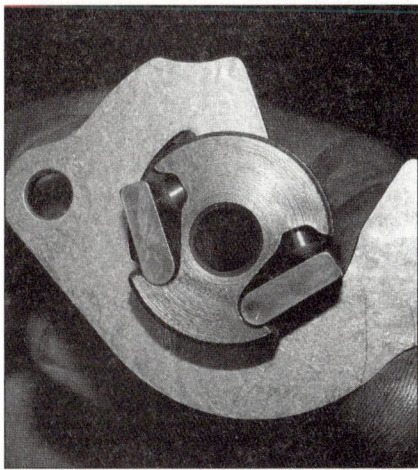

23.7e The pawl assembly goes together like this - note the directions the rounded ends of the springs and pawls face

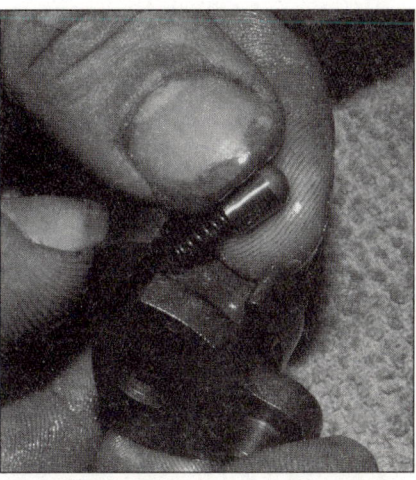

23.7f Separate the pawl holder from the shift guide

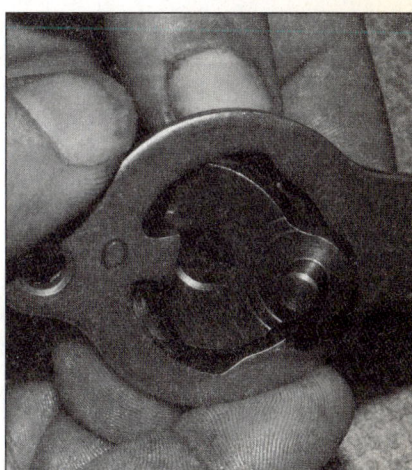

23.7g Remove the pins and springs

2•36 Engine, clutch and transmission

23.7h If the punch mark on the shift drum segment (arrow) is in the position shown . . .

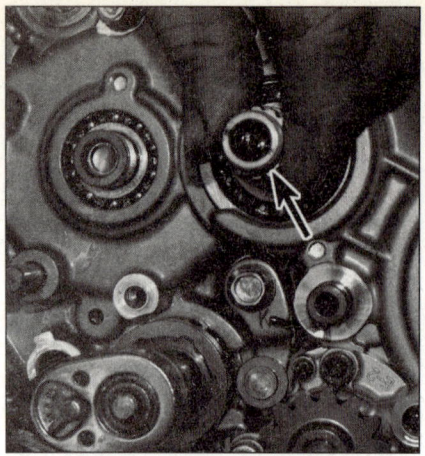

23.7i . . . turn it all the way counterclockwise, turning the transmission shaft (arrow) by hand at the same time to prevent damage to the shift forks . . .

23.7j . . . until the segment stops with its mark in this position

23.7k Unscrew the segment bolt

23.7l Pry the stopper lever out of the way (arrow) and take the segment off

Inspection

8 Check the shift shaft for bends and damage to the splines. If the shaft is bent, you can attempt to straighten it, but if the splines are damaged it will have to be replaced. Check the condition of the return spring, shift arm and the pawl spring. Replace the shift shaft if they're worn, cracked or distorted.

Installation

9 Installation is the reverse of the removal steps, with the following additions:
   a) Tighten the stopper arm bolt and shift drum segment bolt to the torques listed in this Chapter's Specifications.
   b) Check the engine oil level and add some, if necessary (see Chapter 1).

23.7m Locate the dowel pin (arrow) - align the pin and notch (arrow) on installation

23.7n Note how the spring engages the stopper arm and crankcase, then unbolt the stopper arm and take it off

Engine, clutch and transmission 2•37

24.11 Crankcase bolts (YFZ450; others similar)

24.12a Set up a puller like this to push against the crankshaft while pulling the upper case half off

24 Crankcase - disassembly and reassembly

1 To examine and repair or replace the crankshaft, connecting rod, bearings and transmission components, the crankcase must be split into two parts.

Disassembly

2 Remove the engine from the vehicle (see Section 6).
3 Remove the alternator and starter clutch (if equipped) (see Chapter 5).
4 Remove the right crankcase cover and clutch (see Sections 18 and 19).
5 Remove the external shift mechanism (see Section 23).
6 Remove the valve cover, cam chain tensioner, camshafts, cylinder head, cylinder, piston, external oil lines and crankcase oil tube (see Sections 8, 9, 10, 11, 14, 15 and 17).
7 Remove the cam chain and intake side guide (see Section 20).
8 Remove the oil pump (see Section 22).
9 Remove the balancer gears and shaft (see Section 21).
10 Check carefully to make sure there aren't any remaining components that attach the upper and lower halves of the crankcase together.
11 Loosen the crankcase bolts in two or three stages, in a criss-cross pattern **(see illustration)**.
12 Place the engine on blocks so the transmission shafts and crankshaft can extend downward. Set up a three-legged puller against the end of the crankshaft so it can pull the upper case half off the crankshaft **(see illustration)**. Tap gently on the ends of the transmission shafts, balancer shaft and crankshaft as the case halves are being separated. Make sure the case halves separate

24.12b Watch the crankcase seam to make sure the halves are separating evenly

evenly **(see illustration)**. Carefully pry the crankcase apart at the pry points. Don't pry against the mating surfaces or they'll develop leaks.
13 Lift the right crankcase half off the left half **(see illustration)**.
14 Locate the crankcase dowels **(see illustration 24.13)**. If they aren't secure in their holes, remove them and set them aside for safekeeping.
15 Refer to Sections 25 through 27 for information on the internal components of the crankcase.

Reassembly

16 Remove all traces of old gasket and sealant from the crankcase mating surfaces with a sharpening stone or similar tool. Be careful not to let any fall into the case as this is done and be careful not to damage the mating surfaces.
17 Check to make sure the dowel pins are in place in their holes in the mating surface of the crankcase. Be sure to install a new O-ring

24.13 Lift the left case half off the right half and locate the dowels (arrows) - the center dowel has an O-ring

on the center dowel **(see illustration 24.13)**.
18 Coat both crankcase mating surfaces with Yamaha Quick Gasket (ACC-11001-05-01) or equivalent sealant.
19 Pour some engine oil over the transmission gears, balancer shaft (2007 450 models) and crankshaft bearing surfaces and the shift drum. Don't get any oil on the crankcase mating surfaces.
20 Carefully place the removed crankcase half onto the other crankcase half. While doing this, make sure the transmission shafts, shift drum and crankshaft fit into their bearings in the upper crankcase half.
21 Install the crankcase half bolts or screws in the correct holes and tighten them so they are just snug. Then tighten them in two or three stages, in a criss-cross pattern, to the torque listed in this Chapter's Specifications.
22 Turn the transmission shafts to make sure they turn freely. Also make sure the crankshaft and balancer shaft turn freely.
23 The remainder of installation is the reverse of removal.

2•38 Engine, clutch and transmission

25.3 Check the case bearings for roughness, looseness or noise

25.4a Remove the oil strainer bolts (YFZ450) or bolt (YFZ450R)...

25.4b ... and lift it off - YFZ450 models use a dowel

25 Crankcase components - inspection and servicing

1 Separate the crankcase and remove the following:

a) Transmission shafts and gears
b) Crankshaft and main bearings
c) Shift drums and forks

2 Clean the crankcase halves thoroughly with new solvent and dry them with compressed air. All oil passages should be blown out with compressed air and all traces of old gasket sealant should be removed from the mating surfaces.

Caution: Be very careful not to nick or gouge the crankcase mating surfaces or leaks will result. Check both crankcase sections very carefully for cracks and other damage.

3 Check the bearings in the case halves **(see illustration)**. If they don't turn smoothly, replace them, referring to "Tools and Workshop Tips" at the end of this manual.

4 Check the oil strainer screen(s) for clogging or damage. If problems are found, remove the screen(s) for cleaning or replacement. It's a good idea to remove the screen and check its oil passage in the crankcase whenever the crankcase is disassembled **(see illustrations)**.

5 If any damage is found that can't be repaired, replace the crankcase halves as a set.

6 Assemble the case halves (see Section 24) and check to make sure the crankshaft and the transmission shafts turn freely.

26 Transmission shafts and shift drum - removal, inspection and installation

Note: *When disassembling the transmission shafts, place the parts on a long rod or thread a wire through them to keep them in order and facing the proper direction.*

Removal

1 Remove the engine, then separate the case halves (see Sections 6 and 24). The transmission components remain in one case half when the case is separated.

2 Remove the shift drum, shift forks and transmission shafts from the crankcase **(see illustrations)**.

3 Using snap-ring pliers, remove the snap-rings and take the gears off the shafts.

4 Place the gears in order on a coat hanger or dowel so they won't be mixed up.

Inspection

5 Wash all of the components in clean solvent and dry them off.

6 Inspect the shift fork grooves in the gears. If a groove is worn or scored, replace the affected part and inspect its corresponding shift fork.

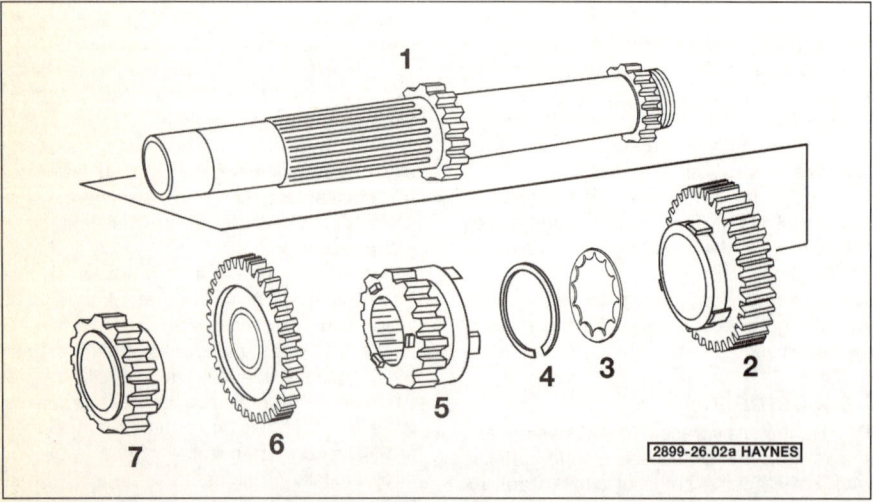

26.2a Mainshaft components

1 Mainshaft
2 Fifth pinion gear
3 Spline washer
4 Snap-ring
5 Third pinion gear
6 Fourth pinion gear
7 Second pinion gear

Engine, clutch and transmission 2•39

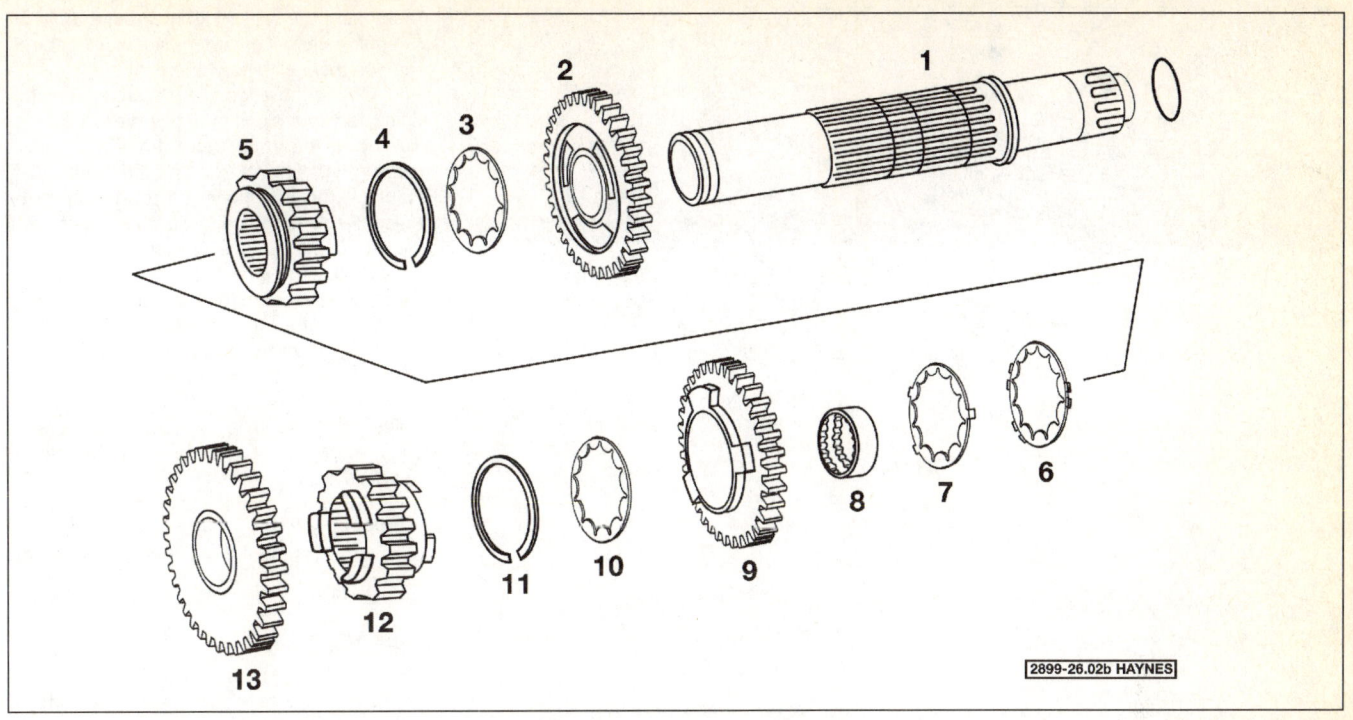

26.2b Countershaft components

1 Countershaft
2 Second wheel gear
3 Spline washer
4 Snap-ring
5 Fourth wheel gear

6 Spline retainer washer
7 Spline lockwasher
8 Spline bushing
9 Third wheel gear

10 Spline washer
11 Snap-ring
12 Fifth wheel gear
13 First wheel gear

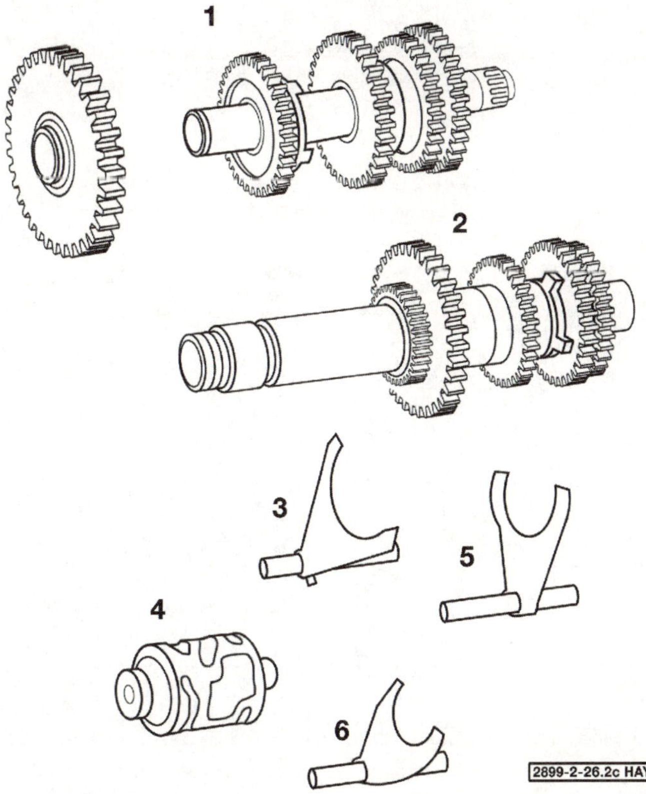

26.2c Shift drum and forks - YFZ450

1 Countershaft
2 Mainshaft
3 Center shift fork
4 Shift drum
5 Left shift fork
6 Right shift fork

2•40 Engine, clutch and transmission

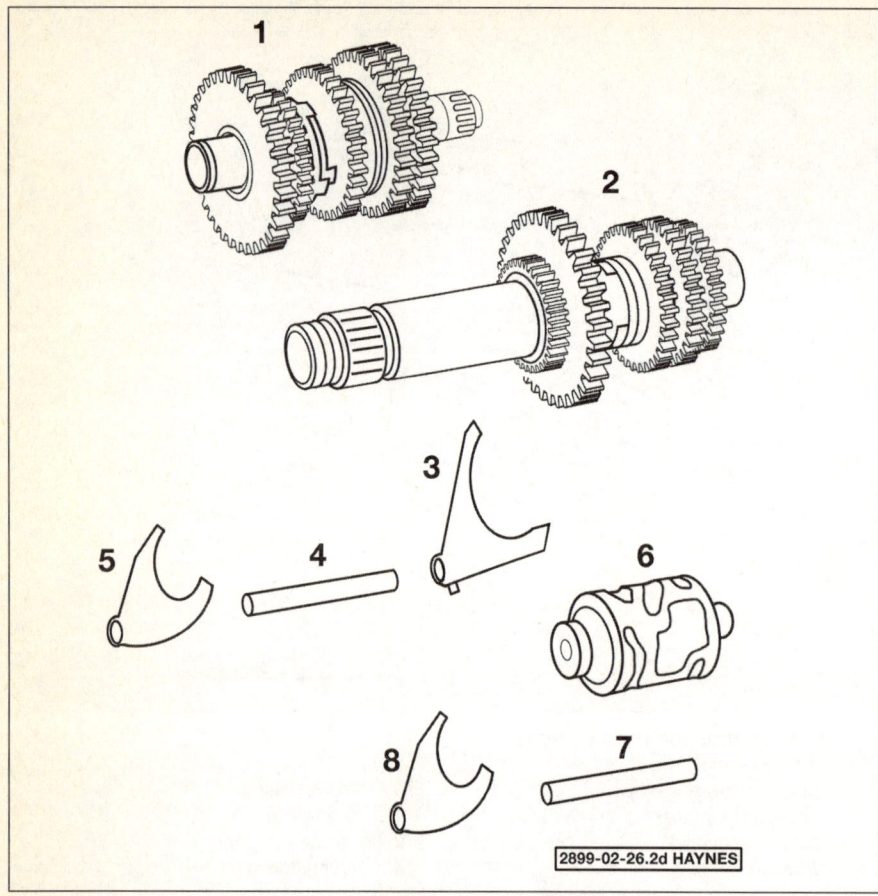

26.2d Shift drum and forks - YFZ450R

1. Countershaft
2. Mainshaft
3. Left shift fork
4. Shift fork guide bar
5. Right shift fork
6. Shift drum
7. Shift fork guide bar
8. Center shift fork

7 Check the shift forks for distortion and wear, especially at the fork ears. If they are discolored or severely worn they are probably bent. Inspect the guide pins for excessive wear and distortion and replace any defective parts with new ones.

8 Check the shift fork guide bars for evidence of wear, galling and other damage.

Make sure the shift forks move smoothly on the guide bars. If the shafts are worn or bent, replace them with new ones.

9 Check the edges of the grooves in the shift drums for signs of excessive wear.

10 Hold the inner race of the shift drum bearing with fingers and spin the outer race. Replace the bearing if it's rough, loose or noisy. Replace the shift drum segment if it's worn or damaged (see Section 23).

11 Check the gear teeth for cracking and other obvious damage. Check the bushing surface in the inner diameter of the free-wheeling gears for scoring or heat discoloration. Replace damaged parts.

12 Inspect the engagement dogs and dog holes on gears so equipped for excessive wear or rounding off. Replace the paired gears as a set if necessary.

13 Check the transmission shaft bearings in the crankcase for wear or heat discoloration and replace them if necessary (see Section 25).

Installation

14 Installation is the basically the reverse of the removal procedure, but take note of the following points:

a) Use new snap-rings. Install the snap-rings with their rounded edges facing the direction of thrust (toward the component they're securing). Refer to "Tools and Workshop Tips" at the end of this manual if necessary.

b) Lubricate the components with engine oil before assembling them.

c) Install the shift forks with their letter/number marks toward the right side of the engine and their L, C and R marks (left, center and right) toward the left side of the engine **(see illustrations)**.

d) After assembly, check the gears to make sure they're installed correctly. Move the shift drums through the gear positions and rotate the gears to make sure they mesh and shift correctly.

26.14a The letter-number codes face the right side of the engine

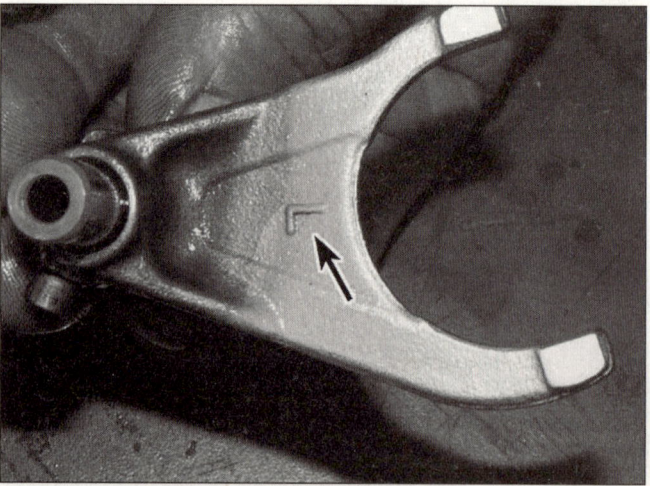

26.14b The L, C and R marks (indicating left, center and right forks) face the left side of the engine

27.2 Use a puller like this to push the crankshaft out of the case half

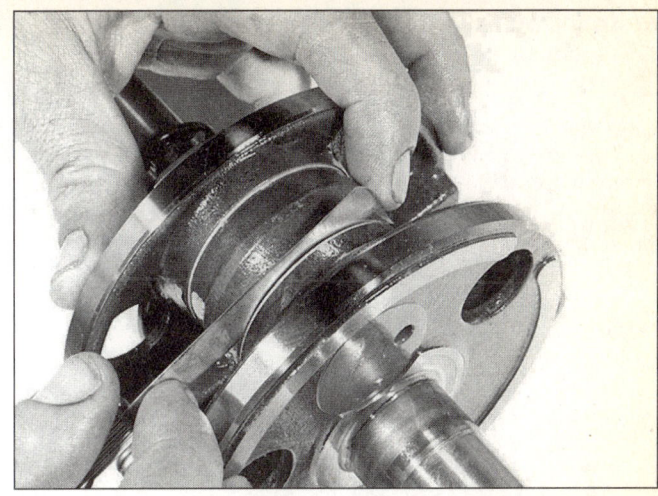

27.3 Measure the gap between the connecting rod and the crankshaft with a feeler gauge

27 Crankshaft and connecting rod - removal, inspection and installation

Note: *The procedures in this section require special tools. If you don't have the necessary equipment or suitable substitutes, have the crankshaft removed and installed by a Yamaha dealer.*

Removal

1 Remove the engine and separate the crankcase halves (see Sections 6, 24 and 25). The transmission shafts need not be removed.
2 The crankshaft may be loose enough in its bearing that you can lift it out of the left crankcase half. If not, push it out with tools YU-A9642 or equivalent **(see illustration)**.

Inspection

3 Measure the side clearance between the connecting rod and crankshaft with a feeler gauge **(see illustration)**. If it's more than the limit listed in this Chapter's Specifications, replace the crankshaft and connecting rod as an assembly.
4 Set up the crankshaft in V-blocks with a dial indicator contacting the big end of the connecting rod. Move the connecting rod side-to-side against the indicator pointer and compare the reading to the value listed in this Chapter's Specifications. If it's beyond the limit, the crankshaft can be disassembled and the needle roller bearing replaced. However, this is a specialized job that should be done by a Yamaha dealer or qualified machine shop.
5 Check the crankshaft splines, the cam chain sprocket, the ball bearing at the sprocket end of the crankshaft and the bearing journals for visible wear or damage **(see illustration)**. Yamaha lists the ball bearing end of the crankshaft as a separately available part, but check with your dealer first; it may be more practical to replace the entire crankshaft if the ball bearing or cam sprocket is worn or damaged. Replace the crankshaft if any of the other conditions are found.
6 Set the crankshaft in a lathe or a pair of V-blocks, with a dial indicator contacting each end **(see illustration)**. Rotate the crankshaft and note the runout. If the runout at either end is beyond the limit listed in this Chapter's Specifications, replace the crankshaft and connecting rod as an assembly.
7 Measure the assembly width of the crankshaft (from the outside of one crank throw to the outside of the other crank throw). If it exceeds the limit listed in this Chapter's Specifications, replace the crankshaft.

27.5 Check the cam chain sprocket and the ball bearing on the end of the crankshaft

27.6 Measure runout on each side of the crankshaft (A); if the assembly width (B) is greater than specified, replace the crankshaft

2•42 Engine, clutch and transmission

Installation

8 Start the crankshaft into the case half. If it doesn't go in easily, pull it in the rest of the way with Yamaha tools YU-90050, YM-01383 and YM-91044 **(see illustration)**.
9 The remainder of installation is the reverse of removal.

28 Initial start-up after overhaul

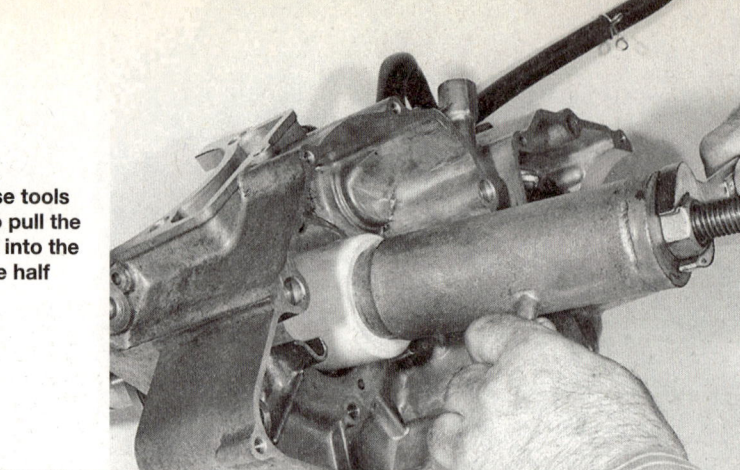

27.8 These tools are used to pull the crankshaft into the left case half

1 Make sure the engine oil level is correct, then remove the spark plug from the engine. Place the engine kill switch in the Off position and unplug the primary (low tension) wires from the coil.
2 Crank the engine over with the starter several times to build up oil pressure. Reinstall the spark plug, connect the wires and turn the switch to On.
3 Make sure there is fuel in the tank, then operate the choke.
4 Refer to the oil change procedure in Chapter 1 to check oil pressure at the check bolt.
Caution: If oil doesn't seep from the check bolt within one minute, stop the engine immediately and locate the problem before running it further.
Once you've made sure that there is oil pressure, allow the engine to run at a moderately fast idle until it reaches operating temperature.
5 Check carefully for oil leaks and make sure the transmission and controls, especially the brakes, function properly before road testing the machine. Refer to Section 29 for the recommended break-in procedure.

6 Upon completion of the road test, and after the engine has cooled down completely, recheck the valve clearances (see Chapter 1).

29 Recommended break-in procedure

1 Any rebuilt engine needs time to break in, even if parts have been installed in their original locations. For this reason, treat the machine gently for the first few miles to make sure oil has circulated throughout the engine and any new parts installed have started to seat.
2 Even greater care is necessary if the cylinder has been rebored or a new crankshaft has been installed. In the case of a rebore, the engine will have to be broken in as if the machine were new. This means greater use of the transmission and a restraining hand on the throttle for the first few operating days. There's no point in keeping to any set speed limit - the main idea is to vary the engine speed, keep from lugging (laboring) the engine and to avoid full-throttle operation. These recommendations can be lessened to an extent when only a new crankshaft is installed. Experience is the best guide, since it's easy to tell when an engine is running freely.
3 If a lubrication failure is suspected (oil doesn't seep from the check bolt, or the engine makes noise), stop the engine immediately and try to find the cause. If an engine is run without oil, even for a short period of time, irreparable damage will occur.

Notes

Notes

Chapter 3
Cooling system

Contents

Coolant change.. See Chapter 1	Cooling system check... See Chapter 1
Coolant hoses - removal and installation..................................... 4	General information... 1
Coolant level check... See Chapter 1	Radiator and fan - removal and installation 6
Coolant reservoir - removal and installation................................. 3	Radiator cap - check... 2
Coolant temperature sensor (YFZ450R)......................See Chapter 4B	Water pump - removal, inspection and installation..................... 7
Coolant temperature warning light................................ See Chapter 5	Water pump seals and bearing - replacement............................ 8
Cooling fan and circuit - check and switch replacement............. 5	

Degrees of difficulty

| Easy, suitable for novice with little experience |  | Fairly easy, suitable for beginner with some experience |  | Fairly difficult, suitable for competent DIY mechanic | | Difficult, suitable for experienced DIY mechanic | | Very difficult, suitable for expert DIY or professional | 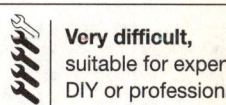 |

Specifications

General
Radiator cap relief pressure
   YFZ450... 15 to 19 psi
   YFZ450R... 16 to 20 psi

Torque specifications
Water pump impeller (YFZ450 only).. 14 Nm (120 inch-lbs)
Water pump bolts.. 10 Nm (86 inch-lbs)
Radiator mounting bolts... 7 Nm (61 inch-lbs)
Coolant reservoir mounting bolts .... 7 Nm (61 inch-lbs)

3•2 Cooling system

3.1a To remove the YFZ450 coolant reservoir, disconnect the overflow hose and radiator hose and unscrew the mounting bolts (arrows)

3.1b To remove the YFZ450R coolant reservoir, pull off the cap (right arrow), disconnect the radiator hose (left arrow), unbolt the tank and lift it out

1 General information

The vehicles covered by this manual are equipped with a liquid cooling system which utilizes a water/antifreeze mixture to carry away excess heat produced during combustion. The combustion chamber and cylinder are surrounded by a water jacket, through which the coolant is circulated by the water pump. The pump is mounted to the right side of the crankcase near the front and is driven by a gear. The radiator is mounted at the front of the frame. The coolant is pumped upward through the cylinder water jacket and cylinder head, then flows from the cylinder head to the radiator where it is cooled, then flows through the radiator bottom hose and water pump, then back into the engine.

The cooling system includes a temperature warning light and fan, but does not include a thermostat. All models have a reservoir tank. As the coolant heats up, it expands and flows into the reservoir tank. As it cools, the coolant is pulled back into the cooling system.

2 Radiator cap - check

If problems such as overheating or loss of coolant occur, check the entire system as described in Chapter 1. The radiator cap opening pressure should be checked by a dealer service department or service station equipped with the special tester required to do the job. If the cap is defective, replace it with a new one.

3 Coolant reservoir - removal and installation

1 The YFZ450 coolant reservoir is located under the left side of the rear fender (see illustration). The YFZ450R coolant reservoir is located forward of the engine on the left side of the vehicle (see illustration).
2 Disconnect the hoses from the tank. Remove the tank mounting bolts and take it off.
3 Installation is the reverse of the removal steps.

4 Coolant hoses - removal and installation

1 The coolant hoses are all secured by screw-type clamps to fittings on the engine and radiator. The water pump hose runs to the bottom of the radiator and another hose runs from the top of the radiator to the engine.
2 To remove a hose, loosen its clamp and carefully pry it off the fitting (see illustrations).
3 If the hose is stuck, pry the edge up

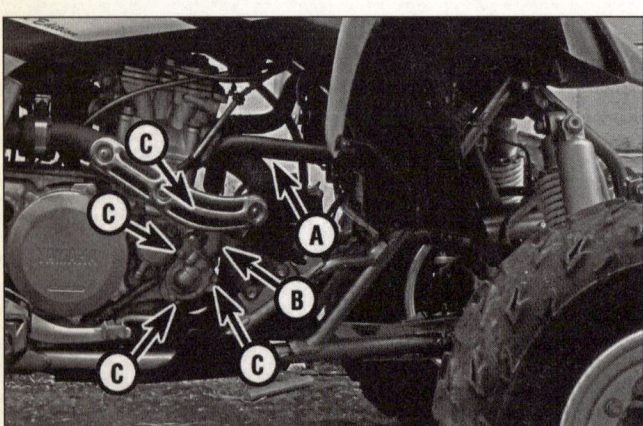

4.2a The YFZ450 water pump to radiator hose (arrow) connects to a metal tube bolted to the water pump

A Hose
B Coolant tube
C Water pump bolts

4.2b Expand the clamp (arrow) and slide it up the hose, then disconnect the hose from the metal tube

Cooling system

4.2c The YFZ450 coolant return hose runs from the cylinder head to the radiator on the left side of the vehicle (arrow)

4.2d The YFZ450R water pump hose connects directly to the pump (arrow)

slightly with a pointed tool and spray brake or electrical contact cleaner into the gap. Work the tool around the fitting, lifting the edge of the hose and spraying into the gap until the hose comes free of the fitting.

4 In extreme cases, you may have to slit the hose and cut it off the fitting with a knife. Make sure you can get a replacement hose before doing this.

5 Cooling fan and circuit - check and switch replacement

Check

1 If the engine is overheating and the cooling fan isn't coming on, first check the main fuse (see Chapter 5). If the fuse is blown, check the fan circuit for a short to ground (see the *Wiring diagrams* at the end of this book).

YFZ450

2 If the main fuse is good, follow the black/blue wire from the main key switch to the fan circuit breaker (it's located at the front of the vehicle near the radiator). Disconnect the circuit breaker from the wiring harness and connect an ohmmeter between the circuit breaker terminals. There should be continuity (zero ohms). If the ohmmeter indicates resistance, replace the circuit breaker with a new one.

YFZ450R

3 If the main fuse is good, remove the front fender (see Chapter 8) and locate the fan motor relay **(see illustration 16.5 in Chapter 5)**.

4 Using a pair of jumper wires, connect a 12-volt battery (the vehicle's battery will do if it's fully charged) to the relay terminals (not the wiring harness terminals) as follows:

4.2e The YFZ450 coolant return hose runs from the cylinder head to the radiator on the left side of the vehicle (arrow)

a) Battery positive to brown wire's terminal
b) Battery negative to blue-red wire's terminal

5 With the battery connected to the relay, connect an ohmmeter between the relay terminals for the red-white wire and red-blue wire. The ohmmeter should show continuity (little or no resistance). If it doesn't, replace the relay with a new one.

6 Disconnect the battery from the relay and recheck continuity between the terminals for the red-white wire and red-blue wire. The ohmmeter should show no continuity (infinite resistance). If it doesn't, replace the relay with a new one.

All models

7 If the preceding steps haven't identified the problem, disconnect the fan motor connector and connect the fan motor directly to a fully charged 12-volt battery using a pair of jumper wires (battery positive to blue; battery negative to black). The fan motor should run. If it doesn't, replace the fan with a new one.

8 If the fan motor runs when connected directly to the battery, disconnect the electrical connector from the fan thermoswitch mounted in the radiator. It can be identified by its wire colors: red-white and black for YFZ450 models; red-white and red for YFZ450R models). **Note:** *Don't mistake the fan thermoswitch for the warning light thermoswitch (all models) or the coolant temperature sensor that's part of the fuel injection system (YFZ450R). The warning light thermoswitch and coolant temperature sensor have different wire colors.*

9 Connect a short jumper wire between the terminals of the fan thermoswitch connector in the wiring harness (not between the terminals of the switch itself). With the ignition key in the ON position, the fan should run. If it does, replace the thermoswitch with a new one.

Switch replacement

10 Drain the cooling system (see Chapter 1).

11 If you haven't already done so, disconnect the electrical connector from the thermoswitch.

3•4 Cooling system

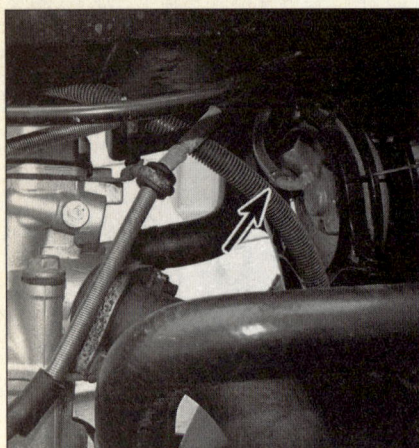

6.3a Disconnect the breather hose from the fan housing (arrow)

6.3b YFZ450 fan details

- A Breather hose
- B Wiring harness and breather hose retainer
- C Fan upper mounting bolts
- D Throttle, clutch and parking brake cables

12 Unscrew the thermoswitch from the radiator.
13 If the thermoswitch uses a gasket, install a new one. If it doesn't, coat the threads with silicone sealant.
14 Tighten the thermoswitch to the torque listed in this Chapter's Specifications.

6 Radiator and fan - removal and installation

⚠ **Warning: The engine must be completely cool before beginning this procedure.**

1 Remove the seat, side covers and front fender (see Chapter 8). Drain the cooling system (see Chapter 1).
2 Disconnect the electrical connectors for the fan and warning light switch. If you're working on a YFZ450R model, also disconnect the electrical connector for the fuel injection system's coolant temperature sensor (see Chapter 4).
3 Disconnect the breather hose from the fan housing **(see illustrations)**.
4 Disconnect the radiator hoses (see Section 4).
5 Remove the radiator mounting bolts. On YFZ450 models, there's one at each of the four corners of the radiator, facing rearward **(see illustration)**. On YFZ450R models, there's a mounting bolt at each of the radiator's four corners, facing outward **(see illustration)**.
6 Lift the radiator away from the frame. Inspect the mounting bolt grommets and replace them if they're worn or deteriorated.
7 Remove the retaining pins from the radiator grille and remove the grille from the radiator.
8 Remove the fan mounting bolts and take the fan motor off the radiator **(see illustration 6.5a or 6.3b)**. The fan and motor are not available separately.
9 Installation is the reverse of the removal steps, with the following additions:

a) Tighten the mounting bolts securely, but don't overtighten them and distort the grommets.
b) Fill the cooling system (see Chapter 1).
c) Run the engine and check for coolant leaks.

7 Water pump - removal, inspection and installation

Removal and disassembly

Note: *The following procedure describes removing the water pump completely. If you're only planning to remove the cover so you can inspect the impeller, ignore the steps that don't apply.*

1 Drain the engine oil and cooling system (see Chapter 1).
2 Remove the exhaust pipe (see Chapter 4).
3 Remove the right footrest (see Chapter 8).

6.5a The YFZ450 radiator is secured by a mounting bolt at each corner of the radiator (left arrow); the fan is secured to the radiator by three bolts, one at the bottom (right arrow) and two at the top

6.5b The YFZ450R radiator is secured by upper and lower mounting bolts on each side (arrows, right side shown)

Cooling system

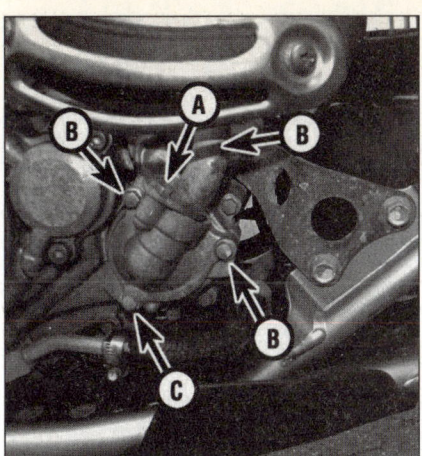

7.5a On YFZ450 models, disconnect the coolant hose and unbolt the coolant tube from the pump

- A Coolant tube bolt
- B Mounting bolts (upper bolt hidden)
- C Drain bolt (with copper washer)

7.5b On YFZ450R models, detach the hose from the pump and remove the pump mounting bolts (arrows)

7.7 Take off the pump housing and remove the O-ring - note the location of the dowel pins (arrows)

4 Remove the brake light switch (see Chapter 5).

5 Disconnect the coolant hose from the water pump **(see illustrations)**. If you're working on a YFZ450, unbolt the coolant tube from the pump.

6 Remove the pump cover bolts **(see illustration 7.5a or 7.5b)**. The bolts are different lengths, so tag them for reinstallation.

7 Take off the pump cover and O-ring **(see illustration)**.

8 To remove the impeller and shaft, remove the right crankcase cover together with the shaft (see Chapter 2).

YFZ450

9 Unscrew the impeller from its shaft and remove the washer **(see illustrations)**.

10 Pull the impeller shaft out of the pump

7.9a On YFZ450 models, place a wrench on the flats of the impeller shaft to keep it from turning ...

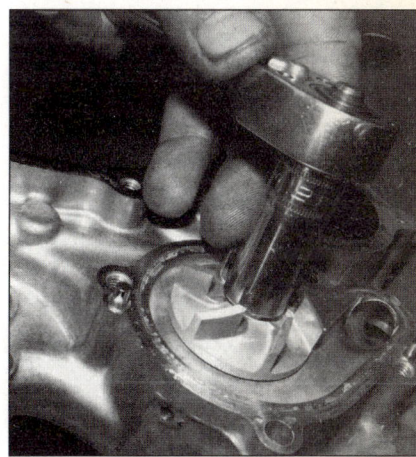

7.9b ... unscrew the impeller ...

7.9c ... take the impeller off and remove the washer (arrow)

7.9d Take the impeller shaft out of the crankcase cover from the inside

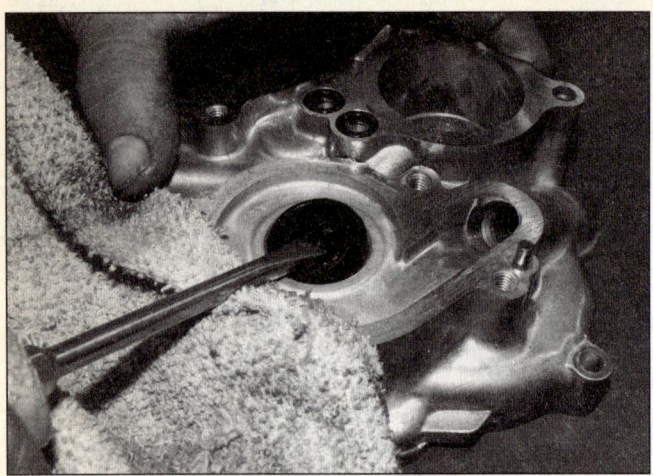

8.3 Pry the seal out of the cover, noting which way the open side faces

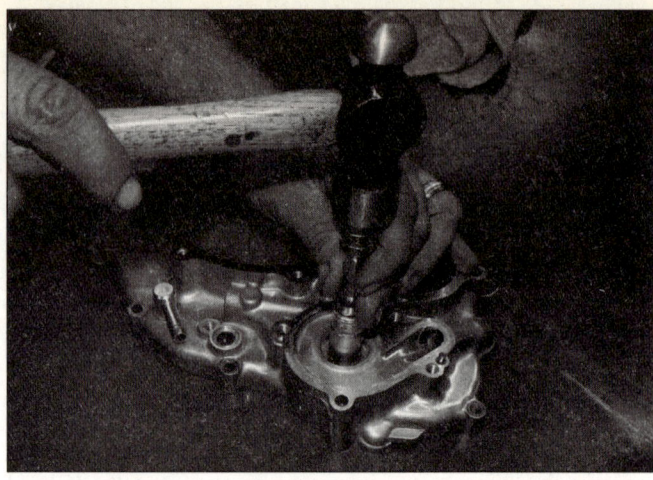

8.4 If the bearing needs to be replaced, drive it out with a socket or bearing driver

body, twisting it as you remove it to prevent damage to the seal.

YFZ450R

11 The impeller and shaft are one piece. To remove them, remove the snap-ring from the inner end of the shaft and pull the impeller and shaft out of the crankcase cover.

Inspection

12 Check the impeller seals for wear or damage. These seals separate the coolant from the engine oil. If the oil is milky or foamy, coolant may have been leaking into it past the seals. Refer to Section 8 and replace them.

13 To inspect the bearing, place the impeller shaft in the bearing, wiggle it and check for play. If it can be wiggled from side to side, the bearing needs to be replaced. Lift the impeller shaft out of the bearing. Spin the bearing and check it for roughness, looseness or noise and replace it as described in Section 8 if any problems are found.

Installation

14 Installation is the reverse of the removal steps, with the following additions:
a) Use a new O-ring.
b) Engage the impeller shaft tang with the drive slot.
c) Tighten the water pump bolts to the torque listed in this Chapter's Specifications.
d) Fill the cooling system and engine oil (see Chapter 1).
e) Run the engine and check for coolant leaks.

8 Water pump seals and bearing - replacement

1 If coolant has been leaking from the weep hole (see Chapter 1), the water pump seal needs to be replaced.

2 Remove the right crankcase cover (see Chapter 2) and the water pump impeller shaft (see Section 7).

3 Carefully pry the seals out of their bore with a screwdriver, being careful not to gouge the crankcase cover **(see illustration)**.

4 The ball bearing is mounted in the right crankcase cover. If it needs to be replaced, drive the bearing out with a socket or bearing driver **(see illustration)**.

5 Drive in a new bearing with a bearing driver or socket that bears against the bearing outer race.

6 Tap in new seals with a socket the same diameter as the seal.

Notes

Notes

Chapter 4 Part A
Fuel and exhaust systems (YFZ450)

Contents

Carburetor - disassembly, cleaning and inspection..................... 5	Exhaust system - removal and installation.................................. 8
Carburetor - reassembly, float check and accelerator pump check 6	Fuel tank - removal and installation 2
	General information.. 1
Carburetor - removal and installation... 4	Throttle cable - removal and installation 7
Carburetor adjustment .... See Chapter 1	Throttle position sensor - check, removal and installation........... 9
Carburetor overhaul - general information 3	

Degrees of difficulty

Easy, suitable for novice with little experience	**Fairly easy,** suitable for beginner with some experience 	**Fairly difficult,** suitable for competent DIY mechanic 	**Difficult,** suitable for experienced DIY mechanic 	**Very difficult,** suitable for expert DIY or professional 

Specifications

General
Fuel type.. See Chapter 1

Carburetor
2004 and 2005
   Type .... Keihin
   ID mark... 5TG1 00
   Main jet.. 158
   Main air jet... 1.0 diameter

Carburetor (continued)

2004 and 2005 (continued)
    Needle/clip position NDSR-4
    Pilot jet 42
    Pilot air jet 100
    Standard pilot screw setting .... Not specified
    Starter jet 90
    Float height .... 8 mm (0.31 inch)
    Accelerator pump adjustment (diameter of measuring pin)............... 3.4 mm (1.34 inch)

2006 and later
    Type .... Keihin FCR39H
    ID mark... 5TGC 30
    Main jet 155
    Main air jet .... 1.0 diameter
    Needle/clip position .... NGNR/not specified
    Pilot jet 42
    Pilot air jet 70
    Standard pilot screw setting .... Not specified
    Starter jet 90
    Float height .... 8 mm (0.31 inch)
    Accelerator pump adjustment (diameter of measuring pin)............... 3.4 mm (1.34 inch)

Fuel and exhaust systems (YFZ450) 4A•3

2.2a If the fuel tap is easy to get to, squeeze the ends of the clamp together, slide it down the hose, then disconnect the fuel line from the tap . . .

2.2b . . . if not, slide the clamp (arrow) up off the carburetor fitting, disconnect the hose and cap the fitting to keep out dirt

1 General information

All YFZ450 models use a flat-slide carburetor with an accelerator pump. The slide acts as the throttle valve. The accelerator pump injects extra gasoline into the fuel mixture during acceleration. For cold starting on all models, a choke plunger is actuated by a knob.

The exhaust system consists of a pipe and muffler with a removable spark arrester.

2 Fuel tank - removal and installation

Warning: *Gasoline is extremely flammable, so take extra precautions when you work on any part of the fuel system. Don't smoke or allow open flames or bare light bulbs near the work area, and don't work in a garage where a gas-type appliance (such as a water heater or clothes dryer) is present. Since gasoline is carcinogenic, wear fuel-resistant gloves when there's a possibility of being exposed to fuel, and, if you spill any fuel on your skin, rinse it off immediately with soap and water. Mop up any spills immediately and do not store fuel-soaked rags where they could ignite. When you perform any kind of work on the fuel system, wear safety glasses and have an extinguisher suitable for a class B type fire (flammable liquids) on hand.*

Removal

1 Remove the seat, fuel tank cover and side covers (see Chapter 8).

2 Turn the fuel tap to Off and disconnect the fuel line **(see illustrations)**. Disconnect it at the tap if there's room. If not, disconnect it at the carburetor fitting. If you disconnect the fuel line at the carburetor, cap it to keep out dirt.
3 Pull the fuel tank vent hose off the fitting on the filler cap **(see illustration)**.
4 Remove one mounting bolt at the rear of the tank and two at the front and lift it off, together with the fuel tap.
5 If necessary, pull up the two trim clips that secure the heat shield under the tank and remove the heat shield.

Installation

6 Before installing the tank, check the condition of the mounting collar at the rear bolt hole, the isolators at the two front bolt holes and the fuel line to the carburetor - if they're hardened, cracked, or show any other signs of deterioration, replace them.
7 When installing the tank, reverse the removal procedure. Make sure the tank does not pinch any wires. Tighten the tank mounting bolts securely, but don't overtighten them and strip the threads.

2.3 Pull the vent hose (arrow) off of the tank fitting or out of the steering stem nut

3 Carburetor overhaul - general information

1 Poor engine performance, hesitation, hard starting, stalling, flooding and backfiring are all signs that major carburetor maintenance may be required.
2 Keep in mind that many so-called carburetor problems are really not carburetor problems at all, but mechanical problems within the engine or ignition system malfunctions. Try to establish for certain that the carburetor is in need of maintenance before beginning a major overhaul.
3 Check the fuel tap and its strainer screen, the fuel lines, the intake manifold clamps, the O-ring between the intake manifold and cylinder head, the vacuum hoses, the air filter element, the cylinder compression, crankcase vacuum and compression, the spark plug and the ignition timing before assuming that a carburetor overhaul is required. If the bike has been unused for more than a few weeks, drain the float cham-

4A•4 Fuel and exhaust systems (YFZ450)

4.3a Loosen the front clamp screws (arrows) . . .

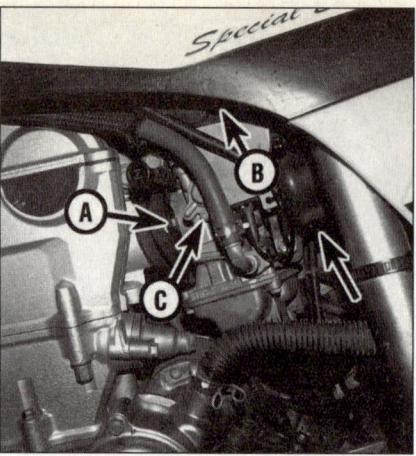

4.3b . . . and the rear clamp screws (arrow, hidden); follow the wiring harnesses from the throttle position sensor and throttle switch to their connectors and unplug them

A Front clamp alignment tab
B Throttle position sensor
C Carburetor switch

ber and refill the tank with fresh fuel.
4   Most carburetor problems are caused by dirt particles, varnish and other deposits which build up in and block the fuel and air passages. Also, in time, gaskets and O-rings shrink or deteriorate and cause fuel and air leaks which lead to poor performance.
5   When the carburetor is overhauled, it is generally disassembled completely and the parts are cleaned thoroughly with a carburetor cleaning solvent and dried with filtered, unlubricated compressed air. The fuel and air passages are also blown through with compressed air to force out any dirt that may have been loosened but not removed by the solvent. Once the cleaning process is complete, the carburetor is reassembled using a new top gasket, O-rings and, generally, a new inlet needle valve and seat.
6   Before disassembling the carburetor, make sure you have the necessary gasket, O-rings and other parts, some carburetor cleaner, a supply of rags, some means of blowing out the carburetor passages and a clean place to work.

4 Carburetor - removal and installation

1   Remove the seat, both side covers and the fuel tank cover (see Chapter 8).
2   Disconnect the fuel line from the carburetor (see Section 2).
3   Loosen the clamping bands at the front and rear of the carburetor (see illustrations).
4   Disconnect the electrical connectors for the throttle position sensor and carburetor switch (see illustration 4.3b).
5   Remove the throttle cable cover from the side of the carburetor and disconnect the throttle cable (see Section 7).
6   Free the carburetor from the intake tube and the air cleaner tube.
7   Note how the hoses are routed and free them from the retainer. Remove the carburetor.
8   Installation is the reverse of the removal steps, with the following additions:
   a) Adjust the throttle freeplay (see Chapter 1).
   b) Adjust the idle speed and, if necessary, the pilot screw (air/fuel mixture) (see Chapter 1).

5 Carburetor - disassembly, cleaning and inspection

⚠ *Warning: Gasoline is extremely flammable, so take extra precautions when you work on any part of the fuel system. See the Warning in Section 2.*

Disassembly
1   Remove the carburetor from the machine as described in Section 4.
2   Set the carburetor on a clean working surface. Take note of how the vent hoses are routed, including locations of hose retainers. Remove the carburetor switch screws and take the switch off the left side of the carburetor **(see illustration 4.3b)**.
3   To disassemble the carburetor, refer to the accompanying **illustrations**.

Cleaning
Caution: Use only a carburetor cleaning solution that is safe for use with plastic parts (be sure to read the label on the container).

4   Submerge the metal components in the carburetor cleaner for approximately thirty minutes (or longer, if the directions recommend it).

5.3a Remove the float chamber screws, take off the float chamber and remove the O-ring (arrow)

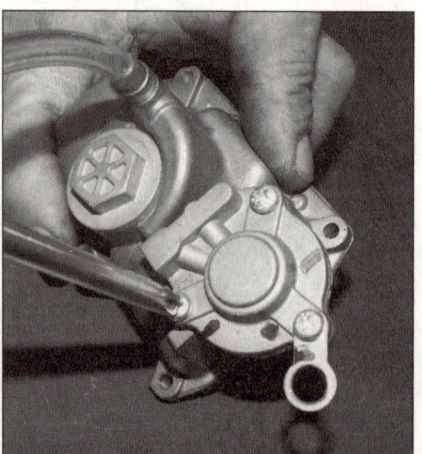

5.3b Remove the accelerator pump cover screws while holding the cover down against the spring pressure . . .

5.3c . . . then lift off the cover and remove the O-rings (arrows)

Fuel and exhaust systems (YFZ450) 4A•5

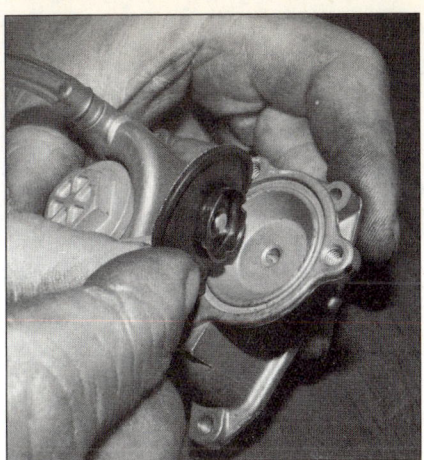

5.3d Remove the accelerator pump diaphragm

5.3e Unscrew the leak jet (lower arrow) and check the spring-loaded ball (upper arrow) for free movement

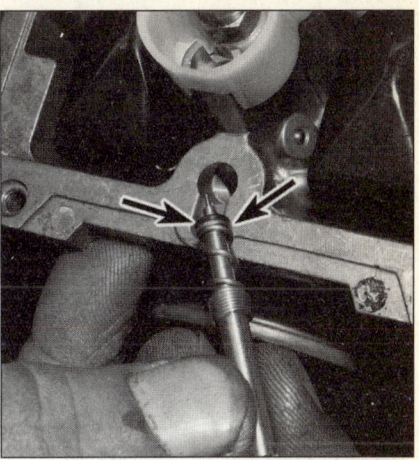

5.3f Bottom the pilot screw lightly, counting the number of turns, then unscrew it all the way and remove the O-ring (left arrow), washer (right arrow) and spring

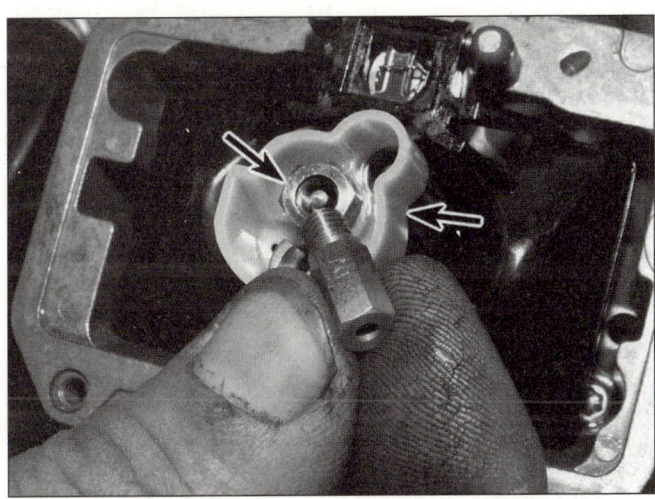

5.3g Unscrew the main jet, then unscrew the needle jet (left arrow) and take off the baffle (right arrow)

5.3h Unscrew the starter jet (upper arrow) and pilot jet (lower arrow)

5.3i Push out the float pivot pin with a piece of wire, then lift off the floats, together with the needle valve (arrow)

5.3j Unscrew the choke valve from the carburetor

5.3k Remove the top cover screws

5.3l Remove the cover and its O-ring - the throttle shaft screw (lower arrow) is not normally removed - the needle holder (upper arrow) . . .

5.3m . . . secures the spring and clip

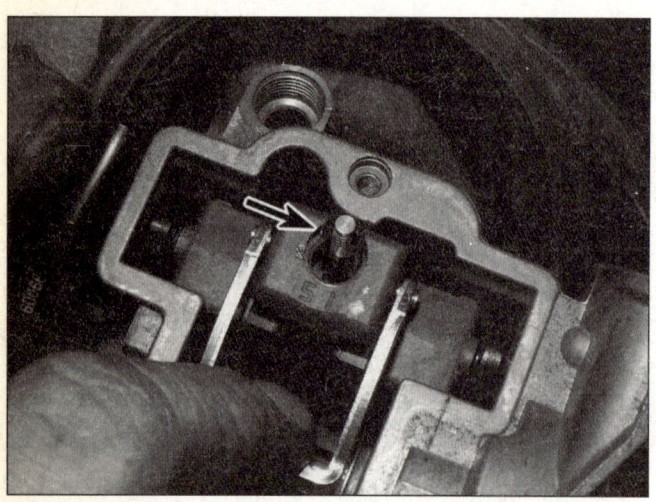

5.3n Lift the throttle piston for access to the jet needle (arrow) . . .

5.3o . . . and lift out the jet needle with its clip

5.3p If you need to remove the throttle valve, remove the throttle shaft screw (illustration 5.3l) and pull out the throttle valve, but do not remove the throttle shaft

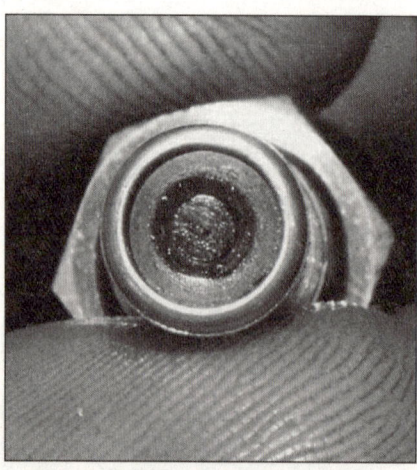

5.6 Check the choke plunger seat for wear or deterioration

5 After the carburetor has soaked long enough for the cleaner to loosen and dissolve most of the varnish and other deposits, use a brush to remove the stubborn deposits. Rinse it again, then dry it with compressed air. Blow out all of the fuel and air passages in the carburetor body.

Caution: Never clean the jets or passages with a piece of wire or a drill bit, as they will be enlarged, causing the fuel and air metering rates to be upset.

Inspection

6 Check the operation of the choke plunger. If it doesn't move smoothly, replace it. Check the plunger seat for wear or damage **(see illustration)** and replace it if problems are found. Inspect the hot start valve in the same manner.

7 Check the tapered portion of the pilot screw for wear or damage. Replace the screw if necessary.

Fuel and exhaust systems (YFZ450) 4A•7

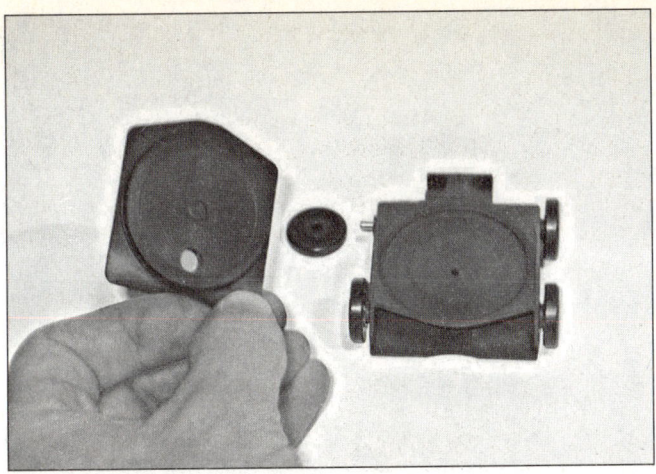

5.13 If the plating has worn off the throttle valve like this, it's time for a new one

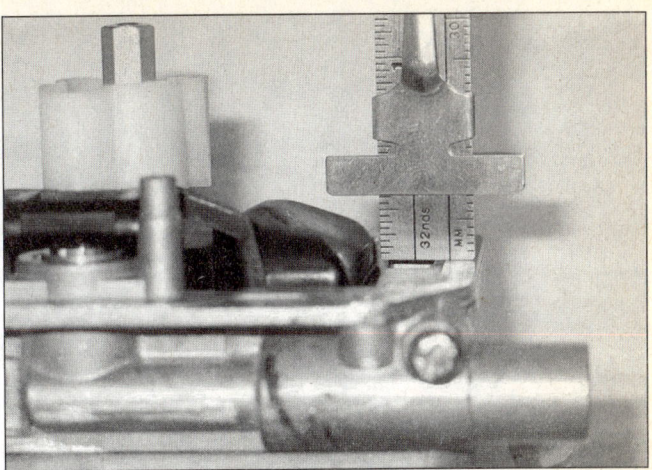

6.5 Measure float height from the float bowl mating surface - the tang on the float should seat the needle, but not compress the spring-loaded pin in the needle

6.9 Carefully tighten the accelerator pump screw (upper arrow) all the way, then back it off until there's no play in the lever (lower arrow)

8 Check the carburetor body, float chamber and carburetor top for cracks, distorted sealing surfaces and other damage. If any defects are found, replace the faulty component, although replacement of the entire carburetor will probably be necessary (check with your parts supplier for the availability of separate components).
9 Check the jet needle for straightness by rolling it on a flat surface (such as a piece of glass). Replace it if it's bent or if the tip is worn.
10 Check the tip of the fuel inlet valve needle. If it has grooves or scratches in it, it must be replaced. Push in on the rod in the other end of the needle, then release it - if it doesn't spring back, replace the valve needle.
11 Check the O-rings on the float chamber and the main jet access plug (in the float chamber). Replace them if they're damaged.
12 Check the floats for damage. This will usually be apparent by the presence of fuel inside one of the floats. If the floats are damaged, they must be replaced.
13 Insert the throttle valve in the carburetor body and see that it moves up-and-down smoothly. Check the rollers and the surface of the throttle valve for wear (see illustration). If it's worn excessively or doesn't move smoothly in the bore, replace it.

6 Carburetor - reassembly, float check and accelerator pump check

Reassembly

Caution: When installing the jets, be careful not to over-tighten them - they're made of soft material and can strip or shear easily.

Note: *When reassembling the carburetor, be sure to use new O-rings.*
Note: *When installing the throttle shaft screw, apply a drop of non-hardening thread locking agent to the screw threads.*

1 Install the clip on the jet needle if it was removed. Place it in the needle groove listed in this Chapter's Specifications. Install the needle and clip in the throttle valve.
2 Install the pilot screw along with its spring, washer and O-ring, turning it in until it seats lightly. Now, turn the screw out the number of turns written down during removal. The manufacturer doesn't specify an initial setting, but if you didn't write down how many turns out the screw was before disassembly, a good starting point would be 1-1/2 turns out (from the seated position). Refer to Chapter 1 for further adjustment if necessary.
3 Reverse the disassembly steps to install the jets.
4 Invert the carburetor. Attach the fuel inlet valve needle to the float. Set the float into position in the carburetor, making sure the valve needle seats correctly. Install the float pivot pin.
5 Measure float height as described in Step 7 before the float chamber is installed (see illustration).
6 Install the float chamber gasket or O-ring. Place the float chamber on the carburetor and install the screws, tightening them securely. Install the main jet access plug in the bottom of the float chamber, using a new O-ring, and tighten it securely.

Float check

7 To check, hold the carburetor so the float hangs down, then tilt it back until the valve needle is just seated (see illustration 6.5). Measure the distance from the float chamber gasket surface to the top of the float and compare your measurement to the float height listed in this Chapter's Specifications. Bend the float tang as necessary to change the adjustment.

Accelerator pump adjustment

8 Raise the throttle piston by hand. Slip a drill bit or similar rod under the throttle valve and let it down against the rod. The diameter is listed in this Chapter's Specifications.
9 Tighten the accelerator pump adjusting screw as far as it will go (but don't over-tighten it) (see illustration).
10 Wiggle the link lever with your fingers and check for freeplay (see illustration 6.9). There should be some.
11 Back out the adjusting screw just far enough to remove the freeplay in the link lever.

7 Throttle cable - removal and installation

1 These vehicles are equipped with a single accelerator cable that operates the

4A•8 Fuel and exhaust systems (YFZ450)

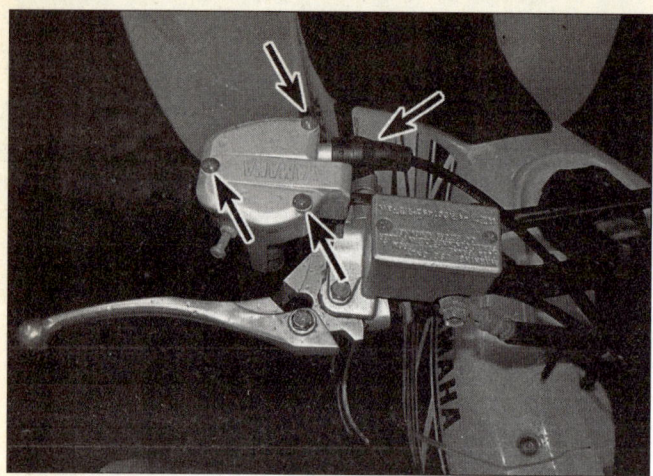

7.5 Slide the rubber boot out of the way and remove the housing screws (arrows)

7.7a Remove the throttle pulley cover screws (arrows, upper screw hidden) and note the location of the rubber piece (arrow)

throttle. Removal and installation procedures are the same as for fuel injected models (see Chapter 4B).

2 Remove the fuel tank (see Section 2).

3 At the handlebar, loosen the throttle cable adjuster all the way (see Chapter 1).

4 Look for a punch mark on the handlebar next to the split in the throttle housing. If you don't see a mark, make one so the throttle housing can be installed in the correct position.

5 Pull back the rubber boot and remove the throttle housing screws **(see illustration)**.

6 Take the cover off the throttle housing and disconnect the throttle cable from the lever (see Section 14 in Chapter 4B).

7 At the carburetor, remove the throttle pulley cover **(see illustrations)**.

8 Loosen the cable locknut to create slack in the cable **(see illustration)**. Lift the cable out of the groove, turn it to align with the removal slot and slip the cable end plug out of the pulley.

9 Note how the cable is routed and remove it from the vehicle.

10 Route the cable into place. Make sure it doesn't interfere with any other components and isn't kinked or bent sharply.

11 Lubricate the carburetor end of the cable with multi-purpose grease. Reverse the disconnection steps to connect the throttle cable to the carburetor throttle pulley.

12 Reverse the disconnection steps to connect the cables to the throttle grip.

13 Operate the throttle and make sure it returns to the idle position by itself under spring pressure.

 Warning: If the throttle doesn't return by itself, find and solve the problem before continuing with installation. A stuck throttle can lead to loss of control of the vehicle.

14 Follow the procedure outlined in Chapter 1, *Throttle and choke operation/grip freeplay*

- *check and adjustment*, to adjust the cable.

15 Turn the handlebars back and forth to make sure the cable does not cause the steering to bind.

16 Once you're sure the cable operates properly, install the fuel tank.

17 With the engine idling, turn the handlebars through their full travel (full left lock to full right lock) and note whether idle speed increases. If it does, the cable is routed incorrectly. Correct this dangerous condition before riding the vehicle.

8 Exhaust system - removal and installation

1 Remove the right side cover (see Chapter 8).

2 Loosen the muffler clamp bolt and unscrew the mounting bolts **(see illustra-**

7.7b Take the cover off, together with the rubber piece, and remove the cover O-ring

7.8 With the cable housing detached from the carburetor, slip the cable out of the pulley, turn it to align with the slot and slip the end plug out

Fuel and exhaust systems (YFZ450) 4A•9

8.2a Loosen the muffler clamp bolt (arrow)...

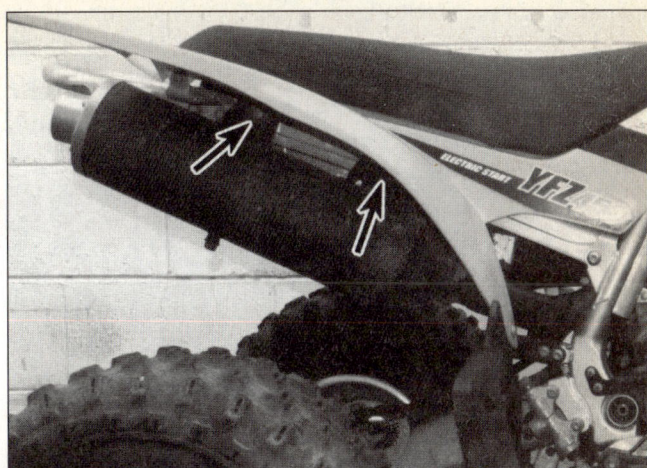

8.2b ...and unbolt the muffler from the frame

tions). Work the muffler free of the pipe and remove the gasket.

3   Detach the front pipe from the cylinder head and remove it from the machine **(see illustration)**.

4   To replace the muffler core, refer to Chapter 1.

5   Installation is the reverse of removal. Use a new gasket in the exhaust port **(see illustration)** and at the joint between pipe and muffler.

9 Throttle position sensor - check, removal and installation

Check

1   Before checking the throttle position sensor, check and adjust engine idle speed (see Chapter 1).

2   Locate the sensor, high on the left side of the carburetor **(see illustration)**. Follow its wiring harness to the connector (remove the side cover if necessary, referring to Chapter 8).

3   Connect the positive probe of a voltmeter (0 to 20 volt scale) to the blue wire's terminal in the connector. Connect the voltmeter negative terminal to the black wire's connector. **Note:** *The wiring connector must be connected during this check. If your voltmeter's terminals are too thick to fit into the connector terminals, insert short pieces of stiff wire into the connector to act as contacts for the voltmeter terminals.*

4   Turn the ignition switch to On (but don't start the engine). The voltmeter should indicate 5 volts (this is the sensor input voltage). If it doesn't, check the wiring from the ECM to the throttle position sensor for breaks or bad connections.

5   Move the voltmeter positive terminal to

8.3 Detach the pipe from the cylinder head (arrows)

8.5 Use a new gasket in the exhaust port (arrow) and at the joint of the muffler and pipe

9.2 Loosen the Torx screw (arrow) to adjust the throttle position sensor

the yellow wire's connector. Leave the voltmeter negative terminal connected to the black wire's terminal. The voltmeter should now indicate 0.58 to 0.87 volts. If the reading is incorrect, adjust the sensor as described below. Do not remove the sensor unless it needs to be replaced, or performance will be impaired.

Adjustment

6 This procedure requires a Torx bit.
7 Loosen the mounting screw **(see illustration 9.2)**. Carefully rotate the sensor back and forth to get the correct output voltage, then tighten the screw.

Replacement

8 Disconnect the electrical connector. Remove the mounting screw and take the sensor off.
9 Install the sensor, making sure its slot aligns with the tab in the carburetor, and tighten the mounting screw, leaving it loose enough so the sensor can be rotated.
10 Adjust the sensor output voltage as described above.
11 Once the correct reading is obtained, mark the sensor position on the carburetor with a felt pen.
12 Tighten the mounting screw, making sure that the felt pen marks stay aligned.
13 Remove the voltmeter and probes.
14 Refer to Chapter 1 and reset idle speed.

Chapter 4 Part B
Fuel and exhaust systems (YFZ450R)

Contents

Air filter element - servicing.. See Chapter 1	
Air filter housing - removal and installation	9
Crankshaft Position (CKP) sensor - check, removal	
and installation	17
Engine control module - removal and installation	20
Engine coolant temperature sensor - check, removal	
and installation...	21
Exhaust system - removal and installation	22
Fuel injection system - check	2
Fuel injection system - general information	1
Fuel pressure relief procedure	4
Fuel pump - removal and installation	6
Fuel pump/fuel pressure - check	5
Fuel rail and injector - removal and installation	13
Fuel system - check and filter replacement .... See Chapter 1	
Fuel tank - cleaning and repair...	8
Fuel tank - removal and installation	7
Idle speed - check and adjustment............................... See Chapter 1	
Idle Speed Control (ISC) valve - check	11
Intake Air Pressure (IAP) sensor - check and replacement	15
Intake Air Temperature (IAT) sensor - check, removal	
and installation	16
Lean angle sensor - check and replacement	19
Self-diagnosis system and trouble codes	3
Throttle body - removal and installation	12
Throttle cable - removal and installation	14
Throttle operation/grip freeplay - check	
and adjustment .... See Chapter 1	
Throttle position sensor - check, adjustment and replacement...	10
Vehicle Speed Sensor (VSS) - check, removal and installation....	18

Degrees of difficulty

Easy, suitable for novice with little experience		Fairly easy, suitable for beginner with some experience		Fairly difficult, suitable for competent DIY mechanic	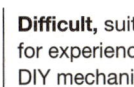	Difficult, suitable for experienced DIY mechanic	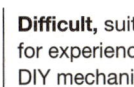	Very difficult, suitable for expert DIY or professional	

Specifications

Fuel injection system
System type .... Single-point throttle body fuel injection
Throttle body
    Model .... Mitsubishi 42EHS/1
    ID number 18P1 00
Idle speed... 1950 to 2050 rpm
Fuel pressure.. 47 psi (324 kPa)
Intake air pressure sensor output voltage.................................. 3.594 to 3.685 volts at sea level

Fuel injection system (continued)

Intake air temperature sensor resistance
    At 32-degrees F (0-degrees C) .... 5400 to 6600 k-ohms
    At 176-degrees F (80-degrees C) .... 290 to 390 ohms
Throttle position sensor
    Maximum resistance.. 2.64 to 6.16 k-ohms
    Output voltage .... 0.679 to 0.681 volts
Engine coolant temperature sensor resistance
    At 32-degrees F .... 5.21 to 6.37 k-ohms
    At 68-degrees F (20-degrees C) .... 2.45 k-ohms
    At 176-degrees F (20-degrees C) .... 290 to 354 ohms
Crankshaft position sensor resistance .... 284 to 372 ohms at 68-degrees F (20-degrees C)

Torque specifications

Fuel tank mounting bolts.. 7 Nm (61 ft-lbs)
Fuel tank top plate nuts... 7 Nm (61 ft-lbs)
Air cleaner housing bolts... 7 Nm (61 ft-lbs)
Fuel rail screws.. 5 Nm (43 inch-lbs)
Throttle position sensor screws .... 3.5 Nm (30 inch-lbs)
Intake manifold mounting bolts.. 10 Nm (86 inch-lbs)
Exhaust pipe to manifold nuts.. 20 Nm (168 inch-lbs)
Exhaust pipe clamp bolt .... 2 Nm (168 inch-lbs)
Exhaust pipe mounting bolts.. 34 Nm (24 ft-lbs)
Exhaust system cover screws.. 7 Nm (61 ft-lbs)*

*Use non-hardening thread locking agent on the screw threads.

Fuel and exhaust systems (YFZ450R) 4B•3

1 Fuel injection system - general information

The fuel injection system is a single-point throttle body system. This means that there is one fuel injector, mounted on a throttle body that attaches to the engine much like a carburetor. The fuel injector injects fuel into the throttle body at the correct point in each engine cycle. The injector is turned on and off by the Engine Control Unit (ECU). When the engine is running, the ECU constantly monitors engine operating conditions with an array of information sensors, calculates the correct amount of fuel, then varies the interval of time during which the injector is open. The fuel injection system provides much better control of the air/fuel mixture than a carburetor, and is therefore able to produce more power, better mileage and lower emissions.

The system uses the ECU and an array of information sensors to determine and deliver the correct air/fuel ratio under all operating conditions. The system consists of three sub-systems: input sensors, the ECU, and output activators.

Input sensors

Throttle Position (TP) sensor

The TP sensor, mounted on the throttle body, is a potentiometer that monitors the opening angle of the throttle plate and sends a variable voltage signal to the Engine Control Unit (ECU).

Intake Air Pressure (IAP) sensor

The IAP sensor is located on the inlet portion of the air cleaner housing. The IAP sensor measures intake manifold pressure and generates a variable voltage signal that's proportionate to the pressure. The ECU uses this data to calculate the load on the engine.

Intake Air Temperature (IAT) sensor

The IAT sensor, mounted on the air cleaner housing, relays a voltage signal to the ECU that varies in accordance with the temperature of the incoming air in the air cleaner housing. The ECU uses this information to calculate how rich or lean the air/fuel mixture should be.

Crankshaft Position (CKP) sensor

The CKP sensor lets the ECU know where the crankshaft is in the induction cycle. The ECU used this information to control timing of the fuel injector opening.

Engine Coolant Temperature (ECT) sensor

The ECT sensor monitors engine temperature and sends a voltage signal to the ECU. The ECU used this information to decide whether to enrich the fuel mixture for cold-engine operation.

Lean angle sensor

This is a safety device that signals the ECU to shut off the engine if the vehicle rolls over.

Vehicle Speed Sensor (VSS)

This device, mounted on the top rear of the engine, signals vehicle speed to the ECU.

Engine Control Unit (ECU)

The ECU is a 32-bit microprocessor, mounted at the rear of the vehicle behind the battery. It receives signals from the input sensors, and uses this information to decide exactly when, and for exactly how long, to open the fuel injector. This controls injection timing as well as the amount of fuel injected.

The ECU also control other functions, such as ignition timing, cooling fan operation, and the warning lights.

Output actuators

The output actuators include an electric fuel pump located in the fuel tank, the fuel rail and the fuel injector. The fuel injector delivers fuel into the intake air stream.

Fuel pump

The fuel pump is part of an assembly that includes the filter screen, fuel level sensor and pressure regulator. Pump components are not available separately. The fuel pressure regulator maintains fuel pressure at a constant 47 psi (324 kPa).

Fuel rail and injector

The fuel rail is mounted on the throttle body, with a fuel injector between the throttle body and fuel rail. Fuel flows from the pump into the fuel rail, and as the injector opens, into the throttle body and then into the engine. A fuel pulsation damper is built into the fuel rail.

Throttle body

The throttle body controls the amount of air entering the engine. It's activated by a cable, which is controlled by the rider through a thumb lever on the right handlebar.

Idle Speed Control (ISC) valve

The ISC valve, which is mounted on the left side of the throttle body, controls the amount of air entering the engine when it's idling. The ISC valve is controlled by the ECU.

2 Fuel injection system - check

Note: *The following procedure is based on the assumption that the fuel pump is working and the fuel pressure is adequate (see Section 5).*

1 Check all electrical connectors that are related to the system. Check the ground wire connections for tightness. Loose connectors and poor grounds can cause many problems that resemble more serious malfunctions.
2 Verify that the battery is fully charged. The Engine Control Unit (ECU), information sensors and output actuators (the fuel injector is an output actuator) depend on a stable voltage supply in order to meter fuel correctly.
3 Inspect the air filter element (see Chapter 1). A dirty or partially blocked filter will severely impede performance and economy.
4 Check the main fuse (see Chapter 5). If you find a blown fuse, replace it and see if it blows again. If it does, look for a wire shorted to ground in the circuit(s) protected by that fuse. Also, refer to Chapter 5 and check the main relay.
5 Check the air induction system between the throttle body and the intake manifold for air leaks, which will cause a lean air/fuel mixture ratio (when the mixture ratio becomes excessively lean, the engine will begin misfiring). Also inspect the condition of all vacuum hoses connected to the intake manifold and to the throttle body. A loose or broken vacuum hose will allow unmetered air into the intake manifold. Unmetered air, especially at idle and during other high-intake-manifold-vacuum conditions, will cause the engine to misfire.
6 Remove the air cleaner housing and check the throttle body for dirt, carbon, varnish, or other residue in the throttle body, particularly around the throttle plate. If it's dirty, clean it with a clean shop towel and a petroleum-based solvent. Do not use caustic carburetor cleaners.
7 With the engine running, place an automotive stethoscope against the injector and listen for a clicking sound that indicates operation. If you don't have a stethoscope, touch the tip of a long screwdriver against the injector and listen through the handle.
8 If you can hear the injector operating, but the engine is misfiring, the electrical circuits are functioning correctly, but the injector might be dirty or clogged. Try a commercial injector cleaning product (available at auto parts stores). If cleaning the injector doesn't help, the injector probably needs to be cleaned professionally, or replaced.
9 If the injector is not operating (it makes no sound), disconnect the injector electrical connector and measure the resistance across the injector terminals with an ohmmeter. If there's an open circuit (infinite resistance) or short circuit (no resistance), replace the injector.
10 If the injector is not operating, but the resistance reading is not infinite or zero, the ECM or the circuit between the ECM and the injector might be faulty.

4B•4 Fuel and exhaust systems (YFZ450R)

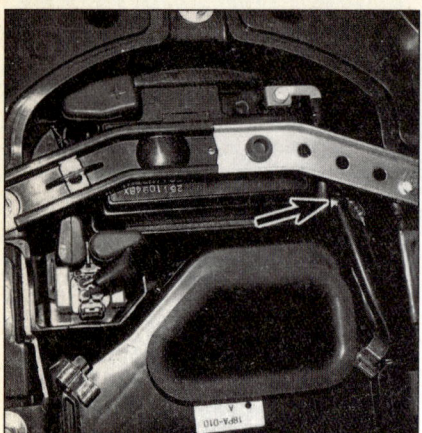

3.4 The diagnostic connector (arrow) is located near the battery

3 Self-diagnosis system and trouble codes

Scan tool information

1 Hand-held scanners are essential for analyzing the engine management system used on these vehicles. On many vehicles equipped with self-diagnosis systems, they're not strictly necessary - the system can also signal trouble codes by flashing the Malfunction Indicator Light (MIL) on the instrument cluster. On the YFZ450R, however, there's no means of accessing the codes without a scanner.

2 Yamaha makes a scanner for the YFZ450R (part no. 90890-03182 [YU-03182]). Aftermarket scan tools, which can diagnose many different makes, are usually a logical choice for independent shops. For the home mechanic working on a YFZ450R, it's more cost-effective to have the codes extracted by a dealer service department or an independent repair shop with a professional scan tool. Most of the components and circuits can be tested with an inexpensive ohmmeter or voltmeter, once you have the code that tells you what to check.

Self-diagnosis system general description

3 All models are equipped with an onboard self-diagnosis system. This system consists of an on-board computer known as the Engine Control Unit (ECU), and information sensors, which monitor various functions of the engine and send data to the ECU. This system incorporates a series of diagnostic monitors that detect and identify fuel injection system faults and store the information in the computer memory. This system also tests sensors and output actuators, diagnoses drive cycles, freezes data and clears codes. In some cases of component failure, the ECU will substitute a fixed value for the variable voltage that the component would normally send to the ECU. This allows the engine to operate in fail-safe mode until the problem can be fixed.

4 This powerful diagnostic computer can be accessed using a scan tool, or code reader, plugged into the diagnostic connector located near the battery (see illustration).

5 It isn't a good idea to attempt diagnosis or replacement of the ECU or emission control components at home while the vehicle is under warranty. Because of the vehicle warranty and because any owner-induced damage to the ECU, sensors and/or control devices might void this warranty, take the vehicle to a dealer service department if the ECU or a system component malfunctions.

Diagnostic Trouble Codes (DTCs)

6 All YFZ450R models are equipped with on-board diagnostics. When the ECU recognizes a malfunction in a monitored fuel injection system component or circuit, it turns on the Malfunction Indicator Light (MIL) on the instrument cluster. The MIL normally illuminates for 1.4 seconds after the main key switch is turned On, and it also illuminates while the starter switch is operated. If a trouble code is set, the MIL will either flash, indicating that the engine can't be started, or glow steadily. A steady glow indicates either that the engine can't start, or that it will start but is running in fail-safe mode. The ECU will continue to display the MIL until the problem is fixed and the Diagnostic Trouble Code (DTC) is cleared from the ECU's memory.

Accessing the DTCs

7 If you have a scan tool, follow the manufacturer's instructions to access the DTCs. If you're using a Yamaha scan tool, plug into the diagnostic connector (see illustration 3.4). Then follow the instructions included with the tool to extract the DTCs.

8 Clear the DTCs with the scan tool, following the instructions provided by the tool's manufacturer.

Diagnostic Trouble Codes

9 The accompanying table is a list of the Diagnostic Trouble Codes (DTCs). If the problem persists after you have checked the component and repaired the related connectors, wire harness and vacuum hoses (if applicable), have the vehicle checked by a dealer service department or other qualified repair shop.

Code	Problem area	Causes	Symptom(s)
12	CKP sensor	Defective sensor or circuit problem	Engine will not start
13	IAP sensor	Open or short circuit	Engine will run
14	IAP sensor	Hose loose or obstructed	Engine will run
15	TPS	Open or short circuit	Engine may or may not run
16	TPS	Sensor jammed	Engine will run
22	Coolant temp sensor	Open or short circuit	Engine will run
30	Lean angle sensor	Vehicle rollover or bad sensor	Engine will not start

Code	Problem area	Causes	Symptom(s)
33	Ignition coil	Bad primary circuit in coil	Engine will not run
37	ISC valve	Valve stuck open	Engine will run - idle abnormally fast
39	Injector	Open or short circuit	Engine won't run
41	Lean angle sensor	Open or short circuit	Engine won't run
42	Speed sensor	Bad sensor or circuit	Engine will run
43	System voltage	ECU can't measure the voltage	Engine will run
44	ECU CO measurement	ECU read error	Engine will run
46	System voltage	System voltage high or low	Engine will run
50	ECU memory failure	Bad ECU	Engine won't start

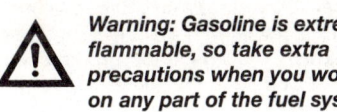

4 Fuel pressure relief procedure

Warning: *Gasoline is extremely flammable, so take extra precautions when you work on any part of the fuel system. Don't smoke or allow open flames or bare light bulbs near the work area, and don't work in a garage where a gas-type appliance (such as a water heater or clothes dryer) is present. Since gasoline is carcinogenic, wear latex gloves when there's a possibility of being exposed to fuel, and, if you spill any fuel on your skin, rinse it off immediately with soap and water. Mop up any spills immediately and do not store fuel-soaked rags where they could ignite. The fuel system is under constant pressure, so, if any fuel lines are to be disconnected, the fuel pressure in the system must be relieved first. When you perform any kind of work on the fuel system, wear safety glasses and have a Class B type fire extinguisher on hand.*

Warning: *Be sure to disconnect the battery (see Chapter 5) before disconnecting any fuel lines.*

Yamaha does not specify a procedure for relieving residual fuel pressure when disconnecting fuel lines, only that you have shop rags handy to catch any spilled fuel. Observe the precautions described in the **Warnings** above. In addition, wear eye protection and catch any spilled fuel in an approved gasoline container.

5 Fuel pump/fuel pressure - check

Warning: *Gasoline is extremely flammable, so take extra precautions when you work on any part of the fuel system. See the Warning in Section 4.*

General checks

1 Verify that there is fuel in the fuel tank.
2 Verify that the fuel pump actually runs. Turn the ignition switch to ON - you should hear a brief whirring noise for a few seconds as the pump comes on and pressurizes the system. **Note:** *If you can't hear the pump, open the fuel filler cap, then have an assistant turn the ignition switch to ON while you listen to the pump through the fuel filler neck.*

Fuel pump/fuel pressure test

3 To measure the fuel pressure, you'll need a fuel pressure gauge capable of reading pressures up to 50 psi (343 kPa). You will also need some fuel hose.
4 Before disconnecting any fuel line fittings, relieve the fuel system pressure (see Section 4).
5 Remove the fuel tank cover (see Chapter 8).
6 Disconnect the fuel line from the fuel pump mounting plate on top of the tank **(see illustrations 6.3a through 6.3c)**. Connect the fuel pressure gauge between the tank fitting and the disconnected end of the hose, using a T-fitting.
7 Start the engine and let it run.
8 Note the indicated fuel pressure reading on the gauge and compare it with the value listed in this Chapter's Specifications.
9 If the indicated pressure is within the specified range, the system is operating correctly.
10 If the indicated pressure is lower than the specified range, the fuel intake might be clogged or the fuel pump or fuel pressure regulator might be defective. There are no individually replaceable parts on the pump unit, installed in the fuel tank; if it won't supply the specified pressure, and the problem can't be solved by cleaning the pump intake, the pump must be replaced as an assembly.
11 After the test is complete, relieve the system fuel pressure (see Section 4).
12 Disconnect the cable from the negative battery terminal.
13 Remove your fuel pressure testing rig, then reconnect the fuel line to the tank fitting.
14 Reconnect the cable to the negative battery terminal (see Chapter 5). Start the engine and check for fuel leaks.
15 Reinstall the fuel tank cover.

4B•6 Fuel and exhaust systems (YFZ450R)

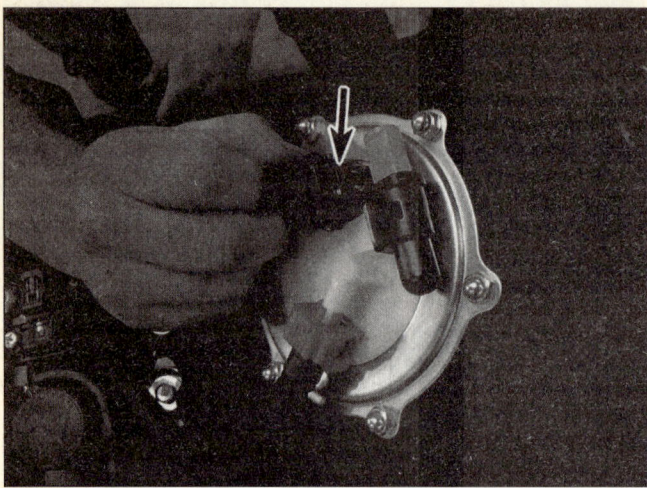

6.2 Squeeze the latch on the fuel pump wiring connector (arrow) and pull it off the terminal

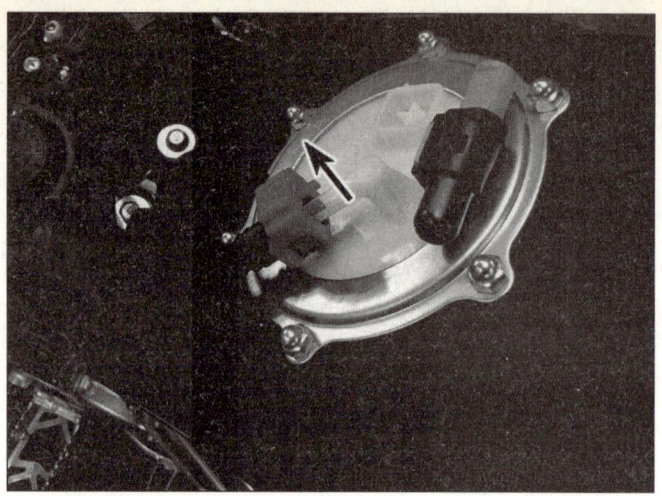

6.3a Pull the fitting cover up (arrow) to expose the latches . . .

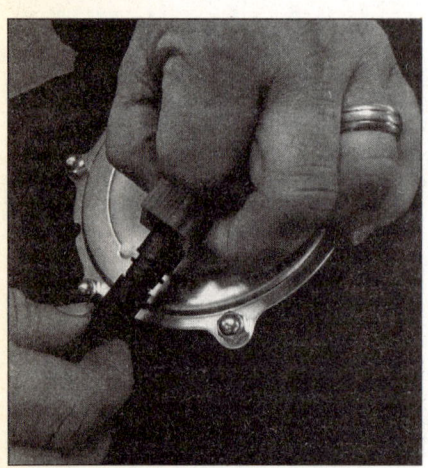

6.3b . . . squeeze the latches to release the hose . . .

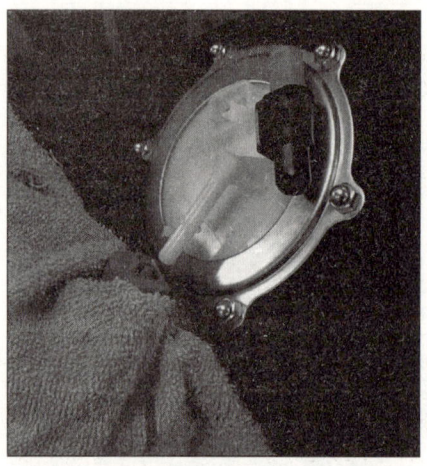

6.3c . . . and pull the hose off the fitting, using fingers only - be sure it's covered with a rag to catch any fuel that might spray out

6 Fuel pump - removal and installation

1 Remove the seat and fuel tank cover (see Chapter 8).
2 Disconnect the wiring connector from the fuel pump **(see illustration)**.
3 Disconnect the fuel line from the tank fitting, referring to the precautions in Section 4 **(see illustrations)**. Cap the fitting and plug the line with the cap and plug mounted on the fuel tank top plate **(see illustrations)**.
4 Remove the screws and lift out the tank top plate, together with the fuel pump **(see illustrations)**. You'll need to turn the pump as it's removed so the fuel level sender will clear the opening.
5 Remove the sealing ring from the opening **(see illustration)**.

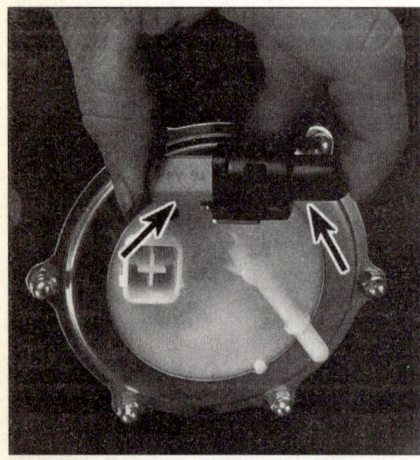

6.3d Slip the plug (left arrow) and cap (right arrow) off their holder tab . . .

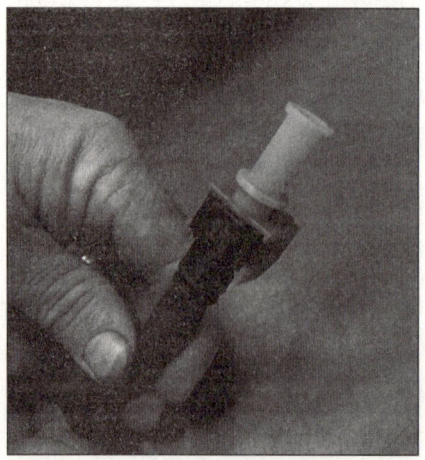

6.3e . . . then insert the plug in the hose and place the cap over the fuel line fitting to keep out dirt

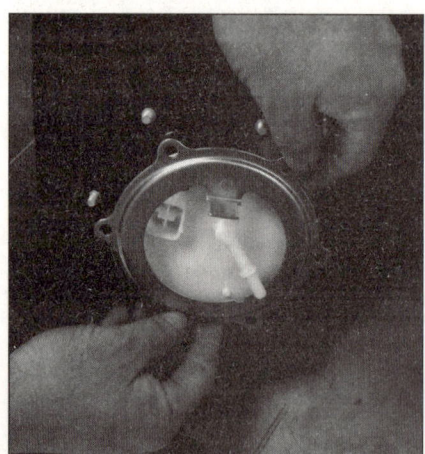

6.4a Remove the nuts and take the cover off the tank . . .

Fuel and exhaust systems (YFZ450R) 4B•7

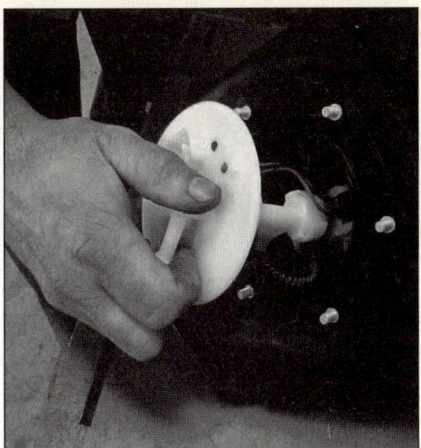

6.4b ... pull the pump unit straight out for a short distance ...

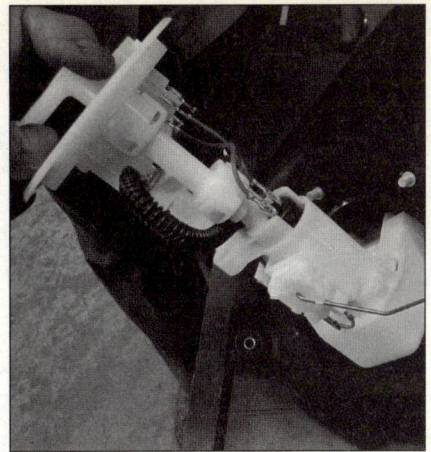

6.4c ... then turn the unit so the bottom can clear the opening

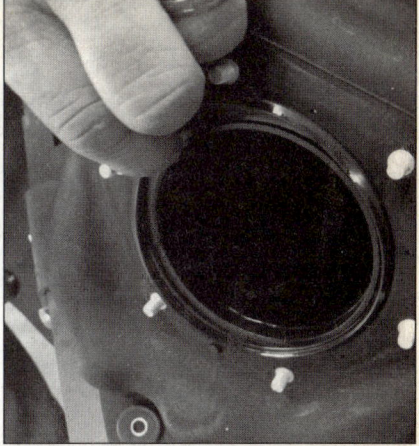

6.5 Remove the sealing ring from the tank opening

6 Installation is the reverse of removal, with the following additions:
 a) Use a new sealing ring if the old one is compressed, brittle or deteriorated.
 b) Note that the fuel hose is directional - if you disconnected both ends of it, it must be installed with the larger fitting connected to the fuel rail.
 c) Push the hose onto the fitting until its latch clicks.

7 Fuel tank - removal and installation

Warning: *Gasoline is extremely flammable, so take extra precautions when you work on any part of the fuel system. See the Warning in Section 4.*

1 The fuel tank is held in place by three bolts.
2 Remove the seat and fuel tank cover (see Chapter 8). **Note:** *The Yamaha factory service manual specifies removing the front fender. However, we were able to remove the fuel tank with the front fender installed.*
3 Unplug the electrical connector, then disconnect the fuel line from the tank top plate (see Section 6).
4 Remove the rear mounting bolt and washer **(see illustrations)**. Loosen the mounting bolt at each front corner.
5 Slide the tank backward to clear the front mounting bolts **(see illustration)**. Disconnect the overflow hose from the handlebar cover and lift the tank off **(see illustration)**.
6 If necessary, unscrew the front tank bolts all the way, disconnect the hose from the underside of the tank heat shield and

7.4a Unscrew the fuel tank rear mounting bolt ...

7.4b ... and remove it together with its washer

7.5a Loosen the bolt at each front corner of the tank (upper arrow), slide the tank back to align the wide part of the hole with the bushing (lower arrow) ...

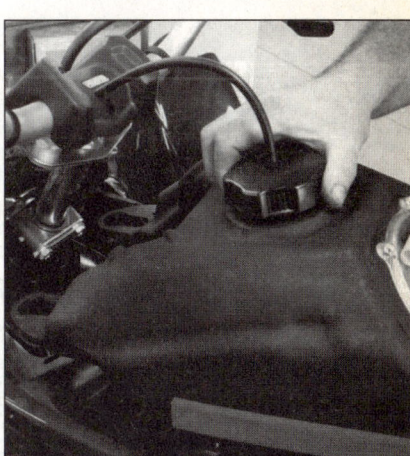

7.5b ... lift the tank off the front bushings, disconnect the overflow hose from the handlebar cover, slide the tank back until the front mounting holes clear the fender and lift it off the vehicle

7.6a Disconnect the hose from the underside of the tank shield

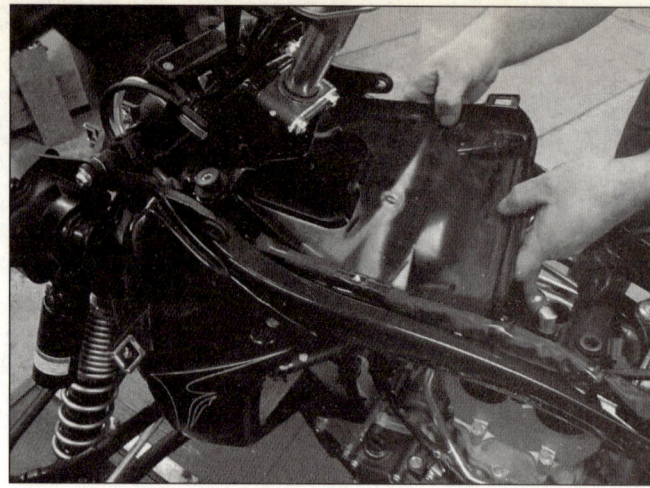

7.6b Remove the tank mounting bolts completely and lift off the tank shield

7.7 Check the fuel tank front bushings (arrow, left bushing shown) and replace them if they're damaged or deteriorated

remove the shield **(see illustrations)**.

7 Before installing the tank, check the condition of the hose and rubber mounting dampers **(see illustration)** - if they're hardened, cracked, or show any other signs of deterioration, replace them.

8 When replacing the tank, reverse the above procedure. Make sure the tank seats properly and does not pinch any control cables or wires.

8 Fuel tank - cleaning and repair

1 All repairs to the fuel tank should be carried out by a professional who has experience in this critical and potentially dangerous work. Even after cleaning and flushing of the fuel system, explosive fumes can remain and ignite during repair of the tank.

2 If the fuel tank is removed from the vehicle, it should not be placed in an area where sparks or open flames could ignite the fumes coming out of the tank. Be especially careful inside garages where a gas-type appliance is located.

9 Air filter housing - removal and installation

1 Remove the air filter element cover (see Chapter 1).
2 Remove the intake air temperature sensor (see Section 16).
3 Remove the housing mounting bolts and collars **(see illustrations)**.
4 Loosen the clamp that connects the front of the air cleaner housing to the throttle body (see Section 12).

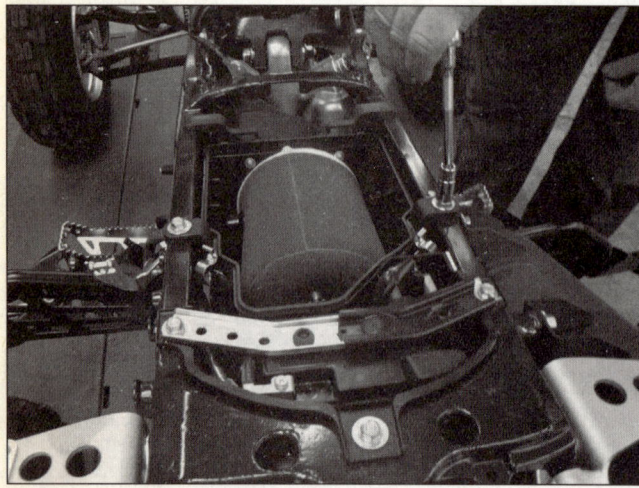

9.3a Remove the air cleaner housing mounting bolts . . .

9.3b . . . and their collars

Fuel and exhaust systems (YFZ450R) 4B•9

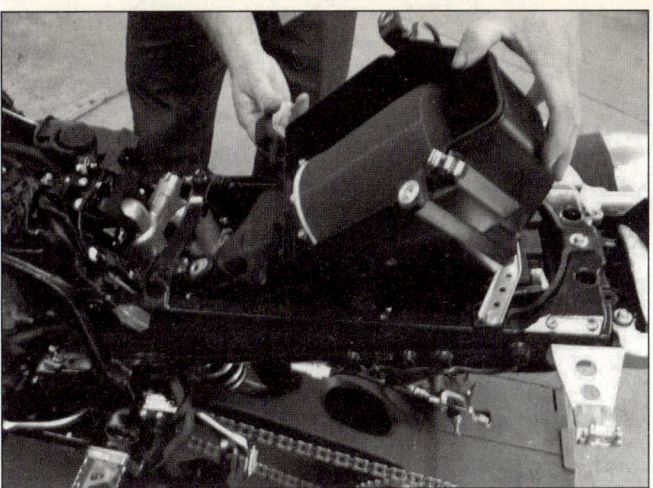

9.5 Tilt the housing and lift it out of the frame

10.1 Here are the idle speed control valve (upper arrow) and throttle position sensor (lower arrow)

5 Tilt the air cleaner housing and lift it out of the frame **(see illustration)**.
6 Installation is the reverse of removal.

10 Throttle position sensor – check, adjustment and replacement

Check
1 Locate the throttle position sensor on the left side of the throttle body **(see illustration)**.
2 Connect the positive probe of a voltmeter (0 to 20 volt scale) to the yellow wire's terminal in the connector. Connect the voltmeter negative terminal to the black/blue wire's connector. **Note:** *The wiring connector must be connected during this check. If your voltmeter's terminals are too thick to fit into the connector terminals, insert short pieces of stiff wire into the connector to act as contacts for the voltmeter terminals.*
3 Turn the ignition switch to On (but don't start the engine). The voltmeter should indicate 0.679 to 0.681 volts (this is the sensor output voltage). If it doesn't, adjust the sensor as described below. Do not remove the sensor unless it needs to be replaced, or performance will be impaired.

Adjustment
4 Loosen the mounting screws **(see illustration 10.1)**. Carefully rotate the sensor back and forth to get the correct output voltage, then tighten the screw. If the correct output voltage can't be obtained, replace the sensor.

Replacement
5 Disconnect the electrical connector, remove the mounting screws and remove the sensor.
6 Install the sensor and tighten the mounting screws, leaving them loose enough so the sensor can be rotated.
7 Adjust the sensor output voltage as described above.
8 Once the correct reading is obtained, mark the sensor position on the throttle body with a felt pen.
9 Tighten the mounting screws, making sure that the felt pen marks stay aligned.
10 Remove the voltmeter and probes.

11 Idle Speed Control (ISC) valve – check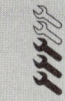

1 The ISC valve is permanently attached to the throttle body and can't be replaced separately. If this procedure indicates a defective ISC valve, the entire throttle body must be replaced.
2 Start by checking the vehicle speed sensor and its circuit (see Section 18). Fix any problems and see if the ISC valve now performs properly.
3 Remove the air cleaner housing (see Section 9) and look at the throttle plate inside the throttle body. With the engine off, operate the throttle lever on the handlebar and make sure the throttle plate closes fully. If it doesn't, adjust the throttle cable (see Chapter 1).
4 Reinstall the air cleaner housing.
5 Start the engine and let it idle. Place a finger on the ISC valve and have an assistant shut the engine off. The ISC valve should vibrate as it closes. If it doesn't, it may be stuck open.
6 Shut off the engine and restart it. The idle speed control valve should move from its fully closed position to the standby position within three seconds. If it doesn't, it may be defective.
7 Check the ISC valve wiring for breaks or bad connections and fix any problems.
8 Check for intake air leaks. These can cause an excessively fast idle.
9 If none of the above checks pinpoint the problem, the ISC valve may be defective. Since the throttle body is an expensive component, it's a good idea to have the diagnosis confirmed by a dealer service department or other qualified shop before replacing it.

12 Throttle body – removal and installation

1 Remove the seat and rear fender (see Chapter 8).
2 Remove the plastic spill shield from the rear brake fluid reservoir and unbolt the reservoir so it can be moved aside (see Chapter 7). It isn't necessary to disconnect the brake fluid hose.
3 Remove the fuel tank (see Section 7).
4 Remove the rear shock absorber (see Chapter 6).
5 Remove the exhaust system (see Section 22).
6 Disconnect the handlebar end of the throttle cable, then the throttle body end (see Section 14). Unless the cable needs to be replaced, it can be left in the vehicle to ease installation.
7 Remove the intake air temperature sensor (see Section 16).
8 Disconnect the wiring connectors for the idle speed control valve and throttle position sensor (see Sections 11 and 10).
9 Disconnect the fuel line from the throttle body and remove the fuel line protective

4B•10 Fuel and exhaust systems (YFZ450R)

12.9a Lift the cover up to expose the latches, squeeze the latches . . .

12.9b . . . cover the fitting with a rag and pull the fuel line off the fuel rail, using fingers only

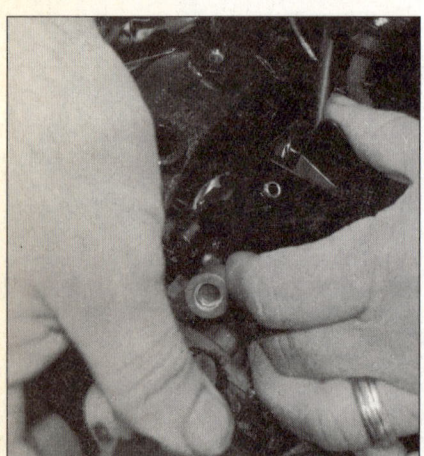

12.9c Remove the fuel rail cover

12.10 Squeeze the latch and disconnect the connector (arrow) from the fuel injector

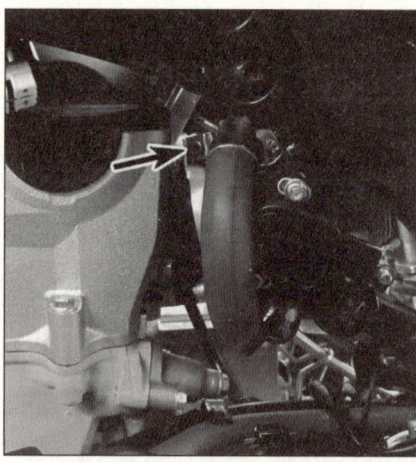

12.11a Loosen the clamp screw at the intake manifold (arrow) . . .

12.11b . . . and at the air cleaner housing (arrow)

12.11c The clamp screw is located behind the frame rail and will be easier to reach with a long Allen bit

cover (see illustrations).

10 Release the latch on the fuel injector wiring connector and disconnect the connector (see illustration).

11 Loosen the clamps at the front and rear of the throttle body and work the throttle body out of the intake manifold and air cleaner housing (see illustrations).

12 Lift the throttle body out and if necessary, remove the intake manifold (see illustration). Cover the opening in the intake manifold or cylinder head with clean rags to keep out dirt, small parts, etc.

13 The fuel injector and throttle position sensor can be replaced separately. The ISC valve is a permanent part of the throttle body; if it has failed, the entire throttle body must be replaced.

Fuel and exhaust systems (YFZ450R) 4B•11

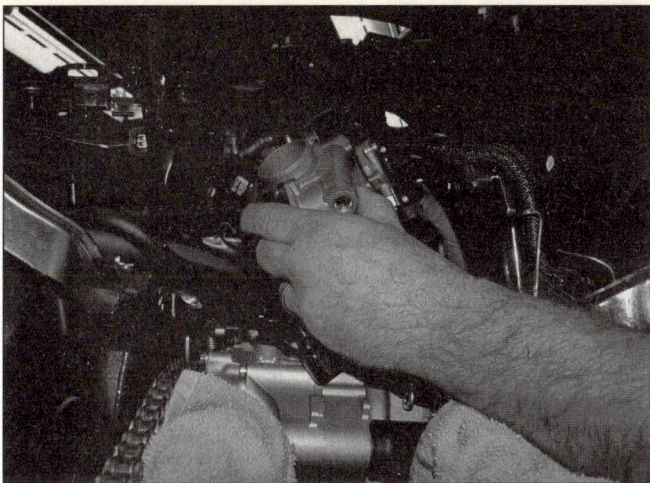

12.12a Work the throttle body free of the manifold and air cleaner housing and remove it

12.12b Remove the intake manifold if necessary - reinstall it with the letters and numbers up (upper arrow) and the notch to the left (lower arrow)

14 If the throttle body needs to be cleaned, use a petroleum-based solvent only. Do not use caustic carburetor cleaning solutions.
15 Installation is the reverse of removal, with the following addition: Position the front insulator notch to the left and the number mark upward **(see illustration 12.12)**.

13 Fuel rail and injector - removal and installation

1 Remove the throttle body (see Section 12)
2 Remove the fuel rail mounting screws, using a no. 3 Phillips screwdriver or bit **(see illustration)**.
3 Take the fuel rail off the throttle body, together with the injector **(see illustration)**.
4 Pull the injector out of the fuel rail **(see illustration)**.
5 Clean all debris from the area around the injector with spray cleaner or compressed air.
6 Installation is the reverse of removal, with the following addition: Use new O-rings on the injector. Lubricate the O-rings with clean engine oil.

14 Throttle cable - removal and installation

1 Loosen the cable adjuster at the handlebar all the way (see Chapter 1).
2 Remove the cover from the throttle

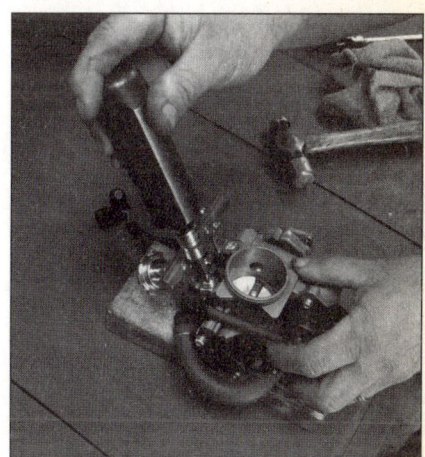

13.2 You may need an impact driver to loosen the fuel rail screws

13.3 Pull the injector and fuel rail away from the throttle body and check the sealing ring and rubber tip (arrows) for damage - use a new sealing ring on installation

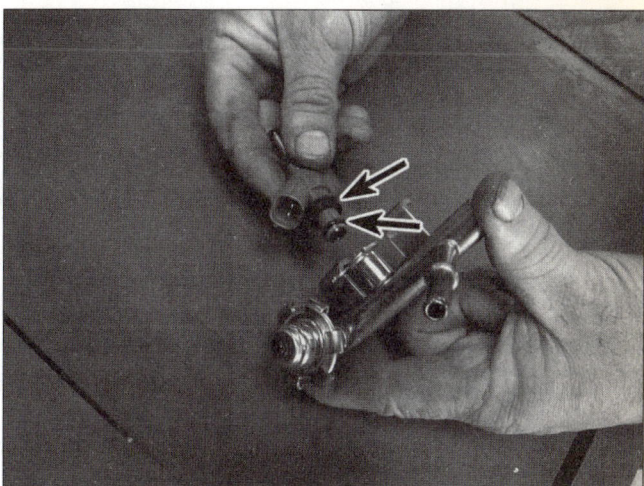

13.4 Pull the injector out of the fuel rail and check the sealing ring and O-ring (arrows) for damage - they're not available separately

4B•12 Fuel and exhaust systems (YFZ450R)

14.2a Remove the screws (arrows) and take the cover off the throttle housing

14.2b Check the gasket for damage, wear or deterioration

14.3a Rotate the cable so it aligns with the notch in the pulley, then lift the cable straight up to remove the end plug from the pulley

14.3b Unscrew the cable nut from the housing, take the end plug off the cable and pull the cable out of the housing

housing and check the gasket (see illustrations).

3 Disconnect the cable end from the throttle pulley inside the cover (see illustration). Unscrew the cable housing nut from the throttle housing and pull the cable out (see illustration).

4 Disconnect the cable from the throttle body pulley (see illustrations).

5 Note how the cable is routed and remove it from its retainers.

6 Route the cable into place. Make sure it doesn't interfere with any other components and isn't kinked or bent sharply.

7 Lubricate the ends of the cables with multi-purpose grease and connect them to the pulleys at the throttle body and at the throttle grip.

8 If it's necessary to remove the throttle cable housing from the handlebar, check for an alignment mark next to the seam in the throttle housing clamp. If there isn't one,

14.4a Hold the locknut and unscrew the adjuster all the way off the cable threads, then remove the cover screws (arrows)

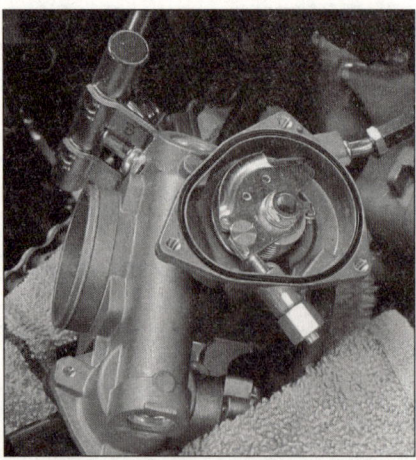

14.4b Remove the cover and inspect the gasket

14.4c Rotate the cable so it aligns with the notch in the pulley, then lift the cable straight up to remove the end plug from the pulley

Fuel and exhaust systems (YFZ450R) 4B•13

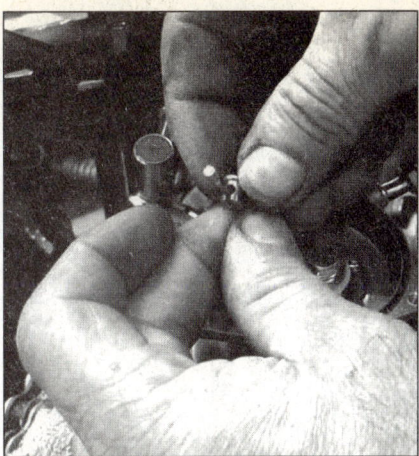

14.4d Slide the end plug slightly down the cable and slip it off, then place it where it won't be lost

14.4e Pull the cable out of the throttle housing

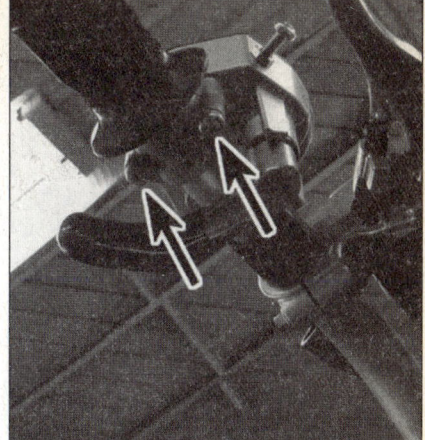

14.8 If necessary, remove the screws (arrows) and take the throttle housing off the handlebar

make your own. Remove the throttle housing clamp screws and take the throttle housing off the handlebar **(see illustration)**.

9 Follow the procedure outlined in Chapter 1, *Throttle operation/grip freeplay - check and adjustment*, to adjust the throttle cable.

10 Turn the handlebars back and forth to make sure the cable doesn't cause the steering to bind. With the engine idling, turn the handlebars back and forth and make sure idle speed doesn't change. If it does, find and fix the cause before riding the vehicle.

11 Install components removed for access.

15 Intake Air Pressure (IAP) sensor - check and replacement

1 The intake air pressure sensor is mounted on top of the intake (forward) part of the air cleaner housing **(see illustration)**.

Check

2 Remove the seat (see Chapter 8).

3 Connect the positive probe of a voltmeter (0 to 20 volt scale) to the pink/blue wire's terminal in the connector. Connect the voltmeter negative terminal to the black/blue wire's connector. **Note:** *The wiring connector must be connected during this check. If your voltmeter's terminals are too thick to fit into the connector terminals, insert short pieces of stiff wire into the connector to act as contacts for the voltmeter terminals.*

4 Turn the ignition switch to On (but don't start the engine). The voltmeter should indicate 3.594 to 3.684 volts with the vehicle at sea level (this is the sensor output voltage). If it doesn't, replace the sensor as described below.

Replacement

5 Disconnect the electrical connector, remove the mounting screws and remove the sensor.

6 Installation is the reverse of removal.

16 Intake Air Temperature (IAT) sensor - check, removal and installation

Caution: The IAT sensor is delicate. Don't strike it with tools or drop it. If it's dropped, it should be replaced with a new one.

Check

1 Remove the seat (see Chapter 8).

2 Unplug the connector from the IAT sensor **(see illustration)**. Connect an ohmmeter between the wire terminals in the sensor.

3 Sensor resistance should be low at low temperatures and high at high temperatures (refer to the values listed in this Chapter's Specifications). If you can't get a definite result by checking it on the vehicle, remove the sensor as described in Step 7 and test it further as described in Step 4.

15.1 The intake air pressure sensor (arrow) is located just forward of the shock absorber upper end

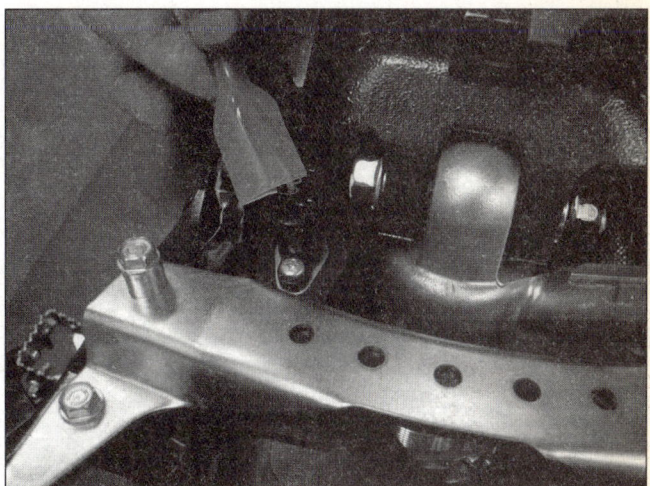

16.2 Slip the cover off the intake air temperature sensor connector and disconnect the connector from the sensor

4B•14 Fuel and exhaust systems (YFZ450R)

16.7a Remove the sensor mounting screw . . .

16.7b . . . and take the sensor out of the air cleaner housing

4   Suspend the sensor in a pan of water, taking care not to get water on the electrical terminals. Cool the water to near freezing with ice. Measure the resistance with an ohmmeter and compare the reading to the value listed in this Chapter's Specifications. Slowly heat the water to the higher specified temperature and check resistance again.

5   If resistance is not within the specified range, replace the sensor with a new one.

Removal and installation

6   Remove the seat (see Chapter 8).

7   Remove the sensor screw and lift the sensor out of the air cleaner housing **(see illustrations)**.

8   Installation is the reverse of removal.

17 Crankshaft Position (CKP) sensor - check, removal and installation

1   The crankshaft position sensor is attached to the inside of the left crankcase cover.

Check

2   Follow the wiring harness from the left crankcase cover to the connector and disconnect it. The CKP sensor harness has two wires, one white and one red.

3   Connect an ohmmeter between the terminals in the sensor side of the harness (not the wiring harness side). Compare the measured resistance with the values listed in this Chapter's Specifications. If it's not within the specified range, replace it as described below.

Replacement

4   Remove the left crankcase cover (see Chapter 2).

5   Remove the sensor screws, remove the sensor and install a new one. Use non-permanent thread locking agent on the threads of the sensor screws.

6   Refer to Chapter 2 and install the left crankcase cover.

18 Vehicle Speed Sensor (VSS) - check, removal and installation

1   The Vehicle Speed Sensor is located on top of the engine behind the clutch cable **(see illustration)**.

Check

2   Follow the wiring harness from the sensor to its connector and disconnect it. Connect a voltmeter (0 to 20 volt setting) between the wires in the sensor side of the connector, positive to the white wire and negative to the black/blue wire.

3   With the engine off, jack up the rear of the vehicle so the tires are off the ground and support it securely.

4   Slowly rotate one of the rear tires and watch the voltmeter. It should cycle back and forth between 0.6 volts and 4.8 volts as the tire is rotated. If it doesn't, replace the sensor.

18.1 The speed sensor (arrow) is mounted on top of the engine behind the clutch cable

18.6 Remove the screw (arrow) and lift the sensor out of the engine

Fuel and exhaust systems (YFZ450R) 4B•15

19.3 The lean angle sensor is mounted under the battery box and secured by two screws (arrows)

20.2 The ECU is mounted behind the battery box and secured by two bolts (arrows)

Removal and installation

5 If you haven't already done so, disconnect the electrical connector from the sensor. Free the wiring harness from any retainers.
6 Unbolt the speed sensor from the engine and pull it out **(see illustration)**. Remove the sensor O-ring.
7 Installation is the reverse of removal. Use a new O-ring, coated with clean engine oil. Tighten the bolt securely, but don't overtighten it and strip the threads.

19 Lean angle sensor - check and replacement

1 The lean angle sensor is located under the battery box.
2 Remove the seat and taillight assembly (see Chapters 8 and 5).
3 Unbolt the lean angle sensor, but leave its wiring connector attached **(see illustration)**.
4 Connect the positive probe of a voltmeter (0 to 20 volt scale) to the yellow/green wire's terminal in the connector. Connect the voltmeter negative terminal to the black/blue wire's terminal. **Note:** *The wiring connector must be connected during this check. If your voltmeter's terminals are too thick to fit into the connector terminals, insert short pieces of stiff wire into the connector to act as contacts for the voltmeter terminals.*
5 Turn the main key switch to On, but don't start the engine.
6 Hold the sensor in its installed position and check the voltage reading - it should be within the range listed in this Chapter's Specifications. Tilt the sensor up so its connector is downward. As it passes 65-degrees from its installed position, the voltage reading should increase to the higher range listed in this Chapter's Specifications.
7 If the sensor performs as specified, it's good. If not, disconnect its connector and replace it with a new one.
8 Installation is the reverse of removal. Make sure the word UP, molded on the sensor case, is upward.

20 Engine control module - removal and installation

1 Remove the seat and taillight assembly (see Chapters 8 and 5).
2 Unbolt the ECU and slide it out for access to the connector **(see illustration)**.
3 Squeeze the connector latch to release and pull the connector out of the ECU **(see illustration)**.
4 Installation is the reverse of removal.

21 Engine coolant temperature sensor - check, removal and installation

1 The engine coolant temperature sensor is screwed into the front of the right-hand radiator tank at the top.
2 Make sure the engine is cool before starting this procedure.
3 Drain the cooling system below the level of the temperature sensor (see Chapter 1).
4 Disconnect the sensor wiring connector and unscrew the sensor from the radiator.
5 Suspend the temperature sensor in a pan of water, making sure water doesn't get into the electrical terminals.

⚠ **Warning: Antifreeze is poisonous. Do not use a cooking pan.**

20.3 Remove the bolts, slide the ECU out of its carrier, squeeze the connector latch and disconnect the connector

6 Cool the water to near freezing with ice. Measure the resistance with an ohmmeter and compare the reading to the value listed in this Chapter's Specifications. Slowly heat the water to the higher specified temperature and check resistance again.
7 If resistance is not within the specified range, replace the sensor with a new one.
8 Installation is the reverse of removal. Use a new sealing washer on the sensor and fill the cooling system (see Chapter 1).

22 Exhaust system - removal and installation

1 Remove the right side cover (see Chapter 8).
2 Loosen the muffler clamp bolt and

22.2a Here are the exhaust pipe clamp (left arrow) and pipe-to-cylinder head nuts (right arrows)

22.2b The muffler is secured to the frame by two bolts (arrows)

unscrew the mounting bolts **(see illustrations)**. Work the muffler free of the pipe and remove the gasket.

3 Detach the front pipe from the cylinder head and remove it from the machine **(see illustration 22.2a)**.

4 To replace the muffler core, refer to Chapter 1.

5 Installation is the reverse of removal. Use a new gasket in the exhaust port and at the joint between the pipe and muffler.

Chapter 5
Ignition and electrical systems

Contents

Alternator and regulator/rectifier - check and replacement	9	Ignition system - check	6
Battery - charging	4	Kill switch - check, removal and installation	10
Battery - inspection and maintenance	3	Lighting circuit - check	16
Brake light switches - check, replacement and adjustment	21	Main key switch - check and replacement	22
Bulb replacement	17	Main relay (YFZ450R) - check and replacement	23
CDI unit (YFZ450) - check, removal and installation	8	Neutral switch - check and replacement	20
Clutch switch - check and replacement	19	Slipper clutch - removal, inspection and installation	15
Electrical troubleshooting	2	Spark plug replacement	See Chapter 1
Fuse - check and replacement	5	Starter circuit - component check and replacement	11
General information	1	Starter clutch - removal, inspection and installation	14
Headlight adjustment	18	Starter motor - check and replacement	12
Ignition coil - check, removal and installation	7	Starter reduction gears - removal and installation	13

Degrees of difficulty

Easy, suitable for novice with little experience 	Fairly easy, suitable for beginner with some experience	Fairly difficult, suitable for competent DIY mechanic	Difficult, suitable for experienced DIY mechanic	Very difficult, suitable for expert DIY or professional

Specifications

Ignition coil resistance

YFZ450
    Primary .... 0.08 to 0.10 ohms
    Secondary .... 4.56 to 6.84 k-ohms
YFZ450R
    Primary .... 2.16 to 2.64 ohms
    Secondary .... 8.64 to 12.96 k-ohms

Ignition and electrical systems

Spark plug cap resistance
YFZ450 .... Not applicable
YFZ450R .... 10 k-ohms

Alternator stator coil resistance
YFZ450
    Charging coil.. 0.288 to 0.432 ohms (white to ground)
    Lighting coil... 0.224 to 0.336 ohms (yellow to ground)
YFZ450R .... 0.32 to 0.48 ohms

Regulator/rectifier
Input voltage at 5000 rpm .... 14.0 volts
Output voltage... 14.1 to 14.9 volts

Alternator pulse generator resistance
YFZ450 .... 248 to 372 ohms
YFZ450R .... Not applicable

Fuse rating
YFZ450 .... 15 amps
YFZ450R .... 20 amps

Torque specifications
Alternator rotor nut .... 65 Nm (47 ft-lbs)
Starter clutch bolts .... 16 Nm (144 inch-lbs)*
Starter mounting bolts... 10 Nm (86 inch-lbs)
Use non-permanent thread locking agent on the bolt threads.

Ignition and electrical systems

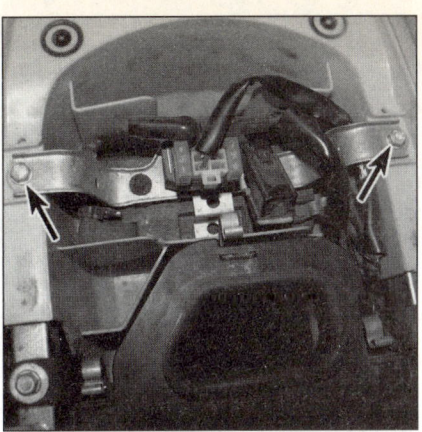

3.3a On YFZ450 models, unbolt the battery retainer (arrows) and lift it off, together with the starter relay

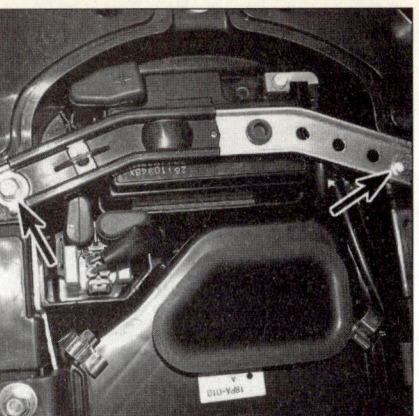

3.3b On YFZ450R models, unbolt the battery retainer (arrows) and lift it off

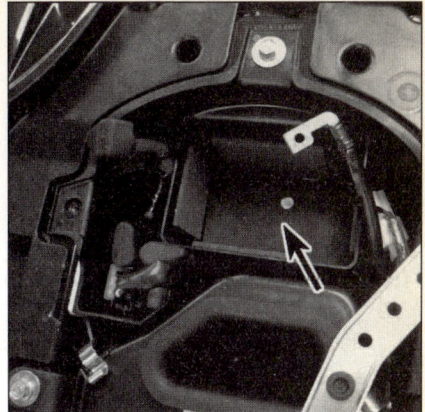

3.3c Check the bottom of the battery case to make sure the pad (or several small pads) is in place

1 General information

The electrical system on all models includes a battery and charging system, lighting system (including warning lights) and an electric starter.

The ignition system on YFZ450 models consists of an alternator that generates the current, a capacitive discharge ignition (CDI) unit that receives and stores it, and a pulse generator that triggers the CDI unit to discharge its current into the ignition coil, where it is stepped up to a voltage high enough to jump the spark plug gap. To aid in locating a problem in the ignition circuit, wiring diagrams are included at the end of this manual.

The CDI ignition system functions on the same principle as a breaker point ignition system with the pulse generator and CDI unit performing the tasks previously associated with the breaker points and mechanical advance system. As a result, adjustment and maintenance of breakerless ignition components is eliminated (with the exception of spark plug replacement).

The YFZ450R ignition system is a transistor controlled ignition (TCI) type. This system is similar to the CDI system used on YFZ450 models, but ignition timing is controlled by the electronic control unit, which also controls the fuel injection system. Ignition system components that are also part of the fuel injection system (the ECU and crankshaft position sensor) are covered in Chapter 4B.

Note: *Keep in mind that electrical parts, once purchased, can't be returned. To avoid unnecessary expense, make very sure the faulty component has been positively identified before buying a replacement part.*

2 Electrical troubleshooting

Electrical problems often stem from simple causes, such as loose or corroded connections. Prior to any electrical troubleshooting, always visually check the condition of the wires and connections in the circuit.

If testing instruments are going to be utilized, use the diagrams to plan where you will make the necessary connections in order to accurately pinpoint the trouble spot.

The basic tools needed for electrical troubleshooting include a test light or voltmeter, an ohmmeter or a continuity tester (which includes a bulb, battery and set of test leads) and a jumper wire, preferably with a circuit breaker incorporated, which can be used to bypass electrical components.

A continuity check is performed to see if a circuit, section of circuit or individual component is capable of passing electricity through it. Connect one lead of a self-powered test light or ohmmeter to one end of the circuit being tested and the other lead to the other end of the circuit. If the bulb lights (or the ohmmeter indicates little or no resistance), there is continuity, which means the circuit is passing electricity through it properly. The kill switch can be checked in the same way.

Remember that the electrical circuit on these vehicles is designed to conduct electricity through the wires, kill switch, etc. to the electrical component (CDI unit, etc.). From there it is directed to the frame (ground) where it is passed back to the alternator. Electrical problems are basically an interruption in the flow of electricity.

Because of their nature, the individual ignition system components can be checked but not repaired. If ignition system troubles occur, and the faulty component can be isolated, the only cure for the problem is to replace the part with a new one. Keep in mind that most electrical parts, once purchased, can't be returned. To avoid unnecessary expense, make very sure the faulty component has been positively identified before buying a replacement part.

Most battery damage is caused by heat, vibration, and/or low electrolyte levels, so keep the battery securely mounted, inspect it at regular intervals and make sure the charging system is functioning properly.

3 Battery - inspection and maintenance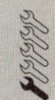

1 The battery used is a maintenance free type.
2 Remove the seat (see Chapter 8). Check around the base inside of the battery for sediment, which is the result of sulfation caused by low electrolyte levels. These deposits will cause internal short circuits, which can quickly discharge the battery. Look for cracks in the case and replace the battery if either of these conditions is found.

 Warning: *Always disconnect the negative cable first and reconnect it last to prevent sparks that could cause the battery to explode.*

3 Check the battery terminals and cable ends for tightness and corrosion. If corrosion is evident, remove the cables from the battery and clean the terminals and cable ends with a wire brush or knife and emery paper. If you need to remove the battery, remove the retainer and lift it out of the carrier **(see illustrations)**. Reconnect the cables and apply a thin coat of petroleum jelly to the connections to slow further corrosion.
4 The battery case should be kept clean to prevent current leakage, which can discharge the battery over a period of time

5•4 Ignition and electrical systems

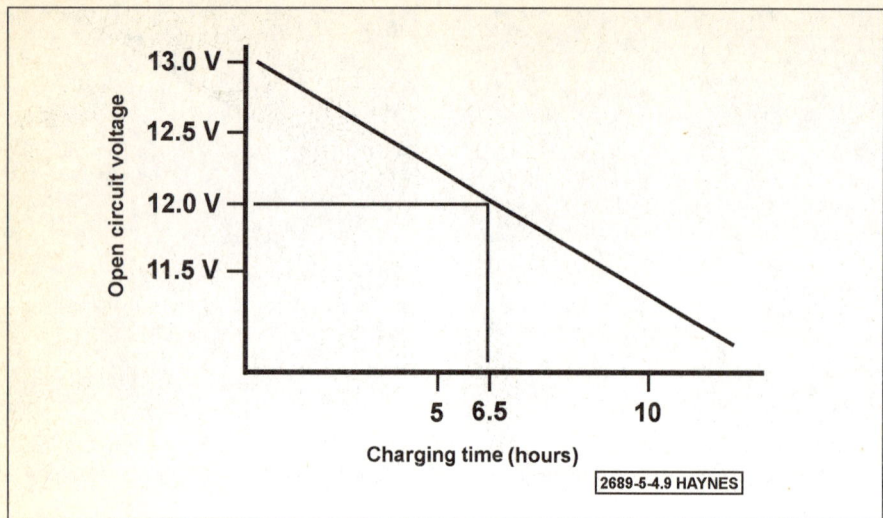

4.5 Draw a line straight across from the open circuit voltage to the bar, then straight down to find the charging time. **Note:** *This is based on a temperature of 68-degrees F (20-degrees C)*

5.1a Here are the YFZ450 main fuse (left) and spare fuse (right)

(especially when it sits unused). Wash the outside of the case with a solution of baking soda and water. Do not get any baking soda solution in the battery cells. Rinse the battery thoroughly, then dry it.

5 If acid has been spilled on the frame or battery box, neutralize it with the baking soda and water solution, dry it thoroughly, then touch up any damaged paint.

6 If the vehicle sits unused for long periods of time, disconnect the cables from the battery terminals. Refer to Section 4 and charge the battery approximately once every month.

4 Battery - charging

1 If the machine sits idle for extended periods or if the charging system malfunctions, the battery can be charged from an external source.

2 Charging the maintenance-free battery requires a variable-voltage charger, digital voltmeter and ammeter. If the charger doesn't have an ammeter built in, you can hook up an external ammeter.

Caution: Never connect an ammeter between the battery terminals. The ammeter's fuse will blow, or if doesn't have a fuse, the ammeter will be ruined.

3 When charging the battery, always remove it from the machine. If the battery case is translucent, check the electrolyte level by looking through the case before hooking up the charger. If the electrolyte level is low, the battery must be discarded; never remove the sealing plug to add water.

4 Disconnect the battery cables (negative cable first), then connect a digital voltmeter between the battery terminals and measure the voltage (open circuit voltage).

5 If open circuit voltage is 12.8 volts or higher, the battery is fully charged. If it's lower, recharge the battery. Refer to the **accompanying illustration** for charging time.

6 A quick charge can be used in an emergency, provided the maximum charge rates and times are not exceeded (exceeding the maximum rate or time may ruin the battery). A quick charge should always be followed as soon as possible by a charge at the standard rate and time.

7 Hook up the battery charger leads (positive lead to battery positive terminal and negative lead to battery negative terminal, then, and only then, plug in the battery charger.

⚠ **Warning: The gas escaping from a charging battery is explosive, so keep open flames and sparks well away from the area. Also, the electrolyte is extremely corrosive and will damage anything it comes in contact with.**

8 Start charging at a high voltage setting (20 to 25 volts, but no more than 25 volts) and watch the ammeter for about 5 minutes. The charging amperage should exceed the maximum charging amperage listed on the battery. If it doesn't, replace the battery with a new one.

9 When the charging current increases beyond the specified maximum, reduce the charging voltage to reduce the charging current to the rate listed on the battery. Do this periodically as the battery charges (at least every five hours).

10 Allow the battery to charge for the time specified in **illustration 4.5**. If the battery overheats or gases excessively, the charging rate is too high. Either disconnect the charger or lower the charging rate to prevent damage to the battery.

11 After the specified time, unplug the charger first, then disconnect the leads from the battery.

12 Wait 30 minutes, then measure voltage between the battery terminals. If it's 12.8 volts or higher, the battery is fully charged. If it's between 12.0 and 12.7 volts, charge the battery again (refer to **illustration 4.5** for charge time).

5 Fuse - check and replacement

1 All models have a single main fuse of the bayonet type, located near the battery **(see illustrations)**. A spare fuse is located near the main fuse.

2 The fuse can be checked visually without removing it from its holder; just look through the plastic to see if the metal element inside is broken. If so, pull the fuse out and push a new one in.

3 If the fuse blows, be sure to check the wiring harnesses very carefully for evidence of a short circuit. Look for bare wires and chafed, melted or burned insulation. If a fuse is replaced before the cause is located, the new fuse will blow immediately.

4 Never, under any circumstances, use a higher rated fuse or bridge the fuse terminals, as damage to the electrical system - or even a fire - could result.

5 Occasionally a fuse will blow or cause an open circuit for no obvious reason. Corrosion of the fuse ends and fuse holder terminals may occur and cause poor fuse contact. If this happens, remove the corrosion with a wire brush or emery paper, then spray the fuse end and terminals with electrical contact cleaner.

Ignition and electrical systems 5•5

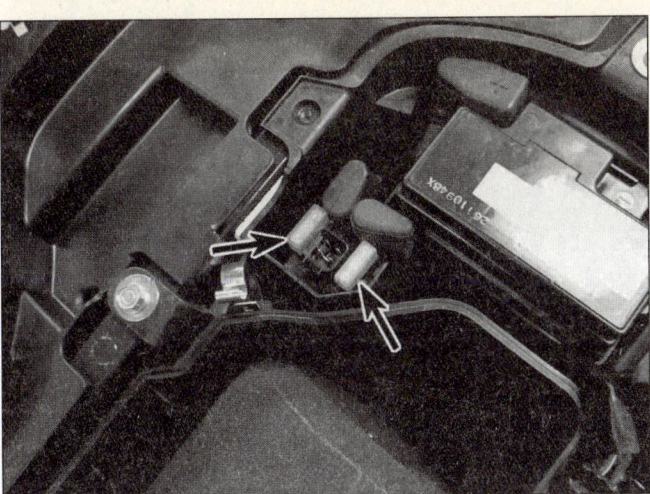

5.1b Here are the YFZ450R main fuse (left) and spare fuse (right)

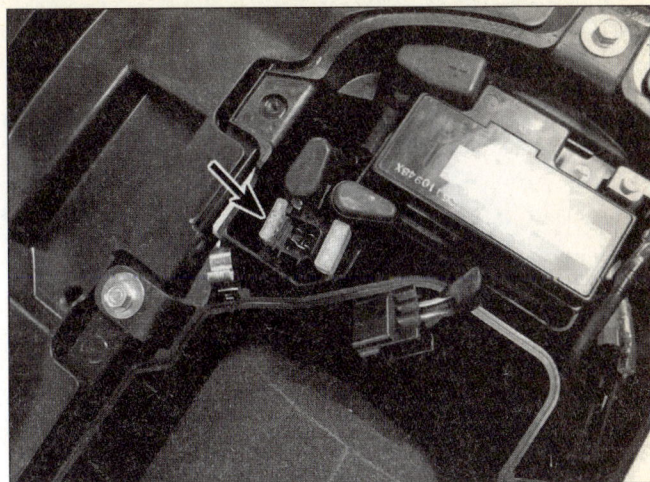

5.1c Pull the cover off to expose the fuse (arrow)

6 Ignition system - check

⚠ **Warning:** *Because of the very high voltage generated by the ignition system, extreme care should be taken when these checks are performed.*

1 If the ignition system is the suspected cause of poor engine performance or failure to start, a number of checks can be made to isolate the problem.

Engine will not start

2 Refer to Chapter 1 and disconnect the spark plug wire. Connect the wire to a spare spark plug and lay the plug on the engine with the threads contacting the engine. If necessary, hold the spark plug with an insulated tool. Crank the engine over and make sure a well-defined, blue spark occurs between the spark plug electrodes.

⚠ **Warning:** *Don't remove the spark plug from the engine to perform this check - atomized fuel being pumped out of the open spark plug hole could ignite, causing severe injury!*

3 If no spark occurs, the following checks should be made:

YFZ450

4 The ignition coil on YFZ450 models is integral with the spark plug cap. Test the ignition coil as described in Section 7.
5 Check the pulse generator (see Section 9).

YFZ450R

6 Unscrew the spark plug cap from the plug wire **(see illustration)** and check its resistance with an ohmmeter **(see illustration)**. If it's not as listed in this Chapter's Specifications, replace the cap.
7 Refer to Section 7 and check the ignition coil primary and secondary resistance.
8 Check the crankshaft position sensor (see Chapter 4B).

All models

9 Make sure all electrical connectors are clean and tight. Check all wires for shorts, opens and correct installation.
10 If the preceding checks produce positive results but there is still no spark at the plug, refer to Section 8 and check the CDI unit (YFZ450) or refer to Chapter 4B and check the ECU (YFZ450R).

Engine starts but misfires

11 If the engine starts but misfires, make the following checks before deciding that the ignition system is at fault.
12 The ignition system must be able to produce a spark across a six-millimeter (1/4-inch) gap (minimum). A simple test fix-

6.6a Pull the cap off the spark plug and unscrew it from the wire . . .

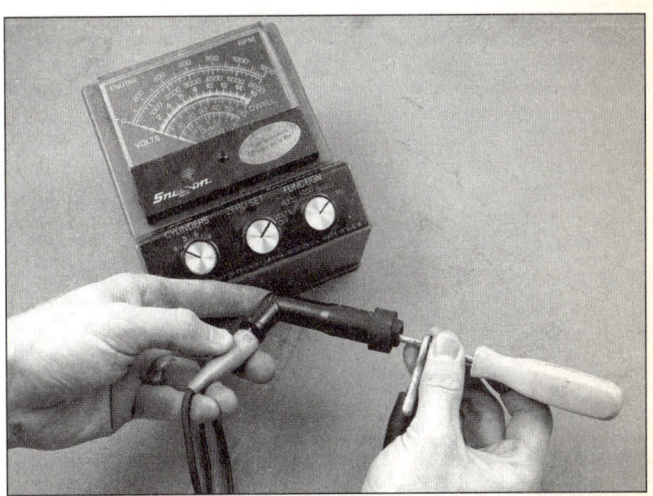

6.6b . . . then check its resistance with an ohmmeter

5•6 Ignition and electrical systems

6.12 A simple spark gap testing fixture can be made from a block of wood, two nails, a large alligator clip, a screw and a piece of wire

7.4 Here's the YFZ450R ignition coil - the two small wire terminals on the left are the primary terminals

ture **(see illustration)** can be constructed to make sure the minimum spark gap can be jumped. Make sure the fixture electrodes are positioned seven millimeters apart.

13 Connect the spark plug wire to the protruding test fixture electrode, then attach the fixture's alligator clip to a good engine ground.

14 Crank the engine over with the starter and see if well-defined, blue sparks occur between the test fixture electrodes. If the minimum spark gap test is positive, the ignition coil is functioning properly. If the spark will not jump the gap, or if it is weak (orange colored), refer to Steps 4 through 10 of this Section and perform the component checks described.

7 Ignition coil - check, removal and installation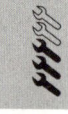

1 The primary and secondary coil resistances can be measured with an ohmmeter. If the coil is undamaged, and if the resistances are as specified, it is probably capable of proper operation.

2 Remove the coil as described below and check it visually for cracks and other damage.

Removal

YFZ450

3 The coil is integral with the spark plug cap. To remove it, refer to the spark plug procedure in Chapter 1.

YFZ450R

4 To remove the coil, remove the fuel tank, then disconnect the spark plug wire from the plug (see Chapter 4B). Label the coil primary circuit electrical wires, then disconnect them **(see illustration)**.

5 Remove the coil mounting bolts, then lift the coil out.

Check

6 If you're working on a YFZ450R, unscrew the spark plug cap from the plug wire.

7 Connect an ohmmeter between the primary (small) terminals **(see illustration)**. Set the ohmmeter selector switch in the Rx1 position and compare the measured resistance to the primary resistance values listed in this Chapter's Specifications. If the resistance is not as specified, the coil is probably defective and should be replaced with a new one.

8 Connect the ohmmeter between the coil primary positive terminal and the spark plug terminal (YFZ450) or spark plug wire (YFZ450R) **(see illustration 7.7)**. Place the ohmmeter selector switch in the Rx100 position and compare the measured resistance to the secondary resistance values listed in this Chapter's Specifications. If the resistance is not as specified, the coil is probably defective and should be replaced with a new one.

9 If you're working on a YFZ450R, connect the ohmmeter to the ends of the spark plug cap and check the resistance **(see illustration 6.6b)**. If the resistance is not as specified, the spark plug cap is bad.

Installation

10 Installation is the reverse of removal.

8 CDI unit (YFZ450) - check, removal and installation

Check

1 The CDI unit is tested by process of elimination (when all other possible causes of ignition problems have been checked and eliminated, the CDI unit is at fault).

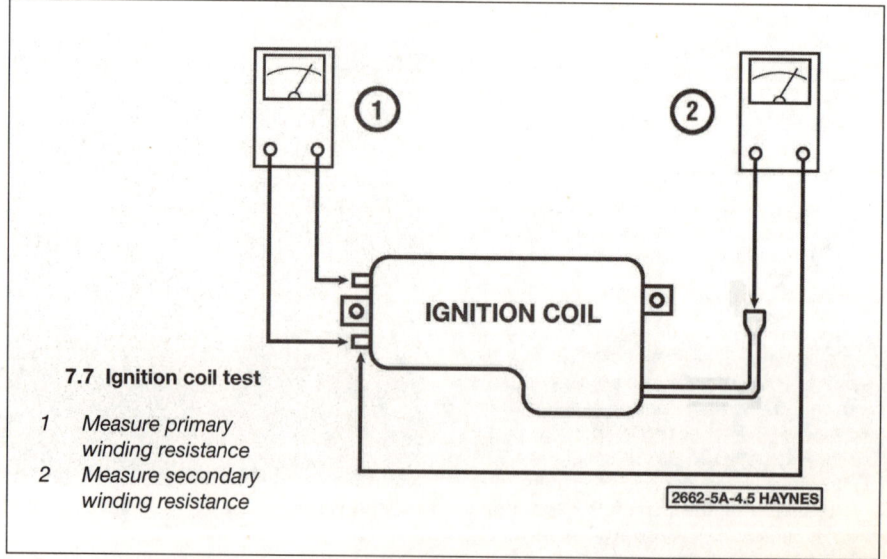

7.7 Ignition coil test
1 Measure primary winding resistance
2 Measure secondary winding resistance

Ignition and electrical systems 5•7

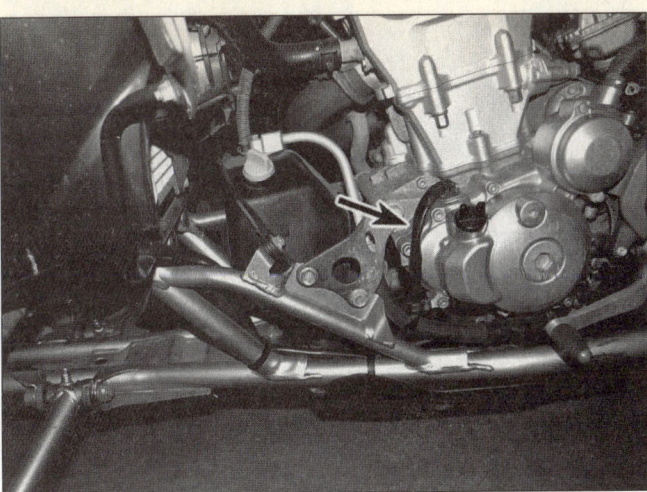

9.1a Follow the alternator wiring harness (arrow) to its connector and unplug it - this is the YFZ450 . . .

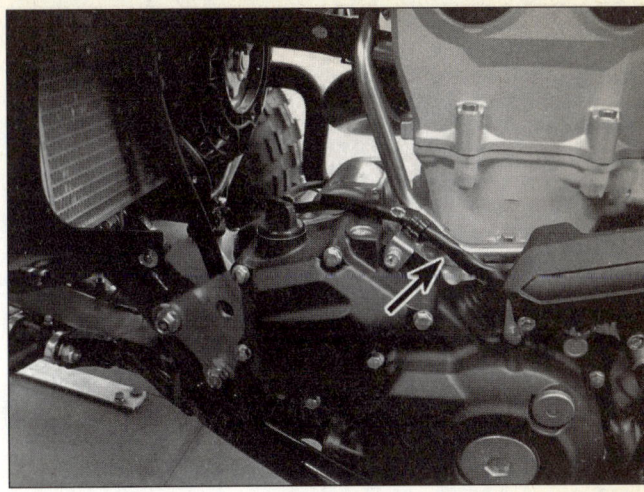

9.1b . . . and this is the YFZ450R

2 Check the ignition coil, alternator exciter coil, pulse generator and kill switch as described elsewhere in this Chapter.
3 Carefully check the wiring harnesses for breaks or bad connections.
4 If the harness and all other system components tested good, the CDI unit may be defective. Before buying a new one, it's a good idea to substitute a known good CDI unit.

Removal and installation

5 Remove the front fender (see Chapter 8).
6 Locate the CDI unit under the fender (it can be identified by its wire colors). Unplug its connector and work the unit out of its mounting band.
7 Installation is the reverse of removal.

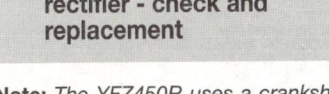

9 Alternator and regulator/rectifier - check and replacement

Note: *The YFZ450R uses a crankshaft position sensor instead of a pickup coil. Refer to Chapter 4B for checking and replacement procedures.*

Alternator check

1 Locate the alternator wiring harness on the left side of the engine and follow it to its connectors **(see illustrations)**.

YFZ450

2 To check the ignition system pickup coil, disconnect the connector for the red and white wires. Connect an ohmmeter to the wires in the alternator side of the connector (not the wiring harness side), positive probe to red and negative probe to white. If the readings are much outside the value listed in this Chapter's Specifications, replace the pulse generator (see Steps 16 through 19).

3 To check the lighting coil, disconnect the connector for the yellow and white wires. Connect the positive probe of an ohmmeter to the yellow wire in the alternator side of the connector (not the wiring harness side) and connect the negative probe to ground (bare metal on the engine). If the readings are much outside the value listed in this Chapter's Specifications, replace the stator (see Steps 16 through 19).
4 To check the charging coil, disconnect the connector for the yellow and white wires. Connect the positive probe of an ohmmeter to the white wire in the alternator side of the connector (not the wiring harness side) and connect the negative probe to ground (bare metal on the engine). If the readings are much outside the value listed in this Chapter's Specifications, replace the stator (see Steps 16 through 19).

YFZ450R

5 To check the stator coils, disconnect the coil connector (three white wires). Connect an ohmmeter between two wires at a time and measure the resistance between each pair. Compare the reading to the value listed in this Chapter's Specifications. If it's not within the specified range, replace the stator coil (see Steps 16 through 19).

Rotor replacement

Note: *To remove the alternator rotor, the special Yamaha puller or an aftermarket equivalent will be required. Don't try to remove the rotor without the proper puller, as it's almost sure to be damaged. Pullers are readily available from motorcycle dealers and aftermarket tool suppliers.*

6 Remove the left crankcase cover (see Chapter 2).
7 Hold the alternator rotor with a universal holder. You can also use a strap wrench. If you don't have one of these tools and the engine is in the frame, the rotor can be locked by placing the transmission in gear and holding the rear brake on. Unscrew the rotor nut and remove the washer **(see illustrations)**.
8 Thread an alternator puller into the cen-

9.7a Unscrew the rotor nut . . .

9.7b . . . and remove the washer - you may need to pry it out

5•8 Ignition and electrical systems

9.8a Thread the puller onto the rotor and tighten the puller screw against the crankshaft, then hold the puller body with a wrench and tighten the puller screw to push the rotor off

9.8b Remove the thrust washer from behind the rotor

9.9a Locate the Woodruff key (arrow); be sure it's in its slot on installation

ter of the rotor and use it to remove the rotor **(see illustrations)**. If the rotor doesn't come off easily, tap sharply on the end of the puller to release the rotor's grip on the tapered crankshaft end.

9 Pull the rotor off **(see illustration)**. Check the Woodruff key; if it's not secure in its slot, pull it out and set it aside for safe-keeping. A convenient method is to stick the Woodruff key to the magnets inside the rotor **(see illustration)**, but be certain not to forget it's there, as serious damage to the rotor and stator coils will occur if the engine is run with anything stuck to the magnets.

Alternator installation

10 Take a look to make sure there isn't anything stuck to the inside of the rotor **(see illustration 9.9b)**.
11 Degrease the center of the rotor and the end of the crankshaft.

12 Make sure the Woodruff key is positioned securely in its slot **(see illustration 9.9a)**.
13 Align the rotor slot with the Woodruff key. Place the rotor on the crankshaft.
14 Install the rotor washer and nut. Hold the rotor from turning with one of the methods described in Step 7 and tighten the nut to the torque listed in this Chapter's Specifications.
15 The remainder of Installation is the reverse of removal.

Stator coil and YFZ450 pulse generator replacement

16 The stator coil and pulse generator are replaced as a unit.
17 Remove the left engine cover and alternator rotor as described above.
18 Remove the screws that secure the stator coils (all models) and pickup coil (YFZ450) **(see illustration)**. Remove them from the

9.9b Be sure there aren't any small metal objects stuck to the rotor magnets; an inconspicuous item like this Woodruff key (arrow) can ruin the rotor and stator if the engine is run

9.18 Remove the stator plate and pulse generator mounting screws with an impact driver (YFZ450 shown)

Ignition and electrical systems 5•9

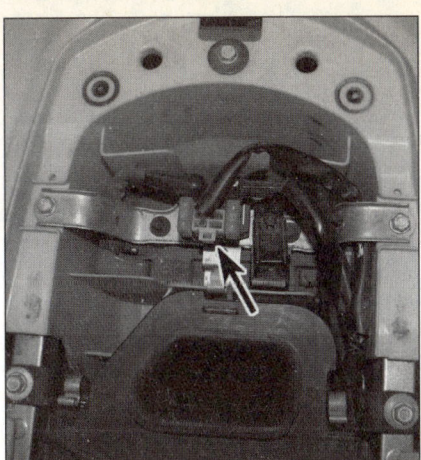

11.3a The YFZ450 starter relay is located on the battery retainer (arrow) . . .

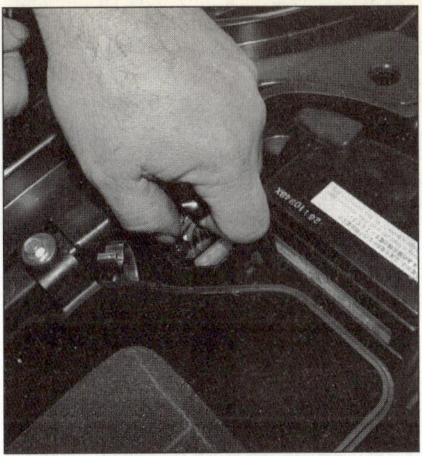

11.3b . . . and here's the YFZ450R starter relay - disconnect the electrical connector

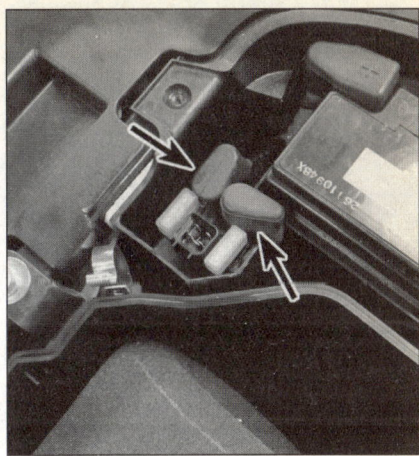

11.4 Connect a 12-volt battery to the relay's battery terminals (arrows)

inside of the left crankcase cover. **Note:** *On YFZ450 models, the stator coils and pickup coil are sold as a unit.*

19 Installation is the reverse of removal. Tighten the base plate screws securely, but don't overtighten them and strip the threads.

Regulator/rectifier

20 The regulator/rectifier is located under the front fender **(see illustration 16.5, YFZ450R; YFZ450 similar)**. Refer to Chapter 8 and remove the front fender to check or replace it.

Check

21 Connect a tune-up tachometer to the engine, following the manufacturer's instructions. The tachometer must be capable of reading 5000 rpm.
22 If you're working on a YFZ450, connect an AC voltmeter to the terminals for the white/black and yellow/red wires in the regulator/rectifier connector. The current from the alternator is not yet rectified to DC at this point, so the voltmeter must be able to measure AC.
23 If you're working on a YFZ450R, you'll need to make connections to each of the three white wires in turn - left to center, left to right, center to right. To do this, insert short pieces of stiff wire into the backs of the connector terminals to act as contacts for the voltmeter probes.
24 Start the engine and run it at 5000 rpm. Measure the input voltage on the voltmeter. If it's not as listed in this Chapter's Specifications, check the alternator charging coil (YFZ450) or stator coils (YFZ450R). Also check the harness from the alternator to the regulator/rectifier for breaks or bad connections.
25 Let the engine idle and move the voltmeter positive probe to the red wire's terminal, and the negative probe to the black wire's terminal. Again run the engine at 5000

rpm and measure the output voltage. If it's not as listed in this Chapter's Specifications, replace the regulator/rectifier.
26 If the regulator/rectifier input and output voltage readings are correct, check the wiring harness from the regulator/rectifier to the battery for breaks or bad connections.

Replacement

27 Disconnect the electrical connector from the regulator/rectifier. Remove its mounting bolts and lift it off.
28 Installation is the reverse of removal.

10 Kill switch - check, removal and installation

1 The kill switch, mounted on the left handlebar, shorts the ignition circuit to ground when its button is pressed.

Check

2 Follow the wires from the switch to their connectors and unplug them.
3 Connect an ohmmeter between the wire terminals in the switch side of the connectors (not the side that leads back to the wiring harness). With the switch in the released position, the ohmmeter should show no continuity (infinite resistance); with the button pushed, the ohmmeter should show continuity (little or no resistance).
4 Repeat the test several times. The ohmmeter should move from continuity to no continuity each time the button is released. If it continues to show continuity after it's released, the ignition system is being shorted out constantly and won't produce a spark.

Removal and installation

5 To remove the switch, remove its mounting screw, separate the clamp and

take it off the handlebar. Remove the wiring harness retainers and unplug the switch electrical connector.
6 Installation is the reverse of removal. Note that the clamp screw secures the switch ground wire.

11 Starter circuit - component check and replacement

1 The electric starter used on these models includes a safety circuit that prevents the starter from operating unless the transmission is in neutral or the clutch lever is pulled in. The YFZ450 uses a starter relay and starting circuit cut-off relay. The YFZ450R uses a starter relay, but the ECU controls starter operation in place of the cut-off relay used on the YFZ450.

Starter relay

2 Remove the seat (see Chapter 8). If you're working on a YFZ450R, remove the battery retainer strap (see Section 3).
3 Disconnect the battery cables from the relay, negative cable first, then disconnect the wiring connector from the starter relay **(see illustrations)**.
4 Connect an ohmmeter between the battery terminals on the relay **(see illustration 11.3a, YFZ450, or the accompanying illustration, YFZ450R)**. The ohmmeter should indicate infinite resistance (no continuity).
5 Connect a fully charged battery (the vehicle's battery will work) to the relay terminals, using lengths of wire. The ohmmeter between the relay's battery terminals should now indicate continuity (little or no resistance).
6 If the relay doesn't perform as described, remove it from its mount and install a new one.

5•10 Ignition and electrical systems

12.1a The YFZ450 starter (arrow) is mounted behind the cylinder

12.1b The YFZ450R starter (arrow) is mounted in front of the cylinder

13.3a YFZ450 models use a set of starter reduction gears . . .

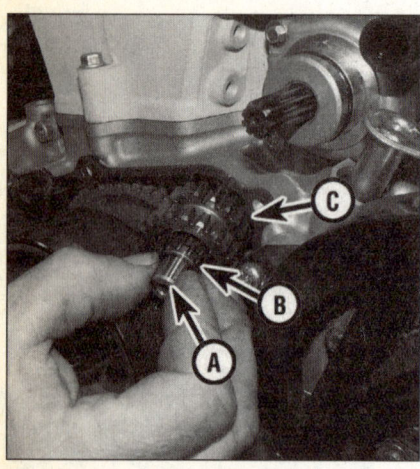

13.3b . . . to remove them, pull out the shaft and bearing

A	Shaft	C	Gears
B	Bearing		

Starting circuit cut-off relay (YFZ450)

7 Remove the seat (see Chapter 8).
8 Remove the relay from its mount and disconnect the wiring connector (see illustration 11.3a).
9 Connect an ohmmeter positive terminal to the relay terminal that connects to the red/black wire. Connect the ohmmeter negative terminal to the relay terminal that connects to the yellow/black wire.
10 Connect the positive terminal of a fully charged battery (the vehicle's battery will work) to the relay terminal that connects to the red/black wire, using a length of wire. Connect the battery negative terminal to the relay terminal that connects to the sky blue wire. The ohmmeter between the relay's battery terminals should indicate continuity (little or no resistance).

11 Repeat Step 10, this time with the battery negative terminal connected to the relay terminal that connects to the sky blue wire. The ohmmeter between the relay's battery terminals should again indicate continuity (little or no resistance).
12 If the relay doesn't perform as described, replace it.
13 Disconnect the battery from the relay.
14 Connect the ohmmeter positive probe to the relay terminal that connects to the sky blue wire. Connect the negative probe to the red/black wire's terminal. The ohmmeter should indicate continuity.
15 Reverse the ohmmeter connections. The ohmmeter should now show no continuity.
16 If the ohmmeter doesn't perform as described in Step 14 or Step 15, the diode is bad. Replace the relay with a new one.

12 Starter motor - check and replacement

Check

Warning: This check may cause sparks. Make sure these is no leaking gasoline or anything else flammable in the vicinity.

Warning: Make sure the transmission is in Neutral or the vehicle will jump forward during Step 2.

Caution: *The jumper cable used for this procedure must be of a gauge at least as heavy as the battery cable, or it may melt.*

1 Locate the starter motor and disconnect its cable (see illustrations).
2 Connect a jumper cable from the battery positive terminal directly to the starter motor

terminal. The starter should crank the engine.
3 If the starter doesn't crank at all, replace it. If it turns but doesn't crank the engine, remove and inspect the starter reduction gears and slipper clutch (see Sections 13 and 15).

Replacement

4 If you haven't already done so, disconnect the starter cable.
5 Remove the starter mounting bolts and lift the starter out of the engine.
6 Installation is the reverse of removal. Use a new O-ring and tighten the bolts to the torque listed in this Chapter's Specifications.

13 Starter reduction gears - removal and installation

1 These vehicles use two reduction gears, an idler gear and a starter clutch drive gear. The idler gear transfers torque from the starter slipper clutch to the starter clutch drive gear (large gear). The starter clutch turns the crankshaft.

Idler gear removal

2 Remove the left crankcase cover (see Chapter 2).

YFZ450

3 The dual idler gear is mounted in the outside of the crankcase (see illustration). Pull the gear shaft and bearing out and remove the gear, noting which direction it faces (see illustration).

YFZ450R

4 The idler gear is mounted in the outside of the crankcase toward the front of the engine. Pull the gear shaft and bearing out and remove the gear. The long shoulder on the gear faces away from the engine.

Ignition and electrical systems

13.6 Take the reduction gear off the crankshaft and note which way it faces

14.3 Remove the starter clutch bolts (shown here from the back side) to separate the starter clutch from the rotor

Starter clutch gear removal

5 Remove the left crankcase cover and alternator rotor (see Chapter 2 and Section 9). Remove the thrust washer behind the rotor.
6 Slip the drive gear off the crankshaft, noting which direction it faces **(see illustration)**.

Inspection

7 Check the gears for wear or damage such as chipped teeth. Check the shaft for scoring or heat damage that might indicate lack of lubrication. Replace the gear if problems are found.
8 Check the bushing on the inside of the starter clutch gear for wear or damage. Replace the gear if problems are found.
9 Since needle roller bearing wear is difficult to see, the idler gear bearing should be replaced if its condition is in doubt.

Installation

10 Installation is the reverse of removal.

14 Starter clutch - removal, inspection and installation

1 If the starter motor spins but doesn't crank the engine, you can perform a quick check to see if the starter clutch could be causing the problem.
2 Remove the slipper clutch (see Section 15). Reach into the slipper clutch recess and spin the starter idler gear with a finger. It should spin freely and smoothly in one direction and not at all in the other direction. If it spins both ways, the starter clutch is probably damaged. If the movement of the gear is rough or uneven, the starter clutch or one of the reduction gears may be damaged. Remove the starter clutch for further inspection as described below.

Removal

3 Remove the alternator rotor (see Section 9). The starter clutch is mounted in the back of the rotor **(see illustration)**.
4 Mark the starter clutch so you can reinstall it facing the correct direction. Remove the six Torx bolts that secure the starter clutch to the alternator rotor and take the starter clutch off.

Inspection

5 Check all parts for visible wear and damage and replace any parts that show problems.
6 Test the starter clutch. Place it in position on the back of the alternator rotor. Place the starter reduction gear in the starter clutch. Hold the rotor steady, with the reduction gear toward you, and try to twist the clutch. It should twist freely in a counterclockwise direction, but not at all in the clockwise direction.
7 If the gear will turn both ways or neither way, the starter clutch is bad. If the gear will turn freely clockwise, but not at all counterclockwise, the starter clutch rollers are installed upside down.

Installation

8 Installation is the reverse of removal. Tighten the starter clutch bolts to the torque listed in this Chapter's Specifications and use non-hardening Loctite on the bolt threads. Be sure to check the starter clutch function as described in Step 6 before completing final installation.

15 Slipper clutch - removal, inspection and installation

1 These vehicles use a torque limiting slipper clutch. The slipper clutch connects the starter pinion to the starter reduction gears. On YFZ450 models, the slipper clutch is mounted inside a cover behind the cylinder. On YFZ450R models, it's mounted forward of the cylinder, inside the left crankcase cover.

Removal

YFZ450

2 Remove the cover mounting bolts **(see illustration)**.

15.2 The YFZ450 slipper clutch cover is secured by two bolts (arrows)

5•12 Ignition and electrical systems

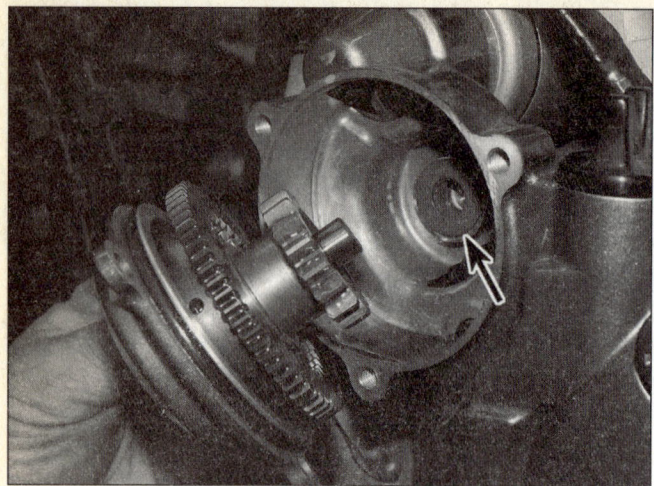

15.3a Remove the cover and take out the thrust washer . . .

15.3b . . . then remove the slipper clutch from the cover and take out the remaining thrust washer

3 Take the cover off, then remove the slipper clutch and washer from the cover **(see illustrations)**.

YFZ450R
4 Remove the left crankcase cover (see Chapter 2). Take the slipper clutch off the engine.

Inspection
5 The slipper clutch components aren't available separately, so if there's wear or damage, replace the slipper clutch as a unit.

Installation
6 Installation is the reverse of removal. If you're working on a YFZ450, use a new cover O-ring, lubricated with clean engine oil.

16 Lighting circuit - check

System check
1 If the headlight or taillight doesn't work, check the bulb. If it's good, check the socket for corrosion and the wiring for breaks or bad connections. The taillight on later models is a light-emitting diode (LED) assembly that's replaced as a unit.
2 If neither light works, check the switch. Disconnect its wiring connector and connect an ohmmeter to the switch terminals. The ohmmeter should show little or no resistance when the switch is On, and infinite resistance when it's Off. If not, replace it.
3 If the brake light doesn't work, check it in the same manner as the headlight and taillight (see Steps 1 and 2). If none of the lights work and the switch is good, check the alternator lighting coil (YFZ450, see Section 9) or the headlight relay (YFZ450R, see Steps 4 through 10).

Relay check (YFZ450R)
4 You'll need a fully charged 12-volt battery and an ohmmeter for this test (the vehicle's battery will work).
5 The headlight relay and cooling fan relay are located under the front fender just above the regulator/rectifier **(see illustration)**. Remove the front fender (see Chapter 8) for access to the relay.
6 Detach the relay from its rubber holder and disconnect it from the wiring harness.
7 Identify the relay terminals. They're arranged in a T. Terminals 1 (yellow), 5 (green) and 2 (black) are across the top of the T. Terminals 3 (blue) and 4 (yellow) are on the leg of the T. Connect the positive terminal of a fully charged 12-volt battery (the vehicle's battery will work) to terminal 1. Connect the battery negative terminal to terminal 2.
8 Connect the ohmmeter positive terminal to relay terminal 3. Connect the ohmmeter negative terminal to relay terminals 4 and 5 in turn. In both cases, the ohmmeter should show continuity (little or no resistance).
9 Disconnect the battery from the relay and repeat the ohmmeter tests. There should be no continuity (infinite resistance).
10 If the relay doesn't perform as described, replace it.

17 Bulb replacement

Headlights
1 Working beneath the fender, pull the removal tab to pull the rubber cap off of the headlight assembly.
2 Press the wiring connector into its socket and turn it counterclockwise, then remove it from the headlight.
3 Pull the bulb out, holding it by the metal base.

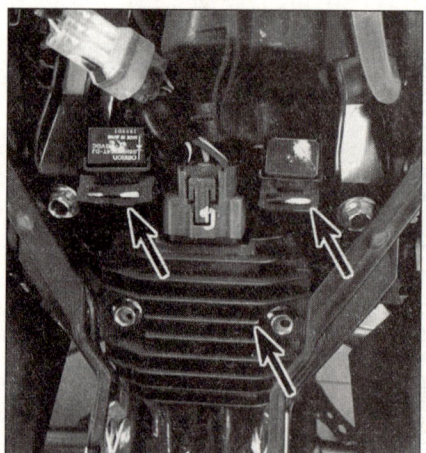

16.5 The YFZ450R headlight relay (left arrow) and cooling fan motor relay (right arrow) are located under the front fender, just above the regulator/rectifier (center arrow)

4 Installation is the reverse of removal. Hold the bulb by its base. Be sure not to touch the bulb glass with your fingers - oil from your skin will cause the bulb to overheat and fail prematurely. If you do touch the bulb, wipe it off with a clean rag dampened with rubbing alcohol.
5 Reinstall the rubber cap, making sure the TOP mark on the cap is upward. If you removed both rubber caps at the same time, refer to the L (left) and R (right) marks to make sure they're reinstalled on the correct sides of the vehicle.

Tail/brake light
Conventional bulb
6 2004 and 2005 models use a conventional bulb for the brake/taillight. To replace it, remove the lens securing screws and take off the lens. Press the bulb into its socket and

Ignition and electrical systems 5•13

17.12 Follow the warning light wiring harness (arrow) to its connector and unplug it, then remove the screws to detach the light unit from the bracket

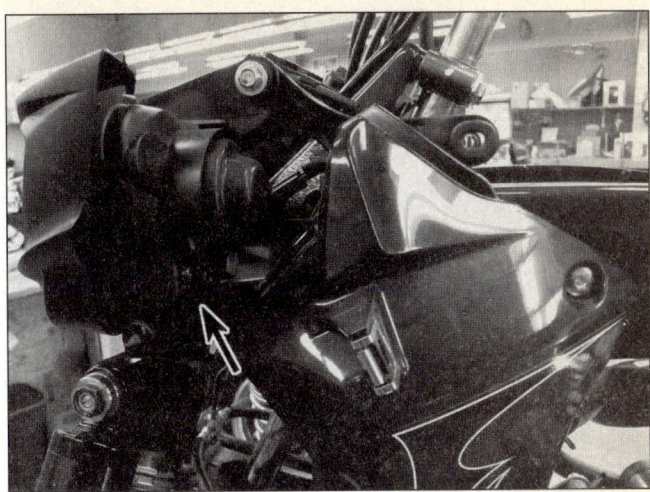

18.1 Turn the adjuster (arrow) to adjust the headlight

turn it counterclockwise to remove. Install in the reverse order.

Light-emitting diode (LED)

7   2006 and later models use a light-emitting diode (LED) unit. If it fails, the entire assembly must be replaced.
8   Remove the seat (see Chapter 8). Detach the cover from the electrical unit bracket.
9   Disconnect the wiring harness from the taillight. Remove the taillight mounting screws and take the assembly out of the cover.
10   Installation is the reverse of removal.

Warning lights

11   If you're working on a YFZ450, remove the instrument light socket from the bracket, then pull the bulb out, push a new one in and reinstall the socket.
12   If you're working on a YFZ450R, disconnect the wiring connector from the light assembly **(see illustration)**. Remove the mounting screws and take the assembly off the vehicle.
13   Installation is the reverse of removal.

18 Headlight adjustment

The headlight can be adjusted vertically by turning the adjuster wheel located under the fender **(see illustration)**.

19 Clutch switch - check and replacement

1   The clutch switch is mounted in the clutch lever pivot **(see illustration)**.
2   Follow the wiring harness from the switch to its connector and disconnect it.
3   Connect an ohmmeter between the terminals in the switch side of the connector. With the clutch lever pulled in, there should be no resistance (zero ohms). With the lever released, there should be infinite resistance.
4   If the switch doesn't perform as described, slide back the lever pivot cover, press the switch retainer prong and pull the switch out of the clutch lever pivot. Push a new switch in until the retainer prong engages, then connect the wiring harness and reposition the cover.

20 Neutral switch - check and replacement

1   Disconnect the electrical connector from the switch **(see illustration)**.

19.1 The clutch switch is located in the lever pivot - slide back the cover and press its release prong (arrow, hidden) to free the switch

20.1 The neutral switch is located near the shift pedal (arrow, YFZ450R shown)

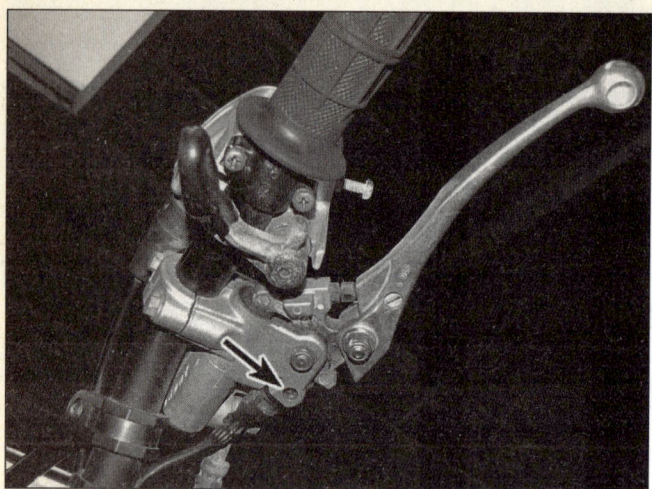

21.1a The front brake light switch is located in the lever pivot - press its release prong (arrow) to free the switch

21.1b The rear brake light switch is located above the brake pedal - turn its nut (arrow) to adjust or remove it

2 Connect one lead of an ohmmeter to a good ground and the other lead to the terminal post on the switch.
3 There should be no resistance between the switch and ground when the transmission is in Neutral. In any other gear, there should be infinite resistance.
4 If the switch doesn't perform as described, unscrew it and screw in a new one, using a new gasket.

21 Brake light switches - check, replacement and adjustment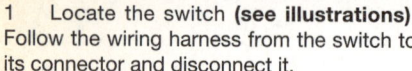

1 Locate the switch **(see illustrations)**. Follow the wiring harness from the switch to its connector and disconnect it.
2 Connect an ohmmeter between the terminals in the switch side of the connector. Operate the brake lever or pedal. With the lever pulled in or the pedal pressed, there should be no resistance (zero ohms). With the lever or pedal released, there should be infinite resistance.
3 If the front brake light switch doesn't perform as described, replace it. The switch is not adjustable. To replace it, press the switch retainer prong and pull the switch out of the brake lever pivot. Push a new switch in until the retainer prong engages, then connect the wiring harness.
4 The rear brake light switch can be adjusted. Hold the switch body so it won't turn and turn the adjusting nut to raise or lower the switch in the bracket **(see illustration 21.1b)**.
5 If adjustment of the rear brake light switch doesn't help, replace the switch with a new one. Unhook the switch from the bake pedal, unscrew the nut off the switch body and take it out of the bracket. Reverse the removal procedure to install the new switch, then adjust it as described in Step 4.

22 Main key switch - check and replacement

1 The main key switch (ignition switch) is located in the rear edge of the right front fender (YFZ450) or in the top of the right front fender (YFZ450R).

Check

2 To check the switch, follow its wiring harness to the connector and disconnect it. Remove the front fender, if necessary for access (see Chapter 8).
3 If you're working on a YFZ450, connect an ohmmeter to the red and brown wires, then to the red/white and brown/blue wires (in the switch side of the wiring harness). In both cases, the ohmmeter should indicate continuity (zero ohms) with the switch in the On position. If it doesn't, replace it.
4 If you're working on a YFZ450R, connect an ohmmeter between the red and brown wires in the switch side of the wiring harness. The ohmmeter should indicate continuity (zero ohms) with the switch in the On position. If it doesn't, replace it.

Replacement

5 Disconnect the switch wiring connector as described above.
6 Unscrew the switch nut and lift the switch out of the fender.
7 Installation is the reverse of removal.

23 Main relay check (YFZ450R) - check and replacement

1 You'll need a fully charged 12-volt battery and an ohmmeter for this test (the vehicle's battery will work).
2 The main relay is located at the rear of the vehicle under the seat. It can be identified by its wire colors. Remove the seat (see Chapter 8) for access to the relay.
3 Detach the relay from its rubber holder and disconnect it from the wiring harness.
4 Identify the relay terminals. They're arranged in a T. Terminals 1 and 2 are on the top of the T, and terminals 3 and 4 are on the leg of the T.
5 Connect the positive terminal of a fully charged 12-volt battery (the vehicle's battery will work) to terminal 1. Connect the battery negative terminal to terminal 2.
6 Connect the ohmmeter positive terminal to relay terminal 3 (red wire). Connect the ohmmeter negative terminal to relay terminal 4 (red/blue wire). The ohmmeter should show continuity (little or no resistance).
7 Disconnect the battery from the relay and repeat the ohmmeter tests. There should be no continuity (infinite resistance).
8 If the relay doesn't perform as described, replace it.

Notes

Notes

Chapter 6
Steering, suspension and final drive

Contents

Drive chain - removal, cleaning, inspection and installation	12	Steering knuckles - removal, inspection, and installation	6
Drive chain adjustment	See Chapter 1	Steering shaft - removal, inspection and installation	3
General information	1	Suspension - check	See Chapter 1
Handlebar - removal and installation	2	Suspension arms and balljoints - removal, inspection and installation	7
Rear axle - removal, inspection and installation	8		
Rear hub and bearings	See Chapter 7	Swingarm bearings - check	9
Shock absorbers - removal, installation and adjustment	4	Swingarm bearings - replacement	11
Shock linkage and swingarm - removal and installation	10	Tie-rods - removal, inspection and installation	5
Sprockets - check and replacement	13		

Degrees of difficulty

| Easy, suitable for novice with little experience | Fairly easy, suitable for beginner with some experience | Fairly difficult, suitable for competent DIY mechanic | Difficult, suitable for experienced DIY mechanic | Very difficult, suitable for expert DIY or professional |

Specifications

Front spring preload (installed length)
  YFZ450
    2004 and 2005
      Standard.. 255 mm (10.04 inches)
      Minimum (hardest setting)... 245 mm (9.65 inches)
      Maximum (softest setting)... 256.5 mm (10.10 inches)
    2006 and later
      Standard.. 255 mm (10.04 inches)
      Minimum (hardest setting)... 246.5 mm (9.70 inches)
      Maximum (softest setting)... 261.5 mm (10.30 inches)
  YFZ450R
    Standard... 289.8 mm (11.42 inches)
    Minimum (hardest setting).. 279.8 mm (11.02 inches)
    Maximum (softest setting).. 299.8 mm (11.80 inches)

6•2 Steering, suspension and final drive

Specifications (continued)

Front shock absorber compression damping (clicks out from fully turned in)
  YFZ450
    2004 and 2005
      Standard.. 12
      Minimum (hardest setting)... 22
      Maximum (softest setting)... 1
    2006 and later
      Standard.. 11
      Minimum (hardest setting)... 22
      Maximum (softest setting)... 1
  YFZ450R
    Slow compression damping
      Standard.. 10
      Minimum (hardest setting)... 18
      Maximum (softest setting)... 1
    Fast compression damping (turns out from fully turned in)
      Standard.. 1
      Minimum (hardest setting)... 2
      Maximum (softest setting)... Fully turned in
Front shock absorber rebound damping
  YFZ450
    2004 and 2005
      Standard.. 12
      Minimum (hardest setting)... 22
      Maximum (softest setting)... 1
    2006 and later
      Standard.. 11
      Minimum (hardest setting)... 22
      Maximum (softest setting)... 1
  YFZ450R
    Standard... 12
    Minimum (hardest setting).. 20
    Maximum (softest setting).. 1
Rear spring preload (installed length)
  YFZ450
    2004 and 2005
      Standard.. 244 mm (9.61 inches)
      Minimum (hardest setting)... 237 mm (9.33 inches)
      Maximum (softest setting)... 251 mm (9.88 inches)
    2006 and later
      Standard.. 257 mm (10.12 inches)
      Minimum (hardest setting)... 250 mm (9.84 inches)
      Maximum (softest setting)... 264 mm (10.39 inches)
  YFZ450R
    Standard... 265.0 mm (10.43 inches)
    Minimum (hardest setting).. 253.5 mm (9.98 inches)
    Maximum (softest setting).. 273.5 mm (10.77 inches)
Rear spring compression damping
  YFZ450
    Standard... 1-3/4 turns out
    Minimum (softest setting)... Fully turned out
    Maximum (hardest setting)... Fully turned in
  YFZ450R
    Slow compression damping
      Standard.. 10
      Minimum (hardest setting)... 18
      Maximum (softest setting)... 1
    Fast compression damping
      Standard.. 1 turn out
      Minimum (softest setting).. Fully turned out
      Maximum (hardest setting).. Fully turned in
Rear axle runout limit.. 1.5 mm (0.06 inch)

Torque specifications

Steering
Handlebar bracket bolts	23 Nm (17 ft-lbs)
Handlebar bracket nuts (YFZ450R)	64 Nm (46 ft-lbs)
Steering shaft nut	180 Nm (130 ft-lbs)
Steering shaft lower bearing	65 Nm (47 ft-lbs)
Steering shaft (upper) bearing bolts	23 Nm (17 ft-lbs)
Tie-rod nuts	25 Nm (18 ft-lbs)
Tie-rod locknuts	
2004 and 2005	13 Nm (132 inch-lbs)
2006 and later (YFZ450 and YFZ450R)	18 Nm (156 inch-lbs)

Front suspension
Front shock absorber bolts and nuts	
YFZ450	
2004 and 2005	45 Nm (32 ft-lbs)
2006 and later	48 Nm (35 ft-lbs)
YFZ450R	
Upper	40 Nm (29 ft-lbs)
Lower	55 Nm (40 ft-lbs)
Balljoint castle nuts	25 Nm (18 ft-lbs)
Front suspension arm pivot bolts and nuts	55 Nm (40 ft-lbs)

Rear suspension
Rear shock absorber	
Upper shock-to-frame bracket bolt and nut	80 Nm (58 ft-lbs)
Shock absorber lower bolt	55 Nm (40 ft-lbs)
Relay arm and connecting rod	
Relay arm-to-frame	55 Nm (40 ft-lbs)
Relay arm-to-connecting arm	55 Nm (40 ft-lbs)
Connecting arm-to-swingarm bolt	55 Nm (40 ft-lbs)
Swingarm pivot bolt and nut	100 Nm (72 ft-lbs)

Final drive
Front sprocket nut	
YFZ450	75 Nm (54 ft-lbs)
YFZ450R	100 Nm (72 ft-lbs)
Rear sprocket nuts	
2004 and 2005	55 Nm (40 ft-lbs)
2006 and later (YFZ450 and YFZ450R)	72 Nm (52 ft-lbs)

2.5 Mark the front side of each bracket, then remove the bracket bolts and lift off the bracket and handlebar

3.4 Bend back the lockwasher tabs, remove the bolts (arrows), separate the bracket halves and remove the upper and lower bearings

3.6 To detach the lower end of the steering shaft from the frame, remove this cotter pin and nut (arrow)

1 General information

The front suspension consists of upper and lower control arms on each side of the vehicle, supported by a shock absorber with a concentric coil spring.

The steering system consists of knuckles mounted at the outer ends of the front suspension and connected to a steering shaft by tie-rods. The steering shaft is turned by a one-piece handlebar.

The rear suspension on all models consists of a single shock absorber with concentric coil spring, progressive linkage and a swingarm. Final drive is by a chain and sprockets.

2 Handlebar - removal and installation

Removing the handlebar to service other components

1 If you're removing the handlebar simply to gain access to the steering shaft, it's not necessary to remove the clutch lever bracket, the left switch housing, the throttle cable housing or the front brake master cylinder.
2 Pull the fuel tank breather hose out of the hole in the handlebar trim cover.
3 Pull the handlebar cover off.
4 Look for a punch mark on the front of each handlebar bracket. If you can't find the factory punch marks, make your own marks to ensure that the brackets are correctly oriented when they're reinstalled.
5 Remove the handlebar bracket bolts **(see illustration)**, remove the upper bracket halves, then lift the handlebar off the lower bracket halves.

Caution: Support the handlebar assembly with a piece of wire or rope; allowing it to hang free will damage the cables, hoses and wiring.

6 If you're working on a YFZ450R, remove the nuts from the underside of the lower bracket halves and lift the bracket halves out of the steering shaft.
7 Installation is the reverse of removal. Make sure that the factory punch marks (or the ones you made prior to disassembly) face to the front. Tighten the handlebar bracket bolts to the torque listed in this Chapter's Specifications.

Caution: Tighten the front bracket bolts first, then the rear bracket bolts. This will leave a gap between the upper and lower bracket halves at the rear of each bracket. Don't try to close the gap by overtightening or you'll break the brackets.

Replacing the handlebar

8 If you're replacing the handlebar, remove all cable ties, then remove the clutch lever bracket, the left switch housing, the throttle cable housing (see Chapter 4), and the front brake master cylinder (see Chapter 7).
9 Follow Steps 2 through 5 above. If you need to remove the lower brackets on a YFZ450R, follow Step 6.
10 Installation is the reverse of removal. Tighten the handlebar bracket bolts to the torque listed in this Chapter's Specifications, observing the **Caution** in Step 7.

3 Steering shaft - removal, inspection and installation

Removal

1 Remove the handlebar and brackets (see Section 2).
2 Remove the front fender (see Chapter 8).
3 Remove the fuel tank (see Chapter 4).
4 Straighten the lockwasher tabs and remove the two nuts, the lockwasher, the washer and the steering shaft bearing halves **(see illustration)**.
5 Disconnect the inner ends of the tie-rods from the steering shaft (see Section 5).
6 Remove the cotter pin and nut from the bottom of the steering shaft **(see illustration)**.
7 Remove the steering shaft from the vehicle.
8 Pry out the seals from the steering shaft's lower pivot in the frame, unscrew the retainer with a hex bit and remove the lower bearing from the frame.

Inspection

9 Clean all the parts with solvent and dry them thoroughly, using compressed air, if available.
10 Inspect the steering shaft bearings and seals for wear, deterioration or damage. Replace them if there's any doubt about their condition.
11 Inspect the steering shaft and its integral steering arm for bending or other signs of damage. Do not attempt to repair any steering components. Replace them with new parts if defects are found.

Installation

12 Installation is the reverse of removal, with the following additions:
   a) *Lubricate the steering shaft upper bearing and seals with grease.*
   b) *Use new locknuts, lockwasher and cotter pins and tighten all fasteners to the torque values listed in this Chapter's Specifications.*

Steering, suspension and final drive 6•5

4.3 Unbolt the upper end of the front shock from the frame bracket and the lower end from the suspension arm

4.7 Place a rag under the shock so it won't scratch the swingarm during removal

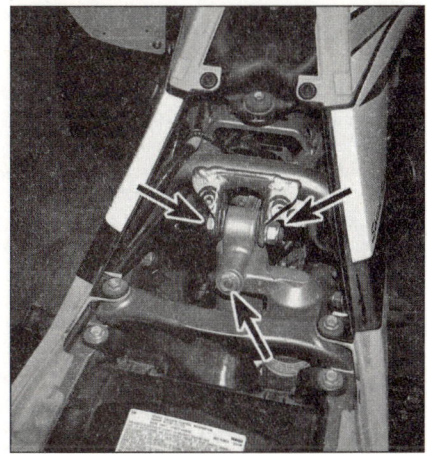

4.8a YFZ450 rear shock bolt (left), nut (right) and compression damping adjuster screw (center) locations

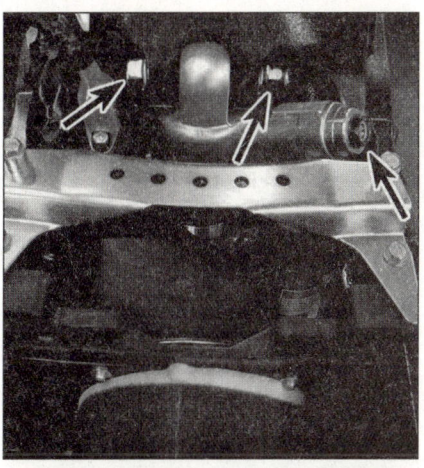

4.8b YFZ450R rear shock bolt (left), nut (center) and compression damping adjuster screw and nut (right) locations

4.8c There's a washer under the nut . . .

4 Shock absorbers - removal, installation and adjustment

Removal and installation

 Warning: *Do not attempt to disassemble these shock absorbers. They are nitrogen-charged under high pressure. Replace the shocks and springs as a unit.*

Front shock absorbers

Note: *This procedure applies to either front shock absorber.*

1 Support the front of the vehicle securely on jackstands and remove the front wheels.
2 Support the outer ends of the front lower arms with jackstands so they won't drop when the shock absorbers are removed.
3 Remove the nuts and bolts that attach the upper end of the shock to the frame bracket and the lower end to the bracket on the lower control arm bracket (see illustrations). Separate the shock from the frame bracket and from the control arm bracket and lift it out.
4 Inspect the shock absorber for signs of wear or damage such as oil leaks, bending, a weak spring and worn bushings. Replace both shock absorbers as a pair if any problems are found.
5 Installation is the reverse of removal. Tighten the nuts and bolts to the torque listed in this Chapter's Specifications.

Rear shock absorber

6 Remove the seat (see Chapter 8).
7 Jack up the rear end of the vehicle and support it securely on jackstands. Slip a rag beneath the shock so the swingarm and shock body won't be scratched (see illustration).
8 Remove the mounting bolt, nut and bushing at the top of the shock (see illustrations).
9 Remove the cotter pin, washer, lower shock mounting bolt and assorted spacers, bushings, etc. at the lower end of the shock

4.8d . . . and a bushing in the mounting hole

4.9a Remove the cotter pin (arrow) and cover from the shock's lower mounting pivot . . .

4.9b . . . and remove the washer, then remove the bolt, cover and washer from the other side

(see illustrations). To ensure that the various washers, spacers, bushings, etc. are installed in the correct sequence and relationship to one another, it's a good idea to immediately install all parts on the lower shock mounting bolt in the order in which they were removed. Separate the shock from the upper mounting bracket and from the relay arm and lift it out of the vehicle.

10 Installation is the reverse of removal, with the following additions:
   a) Make sure that you install all parts, in order, when reattaching the lower end of the shock to the relay arm.
   b) Tighten the nut and bolt to the torque listed in this Chapter's Specifications.
   c) Install a thrust washer on each side of the pivot pin.
   d) Use a new cotter pin in the pivot pin.

Adjustment

Front shock absorbers

11 Front shock absorber spring preload is adjusted by turning the adjuster ring at the top of the shock with a spanner wrench **(see illustration)**. Note: *The spanner should be in your machine's toolkit; if not, you can obtain one at any Yamaha dealer.* Loosen the locknut (the lower nut), turn the adjuster ring to obtain the desired preload, then tighten the locknut.

12 Front shock absorber rebound damping is adjusted by turning the screw on the bottom of the shock absorber. Turning the adjuster clockwise increases the rebound damping force (slower rebound); turning the adjuster counterclockwise decreases the rebound damping force (faster rebound). To set the rebound damping adjuster to its standard position, turn it all the way in, then back it out the number of clicks listed in this Chapter's Specifications.

Caution: Do NOT attempt to turn the rebound adjuster beyond the maximum or minimum setting.

YFZ450

13 Front shock absorber compression damping on YFZ450 models is adjusted by turning the screw on the shock reservoir **(see illustration 4.11)**. Turning the adjuster clockwise increases the compression damping force (slower rebound); turning the adjuster counterclockwise decreases the compression damping force (faster rebound). To set the adjuster to its standard position, turn it all the way in, then back it out the number of clicks listed in this Chapter's Specifications.

Caution: Do NOT attempt to turn the compression damping adjuster beyond the maximum or minimum setting.

YFZ450R

14 YFZ450R models have two compression damping adjustments: slow compression damping and fast compression damping.

15 Slow compression damping is adjusted by turning the adjuster screw **(see illustration 4.11)**. Fast compression damping is adjusted by turning the nut that surrounds the screw.

16 To set the slow adjuster to its standard position, turn it all the way in, then back it out the number of clicks listed in this Chapter's Specifications.

Caution: Do NOT attempt to turn the compression damping adjuster beyond the maximum or minimum setting.

17 To set the fast adjuster to its standard position, turn the nut in all the way, then back it out the number of clicks listed in this Chapter's Specifications.

Caution: Do NOT attempt to turn the compression damping adjuster beyond the maximum or minimum setting.

Rear shock absorber

18 The rear shock absorber is fully adjustable for spring preload, compression damping and rebound damping.

19 Spring preload is adjusted by changing the length of the spring. Loosen the preload adjuster locknut at the top of the shock, then turn the adjuster nut with a spanner wrench **(see illustrations 4.8a and 4.8b)**. Note: *The spanner should be in your machine's toolkit; if not, you can obtain one at any Yamaha dealer.* Turn the adjuster clockwise to reduce spring length or counterclockwise to increase spring length. Measure the spring length and compare your measurement to the values listed in this Chapter's Specifications.

Caution: Do NOT attempt to turn the spring preload adjuster beyond the maximum or minimum setting.

Tighten the locknut.

20 Rebound damping force is adjusted by turning the adjuster at the bottom of the shock

4.11 Spring preload on all models is adjusted with the locknut and adjusting nut (left) - compression damping is adjusted with the screw (right) on all models, and YFZ450R fast compression damping is adjusted with the hex nut that surrounds the screw

Steering, suspension and final drive 6•7

4.20 Rebound damping is adjusted with this screw at the bottom of the shock

5.3 The steering arm is attached to the tie-rod and suspension arms by cotter pins and nuts (arrows)

(see illustration). Turning the adjuster clockwise increases the rebound damping force (slower rebound); turning the adjuster counterclockwise decreases the rebound damping force (faster rebound). To set the rebound damping adjuster to its standard position, turn it all the way in, then back it out the number of clicks listed in this Chapter's Specifications.

Caution: Do NOT attempt to turn the rebound adjuster beyond the maximum or minimum setting.

YFZ450

21 Rear shock absorber compression damping on YFZ450 models is adjusted by turning the screw on the shock reservoir **(see illustration 4.8a).** Turning the adjuster clockwise increases the compression damping force (slower rebound); turning the adjuster counterclockwise decreases the compression damping force (faster rebound). To set the adjuster to its standard position, turn it all the way in, then back it out the number of clicks listed in this Chapter's Specifications.

Caution: Do NOT attempt to turn the compression damping adjuster beyond the maximum or minimum setting.

YFZ450R

22 YFZ450R models have two compression damping adjustments: slow compression damping and fast compression damping.
23 Slow compression damping is adjusted by turning the adjuster screw **(see illustration 4.8b).** Fast compression damping is adjusted by turning the nut that surrounds the screw.
24 To set the slow adjuster to its standard position, turn it all the way in, then back it out the number of clicks listed in this Chapter's Specifications.

Caution: Do NOT attempt to turn the compression damping adjuster beyond the maximum or minimum setting.

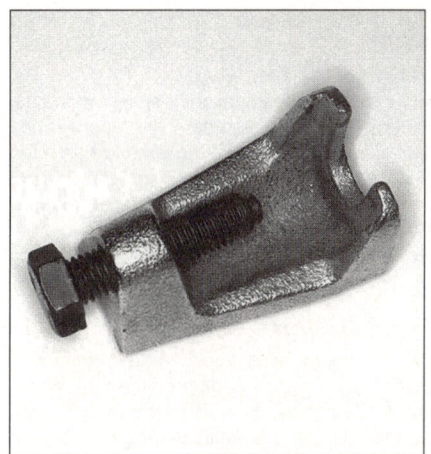

5.4 This automotive tie-rod puller will work on tie-rod ends and balljoints

25 To set the fast adjuster to its standard position, turn the nut in all the way, then back it out the number of clicks listed in this Chapter's Specifications.

Caution: Do NOT attempt to turn the compression damping adjuster beyond the maximum or minimum setting.

5 Tie-rods - removal, inspection and installation

Removal

1 Place the steering in the straight-ahead position.
2 If both of the tie-rods are to be removed, mark them "Left" and "Right" so they're not accidentally switched during reassembly.
3 Remove the cotter pin from the nut at the outer end of the tie-rod and undo the nut **(see illustration).**

5.5 Cotter pins and nuts also secure the inner ends of the tie-rods (arrows)

4 Separate the tie-rod stud from the knuckle with a tie rod puller or pickle fork balljoint separator **(see illustration).**

Caution: It's very easy to damage the rubber boot on the tie-rod with a pickle fork separator. If you're going to use the tie-rod again, it's best to use another type of tool.

5 Repeat Steps 3 and 4 to disconnect the inner end of the tie rod from the steering shaft **(see illustration).**

Inspection

6 Check the tie-rod shaft for bending or other damage and replace it if any problems are found. Don't try to straighten the shaft.
7 Check the tie-rod balljoint boots for cracks or deterioration. Twist and rotate the threaded studs. They should move easily, without roughness or looseness. If a boot or stud show any problems, unscrew the tie-rod end from the tie-rod and install a new one.

6•8 Steering, suspension and final drive

7.4 Remove the pivot bolts and nuts (arrows) to detach the inner ends of the suspension arms from the frame

7.10 The YFZ450R balljoints are secured to the lower suspension arms by snap-rings

Installation

8 Thread the tie-rod ends onto the tie-rods. The length of exposed threads on each end of the tie-rod must be even. The flat on the tie-rod that's used to adjust toe-in goes at the outer end of the tie-rod.
9 The remainder of installation is the reverse of removal, with the following additions:
a) Use new cotter pins and bend them to hold the nuts securely.
b) Check front wheel toe-in and adjust as necessary (see Chapter 1).

6 Steering knuckles - removal, inspection, and installation

Removal

1 Jack up the front end of the vehicle and support it securely on jackstands. Remove the front wheels.
2 Disconnect the outer end of the tie-rod from the steering knuckle (see Section 5).
3 Remove the outer disc cover, the front brake caliper, the wheel hub and the inner disc cover (see Chapter 7).
4 Remove the front shock absorber (see Section 4).
5 Remove the cotter pin and nut from the upper and lower balljoint studs **(see illustration 5.3)**.
6 Separating the balljoints from the steering knuckle requires a separator tool. Automotive tie-rod separator tools are suitable (try it for fit before you buy it, if possible) and can be rented from tool yards or purchased inexpensively **(see illustration 5.4)**.
7 If balljoint separation proves difficult, the knuckle and suspension arms can be removed as a single assembly, then taken to a Yamaha dealer for balljoint removal.

Inspection

8 Inspect the knuckle carefully for cracks, bending or other damage. Replace it if any problems are found. If the vehicle has been in a collision or has been bottomed hard, it's a good idea to have the knuckle magnafluxed by a machine shop to check for hidden cracks.

Installation

9 Installation is the reverse of removal, with the following addition: Use new cotter pins and tighten the nuts to the torque listed in this Chapter's Specifications.

7 Suspension arms and balljoints - removal, inspection and installation

Suspension arms

Removal

1 Securely block both rear wheels so the vehicle won't roll. Loosen the front wheel nuts with the tires still on the ground, then jack up the front end, support it securely on jackstands and remove the front wheels.
2 On Banshee models, remove the front bumper (see Chapter 8). Remove the front fender (see Chapter 8) and expansion chamber (see Chapter 4) from the side you're working on.
3 Remove the steering knuckle (see Section 6). If you're removing an upper arm, remove the brake hose shield and disengage the brake hose from the arm (see Chapter 7).
4 Remove the pivot bolts and nuts and remove the suspension arm **(see illustration)**.

Inspection

5 Inspect the suspension arm(s) for bending, cracks or corrosion. Replace damaged parts. Don't attempt to straighten them.
6 Inspect all rubber bushings for cracks or deterioration. Check the inner collars on the lower suspension arms for damage or corrosion. Inspect the pivot bolts for wear as well. Replace the bushings and pivot bolts if they're worn or deteriorated.
7 Check the balljoint boot for cracks or deterioration. Twist and rotate the threaded stud. It should move easily, without roughness or looseness. On YFZ450 models, the balljoints can't be replaced separately from the suspension arms. If the boot or stud show any problems, replace the suspension arm together with the balljoint. On YFZ450R models, see Step 10.

Installation

8 Installation is the reverse of removal, but don't torque the suspension fasteners while the vehicle is off the ground. Tighten the nuts and bolts *slightly* while the vehicle is jacked up, then tighten them to the torque listed in this Chapter's Specifications after the vehicle is resting on its wheels.

Balljoints

9 On YFZ450 models, the balljoints are an integral part of the suspension arms; they cannot be separated. If the balljoint or the suspension arm is damaged or worn, they must be replaced as a single assembly.
10 On YFZ450R models, the balljoints can be removed from the suspension arms and replaced separately. With the suspension arm disconnected from the knuckle, remove the snap-ring **(see illustration)** and press the balljoint out of the suspension arm. If you don't have a press, have the balljoint pressed out by a dealer service department or other qualified shop.

8.4 Unscrew the axle nut lockbolts (arrows) - they're secured by Loctite

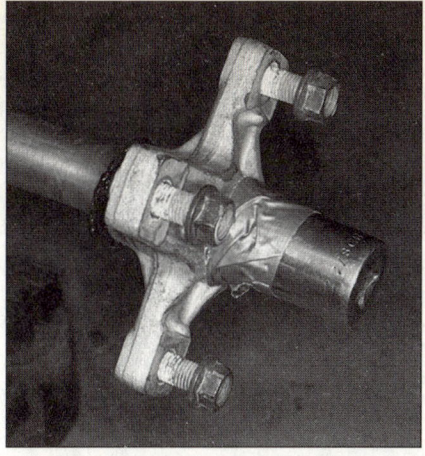

8.7 Tape a large socket over the hub threads, then tap on the socket to free the axle

8 Rear axle - removal, inspection and installation

Warning: *The axle nuts are secured with thread locking agent and tightened to a very high torque. When tightening or loosening them with the vehicle jacked up, be sure the vehicle is securely positioned on jackstands so it can't fall.*

Removal

1 Block the front wheels so the vehicle won't roll.
2 Jack up the rear end of the vehicle and support it securely, positioning the jackstands so they won't obstruct removal of the axle. The supports must be secure enough so the vehicle won't be knocked off of them while the axle is removed. Remove the rear wheels.
3 Remove the rear wheel hubs (see Chapter 7).
4 Remove the axle nut lockbolts **(see illustration)**. **Note:** *The lockbolts are secured with Loctite, so they may be difficult to remove.* Set the parking brake to keep the axle from turning, then unscrew the axle nut with a 46 mm wrench. Once the nut is loose, release the parking brake so the rear caliper can be removed.
5 Loosen the drive chain (see Chapter 1). Disengage the chain from the rear sprocket.
6 Remove the brake caliper and unbolt the brake disc (see Chapter 7). The brake hose and cable can be left connected. Secure the caliper out of the way.
7 Thread the nut back on to the right-hand end of the axle to protect the threads. Tape a socket over the nut **(see illustration)**, then tap on the nut to free the axle from the hub and remove it from the left side of the vehicle.

Inspection

8 Check the axle for obvious damage, such as step wear of the splines or bending, and replace it as necessary **(see illustration)**.
9 Inspect the brake disc and replace it if necessary (see Chapter 7).
10 Place the axle in V-blocks and set up a dial indicator to contact each of the outer ends in turn (see "Tools and Workshop Tips" at the end of this manual for information on dial indicators). Rotate the axle and compare runout to the value listed in this Chapter's Specifications. If runout is excessive, replace the axle.
11 Inspect the hub seals and bearings (see Chapter 7).
12 Inspect the sprockets and drive chain (see Sections 12 and 13).

Installation

13 Installation is the reverse of removal, with the following additions:
 a) Apply non-permanent thread locking agent to the nut threads on the axle. Tighten the axle nut with a torque wrench adapter (Yamaha tool 09890-01498/YM37134 or an equivalent 46 mm crow's foot wrench). Be sure to install the adapter at right angles to the torque wrench centerline. If the adapter is installed in a direct line with the torque wrench centerline, it will amplify the torque and the nut will be overtightened.
 b) Apply non-permanent thread locking agent to the threads of the axle nut lockbolts and tighten them to the torque listed in this Chapter's Specifications.
 c) After installation, adjust the drive chain as described in Chapter 1.

9 Swingarm bearings - check

1 Remove the rear wheels (see Chapter 7), then remove the rear shock absorber (see Section 4).
2 Grasp the rear of the swingarm with one hand and place your other hand at the junction of the swingarm and the frame. Try to move the rear of the swingarm from side-to-side. If the bearings are worn, they will allow some freeplay, which produces movement between the swingarm and the frame at the front (the swingarm will move forward and backward at the front, not from side-to-side). If any play is noted, the bearings should be replaced with new ones (see Sections 10 and 11).
3 Next, move the swingarm up and down through its full travel. It should move freely, without any binding or rough spots. If it does not move freely, remove the swingarm (see Section 10) and inspect the bearings (see Section 11).

10 Shock linkage and swingarm - removal and installation

1 If the swingarm is being removed just for bearing replacement, the brake assembly,

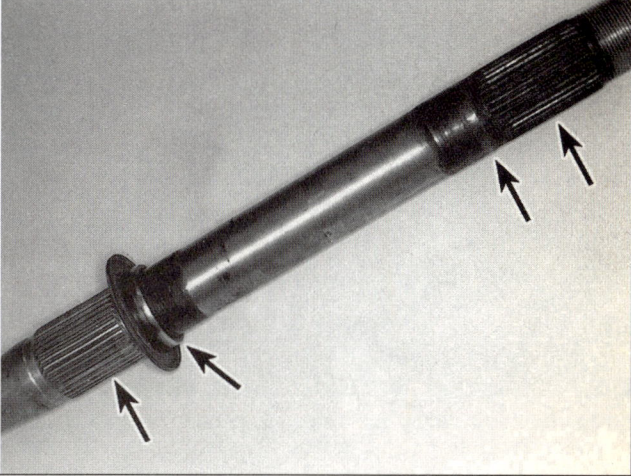

8.8 Inspect the splines and seal contact areas (arrows)

10.7 Here are the suspension linkage connecting arm (left) and relay arm (right)

10.8a On a YFZ450, remove the swingarm locknut...

10.8b ... the YFZ450R has a washer under the locknut

rear hub and rear axle need not be removed from the swingarm.

Removal

2 Raise the rear end of the vehicle and support it securely on jackstands.
3 Remove the rear wheels, the rear wheel hubs, the brake caliper and the brake disc (see Chapter 7).
4 Unbolt the swingarm protector from the underside of the swingarm. Take the drive chain off the sprockets (see Section 12).
5 If you're replacing the swingarm, remove the rear axle (see Section 8).
6 Support the swingarm so it won't drop, then detach the lower end of the shock absorber from the relay arm (see Section 4).
7 Remove the relay arm and the connecting rod (see illustration).
8 Unscrew the locknut, then pull the pivot bolt out of the swingarm (see illustrations).
9 Pull the swingarm back and away from the vehicle.
10 Inspect the pivot bearings in the swingarm for dryness or deterioration (see Section 11).

Installation

11 Lift the swingarm into position in the frame. Install the pivot bolt and locknut to hold the swingarm in the frame, but don't tighten them yet. On YFZ450 models, make sure the hexagonal bolt head fits into its recess in the frame (see illustration). On YFZ450R models, make sure the oval bolt head fits into the recess in the frame (see illustration).
12 Raise and lower the swingarm several times, moving it through its full travel to seat the bearings and pivot bolt.

10.11a On installation make sure the YFZ450's pivot bolt head fits into the hexagonal recess...

10.11b ... the YFZ450R has an oval bolt head - make sure it fits into the recess before trying to tighten it

Steering, suspension and final drive

11.4 Inspect the swingarm bearings for damage or wear

12.2a YFZ450 sprocket cover bolt locations (left arrows) - bend back the lockwasher tab (right arrow) to remove the nut

13 Tighten the pivot bolt and locknut to the torque listed in this Chapter's Specifications.
14 The remainder of installation is the reverse of removal.

11 Swingarm bearings - replacement

1 The swingarm pivot bolt rides on two needle roller bearings.
2 Remove the swingarm (see Section 10).
3 Remove the collar and pry the seal from each side of the swingarm.
4 Inspect the swingarm pivot bearing in each end of the swingarm (see illustration). If either bearing is rough or loose, or has excessive play, replace the bearings as a set.
5 Remove the bearings with a blind hole puller and slide hammer. If you don't have the proper tools, have the bearings replaced by a Yamaha dealer or machine shop.

12.2b YFZ450R sprocket cover bolt locations (left arrows) - grind away the staked portion of the locknut (right arrow) to remove the nut

6 While the bearings are removed, remove the collar, clean it thoroughly, inspect it for burrs, scoring and other damage. If the collar is damaged or worn, replace it. Lubricate the collar with grease and insert it back into the swingarm (make sure that the pivot bore is clean).
7 Tap new bearings into position with a bearing driver or socket just slightly smaller than the diameter of the outer race.
8 Pack the bearings with waterproof lithium-based wheel bearing grease.
9 Tap new seals into position with a seal driver or a socket just slightly smaller than the outside diameter of the seal.

12 Drive chain - removal, cleaning, inspection and installation

Removal

1 Remove the swingarm (see Section 10).
2 Remove the front sprocket cover from the engine (see illustrations).
3 Loosen the chain adjusters as needed to create slack so you can disengage the chain from the rear sprocket (see Chapter 1).
4 Lift the chain off the sprockets and remove it from the vehicle.
5 Check the chain guide and rollers on the swingarm and frame for wear or damage and replace them as necessary (see Chapter 1).

Cleaning and inspection

6 The drive chain has small rubber O-rings between the chain plates. Soak the chain in kerosene and use a brush to work the solvent into the spaces between the links and plates.
Caution: Do NOT use steam, high-pressure washes or solvents to clean the chain, all of which can damage the O-rings. Use only kerosene.
7 Wipe the chain dry, then inspect it carefully for worn or damaged links. Replace the chain if wear or damage is found at any point.
8 If the chain is worn or damaged, inspect the sprockets. If they're worn or damaged, replace them also.
Caution: Do NOT install a new chain on worn sprockets; it will wear out quickly.
9 Lubricate the chain (Yamaha recommends engine oil or chain lube suitable for O-ring chains).

Installation

10 Installation is the reverse of removal.
11 Adjust the chain (see Chapter 1).

13 Sprockets - check and replacement

1 Whenever the sprockets are inspected, the chain should be inspected and replaced if it's worn. Installing a worn chain on new sprockets will cause them to wear quickly.
2 Check the teeth on the engine sprocket and rear sprocket for wear. The engine sprocket is visible through the cover slots.
3 If the sprockets are worn, remove the chain (see Section 12) and the left rear wheel and hub (see Chapter 7).
4 To remove the engine sprocket, bend back the lockwasher (YFZ450) (see illustration 12.2a) or unstake the locknut (YFZ450R) (see illustration 12.2b). Remove the nut. Pull the sprocket off the transmission shaft.
5 Inspect the seal behind the engine sprocket. If it has been leaking, pry it out (take care not to scratch the seal bore) and tap in a new seal with a socket the same diameter as the seal.
6 To remove the rear sprocket, hold the Allen bolts with a wrench and unscrew the

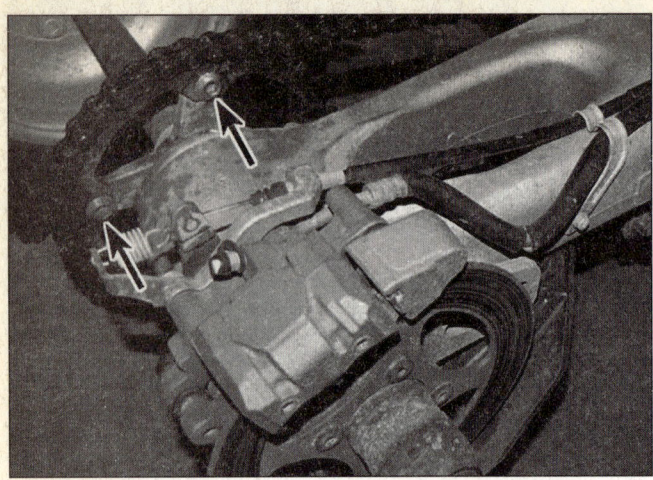

13.6a Hold the Allen bolts (arrows, two bolts hidden) . . .

13.6b . . . and unscrew the nuts (arrows, one nut hidden) to detach the sprocket from the axle hub

nuts **(see illustrations)**. Slip the sprocket over the end of the axle.

7 Installation is the reverse of removal. Be sure to use new a drive sprocket lockwasher (YFZ450) or locknut (YFZ450R). Tighten the drive sprocket nut and driven sprocket nuts and bolts to the torque listed in this Chapter's Specifications.

8 Install the chain (see Section 12).
9 Adjust the chain (see Chapter 1).

Chapter 7
Brakes, wheels and tires

Contents

Brake hoses and lines - inspection and replacement	14	Rear axle hub and bearings - removal, inspection and installation	16
Brake system - bleeding	15	Rear brake caliper - removal, overhaul and installation	9
Brake system - general check	See Chapter 1	Rear brake disc - inspection, removal and installation	11
Front brake caliper - removal, overhaul and installation	6	Rear brake master cylinder - removal, overhaul and installation	13
Front brake disc - inspection, removal and installation	7	Rear brake pads - replacement	8
Front brake master cylinder - removal, overhaul and installation	12	Rear wheel hubs - removal and installation	10
Front brake pads - replacement	5	Tires - general information	3
Front wheel hub and bearing - removal and installation	4	Tires and wheels - general check	See Chapter 1
General information	1	Wheels - inspection, removal and installation	2

Degrees of difficulty

| Easy, suitable for novice with little experience | | Fairly easy, suitable for beginner with some experience |  | Fairly difficult, suitable for competent DIY mechanic | | Difficult, suitable for experienced DIY mechanic |  | Very difficult, suitable for expert DIY or professional |  |

Specifications

Brakes
Brake pedal height .... See Chapter 1
Brake pad thickness (limit)
   Front .... 1.0 mm (0.04 inch)
   Rear .... 1.0 mm (0.04 inch)
Brake disc
   Standard thickness .... 3.5 mm (0.14 inch)
   Maximum runout .... 0.10 mm (0.004 inch)
   Minimum allowable thickness .... 3.0 mm (0.12 inch) (1)
Parking brake cable adjustment length
   2004 and 2005 .... 46 to 50 mm (1.8 to 1.9 inches)
   2006 and later (YFZ450 and YFZ450R) .... 47 to 51 mm (1.85 to 2.01 inches)

Wheels and tires
Tire pressures .... See *Daily (pre-ride) checks* at the beginning of this manual
Tire tread depth .... See *Daily (pre-ride) checks* at the beginning of this manual

Torque specifications

Wheel lug nuts	45 Nm (32 ft-lbs)
Front hub nuts	70 Nm (50 ft-lbs)
Rear hub nuts	
2004 and 2005	100 Nm (72 ft-lbs) (2)
2006 and later YFZ450 and YFZ450R (2,3)	
Step 1	200 Nm (145 ft-lbs)
Step 2	Loosen completely
Step 3	200 Nm (145 ft-lbs)
Front brake caliper	
Mounting bolts	28 Nm (20 ft-lbs)
Brake pad retaining bolts (2)	
2004 and 2005	18 Nm (156 in-lbs)
2006 and later (YFZ450 and YFZ450R)	17 Nm (144 inch-lbs)
Brake hose-to-caliper banjo bolts	27 Nm (19 ft-lbs) (4)
Brake disc retaining bolts	28 Nm (20 ft-lbs) (5)
Rear brake caliper	
Caliper-to-bracket bolts	
2004 and 2005	31 Nm (22 ft-lbs)
2006 and later (YFZ450 and YFZ450R)	43 Nm (31 ft-lbs)
Brake pad retaining bolts (2)	
2004 and 2005	18 Nm (156 in-lbs)
2006 and later (YFZ450 and YFZ450R)	17 Nm (144 inch-lbs)
Brake hose-to-caliper banjo bolt	30 Nm (22 ft-lbs) (4)
Brake disc retaining bolts (2)	
2004 and 2005	28 Nm (20 ft-lbs) (5)
2006 and later (YFZ450 and YFZ450R)	33 Nm (24 ft-lbs)
Parking brake case/bracket bolts (2)	
YFZ450	23 Nm (17 ft-lbs)
YFZ450R	22 Nm (16 ft-lbs)
Parking brake adjusting bolt locknut	
YFZ450	16 Nm (132 inch-lbs)
YFZ450R	17 Nm (144 inch-lbs)
Front master cylinder	
Brake hose banjo bolt	27 Nm (19 ft-lbs) (4)
Handlebar clamp bolts	7 Nm (61 inch-lbs)
Rear master cylinder	
Brake hose banjo bolt (3)	
YFZ450	30 Nm (22 ft-lbs)
YFZ450R	27 Nm (19 ft-lbs)
Rear hub nuts and through-bolts (2004 and 2005 YFZ450)	85 Nm (61 ft-lbs)
Rear axle nut	
2004 and 2005 YFZ450	100 Nm (72 ft-lbs) (5)
2006 and later	
YFZ450	240 Nm (175 ft-lbs) (5)
YFZ450R	250 Nm (181 ft-lbs) (5)
Rear axle nut lockbolts	7 Nm (61 inch-lbs) (3)

1 Refer to marks stamped into the disc (they supersede information printed here).
2 If the cotter pin holes don't line up, tighten the nut just enough to align them. Don't loosen the nut to align the cotter pin holes.
3 Apply rust preventative (WD-40 or equivalent) to the threads and to the seating surfaces of the nut and washer.
4 Use new sealing washers.
5 Apply non-permanent thread locking agent to the threads.

4.2 Remove the outer disc shield from the hub

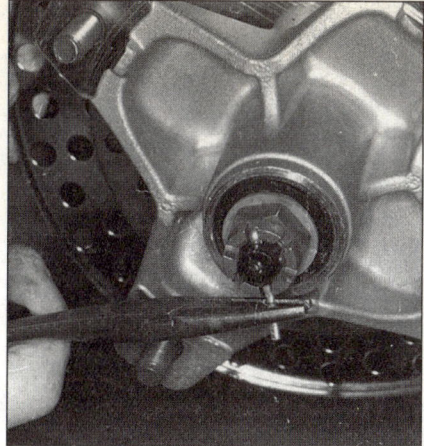

4.3 Bend back the cotter pin and pull it out

4.4 Have an assistant firmly apply the front brakes while you crack the hub nut loose

1 General information

The vehicles covered by this manual are equipped with three hydraulically-operated disc brakes: a disc at each front wheel and a single disc on the rear axle. The front brakes are operated by a lever-actuated master cylinder on the right end of the handlebar; the rear brake is operated by a pedal-actuated master cylinder on the right side of the vehicle, just behind the right footrest. The rear brake caliper is equipped with a parking brake system, which is actuated by a lever on the left end of the handlebar.

All front calipers have dual pistons. The rear caliper on 2004 and 2005 YFZ450 models has a single piston. The rear caliper on 2006 and later YFZ450 and YFZ450R models has dual pistons.

All models are equipped with wheels which require very little maintenance and allow tubeless tires to be used.

Caution: *Brake components rarely require disassembly. Do not disassemble components unless absolutely necessary.*

2 Wheels - inspection, removal and installation

Inspection

1 Clean the wheels thoroughly to remove mud and dirt that may interfere with the inspection procedure or mask defects. Make a general check of the wheels and tires as described in Chapter 1.
2 The wheels should be visually inspected for cracks, flat spots on the rim and other damage. Since tubeless tires are involved, look very closely for dents in the area where the tire bead contacts the rim. Dents in this area may prevent complete sealing of the tire against the rim, which leads to deflation of the tire over a period of time.
3 If damage is evident, the wheel will have to be replaced with a new one. Never attempt to repair a damaged wheel.

Removal

4 Securely block the wheels at the opposite end of the vehicle from the wheel being removed, so it can't roll.
5 Loosen the lug nuts on the wheel being removed. Jack up one end of the vehicle and support it securely on jackstands.
6 Remove the lug nuts and pull the wheel off.

Installation

7 Position the wheel on the studs. Make sure the directional arrow on the tire points in the forward rotating direction of the wheel.
8 Install the wheel nuts with their tapered sides toward the wheel. This is necessary to locate the wheel accurately on the hub.
9 Snug the wheel nuts evenly in a criss-cross pattern.
10 Remove the jackstands, lower the vehicle and tighten the wheel nuts, again in a criss-cross pattern, to the torque listed in this Chapter's Specifications.

3 Tires - general information

1 Tubeless tires are used as standard equipment on this vehicle. Unlike motorcycle tires, they run at very low air pressures and are completely unsuited for use on pavement. Inflating ATV tires to excessive pressures will rupture them, making replacement of the tire necessary.
2 The force required to break the seal between the rim and the bead of the tire is substantial, much more than required for motorcycle tires, and is beyond the capabilities of an individual working with normal tire irons or even a normal bead breaker. A special bead breaker is required for ATV tires; it produces a great deal of force and concentrates it in a relatively small area.
3 Also, repair of the punctured tire and replacement on the wheel rim requires special tools, skills and experience that the average do-it-yourselfer lacks.
4 For these reasons, if a puncture or flat occurs with an ATV tire, the wheel should be removed from the vehicle and taken to a dealer service department or a repair shop for repair or replacement of the tire. The illustrations at the end of this Chapter can be used as a guide to tire replacement in an emergency, provided the necessary bead breaker is available.

4 Front wheel hub and bearing - removal and installation

Removal

Note: *This procedure applies to either front hub.*

1 Remove the front wheel (see Section 2).
2 Remove the disc outer cover **(see illustration)**, if equipped.
3 Bend back the cotter pin and pull it out of the hub nut **(see illustration)**.
4 Have an assistant apply the front brake while you loosen the hub nut **(see illustration)**. Remove the hub nut and the washer.
5 Remove the front brake caliper and inner disc cover (see Section 6). The inner cover itself doesn't interfere with hub removal, but the caliper can't be removed without detaching the inner cover from the steering knuckle. It's not necessary to disconnect the brake hose from the caliper; set the caliper aside and hang it from the suspension with a coat hanger.

4.6 You may need a slide hammer and adapter to pull the hub off the spindle

5.2 Pull on the caliper body to press the pistons in and provide removal clearance for the pads

6 Pull the hub off the spindle. If the hub is stuck, remove it with a puller **(see illustration)**.

Bearing inspection and replacement

7 Wipe off the spindle and hub.

Caution: *Do NOT immerse the hub in any kind of cleaning solvent. The sealed hub bearings, which cannot be disassembled and repacked, could be damaged if any solvent enters them.*

8 Insert your fingers into each hub bearing and turn the bearing. If the bearing feels rough or dry, replace it.
9 Pry out the old seals and discard them.
10 To drive each bearing from the hub, lay the hub on a workbench, with the outer side of the hub facing down, then insert a soft metal (brass) drift into the hub from the inner side of the hub, push the floating spacer to the side and tap gently against the inner face of the outer bearing. Then flip over the hub, inner side facing down, insert the drift from the outer side of the hub, and drive out the inner bearing the same way.
11 To install the new bearings, drive them into place with an old socket. The socket must have an outside diameter that's the same, or slightly smaller than, the outer diameter of the bearings.

Caution: *Do NOT strike the center race or the ball bearings.*

12 Tap new inner and outer seals into place with a block of wood. Do NOT use the old seals.

Installation

13 Installation is the reverse of removal. Lubricate the spindle with wheel bearing grease. Tighten the hub nut to the torque listed in this Chapter's Specifications. If necessary, tighten it an additional amount to align the cotter pin slots. Don't loosen the nut to align the slots. Install a new cotter pin and bend it to secure the nut.

5 Front brake pads - replacement

Note: *Always replace both pairs of brake pads at the same time.*

1 Remove the front wheel (see Section 2). Remove the outer disc cover.
2 Slide the caliper to compress the pistons into the bore, providing removal clearance for the pads **(see illustration)**.
3 Loosen the brake pad retaining bolts **(see illustration)**. The pad retaining bolts are easier to loosen while the caliper is still bolted to the steering knuckle.
4 If you're removing the caliper to overhaul it, remove the brake hose-to-caliper banjo bolt **(see illustrations)** and disconnect the brake hose from the caliper now. If you're only removing the caliper to replace the brake pads, or to remove the steering knuckle, do NOT disconnect the brake hose from the caliper.

5.3 Loosen - but don't remove - the brake pad retaining bolts while the caliper is still bolted to the steering knuckle

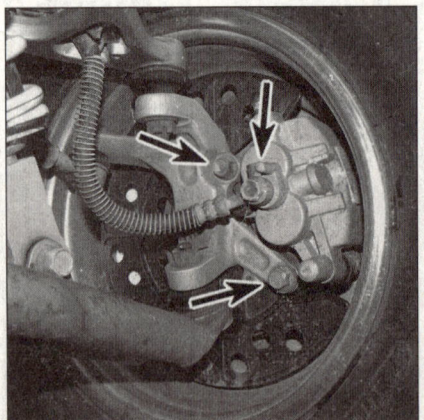

5.4a YFZ450 caliper mounting bolts (left arrows) and brake hose banjo fitting (right arrow); be sure the tab on the brake hose fits against the stop on the caliper as shown

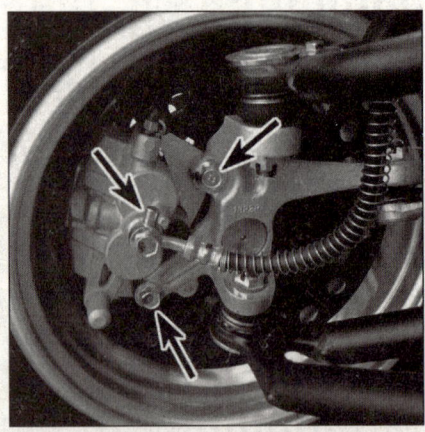

5.4b YFZ450R caliper mounting bolts (right arrows) and brake hose banjo fitting (left arrow); be sure the tab on the brake hose fits against the stop on the caliper as shown

Brakes, wheels and tires 7•5

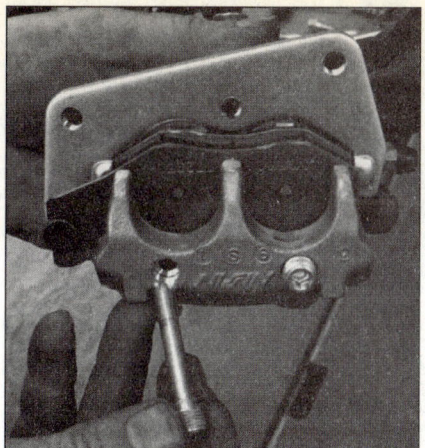

5.7 Remove the caliper, then remove the pad retaining bolts

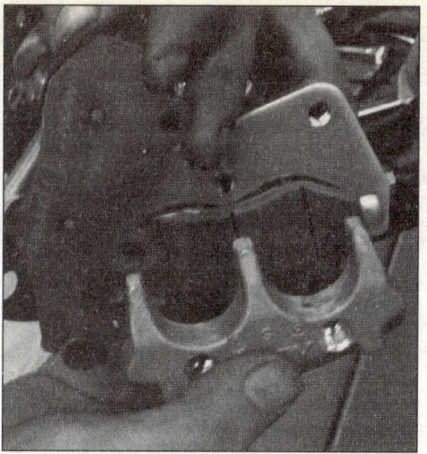

5.8a Remove the outer brake pad, noting how the notches end fits against the pin . . .

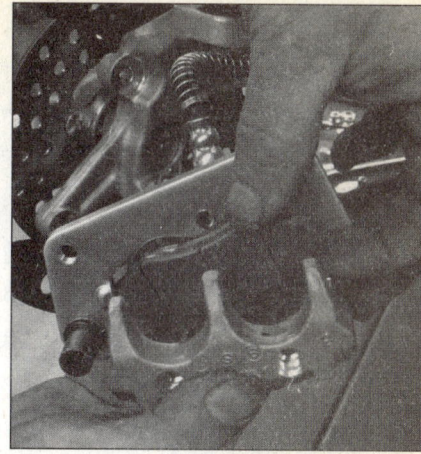

5.8b . . . and the inner pad

5 Unbolt the caliper from the steering knuckle **(see illustration 5.4a or 5.4b)**.
6 Remove the caliper. If you're only removing the caliper to replace the brake pads, hang the caliper from the suspension with a coat hanger.

Caution: Do NOT allow the caliper to hang from its brake hose.

7 Remove the brake pad retaining bolts **(see illustration)**.
8 Remove the brake pads **(see illustrations)**.
9 Inspect the pad spring **(see illustration)**. If it's damaged or distorted, replace it.
10 If the inner brake pad has a shim, remove it and install it on the new inner pad.
11 Check the area around the pistons for fluid leakage **(see illustration)**. If fluid has been leaking past the pistons, overhaul the caliper as described in Section 6.
12 Installation is the reverse of removal. Using a C-clamp, depress the pistons back into the caliper bores to provide enough room for the new pads to clear the disc. Be sure to tighten the caliper bolts to the torque listed in this Chapter's Specifications. Apply non-permanent thread locking agent to the threads of the brake pad bolts and tighten them to the torque listed in this Chapter's Specifications **(see illustration)**.
13 Replace the brake pads on the other front caliper as described above.

6 Front brake caliper - removal, overhaul and installation

Warning: The dust created by the brake system is harmful to your health. Never blow it out with compressed air

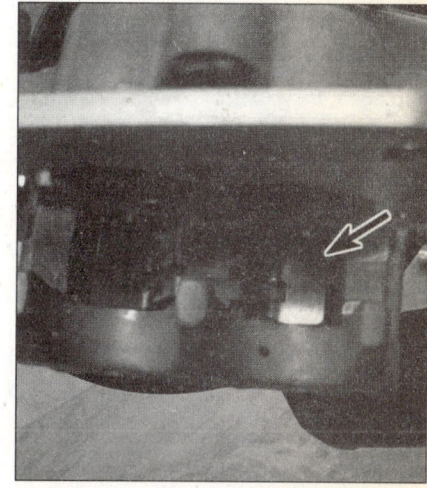

5.9 Check the pad spring and replace it if it's worn or damaged

5.11 Check the area around the pistons (arrows) for fluid leaks

5.12 Apply non-permanent thread locking agent to the threads of the pad retaining pins and tighten them to the torque listed in this Chapter's Specifications

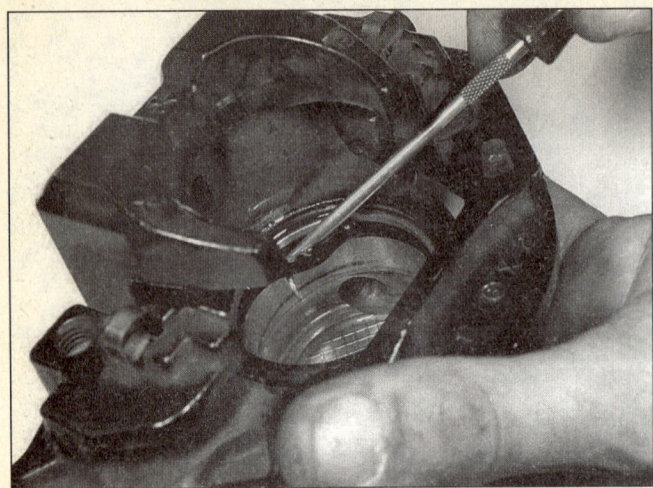

6.6 Remove the old piston seal from its groove in the bore with a toothpick (if you use a metal tool, don't scratch the bore)

7.3 To measure front disc runout, position a dial indicator so that its probe is about half an inch from the outer edge of the disc

and don't inhale any of it. An approved filtering mask should be worn when working on the brakes. Do not, under any circumstances, use petroleum-based solvents to clean brake parts. Use brake cleaner only!

Note: *This procedure applies to both front calipers.*

Removal

1 Disconnect the brake hose from the caliper, remove the caliper from the steering knuckle and remove the brake pads, shim (if equipped) and pad spring (see Section 5).

Overhaul

2 Clean the exterior of the caliper with denatured alcohol or brake system cleaner.
3 Place a few rags between the piston and the caliper frame to act as a cushion, lay the caliper on the work bench so that the piston is facing down, toward the work bench surface, then use compressed air, directed into the fluid inlet, to remove the piston(s). Use only small quick blasts of air to ease the piston out of the bore. If a piston is blown out with too much force, it might be damaged.

 Warning: *Never place your fingers in front of the piston in an attempt to catch or protect it when applying compressed air. Doing so could result in serious injury.*

4 If compressed air isn't available, reconnect the caliper to the brake hose and pump the brake lever until the piston is free. You'll have to put brake fluid in the master cylinder reservoir and get most of the air out of the hose to use this method.
5 Once the piston is protruding from the caliper, remove it and the old dust seal.
6 Using a wood or plastic tool, remove the piston seal **(see illustration)**.
7 Clean the piston and piston bore with denatured alcohol, fresh brake fluid or brake system cleaner and dry them off with filtered, unlubricated compressed air. Inspect the surfaces of the piston and the piston bores for rust, corrosion, nicks, burrs and loss of plating. If you find defects on the surface of either piston or piston bore, replace the piston and caliper assembly (the piston is matched to the caliper). If the caliper is in bad shape, inspect the master cylinder too.
8 Lubricate the new piston seal with clean brake fluid and install it in its groove in the caliper bore. Make sure it's not twisted and is fully and correctly seated.
9 Lubricate the piston with clean brake fluid and install it into its bore in the caliper. Using your thumbs, push the piston all the way in; make sure it doesn't become cocked in the bore.
10 Install the new dust seal. Make sure that the inner lip of the seal is seated in its groove in the piston and the outer circumference of the seal is seated in its groove in the caliper bore.

Installation

11 Install the caliper and brake pads (see Section 5).
12 Install the brake hose-to-caliper banjo bolt **(see illustration 5.4a or 5.4b)**. Be sure to use new sealing washers. Tighten the banjo bolt to the torque listed in this Chapter's Specifications.
13 Remove and overhaul the other front brake caliper.
14 Bleed the front brake system (see Section 15).

7 Front brake disc - inspection, removal and installation

Note: *This procedure applies to both front discs.*

1 Remove the front wheels (see Section 2).

Inspection

2 Visually inspect the surface of the disc for score marks and other damage. Light scratches are normal after use and won't affect brake operation, but deep grooves and heavy score marks will reduce braking efficiency and accelerate pad wear. If the disc is badly grooved it must be machined or replaced.
3 To check disc runout, mount a dial indicator with the plunger on the indicator touching the surface of the disc about 1/2-inch from the outer edge **(see illustration)**. Slowly turn the wheel hub and watch the indicator needle, comparing your reading with the disc runout limit listed in this Chapter's Specifications. If the runout is greater than allowed, replace the disc.
4 The disc must not be machined or allowed to wear to a thickness less than the minimum listed in this Chapter's Specifications. The thickness of the disc can be checked with a micrometer. If the thickness of the disc is less than the minimum, it must be replaced.

Removal and installation

5 Remove the front wheel hub (see Section 4).
6 To detach the brake disc from the hub, remove the four disc retaining bolts.

Brakes, wheels and tires 7•7

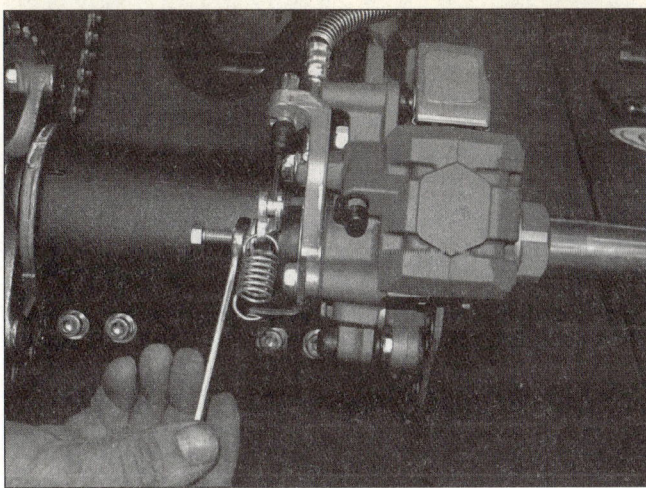

8.1a Loosen the locknut and back off the parking brake adjusting bolt

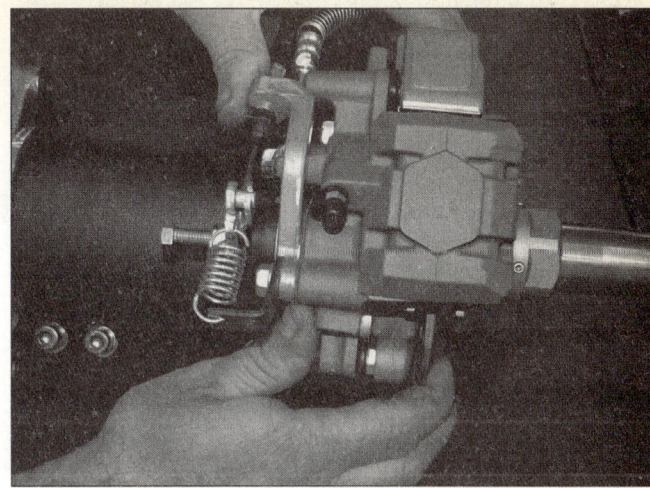

8.1b Slide the caliper, compressing the piston(s) into the bore to provide removal clearance for the pads

7   Installation is the reverse of removal. Tighten the disc retaining bolts to the torque listed in this Chapter's Specifications.

8 Rear brake pads - replacement

Warning: *The dust created by the brake system is harmful to your health. Never blow it out with compressed air and don't inhale any of it. An approved filtering mask should be worn when working on the brakes. Do not, under any circumstances, use petroleum-based solvents to clean brake parts. Use brake cleaner only!*

1   Loosen the parking brake adjusting locknut and back off the bolt, then pull the caliper body toward the bracket to press the piston in slightly **(see illustrations)**. This will free the pads so they will be easier to remove.

2   Loosen the brake pad retaining bolts **(see illustration)**. **Note:** *The brake pad retaining bolts are secured with thread locking agent and will be easier to loosen while the caliper is still bolted onto the caliper bracket.*

3   If you're planning to overhaul the caliper, remove the brake hose-to-caliper banjo bolt **(see illustrations)**, disconnect the brake hose from the caliper and discard the old sealing washers. If you're simply replacing the brake pads, or if you're only removing the caliper to remove other components, such as the axle, do NOT disconnect the brake hose.

8.2 Before removing the rear caliper, loosen both of the brake pad retaining bolts

8.3a Remove the caliper mounting bolts (socket on left bolt, lower arrow indicates right bolt); be sure the tab on the banjo fitting (upper arrow) is against the stop on the caliper when the hose is installed

8.3b Lift the caliper off and remove the pad retaining bolts

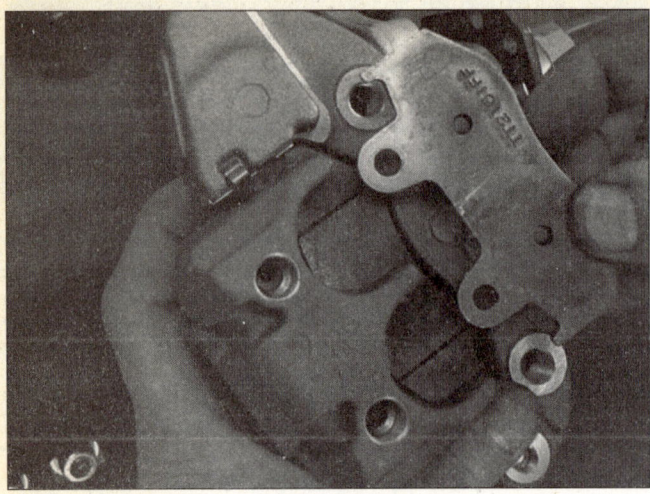

8.5a Remove the outer brake pad - on installation, fit the tab on the end of the pad into the caliper notch and engage the spring . . .

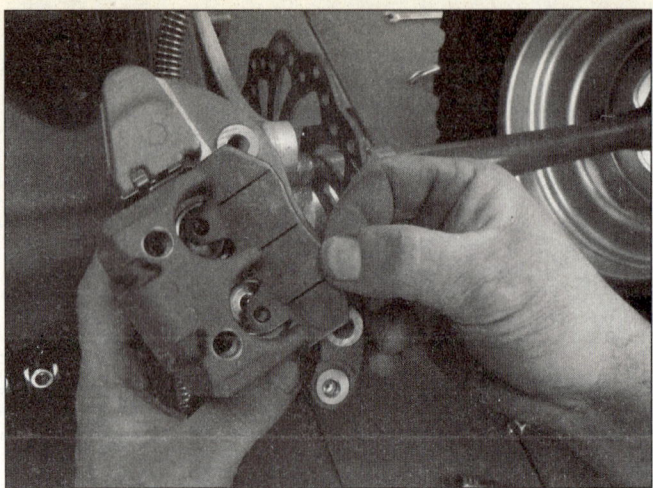

8.5b . . . and the inner pad - its tab also fits into the notch and engages the spring

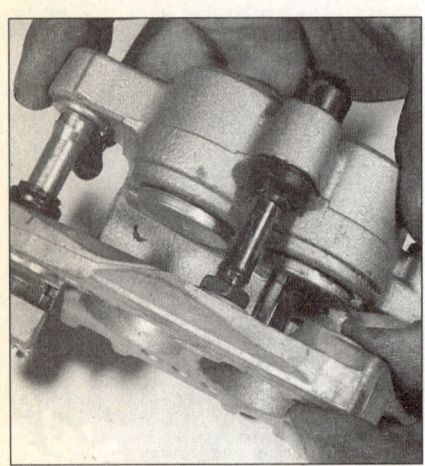

9.6 Slide the caliper off the bracket

4 Remove the brake caliper bolts **(see illustration 8.3a)** and take the caliper off **(see illustration 8.3b)**. While the caliper is off the disc, tie it up out of the way.
5 Remove the brake pad retaining bolts and lockplate, then remove the brake pads **(see illustration 8.3b and the accompanying illustrations)**.
6 Check the area around the pistons for brake fluid leakage. If fluid has been leaking, overhaul the caliper (see Section 9).
7 If you're working on a 2004 or 2005 YFZ450R, remove the shim from the inner pad (the pad closest to the piston) and install it on the new inner pad. Be sure to install the shim so that its arrow mark points in the same direction that the disc rotates when the vehicle is moving forward.
8 Installation is otherwise the reverse of removal. If you disconnected the brake fluid hose from the caliper, reinstall it with its anti-twist stopper against the boss on the caliper **(see illustration 8.3a)**. Use new sealing washers on the banjo fitting and tighten the bolt to the torque listed in this Chapter's Specifications. Be sure to tighten the caliper retaining bolts and the pad retaining bolts to the torque listed in this Chapter's Specifications.

9 Rear brake caliper - removal, overhaul and installation

Warning: The dust created by the brake system is harmful to your health. Never blow it out with compressed air and don't inhale any of it. An approved filtering mask should be worn when working on the brakes. Do not, under any circumstances, use petroleum-based solvents to clean brake parts. Use brake cleaner only!

Removal

1 Disconnect the parking brake cable.
2 Disconnect the brake hose from the caliper, remove the caliper and remove the brake pads (see Section 8).

Overhaul

3 Clean the exterior of the caliper with denatured alcohol or brake system cleaner.
4 Loosen the parking brake adjuster locknut and unscrew the bolt **(see illustration 8.1a)**. Remove the parking brake lever and return spring.
5 Remove the parking brake case Allen bolts, detach the case/bracket assembly from the caliper body and remove the gasket **(see illustration 9.16)**. Set the parking brake case aside for now.
6 Separate the caliper bracket from the caliper **(see illustration)**.
7 Place a few rags between the piston and the caliper frame to act as a cushion, lay the caliper on the work bench so that the piston is facing down, toward the work bench surface, then use compressed air, directed into the fluid inlet, to remove the piston. Use only small quick blasts of air to ease the piston out of the bore. If a piston is blown out with too much force, it might be damaged.

Warning: Never place your fingers in front of the piston in an attempt to catch or protect it when applying compressed air. Doing so could result in serious injury.

8 If compressed air isn't available, reconnect the caliper to the brake hose and pump the brake lever until the piston is free. You'll have to put brake fluid in the master cylinder reservoir and get most of the air out of the hose to use this method.
9 Once the piston is protruding from the caliper, remove it **(see illustration)** and remove the old dust seal **(see illustration)**.
10 Using a wood or plastic tool, remove the piston seal **(see illustration 9.9b)**.
11 Clean the piston and piston bore with denatured alcohol, fresh brake fluid or brake system cleaner and dry them off with filtered, unlubricated compressed air. Inspect the surfaces of the piston and the piston bores for rust, corrosion, nicks, burrs and loss of plating. If you find defects on the surface of either piston or piston bore, replace the piston and caliper assembly (the piston is matched to the caliper). If the caliper is in bad shape, also inspect the master cylinder. Check the pin boot **(see illustration)** for damage or deterioration and replace it if problems are found.
12 Lubricate the new piston seal with clean brake fluid and install it in its groove in the caliper bore. Make sure it's not twisted and is fully and correctly seated.
13 Lubricate the piston with clean brake

Brakes, wheels and tires

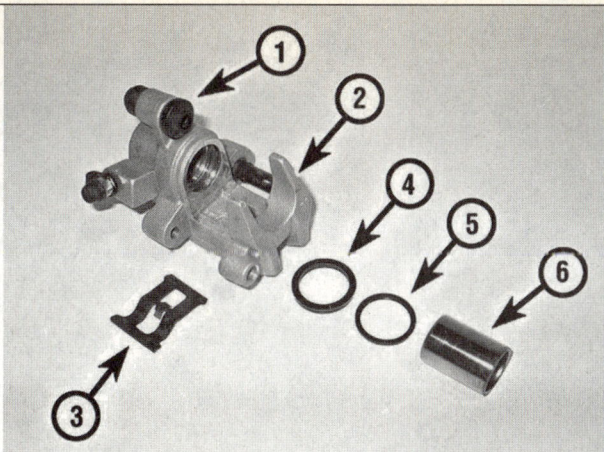

9.9a Rear caliper details (single-piston model shown; later models have an additional piston)

1. Pin boot
2. Caliper body
3. Pad spring
4. Piston seal
5. Dust seal
6. Piston

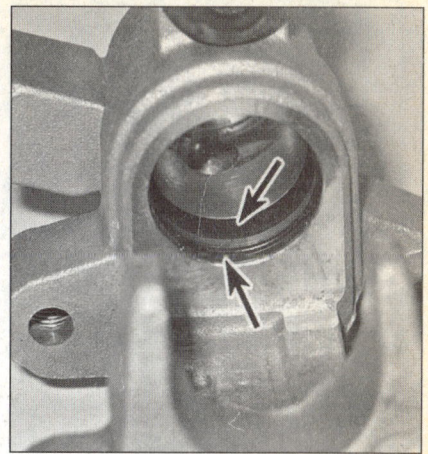

9.9b Remove the dust seal (lower arrow) and piston seal (upper arrow) with a wood or plastic tool

fluid and install it into its bore in the caliper. Using your thumbs, push the piston all the way in; make sure it doesn't become cocked in the bore.

14 Install the new dust seal. Make sure that the inner lip of the seal is seated in its groove in the piston and the outer circumference of the seal is seated in its groove in the caliper bore.

15 If you're working on a 2004 or 2005 YFZ450, remove the spring, adjuster nut and bearing from the parking brake case. The bearing consists of three parts: a bearing race without a tab on its outer edge, three balls, and another bearing race with a tab on its outer edge.

16 If you're working on a 2006 or later YFZ450 or YFZ450R, remove the case cover from the case **(see illustration)**. Unscrew the parking brake shaft from the parking brake case.

2004 and 2005 YFZ450

17 Reassembly of the parking brake case is essentially the reverse of disassembly. Make sure that the tab on the bearing race is aligned with the slit in the parking brake case and the bearing race grooves face toward the balls. Be sure to grease the bearing balls and races. Tighten the parking brake case bolts to the torque listed in this Chapter's Specifications. When installing the parking brake lever, make sure it's positioned as shown in the parking brake adjustment procedure in Chapter 1.

2006 and later YFZ450 and YFZ450R

18 Lubricate the parking brake shaft with grease and install it in the case. The notch in the hex end of the parking brake shaft is installed between the two notches on the case next to the shaft bore.

19 When installing the parking brake lever, make sure it's positioned as shown in the parking brake adjustment procedure in Chapter 1.

Installation

20 Install the caliper and brake pads (see Section 8).
21 Connect the brake hose-to-caliper banjo bolt, making sure its stop is against the boss on the caliper **(see illustration 8.3a)**. Be sure to use new sealing washers. Tighten the banjo bolt to the torque listed in this Chapter's Specifications.
22 Bleed the front brake system (see Section 15).
23 Adjust the parking brake (see Chapter 1).

10 Rear wheel hubs - removal and installation

1 Remove the rear wheels (see Section 2).
2 Bend back the cotter pin and pull it out of the hub nut **(see illustration)**.
3 Apply the parking brake to lock the rear axle. Unscrew the hub nut and remove the washer.

9.11 Check the pin boot for deterioration or damage

9.16 The rubber boot (left arrow) is installed in the parking brake case/bracket (right arrow)

10.2 Remove the cotter pin, then unscrew the nut and remove the washer

7•10 Brakes, wheels and tires

10.4 Pull the hub off and clean the splines

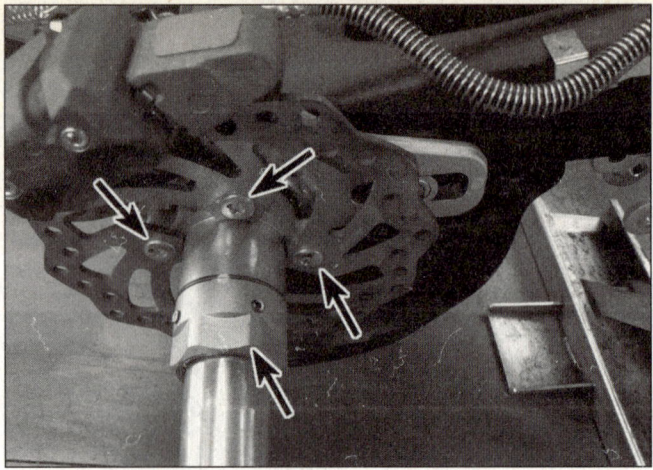

11.6 To detach the rear disc from the axle, remove these four Allen bolts (lower bolt hidden)

4 Pull the hub off the axle shaft (see illustration). Clean the hub and the axle splines.
5 Installation is the reverse of removal.

11 Rear brake disc - inspection, removal and installation

Inspection

1 Visually inspect the surface of the disc for score marks and other damage. Light scratches are normal after use and won't affect brake operation, but deep grooves and heavy score marks will reduce braking efficiency and accelerate pad wear. If the disc is badly grooved, it must be machined or replaced.
2 To check disc runout, mount a dial indicator with the plunger on the indicator touching the surface of the disc about 1/2-inch from the outer edge (see illustration 7.3). Slowly turn the wheel hub and watch the indicator needle, comparing your reading with the disc runout limit listed in this Chapter's Specifications. If the runout is greater than allowed, replace the disc.
3 The disc must not be machined, or allowed to wear, to a thickness less than the minimum listed in this Chapter's Specifications. The thickness of the disc can be checked with a micrometer. If the thickness of the disc is less than the minimum, it must be replaced.

Removal and installation

4 Remove the right rear wheel hub (see Section 10).
5 Remove the rear caliper (see Section 9).
6 Remove the disc retaining bolts (see illustration) and remove the disc.
7 Installation is the reverse of removal. Be sure to tighten the disc retaining bolts to the torque listed in this Chapter's Specifications.

12 Front brake master cylinder - removal, overhaul and installation

1 If the front brake master cylinder is leaking fluid, or if the lever does not produce a firm feel when the brake lever is applied, and bleeding the brakes does not help, master cylinder overhaul is recommended.
2 Before disassembling the master cylinder, read through the entire procedure and make sure that you have the correct rebuild kit. Also, you will need some new, clean brake fluid of the recommended type, some clean rags and internal snap-ring pliers.
Note: *To prevent damage to the paint from spilled brake fluid, always cover the top cover or upper fuel tank when working on the master cylinder.*

Caution: *Disassembly, overhaul and reassembly of the brake master cylinder must be done in a spotlessly clean work area to avoid contamination and possible failure of the brake hydraulic system components.*

Removal

3 Remove the reservoir cover retaining screw. Remove the reservoir and the rubber diaphragm. Siphon as much brake fluid from the reservoir as you can to avoid spilling it on the bike.
4 Pull back the rubber dust boot and loosen the brake hose banjo bolt (see illustration), then separate the brake hose from the master cylinder. Wrap the end of the hose in a clean rag and suspend the hose in an upright position or bend it down carefully and place the open end in a clean container. The objective is to prevent excessive loss of brake fluid, fluid spills and system contamination.
5 Remove the master cylinder mounting bolts (see illustration) and separate the master cylinder from the handlebar.

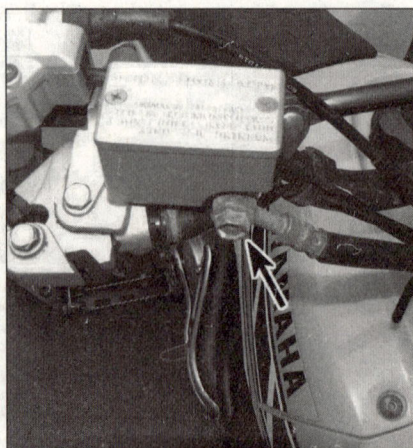

12.4 Remove the banjo bolt (arrow); use new sealing washers on assembly

12.5 Remove the master cylinder clamp bolts (arrows); the arrow on the clamp must point up when installed

Brakes, wheels and tires 7•11

12.6 Front brake lever position adjusting bolt (lower arrow) and pivot bolt (upper arrow)

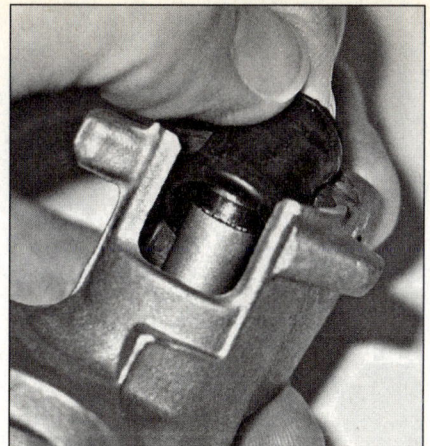

12.7a Remove the rubber boot . . .

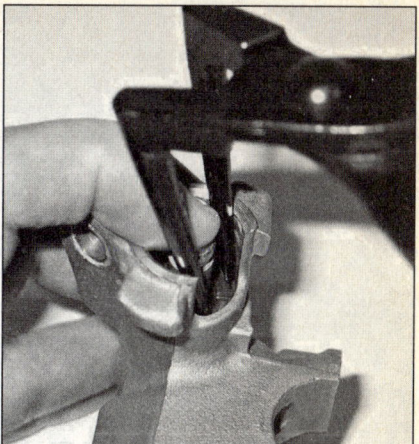

12.7b . . . compress the piston and remove the snap-ring

Caution: *Do not tip the master cylinder upside down or any brake fluid still in the reservoir will run out.*

Overhaul

6 Remove the brake lever pivot bolt nut, remove the pivot bolt and remove the lever **(see illustration)**.

7 Carefully remove the rubber dust boot from the end of the piston **(see illustration)**. Using snap-ring pliers, remove the snap-ring and slide out the piston assembly and the spring **(see illustrations)**.

8 Lay the parts out in the order in which they are removed to prevent confusion during reassembly.

9 Clean all of the parts with brake system cleaner (available at motorcycle dealerships and auto parts stores), isopropyl alcohol or clean brake fluid. Make sure the delivery port at the bottom of the master cylinder reservoir is clear **(see illustration)**.

Caution: *Do not, under any circumstances, use a petroleum-based solvent to clean brake parts. If compressed air is available, use it to dry the parts thoroughly (make sure it's filtered and unlubricated). Check the master cylinder bore for corrosion, scratches, nicks and score marks. If damage is evident, the master cylinder must be replaced with a new one. If the master cylinder is in poor condition, then the calipers should be checked as well.*

10 The dust seal, piston assembly and spring are included in the rebuild kit. Use all of the new parts, regardless of the apparent condition of the old ones.

11 Before reassembling the master cylinder, soak the piston and the rubber cup seals in clean brake fluid for ten or fifteen minutes. Lubricate the master cylinder bore with clean brake fluid, then carefully insert the piston and related parts in the reverse order of disassembly. Make sure the lips on the cup seals do not turn inside out when they are slipped into the bore.

12 Depress the piston, then install the snap-ring (make sure the snap-ring is properly seated in the groove). Install the rubber dust boot (make sure the lip is seated properly in the piston groove).

13 Lubricate the brake lever pivot bolt and the friction surface on the lever that pushes against the piston assembly.

Installation

14 Attach the master cylinder to the handlebar. Make sure that the arrow on the clamp is pointing up **(see illustration 12.5)**. Tighten the bolts to the torque listed in this Chapter's Specifications.

15 Connect the brake hose to the master cylinder, using new sealing washers. Tighten the banjo bolt to the torque listed in this Chapter's Specifications.

16 Fill the master cylinder with the recommended brake fluid (see Chapter 1), then bleed the front brake system (see Section 15).

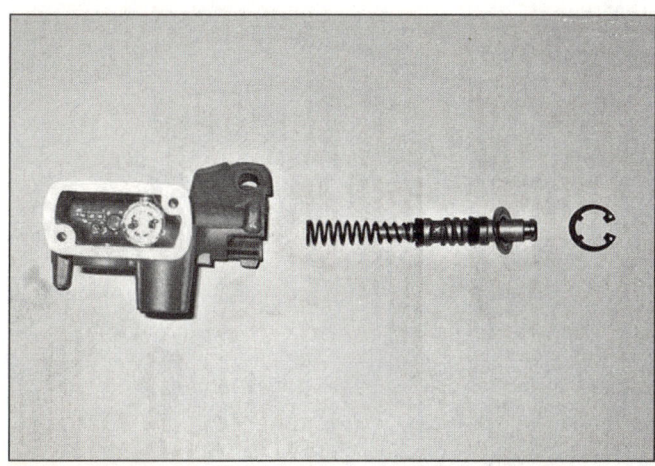

12.7c Remove the piston and spring from the bore

12.9 Make sure the fluid port in the bottom of the reservoir is clear - if there's a baffle plate, make sure it's securely installed

7•12 Brakes, wheels and tires

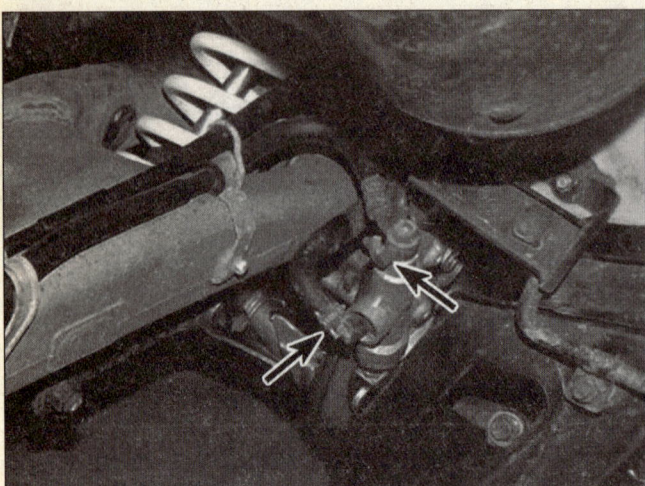

13.4a Reservoir hose clamp (left arrow) and banjo fitting stop (right arrow) locations (YFZ450)

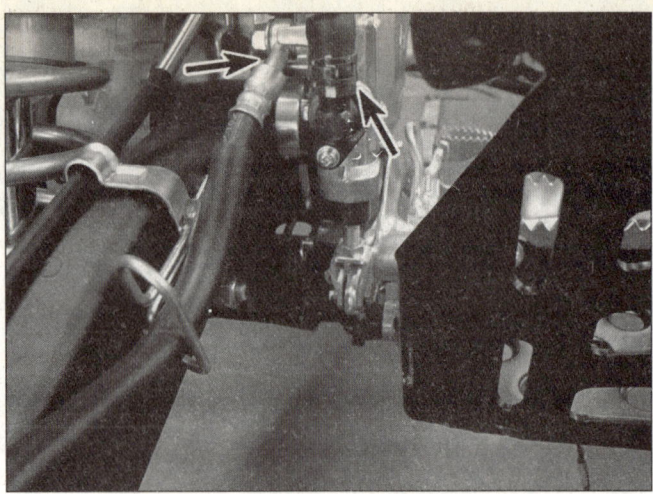

13.4b Disconnect the YFZ450R reservoir hose (right arrow) - on installation, position the neck of the master cylinder hose (left arrow) between the stops on the cylinder body

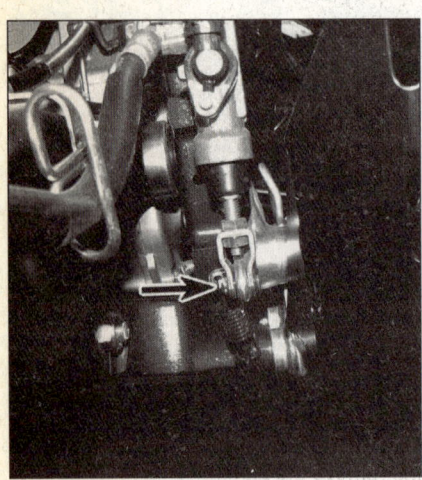

13.5 Remove the cotter pin (arrow) and push out the clevis pin to detach the master cylinder from the brake pedal

13 Rear brake master cylinder - removal, overhaul and installation

1 If the rear brake master cylinder is leaking fluid, or if the lever does not produce a firm feel when the brake pedal is applied, and bleeding the brakes does not help, master cylinder overhaul is recommended.

2 Before disassembling the master cylinder, read through the entire procedure and make sure that you have the correct rebuild kit. Also, you will need some new, clean brake fluid of the recommended type, some clean rags and internal snap-ring pliers. **Note:** *To prevent damage to the paint from spilled brake fluid, always cover the top cover or upper fuel tank when working on the master cylinder.*

Caution: Disassembly, overhaul and reassembly of the brake master cylinder must be done in a spotlessly clean work area to avoid contamination and possible failure of the brake hydraulic system components.

Removal

3 Unscrew the reservoir cover and siphon as much brake fluid from the reservoir as you can to avoid spilling it on the bike.

4 Squeeze the brake hose clamp **(see illustrations)** and slide it down the hose. Detach the brake hose coming from the master cylinder reservoir. Plug or pinch off the end of the hose and suspend the hose in an upright position or bend it down carefully and place the open end in a clean container. Try to prevent excessive loss of brake fluid, fluid spills and system contamination.

5 Remove the cotter pin and clevis pin, then disconnect the pushrod clevis from the rear brake pedal **(see illustration)**.

6 Remove the master cylinder mounting bolts **(see illustrations)** and detach the

13.6a Rear master cylinder banjo bolt (upper arrow) and mounting bolt (lower arrows) locations (YFZ450)

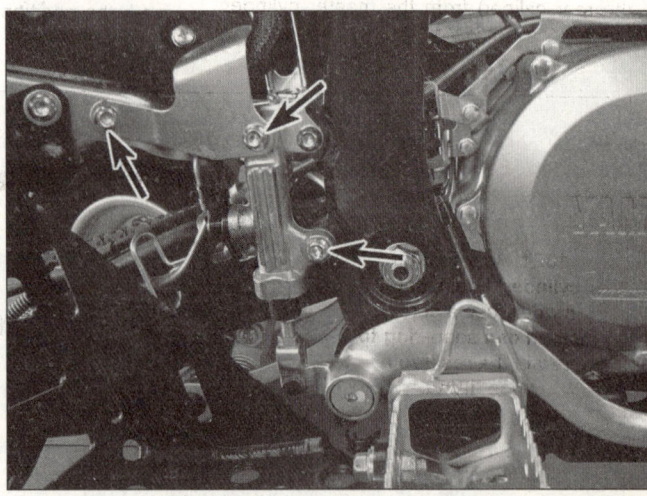

13.6b On YFZ450R models, remove the protective cover bolts and lower mounting bolt (arrow)

Brakes, wheels and tires 7•13

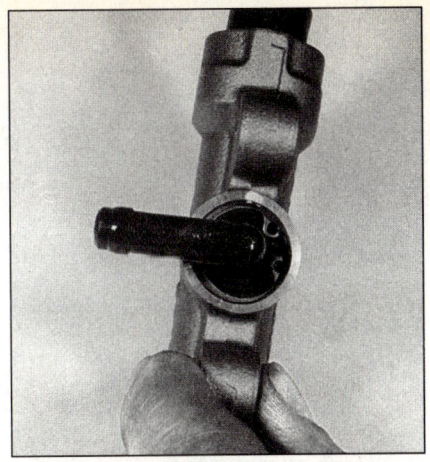

13.7a Remove the snap-ring (early models, shown) or screw (later models) to detach the reservoir hose fitting from the master cylinder

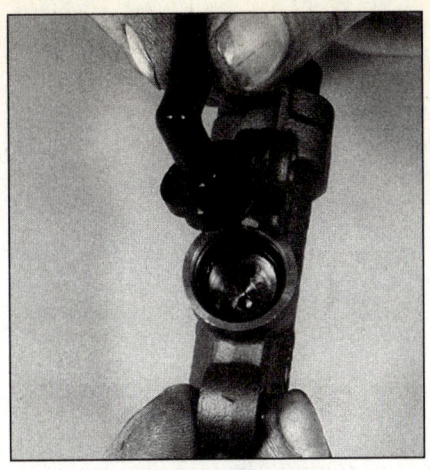

13.7b Lift the fitting out and remove its O-ring

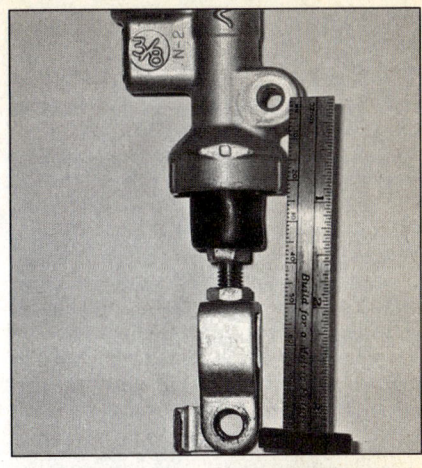

13.7c Measure the length of the pushrod and record it for later installation

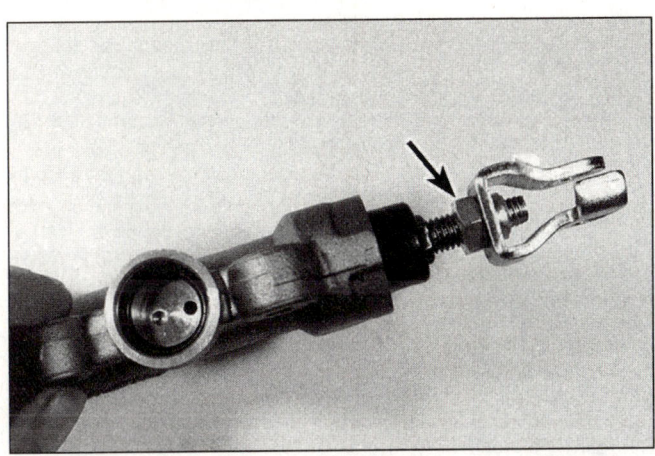

13.7d Loosen the locknut (arrow) and unscrew the pushrod clevis from the pushrod

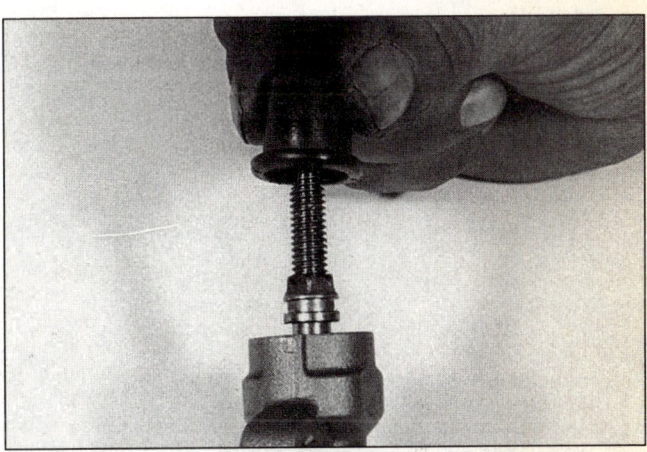

13.7e Take the dust boot off, then compress the piston, remove its snap-ring and remove the piston from the bore

master cylinder from the frame. Remove the banjo bolt to disconnect the brake hose (to the rear caliper) from the master cylinder. Discard the old sealing washers.

Overhaul

7 Back off the pushrod clevis locknut, mark the position of the clevis by marking the threads with a large felt pen or some other suitable marking agent, then unscrew the clevis from the pushrod. Unscrew and remove the locknut from the pushrod. Carefully remove the rubber dust boot from the pushrod. Using snap-ring pliers, remove the snap-ring and slide out the piston assembly and the spring (see illustrations).

8 Lay the parts out in the order in which they're removed to prevent confusion during reassembly.

9 Clean all of the parts with brake system cleaner (available at motorcycle dealerships and auto parts stores), isopropyl alcohol or clean brake fluid.

Caution: Do not, under any circumstances, use a petroleum-based solvent to clean brake parts. If compressed air is available, use it to dry the parts thoroughly (make sure it's filtered and unlubricated). Check the master cylinder bore for corrosion, scratches, nicks and score marks. If damage is evident, the master cylinder

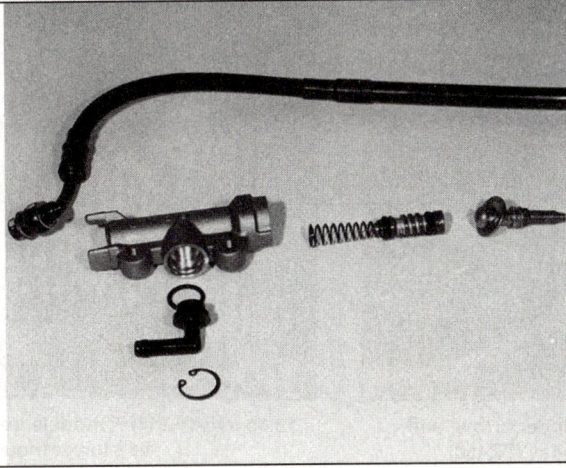

13.7f Rear master cylinder details (later models use a screw instead of a snap-ring to retain the reservoir hose fitting)

7•14 Brakes, wheels and tires

must be replaced with a new one. If the master cylinder is in poor condition, then the calipers should be checked as well.

10 The dust seal, piston assembly and spring are included in the rebuild kit. Use all of the new parts, regardless of the apparent condition of the old ones.

11 Before reassembling the master cylinder, soak the piston and the rubber cup seals in clean brake fluid for ten or fifteen minutes. Lubricate the master cylinder bore with clean brake fluid, then carefully insert the piston and related parts in the reverse order of disassembly. Make sure the lips on the cup seals do not turn inside out when they are slipped into the bore.

12 Depress the piston, then install the snap-ring (make sure the snap-ring is properly seated in the groove) **(see illustration)**.

13 Install the rubber dust boot onto the pushrod, push it all the way on and make sure the lip is seated correctly over the ridge on the end of the master cylinder. Install the locknut on the pushrod. Screw it on beyond the mark you made for the clevis prior to disassembly. Screw the clevis onto the pushrod. Make sure that it's aligned with the mark you made before disassembly. Tighten the locknut securely.

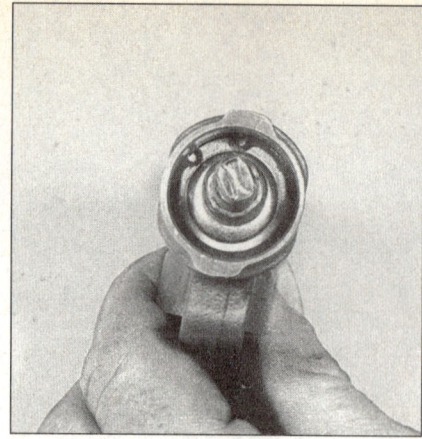

13.12 Make sure the snap-ring is seated in its groove

Installation

14 Connect the rear caliper brake hose to the master cylinder, using new sealing washers. Tighten the banjo bolt to the torque listed in this Chapter's Specifications.

15 Install the master cylinder on the frame and install - but don't tighten - the master cylinder retaining bolts.

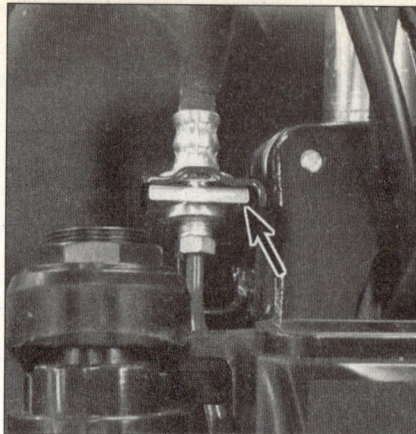

14.2a This clip (arrow) secures the front master cylinder hose to the metal line (YFZ450R shown) . . .

16 Reattach the pushrod clevis to the rear brake pedal.

17 Tighten the rear brake master cylinder retaining bolts to the torque listed in this Chapter's Specifications.

18 Reattach the reservoir hose to the master cylinder. Use a new hose clamp.

19 Fill the master cylinder with the recommended brake fluid (see Chapter 1), then bleed the front brake system (see Section 15).

14 Brake hoses and lines - inspection and replacement

Inspection

1 Once a week or, if the vehicle is used less frequently, before every ride, check the condition of the brake hoses.

2 Twist and flex the rubber hoses while looking for cracks, bulges and seeping fluid **(see illustrations)**. Check extra carefully

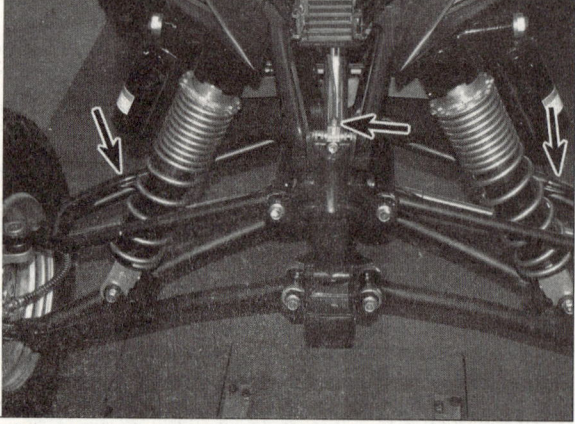

14.2b . . . the metal line is secured to a T-fitting (center arrow) by a flare nut - the front brake hoses run along the upper suspension arms and are protected by covers (left and right arrows)

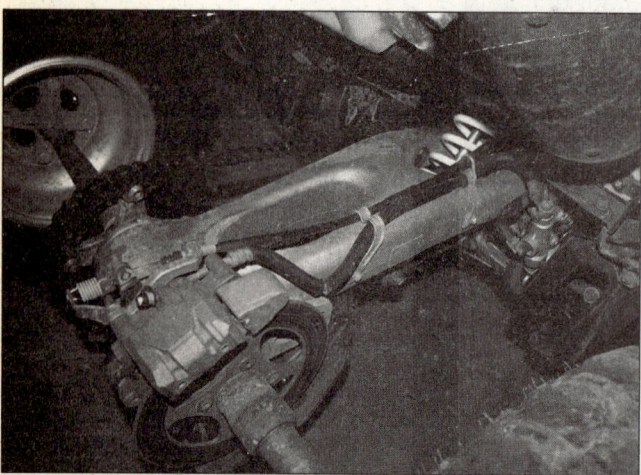

14.2c Rear brake hose and parking brake cable locations (YFZ450)

14.2d Rear brake hose and parking brake cable locations (YFZ450R)

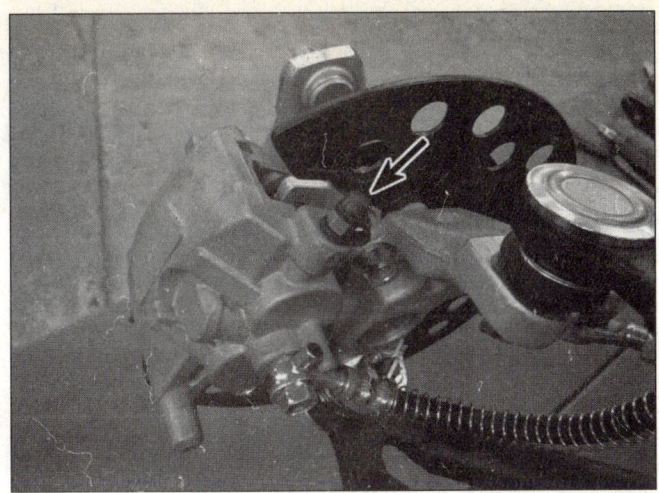

15.5a Front caliper bleed valve location

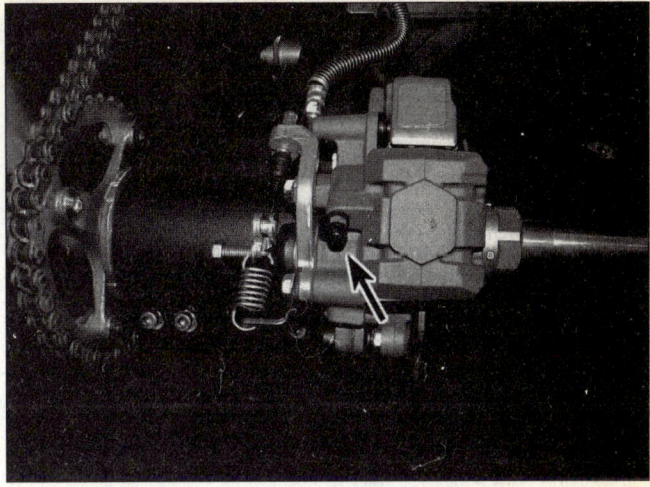

15.5b Rear caliper bleed valve location (2006 and later shown; earlier models similar)

around the areas where the hoses connect with the metal fittings, as these are common areas for hose failure.

3 Inspect the metal banjo fittings connected to the brake hoses. If the fittings are rusted, scratched or cracked, replace them.

Replacement

4 Cover the surrounding area with plenty of rags, then disconnect the ends of the hose. If you're replacing a brake hose, remove the banjo bolt from the caliper and disconnect the hose. Discard the old sealing washers.

5 To disconnect a front brake hose from a metal line, pull off the metal clip (see illustration 14.2a) with a pair of pliers, then unscrew the fitting with a flare nut wrench.

6 All rear brake hoses are attached to the rear master cylinder and to the rear caliper by banjo bolts.

7 Position the new hose, making sure it isn't twisted or otherwise strained, between the two components. Where a hose is attached by a banjo bolt, use new sealing washers on both sides of the fitting, and tighten banjo bolts to the torque listed in this Chapter's Specifications. On non-banjo fittings, tighten the fitting securely.

8 Flush the old brake fluid from the system, refill the system with the recommended fluid (see Chapter 1) and bleed the air from the system (see Section 15). Check the operation of the brakes carefully before riding the vehicle.

15 Brake system - bleeding

1 Bleeding the brake system removes all the air bubbles from the brake fluid reservoirs, the lines and the brake calipers. Bleeding is necessary whenever a brake system hydraulic connection is loosened, when a component or hose is replaced, or when the master cylinder or caliper is overhauled. Leaks in the system may also allow air to enter, but leaking brake fluid will reveal their presence and warn you of the need for repair.

2 To bleed the brakes, you will need some new, clean brake fluid of the recommended type (see Chapter 1), a length of clear vinyl or plastic tubing, a small container partially filled with clean brake fluid, some rags and a wrench to fit the brake caliper bleeder valves.

3 Cover the fuel tank and any other painted surfaces near the reservoir to prevent damage in the event that brake fluid is spilled.

4 Remove the front reservoir cover screws and remove the cover and diaphragm (or, on rear brakes, simply unscrew the reservoir cover). Slowly pump the brake lever (or brake pedal) a few times, until no air bubbles can be seen floating up from the holes at the bottom of the reservoir. Doing this bleeds the air from the master cylinder end of the line. Top up the reservoir with new fluid, then install the reservoir diaphragm and cover, but don't tighten the screws (or cover); you may have to remove the cover and diaphragm several times during the procedure.

5 Remove the rubber dust cover from the bleeder valve on the caliper (see illustrations) and slip a box wrench over the bleeder. Attach one end of the clear vinyl or plastic tubing to the bleed valve and submerge the other end in the brake fluid in the container.

6 Carefully pump the brake lever or brake pedal three or four times and hold it while opening the caliper bleeder valve. When the valve is opened, brake fluid will flow out of the caliper into the clear tubing and the lever will move toward the handlebar (or the pedal will move down). Retighten the bleeder valve, then release the brake lever or pedal.

7 Repeat this procedure until no air bubbles are visible in the brake fluid leaving the caliper and the lever or pedal is firm when applied. Note: *Remember to add fluid to the reservoir as the level drops. Use only new, clean brake fluid of the recommended type. Never re-use the fluid lost during bleeding.*

8 Keep an eye on the fluid level in the reservoir, especially if there's a lot of air in the system. Every time you crack open the bleeder valve, the fluid level in the reservoir drops a little. Do not allow the fluid level to drop below the lower mark during the bleeding process. If the level looks low, remove the reservoir cover and add some fluid.

9 Inspect the fluid level in the reservoir one more time, add some fluid if necessary, then install the diaphragm and reservoir cover and tighten the screws securely. Wipe up any spilled brake fluid and check the entire system for leaks. Note: *If bleeding is difficult, it may be necessary to let the brake fluid in the system stabilize for a few hours (it may be aerated). Repeat the bleeding procedure when the tiny bubbles in the system have settled out.*

16 Rear axle hub and bearings - removal, inspection and installation

Removal

1 Jack up the rear end of the vehicle and support it securely on jackstands.

2 Remove the rear wheels (see Section 2).

3 Remove the drive chain and rear axle (see Chapter 6).

4 If you need to remove the hub to replace it or the swingarm, unbolt it from the swing-

16.5 Pry the seal out of each end of the hub

16.6 Check the bearings for roughness, looseness or noise . . .

16.7 . . . and if problems are found, remove them and the spacer (arrow) (see text)

16.12 Align the arrowhead cast in the hub with the indicator cast on the swingarm (arrow)

arm and take it off the vehicle. The seals and hub bearings can be inspected and replaced with the hub installed on the vehicle.

Inspection and bearing replacement

5 Pry out the seal from each side of the hub **(see illustration)**.
6 Spin the bearing inside each end of the hub and check for roughness, looseness or noise **(see illustration)**.
7 Insert a metal drift or punch into the hub and tilt it so it pushes the spacer aside and catches the edge of the bearing on the far side **(see illustration)**. Tap gently against the bearing, on opposite sides of the bearing, to drive it from the hub. Insert the drift from the other side and drive the other bearing out in the same way. Remove the spacers.
8 The new bearings should be sealed on both sides. Place one of the new bearings in the hub. Tap the bearing into position with a bearing driver or socket the same diameter as the bearing outer race.
9 Install the spacers, with the shorter one on the left side of the hub.
10 Install the remaining bearing in the same manner.
11 Install a new seal in each side of the hub with its lip facing into the hub. Coat the seal lips with multi-purpose grease.

Installation

12 Installation is the reverse of removal. If you're working on a YFZ450R, use new O-rings on the outside of the hub and align the center of the hub indicator with the case mark on the swingarm, **(see illustration)**. Be sure to tighten the hub nuts and bolts to the torque listed in this Chapter's Specifications.
13 Adjust the drive chain when you're done (see Chapter 1).

Brakes, wheels and tires 7•17

TIRE CHANGING SEQUENCE

Deflate the tire and remove the valve core. Release the bead on the side opposite the tire valve with an ATV bead breaker, following the manufacturer's instructions. Make sure you have the correct blades for the tire size (using the wrong size blade may damage the wheel, the tire or the blade). Lubricate the bead with water before removal (don't use soap or any type of lubricant).

Turn the tire over and release the other bead.

If one side of the wheel has a smaller flange, remove and install the tire from that side. Use two tire levers to work the bead over the edge of the rim.

Before installing, ensure that tire is suitable for wheel. Take note of any sidewall markings such as direction of rotation arrows, then work the first bead over the rim flange.

Use tire levers to start the second bead over the rim flange.

Hold the bead while you work the last section of it over the rim flange. Install the valve core and inflate the tire, making sure not to overinflate it.

Notes

Chapter 8
Bodywork and frame

Contents

Footrests - removal and installation	8	General information	1
Frame - general information, inspection and repair	10	Rear fender - removal and installation	7
Front bumper - removal and installation	3	Seat - removal and installation	2
Front fender - removal and installation	6	Side covers - removal and installation	5
Fuel tank cover - removal and installation	4	Skid plates - removal and installation	9

Degrees of difficulty

| Easy, suitable for novice with little experience | | Fairly easy, suitable for beginner with some experience | | Fairly difficult, suitable for competent DIY mechanic | | Difficult, suitable for experienced DIY mechanic |  | Very difficult, suitable for expert DIY or professional | |

1 General information

This Chapter covers the procedures necessary to remove and install the body panels and other body parts. Since many service and repair operations on these vehicles require removal of the panels and/or other body parts, the procedures are grouped here and referred to from other Chapters.

In the case of damage to the panels or other body parts, it is usually necessary to remove the broken component and replace it with a new (or used) one. The material that the plastic body parts is composed of doesn't lend itself to conventional repair techniques. There are, however, some shops that specialize in plastic welding, so it would be advantageous to check around first before throwing the damaged part away.

Note: *When attempting to remove any body panel, first study the panel closely, noting any fasteners and associated fittings, to be sure of returning everything to its correct place on installation. In some cases, the aid of an assistant will be required when removing panels, to help avoid damaging the surface. Once the visible fasteners have been removed, try to lift off the panel as described but DO NOT FORCE the panel - if it will not release, check that all fasteners have been removed and try again. Where a panel engages another by means of tabs and slots, be careful not to break the tabs or to damage the bodywork. Remember that a few moments of patience at this stage will save you a lot of money in replacing broken panels!*

8•2 Bodywork and frame

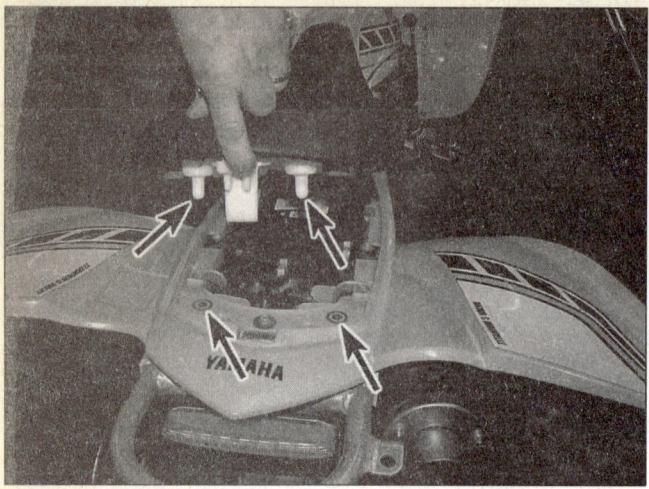

2.1a To release the seat, pull up this latch – the posts (upper arrows) go in the holes (lower arrows) on installation

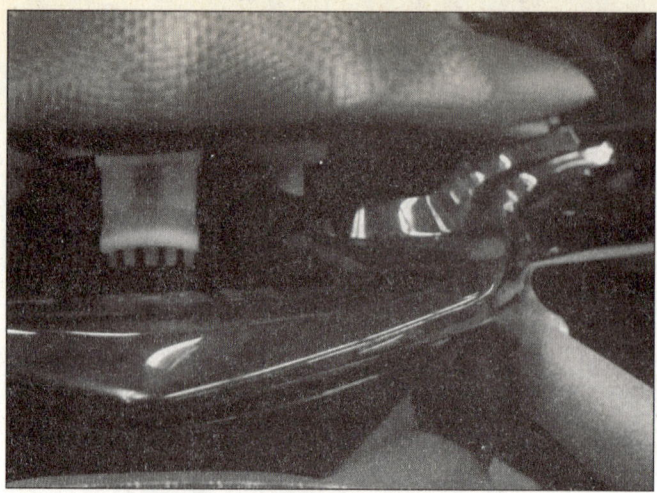

2.1b YFZ450R seat latch location

2.3a Make sure the hooks on the seat engage the catches on the frame (arrows)

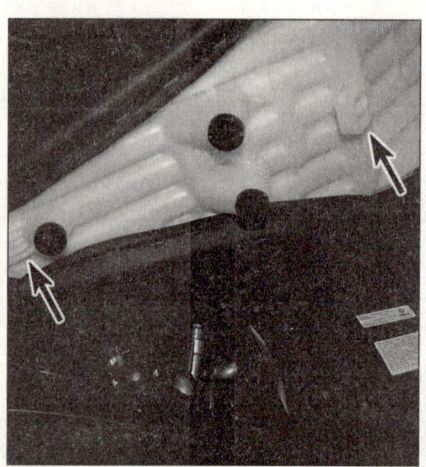

2.3b Here are the hooks that engage the catches on the frame (arrows)

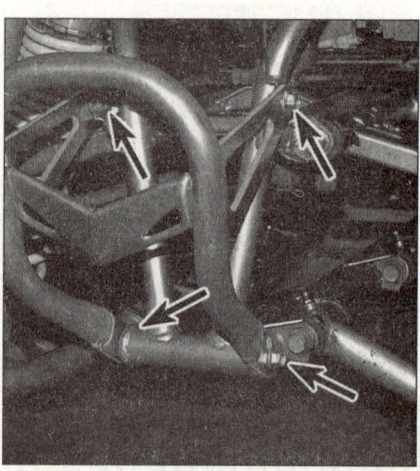

3.1a Front bumper mounting bolts (YFZ450)

3.1b Front bumper mounting bolts (YFZ450R)

2 Seat – removal and installation

1 Lift the latch at the rear of the seat (see illustration) and lift the back end of the seat.
2 Disengage the lobes at the front end of the seat from their corresponding receptacles in the frame and lift the seat off the vehicle.
3 Installation is the reverse of removal. Insert the lobe(s) at the front of the seat into the corresponding receptacle(s) in the frame (see illustrations).

3 Front bumper – removal and installation

1 Remove the bumper mounting bolts (see illustrations) and separate the bumper from the vehicle.
2 Installation is the reverse of removal. Tighten the bumper bolts securely.

4 Fuel tank cover – removal and installation

1 Remove two screws (YFZ450) or two quick-release fasteners (YFZ450R) at the front corners of the cover (see illustration).
2 Pull the fuel tank overflow hose out of the handlebar cover and remove the fuel tank filler cap (see illustration).
3 Remove the trim clips at the rear corners of the cover (see illustrations).
4 Disengage the tabs along the sides of the cover (see illustration). On YFZ450R models, disengage the tabs at the lower front

Bodywork and frame 8•3

4.1 Undo the quick-release fasteners (YFZ450R shown) or remove the screws at the front of the fuel tank cover

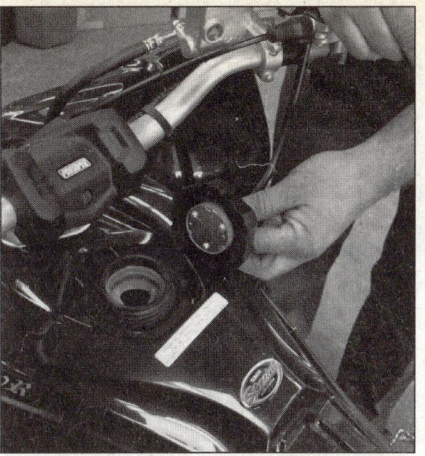

4.2 Pull the overflow hose out of the handlebar cover and unscrew the fuel tank cap

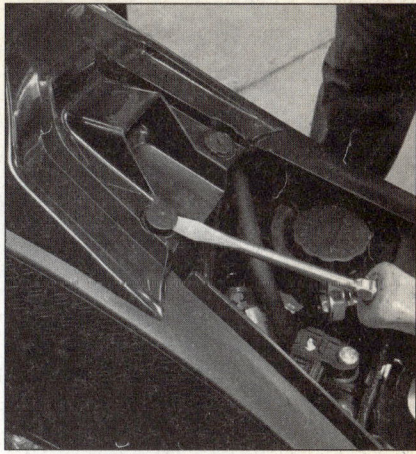

4.3a Pry up the centers of the trim clips . . .

4.3b . . . and pull them out

4.4a Disengage the tabs (arrows) from their slots

corners **(see illustration)**.

5 Installation is the reverse of removal. Make sure that the tabs on the lower edges of the cover are inserted into their corresponding slots in the front fender.

5 Side covers - removal and installation

1 Remove the seat and fuel tank cover (see Sections 2 and 4).
2 If you're working on a YFZ450, remove one screw at the rear corner, one at the upper front corner and one at the lower front corner. Take the side cover off.
3 If you're working on a YFZ450R, carefully pull the post at the front out of its grommet, then disengage the tab from the slot at the rear.

4 Installation is the reverse of the removal steps.

6 Front fender - removal and installation

1 Remove the seat, fuel tank cover and side covers (see Sections 2, 4 and 5).

YFZ450
2 Working under the front fender, locate and disconnect the wiring connectors for the headlights, indicator light panel and main key switch. Remove both headlights (see Chapter 5 if necessary).
3 Working under the fender, remove two screws with their heads facing the rear vehicle and two screws with their heads facing outward (away from the center of the vehicle). Remove two additional screws from each

4.4b On YFZ450R models, disengage the tab at each lower front corner (arrow)

8•4 Bodywork and frame

6.3 Remove the upper and rear fasteners on each side of the vehicle (arrows)

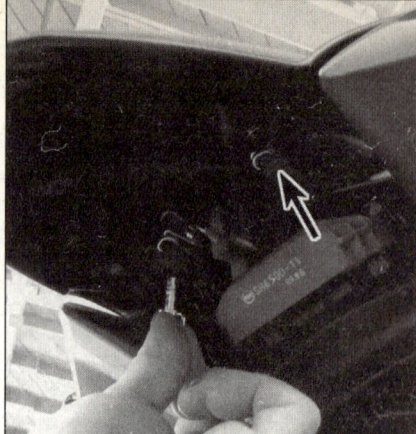

6.5 Undo the quick-release fasteners under the front of the fender

6.6 Remove the Allen screw (upper arrow) and bolt (lower arrow) on each side of the vehicle

side of the fender, one near the top of the fender on the inside and one at the lower rear corner **(see illustration)**. Lift the fender off.
4 Installation is the reverse of the removal steps.

YFZ450R

5 Working under the front of the front fender, remove two quick-release fasteners **(see illustration)**.
6 At the rear of the fender, remove an Allen screw and bolt from each side **(see illustration)**.
7 Lift the fender off, together with its side pieces.
8 Installation is the reverse of the removal steps.

7 Rear fender - removal and installation

1 Remove the seat (see Section 2).

2 If you're working on a YFZ450, remove the battery (see Chapter 5) and air cleaner housing (see Chapter 4A or 4B). Remove the rear fender retaining screws **(see illustration)** and lift the fender off.
3 If you're working on a YFZ450R, remove the quick release fasteners at the rear **(see illustrations)**. Remove two more, one at each front corner of the rear fender above the footrest, and lift the fender off.
4 Installation is the reverse of removal.

8 Footrests - removal and installation

1 To detach a footrest, remove the two Allen bolts that attach it to the foot plate and remove the two bolts that attach it to the frame.
2 To detach the plate, remove the footrest (see Step 1), then remove the nut that attaches the plate to the frame.
3 Installation is the reverse of removal.

9 Skid plates - removal and installation

1 Remove the protector bolts and nuts and remove the protector **(see illustration)**.
2 Installation is the reverse of removal.

10 Frame - general information, inspection and repair

1 All models use an aluminum frame. The YFZ450 frame is made in one piece, with a detachable rear extension made of steel tubing **(see illustration)**. The YFZ450R frame is made in sections, bolted together with safety Torx bolts (except for the rear sub-frame, which is secured by Allen bolts) **(see illustration)**. The frame, except for the rear sub-frame, is available only as a complete unit. The sub-frame is available separately.
2 The frame shouldn't require attention

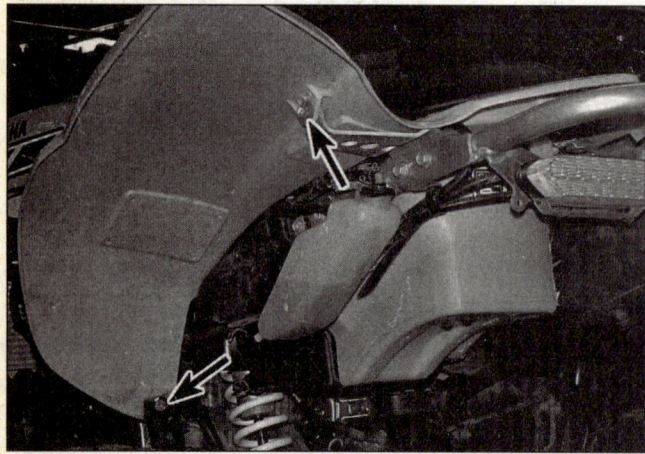

7.2 Remove the fasteners on each side of the vehicle (arrows)

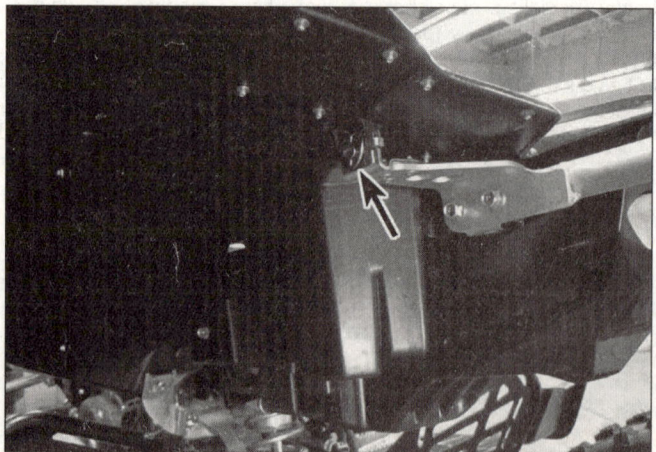

7.3a Undo the quick-release fasteners under the left rear side of the fender (arrow) . . .

Bodywork and frame 8•5

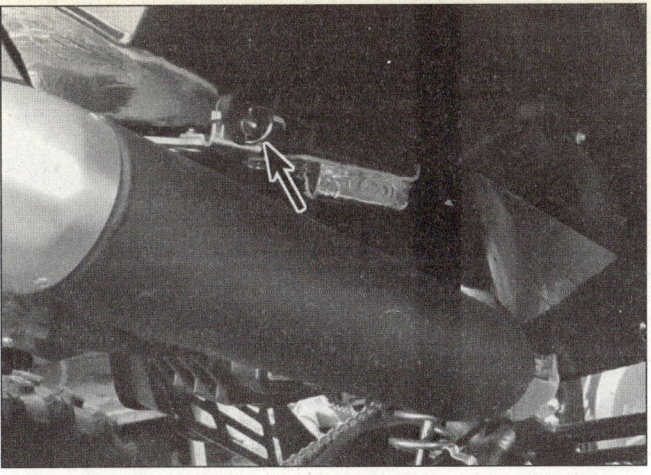

7.3b ... under the right rear side (arrow) ...

7.3c ... and one at each lower front corner (arrow)

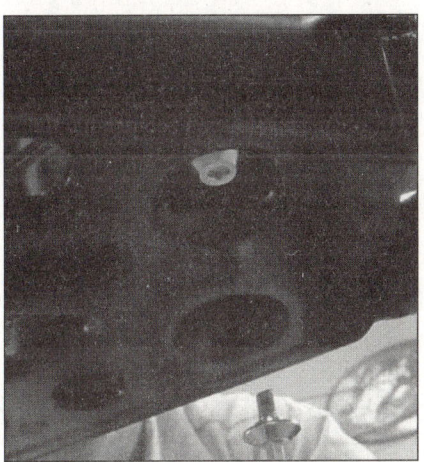

9.1 The engine and rear axle skid plates are bolted to the frame

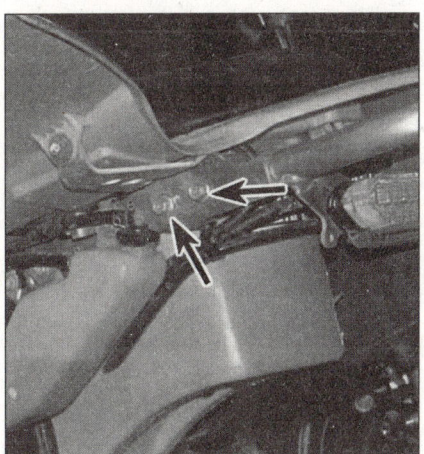

10.1a The YFZ450 frame tailpiece is secured by bolts on each side (arrows)

10.1b The YFZ450R subframe is secured by two Allen bolts on each side (arrows)

unless accident damage has occurred. In most cases, frame replacement is the only satisfactory remedy for such damage. A few frame specialists have the jigs and other equipment necessary for straightening the frame to the required standard of accuracy, but even then there is no simple way of assessing to what extent the frame may have been over-stressed.

3 After the machine has accumulated a lot of miles, the frame should be examined closely for signs of cracking or splitting at the welded joints. Corrosion can also cause weakness at these joints. Loose engine mount bolts can cause elongation of the bolt holes and can fracture the engine mounting points. Minor damage can often be repaired by welding, depending on the nature and extent of the damage.

4 Remember that a frame that is out of alignment will cause handling problems. If misalignment is suspected as the result of an accident, it will be necessary to strip the machine completely so the frame can be thoroughly checked.

Notes

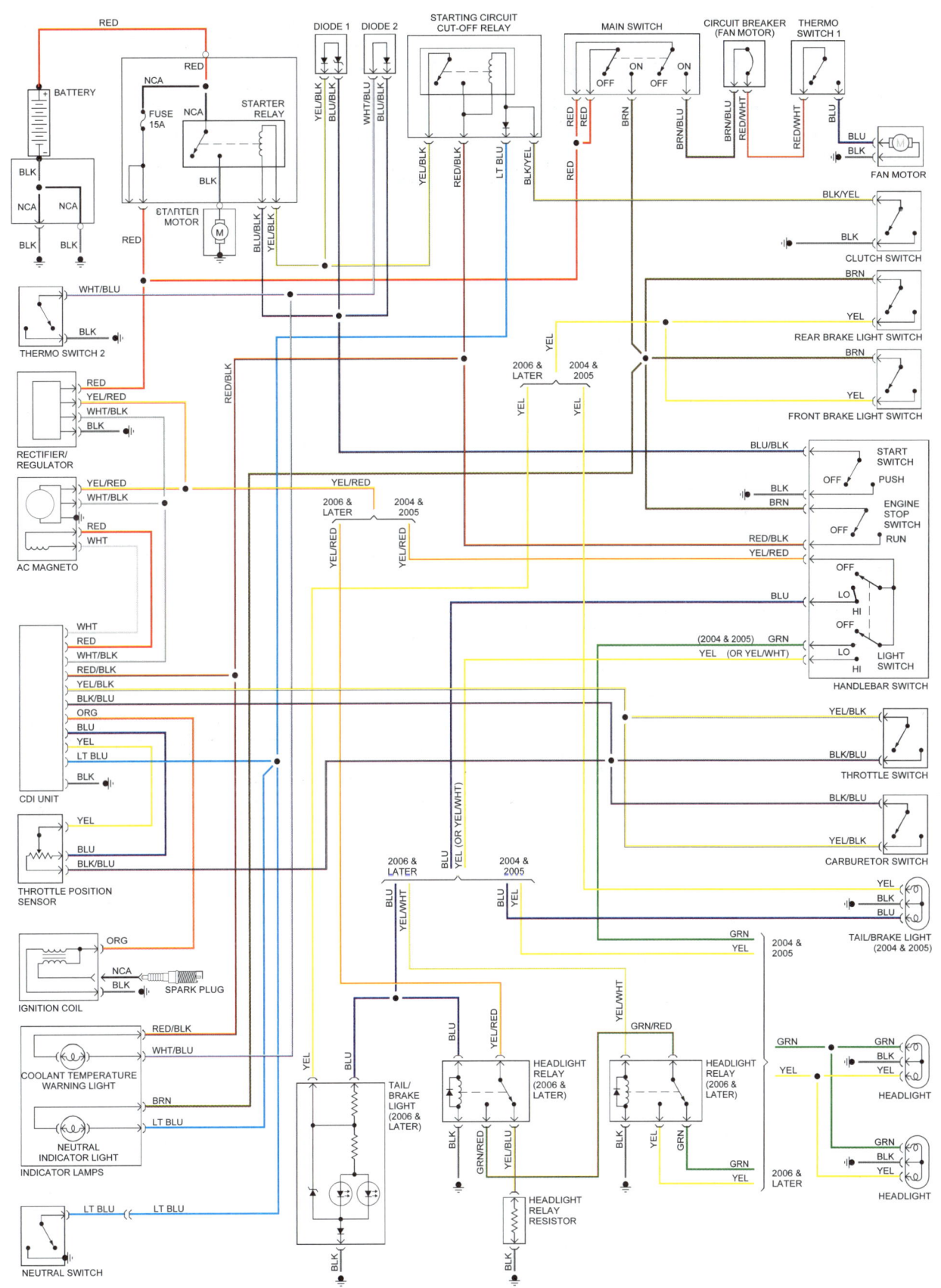

Wiring diagram - YFZ450

9•2 Wiring diagrams

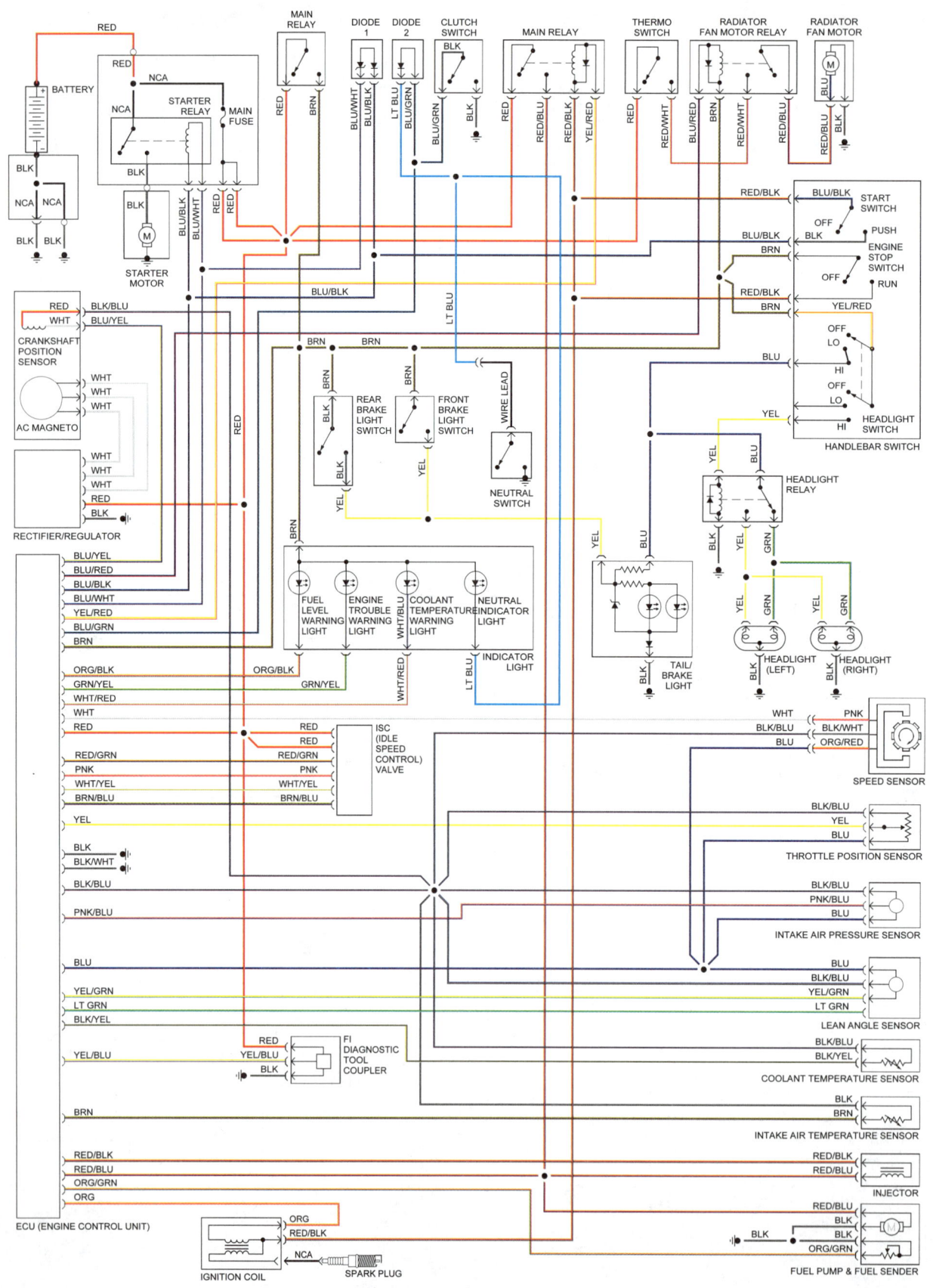

Wiring diagram - YFZ450R

Reference REF•1

Dimensions and Weights . . . . **REF•1**	Troubleshooting Equipment . . . . **REF•38**
Tools and Workshop Tips . . . . **REF•4**	ATV Chemicals and Lubricants . . . . **REF•42**
Conversion Factors . . . . **REF•22**	Technical Terms Explained . . . . **REF•43**
Fraction/decimal/millimeter equivalents . . . . **REF•23**	Trail rules . . . . **REF•50**
Storage . . . . **REF•24**	Index . . . . **REF•51**
Troubleshooting . . . . **REF•27**	

Dimensions and weights

REF•2 Reference

Reference

General Specifications

YFZ450

Wheelbase	1280 mm (50.4 inches)
Overall length	1840 mm (72.4 inches)
Overall width	1170 mm (46.1 inches)
Overall height	1090 mm (42.9 inches)
Seat height	
2004 and 2005	800 mm (31.5 inches)
2006 and later	810 mm (31.9 inches)
Ground clearance	255 mm (10.04 inches)
Weight with oil and full fuel tank	
2004 and 2005	169 kg (373 lbs)
2006 and later	Not specified

YFZ450R

Wheelbase	1270 mm (50.0 inches)
Overall length	1795 mm (70.7 inches)
Overall width	1240 mm (48.8 inches)
Overall height	1065 mm (41.9 inches)
Seat height	810 mm (31.9 inches)
Ground clearance	235 mm (9.25 inches)
Weight with oil and full fuel tank	184 kg (406 lbs)

REF•4 Tools and Workshop Tips

Buying tools

A good set of tools is a fundamental requirement for servicing and repairing a motorcycle. Although there will be an initial expense in building up enough tools for servicing, this will soon be offset by the savings made by doing the job yourself. As experience and confidence grow, additional tools can be added to enable the repair and overhaul of the motorcycle. Many of the special tools are expensive and not often used so it may be preferable to rent them, or for a group of friends or motorcycle club to join in the purchase.

As a rule, it is better to buy more expensive, good quality tools. Cheaper tools are likely to wear out faster and need to be replaced more often, nullifying the original savings.

> **Warning:** To avoid the risk of a poor quality tool breaking in use, causing injury or damage to the component being worked on, always aim to purchase tools which meet the relevant national safety standards.

The following lists of tools do not represent the manufacturer's service tools, but serve as a guide to help the owner decide which tools are needed for this level of work. In addition, items such as an electric drill, hacksaw, files, soldering iron and a workbench equipped with a vise, may be needed. Although not classed as tools, a selection of bolts, screws, nuts, washers and pieces of tubing always come in useful.

For more information about tools, refer to the Haynes *Motorcycle Workshop Practice Techbook* (Bk. No. 3470).

Manufacturer's service tools

Inevitably certain tasks require the use of a service tool. Where possible an alternative tool or method of approach is recommended, but sometimes there is no option if personal injury or damage to the component is to be avoided. Where required, service tools are referred to in the relevant procedure.

Service tools can usually only be purchased from a motorcycle dealer and are identified by a part number. Some of the commonly-used tools, such as rotor pullers, are available in aftermarket form from mail-order motorcycle tool and accessory suppliers.

Maintenance and minor repair tools

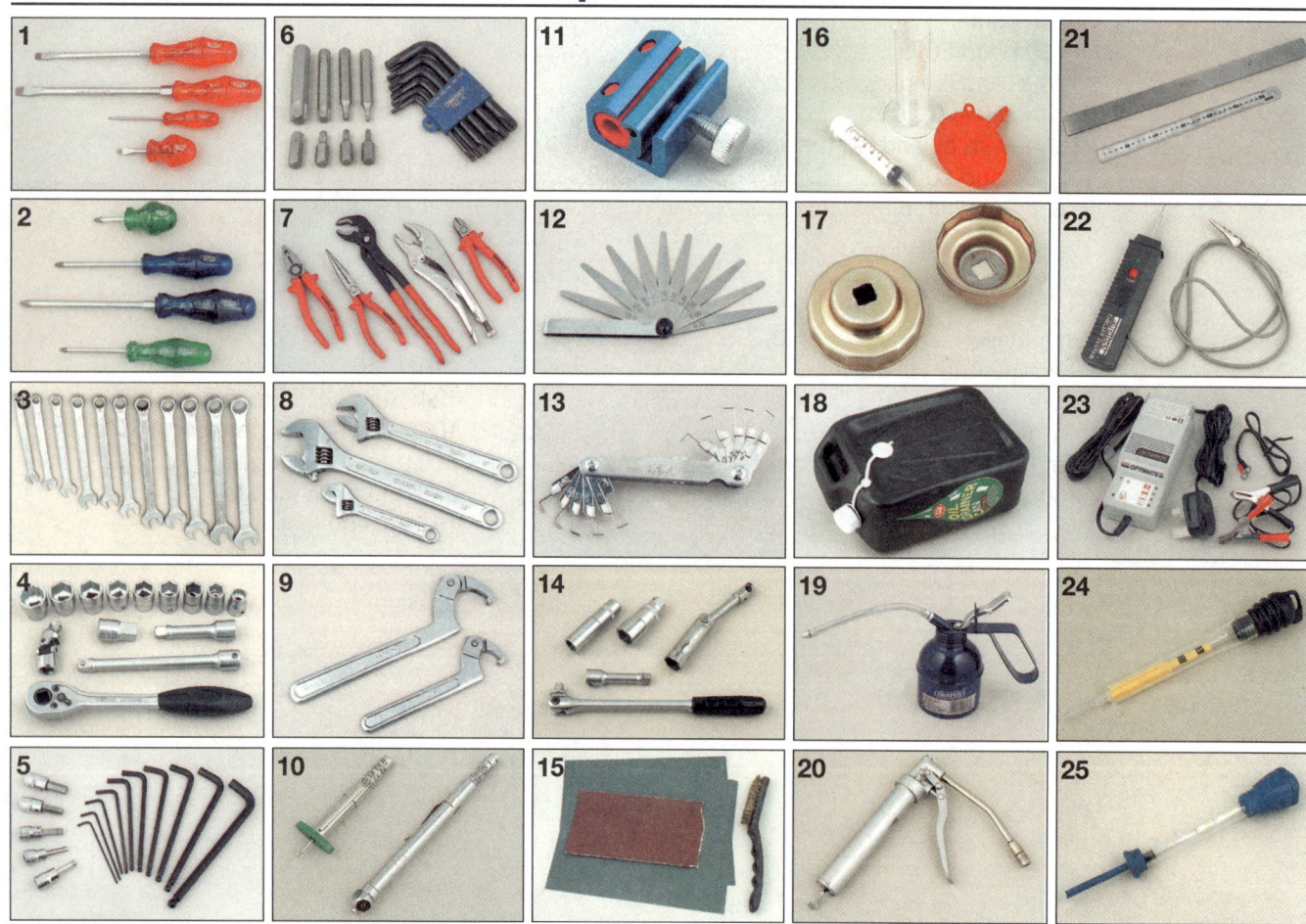

1. Set of flat-bladed screwdrivers
2. Set of Phillips head screwdrivers
3. Combination open-end and box wrenches
4. Socket set (3/8 inch or 1/2 inch drive)
5. Set of Allen keys or bits
6. Set of Torx keys or bits
7. Pliers, cutters and self-locking grips (vise grips)
8. Adjustable wrenches
9. C-spanners
10. Tread depth gauge and tire pressure gauge
11. Cable oiler clamp
12. Feeler gauges
13. Spark plug gap measuring tool
14. Spark plug wrench or deep plug sockets
15. Wire brush and emery paper
16. Calibrated syringe, measuring cup and funnel
17. Oil filter adapters
18. Oil drainer can or tray
19. Pump type oil can
20. Grease gun
21. Straight-edge and steel rule
22. Continuity tester
23. Battery charger
24. Hydrometer (for battery specific gravity check)
25. Antifreeze tester (for liquid-cooled engines)

Tools and Workshop Tips

Repair and overhaul tools

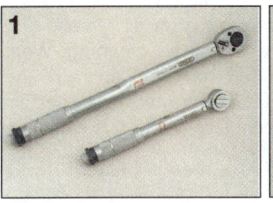
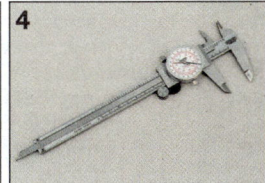
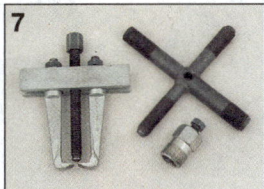
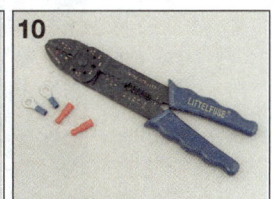
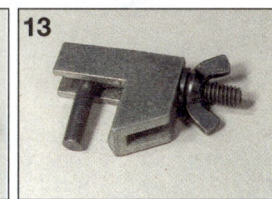

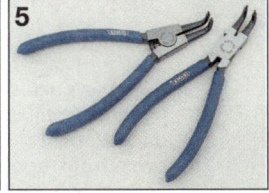
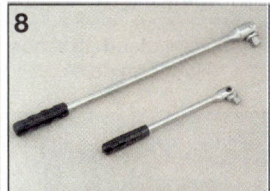

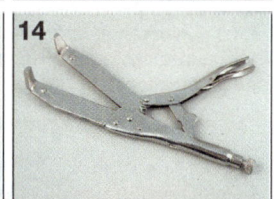

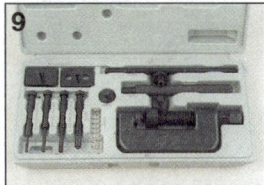

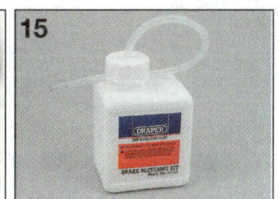

1 Torque wrench (small and mid-ranges)
2 Conventional, plastic or soft-faced hammers
3 Impact driver set
4 Vernier caliper
5 Snap-ring pliers (internal and external, or combination)
6 Set of cold chisels and punches
7 Selection of pullers
8 Breaker bars
9 Chain breaking/riveting tool set
10 Wire stripper and crimper tool
11 Multimeter (measures amps, volts and ohms)
12 Stroboscope (for dynamic timing checks)
13 Hose clamp (wingnut type shown)
14 Clutch holding tool
15 One-man brake/clutch bleeder kit

Special tools

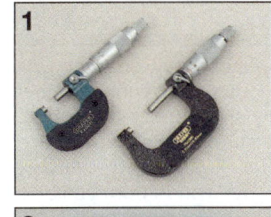
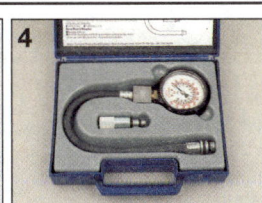
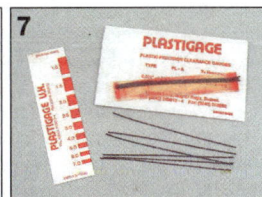
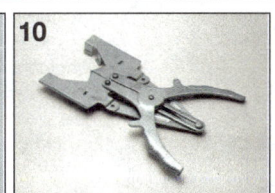

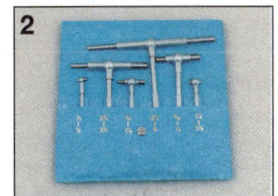
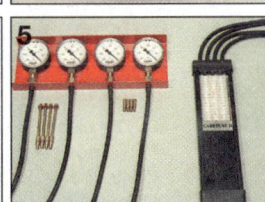
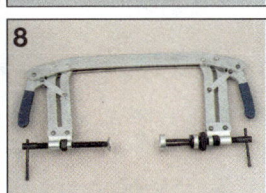
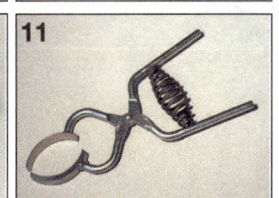
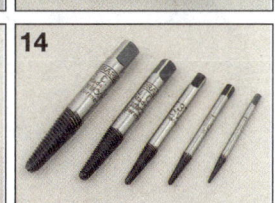

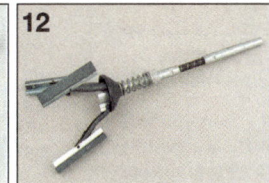
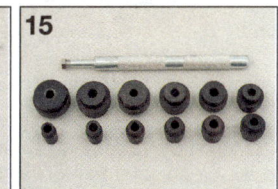

1 Micrometers (external type)
2 Telescoping gauges
3 Dial gauge
4 Cylinder compression gauge
5 Vacuum gauges (left) or manometer (right)
6 Oil pressure gauge
7 Plastigage kit
8 Valve spring compressor (4-stroke engines)
9 Piston pin drawbolt tool
10 Piston ring removal and installation tool
11 Piston ring clamp
12 Cylinder bore hone (stone type shown)
13 Stud extractor
14 Screw extractor set
15 Bearing driver set

REF•6 Tools and Workshop Tips

1 Workshop equipment and facilities

The workbench

● Work is made much easier by raising the bike up on a ramp - components are much more accessible if raised to waist level. The hydraulic or pneumatic types seen in the dealer's workshop are a sound investment if you undertake a lot of repairs or overhauls **(see illustration 1.1)**.

1.1 Hydraulic motorcycle ramp

● If raised off ground level, the bike must be supported on the ramp to avoid it falling. Most ramps incorporate a front wheel locating clamp which can be adjusted to suit different diameter wheels. When tightening the clamp, take care not to mark the wheel rim or damage the tire - use wood blocks on each side to prevent this.

● Secure the bike to the ramp using tie-downs **(see illustration 1.2)**. If the bike has only a sidestand, and hence leans at a dangerous angle when raised, support the bike on an auxiliary stand.

1.2 Tie-downs are used around the passenger footrests to secure the bike

● Auxiliary (paddock) stands are widely available from mail order companies or motorcycle dealers and attach either to the wheel axle or swingarm pivot **(see illustration 1.3)**. If the motorcycle has a centerstand, you can support it under the crankcase to prevent it toppling while either wheel is removed **(see illustration 1.4)**.

1.3 This auxiliary stand attaches to the swingarm pivot

1.4 Always use a block of wood between the engine and jack head when supporting the engine in this way

Fumes and fire

● Refer to the Safety first! page at the beginning of the manual for full details. Make sure your workshop is equipped with a fire extinguisher suitable for fuel-related fires (Class B fire - flammable liquids) - it is not sufficient to have a water-filled extinguisher.

● Always ensure adequate ventilation is available. Unless an exhaust gas extraction system is available for use, ensure that the engine is run outside of the workshop.

● If working on the fuel system, make sure the workshop is ventilated to avoid a build-up of fumes. This applies equally to fume build-up when charging a battery. Do not smoke or allow anyone else to smoke in the workshop.

Fluids

● If you need to drain fuel from the tank, store it in an approved container marked as suitable for the storage of gasoline **(see illustration 1.5)**. Do not store fuel in glass jars or bottles.

● Use proprietary engine degreasers or solvents which have a high flash-point, such as kerosene, for cleaning off oil, grease and dirt - never use gasoline for cleaning. Wear rubber gloves when handling solvent and engine degreaser. The fumes from certain solvents can be dangerous - always work in a well-ventilated area.

Dust, eye and hand protection

● Protect your lungs from inhalation of dust particles by wearing a filtering mask over the nose and mouth. Many frictional materials still contain asbestos which is dangerous to your health. Protect your eyes from spouts of liquid and sprung components by wearing a pair of protective

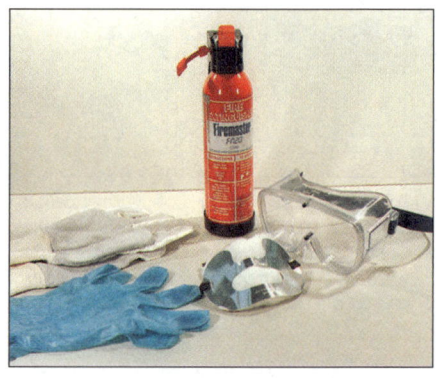

1.6 A fire extinguisher, goggles, mask and protective gloves should be at hand in the workshop

goggles **(see illustration 1.6)**.

● Protect your hands from contact with solvents, fuel and oils by wearing rubber gloves. Alternatively apply a barrier cream to your hands before starting work. If handling hot components or fluids, wear suitable gloves to protect your hands from scalding and burns.

What to do with old fluids

● Old cleaning solvent, fuel, coolant and oils should not be poured down domestic drains or onto the ground. Package the fluid up in old oil containers, label it accordingly, and take it to a garage or disposal facility. Contact your local disposal company for location of such sites.

1.5 Use an approved can only for storing gasoline

> *Note: It is illegal to dump oil down the drain. Check with your local auto parts store, disposal facility or environmental agency to see if they accept the oil for recycling.*

Tools and Workshop Tips

2 Fasteners - screws, bolts and nuts

Fastener types and applications

Bolts and screws

● Fastener head types are either of hexagonal, Torx or splined design, with internal and external versions of each type (see illustrations 2.1 and 2.2); splined head fasteners are not in common use on motorcycles. The conventional slotted or Phillips head design is used for certain screws. Bolt or screw length is always measured from the underside of the head to the end of the item (see illustration 2.11).

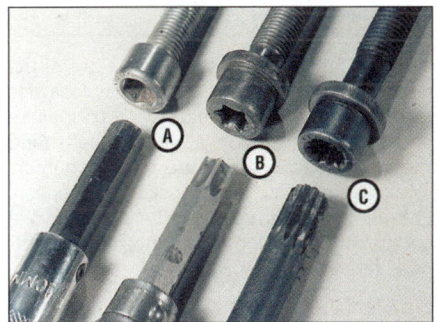

2.1 Internal hexagon/Allen (A), Torx (B) and splined (C) fasteners, with corresponding bits

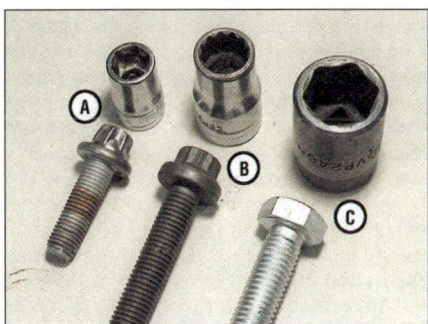

2.2 External Torx (A), splined (B) and hexagon (C) fasteners, with corresponding sockets

● Certain fasteners on the motorcycle have a tensile marking on their heads, the higher the marking the stronger the fastener. High tensile fasteners generally carry a 10 or higher marking. Never replace a high tensile fastener with one of a lower tensile strength.

Washers (see illustration 2.3)

● Plain washers are used between a fastener head and a component to prevent damage to the component or to spread the load when torque is applied. Plain washers can also be used as spacers or shims in certain assemblies. Copper or aluminum plain washers are often used as sealing washers on drain plugs.

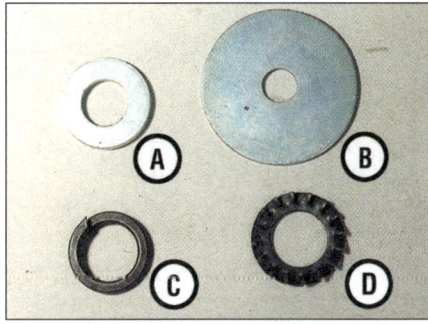

2.3 Plain washer (A), penny washer (B), spring washer (C) and serrated washer (D)

● The split-ring spring washer works by applying axial tension between the fastener head and component. If flattened, it is fatigued and must be replaced. If a plain (flat) washer is used on the fastener, position the spring washer between the fastener and the plain washer.
● Serrated star type washers dig into the fastener and component faces, preventing loosening. They are often used on electrical ground connections to the frame.
● Cone type washers (sometimes called Belleville) are conical and when tightened apply axial tension between the fastener head and component. They must be installed with the dished side against the component and often carry an OUTSIDE marking on their outer face. If flattened, they are fatigued and must be replaced.
● Tab washers are used to lock plain nuts or bolts on a shaft. A portion of the tab washer is bent up hard against one flat of the nut or bolt to prevent it loosening. Due to the tab washer being deformed in use, a new tab washer should be used every time it is removed.
● Wave washers are used to take up endfloat on a shaft. They provide light springing and prevent excessive side-to-side play of a component. Can be found on rocker arm shafts.

Nuts and cotter pins

● Conventional plain nuts are usually six-sided (see illustration 2.4). They are sized by thread diameter and pitch. High tensile nuts carry a number on one end to denote their tensile strength.

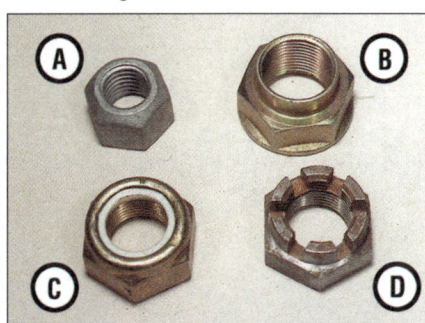

2.4 Plain nut (A), shouldered locknut (B), nylon insert nut (C) and castellated nut (D)

● Self-locking nuts either have a nylon insert, or two spring metal tabs, or a shoulder which is staked into a groove in the shaft - their advantage over conventional plain nuts is a resistance to loosening due to vibration. The nylon insert type can be used a number of times, but must be replaced when the friction of the nylon insert is reduced, i.e. when the nut spins freely on the shaft. The spring tab type can be reused unless the tabs are damaged. The shouldered type must be replaced every time it is removed.
● Cotter pins are used to lock a castellated nut to a shaft or to prevent loosening of a plain nut. Common applications are wheel axles and brake torque arms. Because the cotter pin arms are deformed to lock around the nut a new cotter pin must always be used on installation - always use the correct size cotter pin which will fit snugly in the shaft hole. Make sure the cotter pin arms are correctly located around the nut (see illustrations 2.5 and 2.6).

2.5 Bend cotter pin arms as shown (arrows) to secure a castellated nut

2.6 Bend cotter pin arms as shown to secure a plain nut

Caution: If the castellated nut slots do not align with the shaft hole after tightening to the torque setting, tighten the nut until the next slot aligns with the hole - never loosen the nut to align its slot.

● R-pins (shaped like the letter R), or slip pins as they are sometimes called, are sprung and can be reused if they are otherwise in good condition. Always install R-pins with their closed end facing forwards (see illustration 2.7).

REF•8 Tools and Workshop Tips

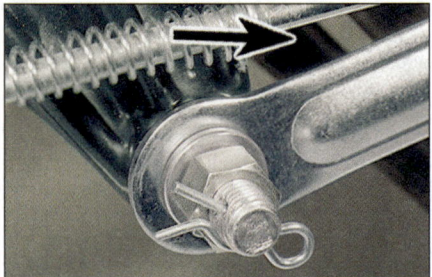

2.7 Correct fitting of R-pin. Arrow indicates forward direction

Snap-rings (see illustration 2.8)

● Snap-rings (sometimes called circlips) are used to retain components on a shaft or in a housing and have corresponding external or internal ears to permit removal. Parallel-sided (machined) snap-rings can be installed either way round in their groove, whereas stamped snap-rings (which have a chamfered edge on one face) must be installed with the chamfer facing the thrust load **(see illustration 2.9)**.

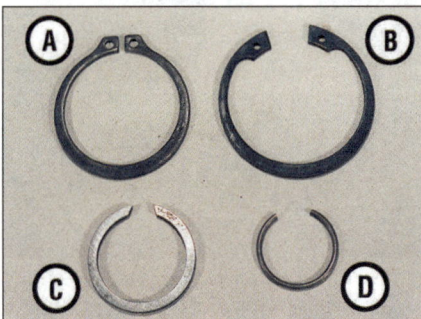

2.8 External stamped snap-ring (A), internal stamped snap-ring (B), machined snap-ring (C) and wire snap-ring (D)

● Always use snap-ring pliers to remove and install snap-rings; expand or compress them just enough to remove them. After installation, rotate the snap-ring in its groove to ensure it is securely seated. If installing a snap-ring on a splined shaft, always align its opening with a shaft channel to ensure the snap-ring ends are well supported and unlikely to catch **(see illustration 2.10)**.

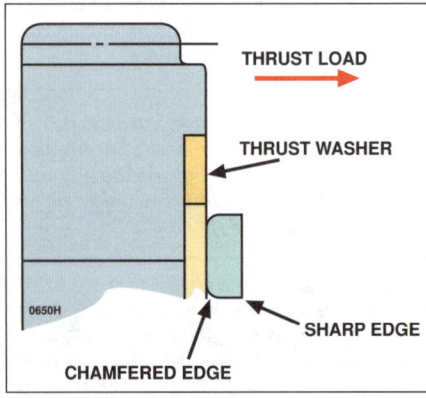

2.9 Correct fitting of a stamped snap-ring

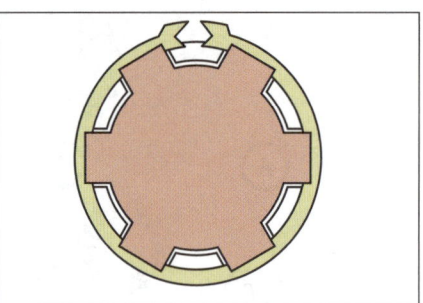

2.10 Align snap-ring opening with shaft channel

● Snap-rings can wear due to the thrust of components and become loose in their grooves, with the subsequent danger of becoming dislodged in operation. For this reason, replacement is advised every time a snap-ring is disturbed.

● Wire snap-rings are commonly used as piston pin retaining clips. If a removal tang is provided, long-nosed pliers can be used to dislodge them, otherwise careful use of a small flat-bladed screwdriver is necessary. Wire snap-rings should be replaced every time they are disturbed.

Thread diameter and pitch

● Diameter of a male thread (screw, bolt or stud) is the outside diameter of the threaded portion **(see illustration 2.11)**. Most motorcycle manufacturers use the ISO (International Standards Organization) metric system expressed in millimeters. For example, M6 refers to a 6 mm diameter thread. Sizing is the same for nuts, except that the thread diameter is measured across the valleys of the nut.

● Pitch is the distance between the peaks of the thread **(see illustration 2.11)**. It is expressed in millimeters, thus a common bolt size may be expressed as 6.0 x 1.0 mm (6 mm thread diameter and 1 mm pitch). Generally pitch increases in proportion to thread diameter, although there are always exceptions.

● Thread diameter and pitch are related for conventional fastener applications and the accompanying table can be used as a guide. Additionally, the AF (Across Flats), wrench or socket size dimension of the bolt or nut **(see illustration 2.11)** is linked to thread and pitch specification. Thread pitch can be measured with a thread gauge **(see illustration 2.12)**.

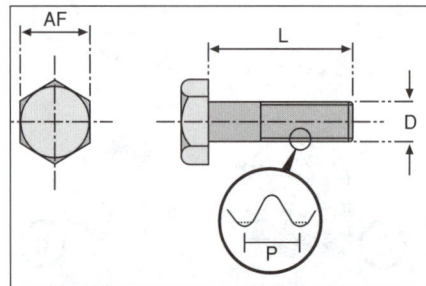

2.11 Fastener length (L), thread diameter (D), thread pitch (P) and head size (AF)

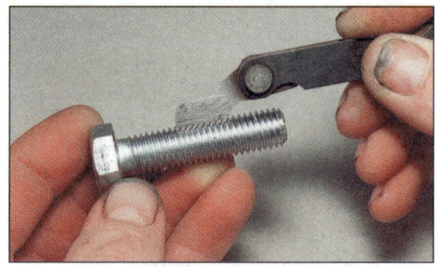

2.12 Using a thread gauge to measure pitch

AF size	Thread diameter x pitch (mm)
8 mm	M5 x 0.8
8 mm	M6 x 1.0
10 mm	M6 x 1.0
12 mm	M8 x 1.25
14 mm	M10 x 1.25
17 mm	M12 x 1.25

● The threads of most fasteners are of the right-hand type, ie they are turned clockwise to tighten and counterclockwise to loosen. The reverse situation applies to left-hand thread fasteners, which are turned counterclockwise to tighten and clockwise to loosen. Left-hand threads are used where rotation of a component might loosen a conventional right-hand thread fastener.

Seized fasteners

● Corrosion of external fasteners due to water or reaction between two dissimilar metals can occur over a period of time. It will build up sooner in wet conditions or in countries where salt is used on the roads during the winter. If a fastener is severely corroded it is likely that normal methods of removal will fail and result in its head being ruined. When you attempt removal, the fastener thread should be heard to crack free and unscrew easily - if it doesn't, stop there before damaging something.

● A smart tap on the head of the fastener will often succeed in breaking free corrosion which has occurred in the threads **(see illustration 2.13)**.

● An aerosol penetrating fluid (such as WD-40) applied the night beforehand may work its way down into the thread and ease removal. Depending on the location, you may be able to make up a modeling-clay well around the fastener head and fill it with penetrating fluid.

2.13 A sharp tap on the head of a fastener will often break free a corroded thread

Tools and Workshop Tips

- If you are working on an engine internal component, corrosion will most likely not be a problem due to the well lubricated environment. However, components can be very tight and an impact driver is a useful tool in freeing them **(see illustration 2.14)**.

2.14 Using an impact driver to free a fastener

- Where corrosion has occurred between dissimilar metals (e.g. steel and aluminum alloy), the application of heat to the fastener head will create a disproportionate expansion rate between the two metals and break the seizure caused by the corrosion. Whether heat can be applied depends on the location of the fastener - any surrounding components likely to be damaged must first be removed **(see illustration 2.15)**. Heat can be applied using a paint stripper heat gun or clothes iron, or by immersing the component in boiling water - wear protective gloves to prevent scalding or burns to the hands.

2.15 Using heat to free a seized fastener

- As a last resort, it is possible to use a hammer and cold chisel to work the fastener head unscrewed **(see illustration 2.16)**. This will damage the fastener, but more importantly extreme care must be taken not to damage the surrounding component.

> **Caution:** Remember that the component being secured is generally of more value than the bolt, nut or screw - when the fastener is freed, do not unscrew it with force, instead work the fastener back and forth when resistance is felt to prevent thread damage.

2.16 Using a hammer and chisel to free a seized fastener

Broken fasteners and damaged heads

- If the shank of a broken bolt or screw is accessible you can grip it with self-locking grips. The knurled wheel type stud extractor tool or self-gripping stud puller tool is particularly useful for removing the long studs which screw into the cylinder mouth surface of the crankcase or bolts and screws from which the head has broken off **(see illustration 2.17)**. Studs can also be removed by locking two nuts together on the threaded end of the stud and using a wrench on the lower nut **(see illustration 2.18)**.

2.17 Using a stud extractor tool to remove a broken crankcase stud

2.18 Two nuts can be locked together to unscrew a stud from a component

- A bolt or screw which has broken off below or level with the casing must be extracted using a screw extractor set. Centerpunch the fastener to centralize the drill bit, then drill a hole in the fastener **(see illustration 2.19)**. Select a drill bit which is approximately half to three-quarters the diameter of the fastener

2.19 When using a screw extractor, first drill a hole in the fastener . . .

and drill to a depth which will accommodate the extractor. Use the largest size extractor possible, but avoid leaving too small a wall thickness otherwise the extractor will merely force the fastener walls outwards wedging it in the casing thread.

- If a spiral type extractor is used, thread it counterclockwise into the fastener. As it is screwed in, it will grip the fastener and unscrew it from the casing **(see illustration 2.20)**.

2.20 . . . then thread the extractor counterclockwise into the fastener

- If a taper type extractor is used, tap it into the fastener so that it is firmly wedged in place. Unscrew the extractor (counter-clockwise) to draw the fastener out.
- Alternatively, the broken bolt/screw can

 Warning: Stud extractors are very hard and may break off in the fastener if care is not taken - ask a machine shop about spark erosion if this happens.

be drilled out and the hole retapped for an oversize bolt/screw or a diamond-section thread insert. It is essential that the drilling is carried out squarely and to the correct depth, otherwise the casing may be ruined - if in doubt, entrust the work to a machine shop.

- Bolts and nuts with rounded corners cause the correct size wrench or socket to slip when force is applied. Of the types of wrench/socket available always use a six-point type rather than an eight or twelve-point type - better grip

Tools and Workshop Tips

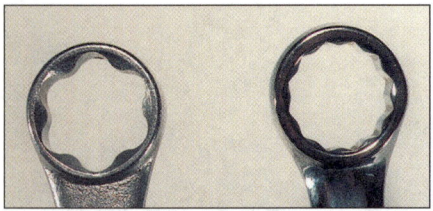

2.21 Comparison of surface drive box wrench (left) with 12-point type (right)

is obtained. Surface drive wrenches grip the middle of the hex flats, rather than the corners, and are thus good in cases of damaged heads **(see illustration 2.21)**.

● Slotted-head or Phillips-head screws are often damaged by the use of the wrong size screwdriver. Allen-head and Torx-head screws are much less likely to sustain damage. If enough of the screw head is exposed you can use a hacksaw to cut a slot in its head and then use a conventional flat-bladed screwdriver to remove it. Alternatively use a hammer and cold chisel to tap the head of the fastener around to loosen it. Always replace damaged fasteners with new ones, preferably Torx or Allen-head type.

HAYNES HiNT

A dab of valve grinding compound between the screw head and screwdriver tip will often give a good grip.

Thread repair

● Threads (particularly those in aluminum alloy components) can be damaged by overtightening, being assembled with dirt in the threads, or from a component working loose and vibrating. Eventually the thread will fail completely, and it will be impossible to tighten the fastener.

● If a thread is damaged or clogged with old locking compound it can be renovated with a thread repair tool (thread chaser) **(see illustrations 2.22 and 2.23)**; special thread

2.22 A thread repair tool being used to correct an internal thread

2.23 A thread repair tool being used to correct an external thread

chasers are available for spark plug hole threads. The tool will not cut a new thread, but clean and true the original thread. Make sure that you use the correct diameter and pitch tool. Similarly, external threads can be cleaned up with a die or a thread restorer file **(see illustration 2.24)**.

2.24 Using a thread restorer file

● It is possible to drill out the old thread and retap the component to the next thread size. This will work where there is enough surrounding material and a new bolt or screw can be obtained. Sometimes, however, this is not possible - such as where the bolt/screw passes through another component which must also be suitably modified, also in cases where a spark plug or oil drain plug cannot be obtained in a larger diameter thread size.

● The diamond-section thread insert (often known by its popular trade name of Heli-Coil) is a simple and effective method of replacing the thread and retaining the original size. A kit can be purchased which contains the tap, insert and installing tool **(see illustration 2.25)**. Drill out the damaged thread with the size drill specified **(see illustration 2.26)**. Carefully retap the thread **(see illustration 2.27)**. Install the

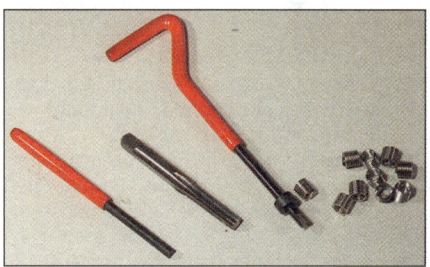

2.25 Obtain a thread insert kit to suit the thread diameter and pitch required

2.26 To install a thread insert, first drill out the original thread . . .

2.27 . . . tap a new thread . . .

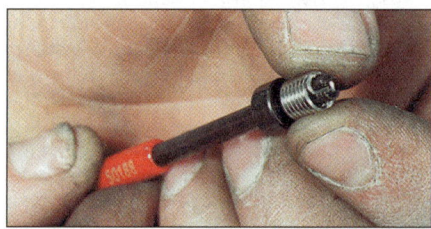

2.28 . . . fit insert on the installing tool . . .

2.29 . . . and thread into the component . . .

2.30 . . . break off the tang when complete

insert on the installing tool and thread it slowly into place using a light downward pressure **(see illustrations 2.28 and 2.29)**. When positioned between a 1/4 and 1/2 turn below the surface withdraw the installing tool and use the break-off tool to press down on the tang, breaking it off **(see illustration 2.30)**.

● There are epoxy thread repair kits on the market which can rebuild stripped internal threads, although this repair should not be used on high load-bearing components.

Tools and Workshop Tips

Thread locking and sealing compounds

● Locking compounds are used in locations where the fastener is prone to loosening due to vibration or on important safety-related items which might cause loss of control of the motorcycle if they fail. It is also used where important fasteners cannot be secured by other means such as lockwashers or cotter pins.

● Before applying locking compound, make sure that the threads (internal and external) are clean and dry with all old compound removed. Select a compound to suit the component being secured - a non-permanent general locking and sealing type is suitable for most applications, but a high strength type is needed for permanent fixing of studs in castings. Apply a drop or two of the compound to the first few threads of the fastener, then thread it into place and tighten to the specified torque. Do not apply excessive thread locking compound otherwise the thread may be damaged on subsequent removal.

● Certain fasteners are impregnated with a dry film type coating of locking compound on their threads. Always replace this type of fastener if disturbed.

● Anti-seize compounds, such as copper-based greases, can be applied to protect threads from seizure due to extreme heat and corrosion. A common instance is spark plug threads and exhaust system fasteners.

3 Measuring tools and gauges

Feeler gauges

● Feeler gauges (or blades) are used for measuring small gaps and clearances **(see illustration 3.1)**. They can also be used to measure endfloat (sideplay) of a component on a shaft where access is not possible with a dial gauge.

● Feeler gauge sets should be treated with care and not bent or damaged. They are etched with their size on one face. Keep them clean and very lightly oiled to prevent corrosion build-up.

3.1 Feeler gauges are used for measuring small gaps and clearances - thickness is marked on one face of gauge

● When measuring a clearance, select a gauge which is a light sliding fit between the two components. You may need to use two gauges together to measure the clearance accurately.

Micrometers

● A micrometer is a precision tool capable of measuring to 0.01 or 0.001 of a millimeter. It should always be stored in its case and not in the general toolbox. It must be kept clean and never dropped, otherwise its frame or measuring anvils could be distorted resulting in inaccurate readings.

● External micrometers are used for measuring outside diameters of components and have many more applications than internal micrometers. Micrometers are available in different size ranges, typically 0 to 25 mm, 25 to 50 mm, and upwards in 25 mm steps; some large micrometers have interchangeable anvils to allow a range of measurements to be taken. Generally the largest precision measurement you are likely to take on a motorcycle is the piston diameter.

● Internal micrometers (or bore micrometers) are used for measuring inside diameters, such as valve guides and cylinder bores. Telescoping gauges and small hole gauges are used in conjunction with an external micrometer, whereas the more expensive internal micrometers have their own measuring device.

External micrometer

Note: *The conventional analogue type instrument is described. Although much easier to read, digital micrometers are considerably more expensive.*

● Always check the calibration of the micrometer before use. With the anvils closed (0 to 25 mm type) or set over a test gauge

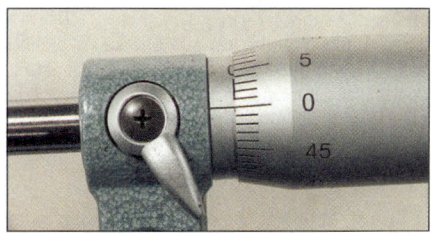

3.2 Check micrometer calibration before use

(for the larger types) the scale should read zero **(see illustration 3.2)**; make sure that the anvils (and test piece) are clean first. Any discrepancy can be adjusted by referring to the instructions supplied with the tool. Remember that the micrometer is a precision measuring tool - don't force the anvils closed, use the ratchet (4) on the end of the micrometer to close it. In this way, a measured force is always applied.

● To use, first make sure that the item being measured is clean. Place the anvil of the micrometer (1) against the item and use the thimble (2) to bring the spindle (3) lightly into contact with the other side of the item **(see illustration 3.3)**. Don't tighten the thimble down because this will damage the micrometer - instead use the ratchet (4) on the end of the micrometer. The ratchet mechanism applies a measured force preventing damage to the instrument.

● The micrometer is read by referring to the linear scale on the sleeve and the annular scale on the thimble. Read off the sleeve first to obtain the base measurement, then add the fine measurement from the thimble to obtain the overall reading. The linear scale on the sleeve represents the measuring range of the micrometer (eg 0 to 25 mm). The annular scale

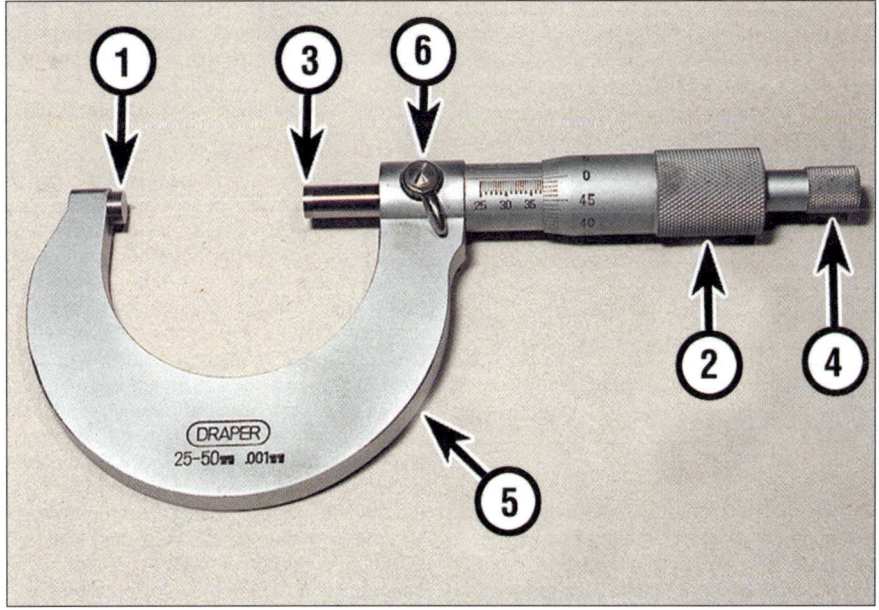

3.3 Micrometer component parts

| 1 Anvil | 3 Spindle | 5 Frame |
| 2 Thimble | 4 Ratchet | 6 Locking lever |

REF•12 Tools and Workshop Tips

on the thimble will be in graduations of 0.01 mm (or as marked on the frame) - one full revolution of the thimble will move 0.5 mm on the linear scale. Take the reading where the datum line on the sleeve intersects the thimble's scale. Always position the eye directly above the scale otherwise an inaccurate reading will result.

In the example shown the item measures 2.95 mm **(see illustration 3.4)**:

Linear scale	2.00 mm
Linear scale	0.50 mm
Annular scale	0.45 mm
Total figure	**2.95 mm**

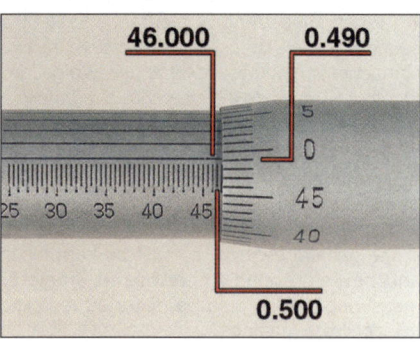

3.5 Micrometer reading of 46.99 mm on linear and annular scales . . .

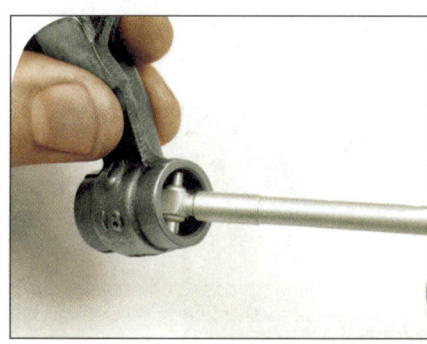

3.7 Expand the telescoping gauge in the bore, lock its position . . .

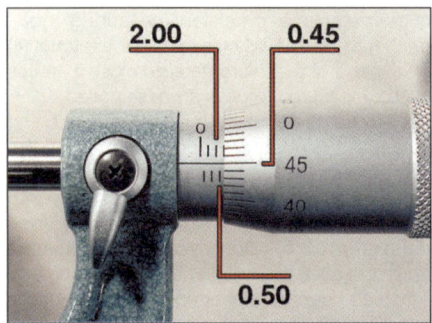

3.4 Micrometer reading of 2.95 mm

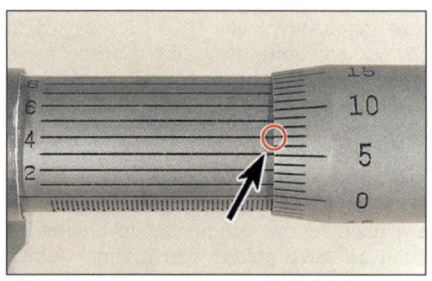

3.6 . . . and 0.004 mm on vernier scale

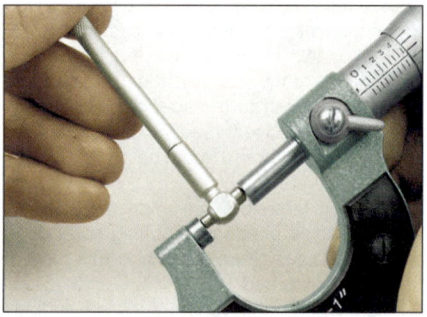

3.8 . . . then measure the gauge with a micrometer

Most micrometers have a locking lever (6) on the frame to hold the setting in place, allowing the item to be removed from the micrometer.

● Some micrometers have a vernier scale on their sleeve, providing an even finer measurement to be taken, in 0.001 increments of a millimeter. Take the sleeve and thimble measurement as described above, then check which graduation on the vernier scale aligns with that of the annular scale on the thimble **Note:** *The eye must be perpendicular to the scale when taking the vernier reading - if necessary rotate the body of the micrometer to ensure this.* Multiply the vernier scale figure by 0.001 and add it to the base and fine measurement figures.

In the example shown the item measures 46.994 mm **(see illustrations 3.5 and 3.6)**:

Linear scale (base)	46.000 mm
Linear scale (base)	00.500 mm
Annular scale (fine)	00.490 mm
Vernier scale	00.004 mm
Total figure	**46.994 mm**

Internal micrometer

● Internal micrometers are available for measuring bore diameters, but are expensive and unlikely to be available for home use. It is suggested that a set of telescoping gauges and small hole gauges, both of which must be used with an external micrometer, will suffice for taking internal measurements on a motorcycle.

● Telescoping gauges can be used to measure internal diameters of components. Select a gauge with the correct size range, make sure its ends are clean and insert it into the bore. Expand the gauge, then lock its position and withdraw it from the bore **(see illustration 3.7)**. Measure across the gauge ends with a micrometer **(see illustration 3.8)**.

● Very small diameter bores (such as valve guides) are measured with a small hole gauge. Once adjusted to a slip-fit inside the component, its position is locked and the gauge withdrawn for measurement with a micrometer **(see illustrations 3.9 and 3.10)**.

Vernier caliper

Note: *The conventional linear and dial gauge type instruments are described. Digital types are easier to read, but are far more expensive.*

● The vernier caliper does not provide the precision of a micrometer, but is versatile in being able to measure internal and external diameters. Some types also incorporate a depth gauge. It is ideal for measuring clutch plate friction material and spring free lengths.

● To use the conventional linear scale vernier, loosen off the vernier clamp screws (1) and set its jaws over (2), or inside (3), the item to be measured **(see illustration 3.11)**. Slide the jaw into contact, using the thumb-wheel (4) for fine movement of the sliding scale (5) then tighten the clamp screws (1). Read off the main scale (6) where the zero on the sliding scale (5) intersects it, taking the whole number to the left of the zero; this provides the base measurement. View along the sliding scale and select the division which lines up exactly

3.9 Expand the small hole gauge in the bore, lock its position . . .

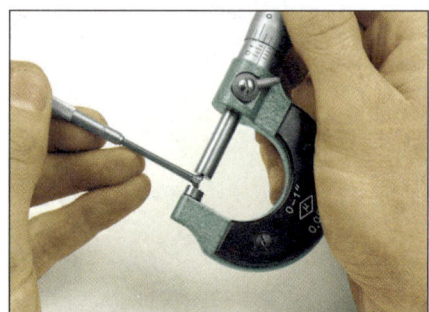

3.10 . . . then measure the gauge with a micrometer

with any of the divisions on the main scale, noting that the divisions usually represents 0.02 of a millimeter. Add this fine measurement to the base measurement to obtain the total reading.

Tools and Workshop Tips   REF•13

Plastigage

● Plastigage is a plastic material which can be compressed between two surfaces to measure the oil clearance between them. The width of the compressed Plastigage is measured against a calibrated scale to determine the clearance.

● Common uses of Plastigage are for measuring the clearance between crankshaft journal and main bearing inserts, between crankshaft journal and big-end bearing inserts, and between camshaft and bearing surfaces. The following example describes big-end oil clearance measurement.

● Handle the Plastigage material carefully to prevent distortion. Using a sharp knife, cut a length which corresponds with the width of the bearing being measured and place it carefully across the journal so that it is parallel with the shaft (see illustration 3.15). Carefully install both bearing shells and the connecting rod. Without rotating the rod on the journal tighten its bolts or nuts (as applicable) to the specified torque. The connecting rod and bearings are then disassembled and the crushed Plastigage examined.

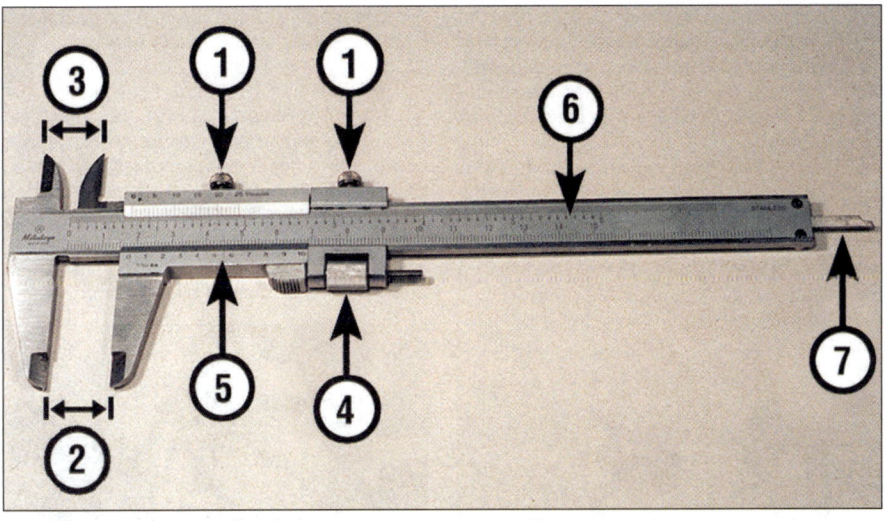

3.11 Vernier component parts (linear gauge)

| 1 Clamp screws | 3 Internal jaws | 5 Sliding scale | 7 Depth gauge |
| 2 External jaws | 4 Thumbwheel | 6 Main scale | |

In the example shown the item measures 55.92 mm (see illustration 3.12):

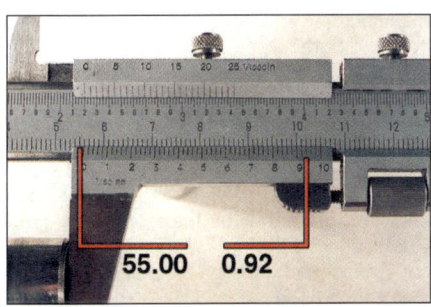

3.12 Vernier gauge reading of 55.92 mm

Base measurement	55.00 mm
Fine measurement	00.92 mm
Total figure	**55.92 mm**

● Some vernier calipers are equipped with a dial gauge for fine measurement. Before use, check that the jaws are clean, then close them fully and check that the dial gauge reads zero. If necessary adjust the gauge ring accordingly. Slacken the vernier clamp screw (1) and set its jaws over (2), or inside (3), the item to be measured (see illustration 3.13). Slide the jaws into contact, using the thumbwheel (4) for fine movement. Read off the main scale (5) where the edge of the sliding scale (6) intersects it, taking the whole number to the left of the zero; this provides the base measurement. Read off the needle position on the dial gauge (7) scale to provide the fine measurement; each division represents 0.05 of a millimeter. Add this fine measurement to the base measurement to obtain the total reading.

In the example shown the item measures 55.95 mm (see illustration 3.14):

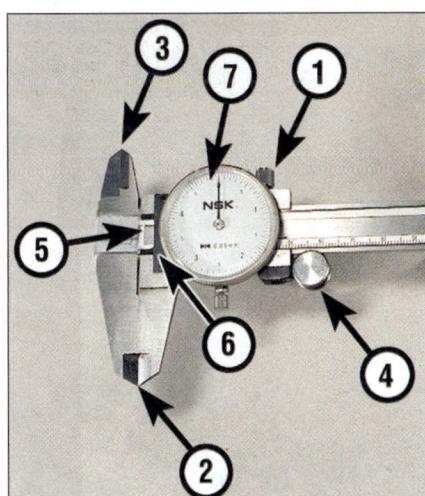

3.13 Vernier component parts (dial gauge)

1 Clamp screw	5 Main scale
2 External jaws	6 Sliding scale
3 Internal jaws	7 Dial gauge
4 Thumbwheel	

Base measurement	55.00 mm
Fine measurement	00.95 mm
Total figure	**55.95 mm**

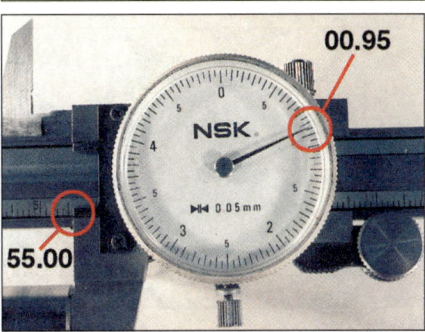

3.14 Vernier gauge reading of 55.95 mm

3.15 Plastigage placed across shaft journal

● Using the scale provided in the Plastigage kit, measure the width of the material to determine the oil clearance (see illustration 3.16). Always remove all traces of Plastigage after use using your fingernails.

Caution: Arriving at the correct clearance demands that the assembly is torqued correctly, according to the settings and sequence (where applicable) provided by the motorcycle manufacturer.

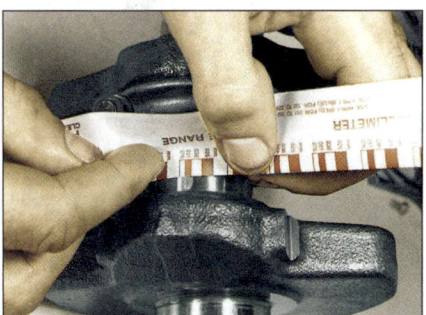

3.16 Measuring the width of the crushed Plastigage

REF•14 Tools and Workshop Tips

Dial gauge or DTI (Dial Test Indicator)

- A dial gauge can be used to accurately measure small amounts of movement. Typical uses are measuring shaft runout or shaft endfloat (sideplay) and setting piston position for ignition timing on two-strokes. A dial gauge set usually comes with a range of different probes and adapters and mounting equipment.
- The gauge needle must point to zero when at rest. Rotate the ring around its periphery to zero the gauge.
- Check that the gauge is capable of reading the extent of movement in the work. Most gauges have a small dial set in the face which records whole millimeters of movement as well as the fine scale around the face periphery which is calibrated in 0.01 mm divisions. Read off the small dial first to obtain the base measurement, then add the measurement from the fine scale to obtain the total reading.

Base measurement	1.00 mm
Fine measurement	0.48 mm
Total figure	**1.48 mm**

3.17 Dial gauge reading of 1.48 mm

In the example shown the gauge reads 1.48 mm **(see illustration 3.17)**:
- If measuring shaft runout, the shaft must be supported in vee-blocks and the gauge mounted on a stand perpendicular to the shaft. Rest the tip of the gauge against the center of the shaft and rotate the shaft slowly while watching the gauge reading **(see illustration 3.18)**. Take several measurements along the length of the shaft and record the maximum gauge reading as the amount of runout in the shaft. **Note:** *The reading obtained will be total runout at that point - some manufacturers specify that the runout figure is halved to compare with their specified runout limit.*
- Endfloat (sideplay) measurement requires that the gauge is mounted securely to the surrounding component with its probe touching the end of the shaft. Using hand pressure, push and pull on the shaft noting the maximum endfloat recorded on the gauge **(see illustration 3.19)**.

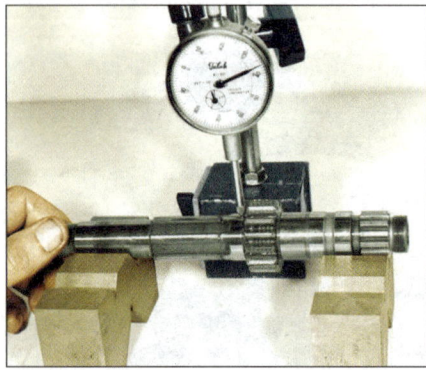

3.18 Using a dial gauge to measure shaft runout

3.19 Using a dial gauge to measure shaft endfloat

- A dial gauge with suitable adapters can be used to determine piston position BTDC on two-stroke engines for the purposes of ignition timing. The gauge, adapter and suitable length probe are installed in the place of the spark plug and the gauge zeroed at TDC. If the piston position is specified as 1.14 mm BTDC, rotate the engine back to 2.00 mm BTDC, then slowly forwards to 1.14 mm BTDC.

Cylinder compression gauges

- A compression gauge is used for measuring cylinder compression. Either the rubber-cone type or the threaded adapter type can be used. The latter is preferred to ensure a perfect seal against the cylinder head. A 0 to 300 psi (0 to 20 Bar) type gauge (for gasoline engines) will be suitable for motorcycles.
- The spark plug is removed and the gauge either held hard against the cylinder head (cone type) or the gauge adapter screwed into the cylinder head (threaded type) **(see illustration 3.20)**. Cylinder compression is measured with the engine turning over, but not running - carry out the compression test as described in *Troubleshooting Equipment*. The gauge will hold the reading until manually released.

Oil pressure gauge

- An oil pressure gauge is used for measuring engine oil pressure. Most gauges come with a set of adapters to fit the thread of the take-off point **(see illustration 3.21)**. If the take-off point specified by the motorcycle manufacturer is an external oil pipe union, make sure that the specified replacement union is used to prevent oil starvation.

3.21 Oil pressure gauge and take-off point adapter (arrow)

- Oil pressure is measured with the engine running (at a specific rpm) and often the manufacturer will specify pressure limits for a cold and hot engine.

Straight-edge and surface plate

- If checking the gasket face of a component for warpage, place a steel rule or precision straight-edge across the gasket face and measure any gap between the straight-edge and component with feeler gauges **(see illustration 3.22)**. Check diagonally across the component and between mounting holes **(see illustration 3.23)**.

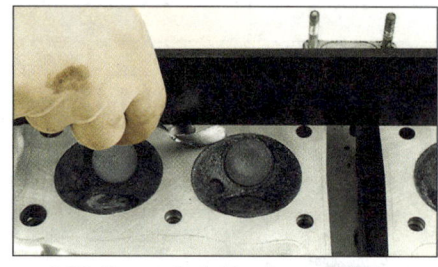

3.22 Use a straight-edge and feeler gauges to check for warpage

3.20 Using a rubber-cone type cylinder compression gauge

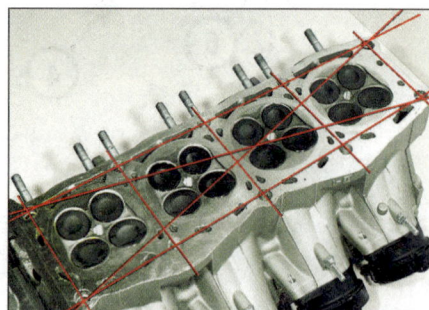

3.23 Check for warpage in these directions

Tools and Workshop Tips

● Checking individual components for warpage, such as clutch plain (metal) plates, requires a perfectly flat plate or piece of plate glass and feeler gauges.

4 Torque and leverage

What is torque?

● Torque describes the twisting force around a shaft. The amount of torque applied is determined by the distance from the center of the shaft to the end of the lever and the amount of force being applied to the end of the lever; distance multiplied by force equals torque.

● The manufacturer applies a measured torque to a bolt or nut to ensure that it will not loosen in use and to hold two components securely together without movement in the joint. The actual torque setting depends on the thread size, bolt or nut material and the composition of the components being held.

● Too little torque may cause the fastener to loosen due to vibration, whereas too much torque will distort the joint faces of the component or cause the fastener to shear off. Always stick to the specified torque setting.

Using a torque wrench

● Check the calibration of the torque wrench and make sure it has a suitable range for the job. Torque wrenches are available in Nm (Newton-meters), kgf m (kilograms-force meter), lbf ft (pounds-feet), lbf in (inch-pounds). Do not confuse lbf ft with lbf in.

● Adjust the tool to the desired torque on the scale (see illustration 4.1). If your torque wrench is not calibrated in the units specified, carefully convert the figure (see *Conversion Factors*). A manufacturer sometimes gives a torque setting as a range (8 to 10 Nm) rather than a single figure - in this case set the tool midway between the two settings. The same torque may be expressed as 9 Nm ± 1 Nm. Some torque wrenches have a method of locking the setting so that it isn't inadvertently altered during use.

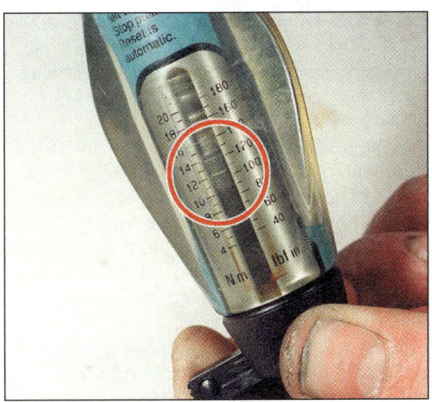

4.1 Set the torque wrench index mark to the setting required, in this case 12 Nm

● Install the bolts/nuts in their correct location and secure them lightly. Their threads must be clean and free of any old locking compound. Unless specified the threads and flange should be dry - oiled threads are necessary in certain circumstances and the manufacturer will take this into account in the specified torque figure. Similarly, the manufacturer may also specify the application of thread-locking compound.

● Tighten the fasteners in the specified sequence until the torque wrench clicks, indicating that the torque setting has been reached. Apply the torque again to double-check the setting. Where different thread diameter fasteners secure the component, as a rule tighten the larger diameter ones first.

● When the torque wrench has been finished with, release the lock (where applicable) and fully back off its setting to zero - do not leave the torque wrench tensioned. Also, do not use a torque wrench for loosening a fastener.

Angle-tightening

● Manufacturers often specify a figure in degrees for final tightening of a fastener. This usually follows tightening to a specific torque setting.

● A degree disc can be set and attached to the socket (see illustration 4.2) or a protractor can be used to mark the angle of movement on the bolt/nut head and the surrounding casting (see illustration 4.3).

4.2 Angle tightening can be accomplished with a torque-angle gauge . . .

4.3 . . . or by marking the angle on the surrounding component

Loosening sequences

● Where more than one bolt/nut secures a component, loosen each fastener evenly a little at a time. In this way, not all the stress of the joint is held by one fastener and the components are not likely to distort.

● If a tightening sequence is provided, work in the REVERSE of this, but if not, work from the outside in, in a criss-cross sequence (see illustration 4.4).

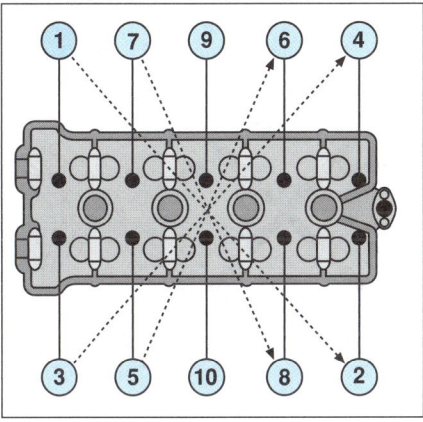

4.4 When loosening, work from the outside inwards

Tightening sequences

● If a component is held by more than one fastener it is important that the retaining bolts/nuts are tightened evenly to prevent uneven stress build-up and distortion of sealing faces. This is especially important on high-compression joints such as the cylinder head.

● A sequence is usually provided by the manufacturer, either in a diagram or actually marked in the casting. If not, always start in the center and work outwards in a criss-cross pattern (see illustration 4.5). Start off by securing all bolts/nuts finger-tight, then set the torque wrench and tighten each fastener by a small amount in sequence until the final torque is reached. By following this practice,

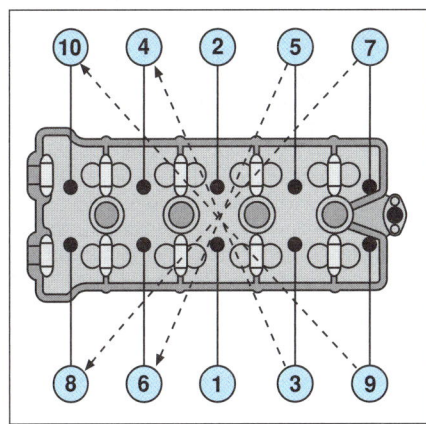

4.5 When tightening, work from the inside outwards

Tools and Workshop Tips

the joint will be held evenly and will not be distorted. Important joints, such as the cylinder head and big-end fasteners often have two- or three-stage torque settings.

Applying leverage

● Use tools at the correct angle. Position a socket or wrench on the bolt/nut so that you pull it towards you when loosening. If this can't be done, push the wrench without curling your fingers around it **(see illustration 4.6)** - the wrench may slip or the fastener loosen suddenly, resulting in your fingers being crushed against a component.

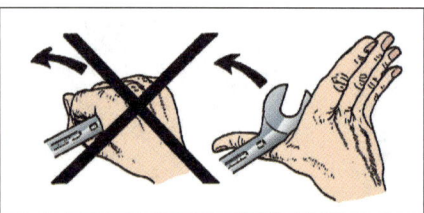

4.6 If you can't pull on the wrench to loosen a fastener, push with your hand open

● Additional leverage is gained by extending the length of the lever. The best way to do this is to use a breaker bar instead of the regular length tool, or to slip a length of tubing over the end of the wrench or socket.
● If additional leverage will not work, the fastener head is either damaged or firmly corroded in place (see *Fasteners*).

5 Bearings

Bearing removal and installation

Drivers and sockets

● Before removing a bearing, always inspect the casing to see which way it must be driven out - some casings will have retaining plates or a cast step. Also check for any identifying markings on the bearing and, if installed to a certain depth, measure this at this stage. Some roller bearings are sealed on one side - take note of the original installed position.
● Bearings can be driven out of a casing using a bearing driver tool (with the correct size head) or a socket of the correct diameter. Select the driver head or socket so that it contacts the outer race of the bearing, not the balls/rollers or inner race. Always support the casing around the bearing housing with wood blocks, otherwise there is a risk of fracture. The bearing is driven out with a few blows on the driver or socket from a heavy mallet. Unless access is severely restricted (as with wheel bearings), a pin-punch is not recommended unless it is moved around the bearing to keep it square in its housing.

● The same equipment can be used to install bearings. Make sure the bearing housing is supported on wood blocks and line up the bearing in its housing. Install the bearing as noted on removal - generally they are installed with their marked side facing outwards. Tap the bearing squarely into its housing using a driver or socket which bears only on the bearing's outer race - contact with the bearing balls/rollers or inner race will destroy it **(see illustrations 5.1 and 5.2)**.
● Check that the bearing inner race and balls/rollers rotate freely.

5.1 Using a bearing driver against the bearing's outer race

5.2 Using a large socket against the bearing's outer race

Pullers and slide-hammers

● Where a bearing is pressed on a shaft a puller will be required to extract it **(see illustration 5.3)**. Make sure that the puller clamp or legs fit securely behind the bearing and are unlikely to slip out. If pulling a bearing

5.3 This bearing puller clamps behind the bearing and pressure is applied to the shaft end to draw the bearing off

off a gear shaft for example, you may have to locate the puller behind a gear pinion if there is no access to the race and draw the gear pinion off the shaft as well **(see illustration 5.4)**.

> **Caution: Ensure that the puller's center bolt locates securely against the end of the shaft and will not slip when pressure is applied. Also ensure that puller does not damage the shaft end.**

5.4 Where no access is available to the rear of the bearing, it is sometimes possible to draw off the adjacent component

● Operate the puller so that its center bolt exerts pressure on the shaft end and draws the bearing off the shaft.
● When installing the bearing on the shaft, tap only on the bearing's inner race - contact with the balls/rollers or outer race will destroy the bearing. Use a socket or length of tubing as a drift which fits over the shaft end **(see illustration 5.5)**.

5.5 When installing a bearing on a shaft use a piece of tubing which bears only on the bearing's inner race

● Where a bearing locates in a blind hole in a casing, it cannot be driven or pulled out as described above. A slide-hammer with knife-edged bearing puller attachment will be required. The puller attachment passes through the bearing and when tightened expands to fit firmly behind the bearing **(see illustration 5.6)**. By operating the slide-hammer part of the tool the bearing is jarred out of its housing **(see illustration 5.7)**.
● It is possible, if the bearing is of reasonable weight, for it to drop out of its housing if the casing is heated as described opposite. If

Tools and Workshop Tips

5.6 Expand the bearing puller so that it locks behind the bearing . . .

5.7 . . . attach the slide hammer to the bearing puller

this method is attempted, first prepare a work surface which will enable the casing to be tapped face down to help dislodge the bearing - a wood surface is ideal since it will not damage the casing's gasket surface. Wearing protective gloves, tap the heated casing several times against the work surface to dislodge the bearing under its own weight **(see illustration 5.8)**.

5.8 Tapping a casing face down on wood blocks can often dislodge a bearing

● Bearings can be installed in blind holes using the driver or socket method described above.

Drawbolts

● Where a bearing or bushing is set in the eye of a component, such as a suspension linkage arm or connecting rod small-end, removal by drift may damage the component. Furthermore, a rubber bushing in a shock absorber eye cannot successfully be driven out of position. If access is available to a hydraulic press, the task is straightforward. If not, a drawbolt can be fabricated to extract the bearing or bushing.

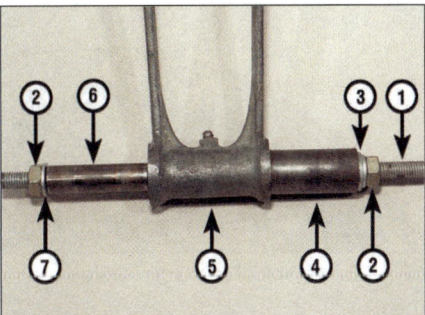

5.9 Drawbolt component parts assembled on a suspension arm

1. Bolt or length of threaded bar
2. Nuts
3. Washer (external diameter greater than tubing internal diameter)
4. Tubing (internal diameter sufficient to accommodate bearing)
5. Suspension arm with bearing
6. Tubing (external diameter slightly smaller than bearing)
7. Washer (external diameter slightly smaller than bearing)

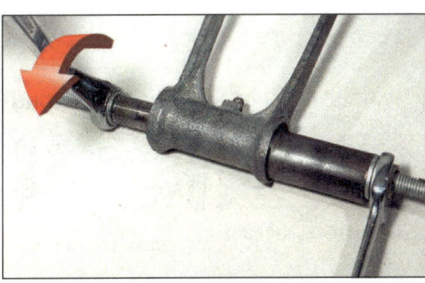

5.10 Drawing the bearing out of the suspension arm

● To extract the bearing/bushing you will need a long bolt with nut (or piece of threaded bar with two nuts), a piece of tubing which has an internal diameter larger than the bearing/bushing, another piece of tubing which has an external diameter slightly smaller than the bearing/bushing, and a selection of washers **(see illustrations 5.9 and 5.10)**. Note that the pieces of tubing must be of the same length, or longer, than the bearing/bushing.

● The same kit (without the pieces of tubing) can be used to draw the new bearing/bushing back into place **(see illustration 5.11)**.

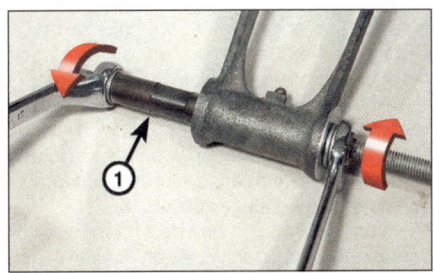

5.11 Installing a new bearing (1) in the suspension arm

Temperature change

● If the bearing's outer race is a tight fit in the casing, the aluminum casing can be heated to release its grip on the bearing. Aluminum will expand at a greater rate than the steel bearing outer race. There are several ways to do this, but avoid any localized extreme heat (such as a blow torch) - aluminum alloy has a low melting point.

● Approved methods of heating a casing are using a domestic oven (heated to 100°C/200°F) or immersing the casing in boiling water **(see illustration 5.12)**. Low temperature range localized heat sources such as a paint stripper heat gun or clothes iron can also be used **(see illustration 5.13)**. Alternatively, soak a rag in boiling water, wring it out and wrap it around the bearing housing.

> ⚠ **Warning: All of these methods require care in use to prevent scalding and burns to the hands. Wear protective gloves when handling hot components.**

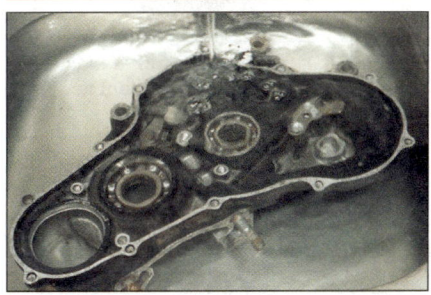

5.12 A casing can be immersed in a sink of boiling water to aid bearing removal

5.13 Using a localized heat source to aid bearing removal

● If heating the whole casing note that plastic components, such as the neutral switch, may suffer - remove them beforehand.

● After heating, remove the bearing as described above. You may find that the expansion is sufficient for the bearing to fall out of the casing under its own weight or with a light tap on the driver or socket.

● If necessary, the casing can be heated to aid bearing installation, and this is sometimes the recommended procedure if the motorcycle manufacturer has designed the housing and bearing fit with this intention.

REF•18 Tools and Workshop Tips

- Installation of bearings can be eased by placing them in a freezer the night before installation. The steel bearing will contract slightly, allowing easy insertion in its housing. This is often useful when installing steering head outer races in the frame.

Bearing types and markings

- Plain shell bearings, ball bearings, needle roller bearings and tapered roller bearings will all be found on motorcycles **(see illustrations 5.14 and 5.15)**. The ball and roller types are usually caged between an inner and outer race, but uncaged variations may be found.

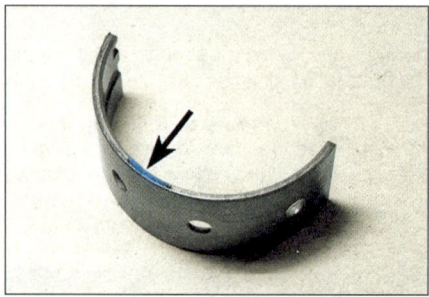

5.14 Shell bearings are either plain or grooved. They are usually identified by color code (arrow)

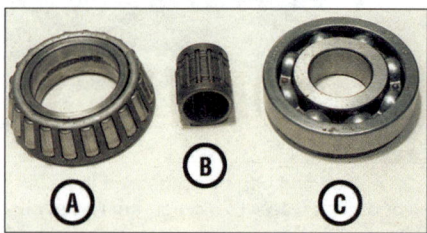

5.15 Tapered roller bearing (A), needle roller bearing (B) and ball journal bearing (C)

- Shell bearings (often called inserts) are usually found at the crankshaft main and connecting rod big-end where they are good at coping with high loads. They are made of a phosphor-bronze material and are impregnated with self-lubricating properties.
- Ball bearings and needle roller bearings consist of a steel inner and outer race with the balls or rollers between the races. They require constant lubrication by oil or grease and are good at coping with axial loads. Taper roller bearings consist of rollers set in a tapered cage set on the inner race; the outer race is separate. They are good at coping with axial loads and prevent movement along the shaft - a typical application is in the steering head.
- Bearing manufacturers produce bearings to ISO size standards and stamp one face of the bearing to indicate its internal and external diameter, load capacity and type **(see illustration 5.16)**.
- Metal bushings are usually of phosphor-bronze material. Rubber bushings are used in suspension mounting eyes. Fiber bushings have also been used in suspension pivots.

5.16 Typical bearing marking

Bearing troubleshooting

- If a bearing outer race has spun in its housing, the housing material will be damaged. You can use a bearing locking compound to bond the outer race in place if damage is not too severe.
- Shell bearings will fail due to damage of their working surface, as a result of lack of lubrication, corrosion or abrasive particles in the oil **(see illustration 5.17)**. Small particles of dirt in the oil may embed in the bearing material whereas larger particles will score the bearing and shaft journal. If a number of short journeys are made, insufficient heat will be generated to drive off condensation which has built up on the bearings.

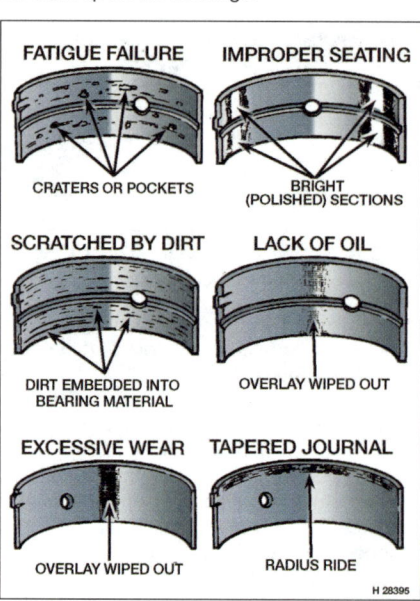

5.17 Typical bearing failures

- Ball and roller bearings will fail due to lack of lubrication or damage to the balls or rollers. Tapered-roller bearings can be damaged by overloading them. Unless the bearing is sealed on both sides, wash it in kerosene to remove all old grease then allow it to dry. Make a visual inspection looking to dented balls or rollers, damaged cages and worn or pitted races **(see illustration 5.18)**.
- A ball bearing can be checked for wear by listening to it when spun. Apply a film of light oil to the bearing and hold it close to the ear - hold the outer race with one hand and spin the inner race with the other hand **(see illustration 5.19)**. The bearing should be almost silent when spun; if it grates or rattles it is worn.

5.18 Example of ball journal bearing with damaged balls and cages

5.19 Hold outer race and listen to inner race when spun

6 Oil seals

Oil seal removal and installation

- Oil seals should be replaced every time a component is dismantled. This is because the seal lips will become set to the sealing surface and will not necessarily reseal.
- Oil seals can be pried out of position using a large flat-bladed screwdriver **(see illustration 6.1)**. In the case of crankcase seals, check first that the seal is not lipped on the inside, preventing its removal with the crankcases joined.

6.1 Pry out oil seals with a large flat-bladed screwdriver

- New seals are usually installed with their marked face (containing the seal reference code) outwards and the spring side towards the fluid being retained. In certain cases, such as a two-stroke engine crankshaft seal, a double lipped seal may be used due to there being fluid or gas on each side of the joint.

Tools and Workshop Tips

● Use a bearing driver or socket which bears only on the outer hard edge of the seal to install it in the casing - tapping on the inner edge will damage the sealing lip.

Oil seal types and markings

● Oil seals are usually of the single-lipped type. Double-lipped seals are found where a liquid or gas is on both sides of the joint.
● Oil seals can harden and lose their sealing ability if the motorcycle has been in storage for a long period - replacement is the only solution.
● Oil seal manufacturers also conform to the ISO markings for seal size - these are molded into the outer face of the seal **(see illustration 6.2)**.

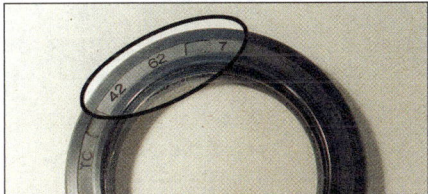

6.2 These oil seal markings indicate inside diameter, outside diameter and seal thickness

7 Gaskets and sealants

Types of gasket and sealant

● Gaskets are used to seal the mating surfaces between components and keep lubricants, fluids, vacuum or pressure contained within the assembly. Aluminum gaskets are sometimes found at the cylinder joints, but most gaskets are paper-based. If the mating surfaces of the components being joined are undamaged the gasket can be installed dry, although a dab of sealant or grease will be useful to hold it in place during assembly.
● RTV (Room Temperature Vulcanizing) silicone rubber sealants cure when exposed to moisture in the atmosphere. These sealants are good at filling pits or irregular gasket faces, but will tend to be forced out of the joint under very high torque. They can be used to replace a paper gasket, but first make sure that the width of the paper gasket is not essential to the shimming of internal components. RTV sealants should not be used on components containing gasoline.
● Non-hardening, semi-hardening and hard setting liquid gasket compounds can be used with a gasket or between a metal-to-metal joint. Select the sealant to suit the application: universal non-hardening sealant can be used on virtually all joints; semi-hardening on joint faces which are rough or damaged; hard setting sealant on joints which require a permanent bond and are subjected to high temperature and pressure. **Note:** *Check first if the paper gasket has a bead of sealant impregnated in its surface before applying additional sealant.*
● When choosing a sealant, make sure it is suitable for the application, particularly if being applied in a high-temperature area or in the vicinity of fuel. Certain manufacturers produce sealants in either clear, silver or black colors to match the finish of the engine. This has a particular application on motorcycles where much of the engine is exposed.
● Do not over-apply sealant. That which is squeezed out on the outside of the joint can be wiped off, whereas an excess of sealant on the inside can break off and clog oilways.

Breaking a sealed joint

● Age, heat, pressure and the use of hard setting sealant can cause two components to stick together so tightly that they are difficult to separate using finger pressure alone. Do not resort to using levers unless there is a pry point provided for this purpose **(see illustration 7.1)** or else the gasket surfaces will be damaged.
● Use a soft-faced hammer **(see illustration 7.2)** or a wood block and conventional hammer to strike the component near the mating surface. Avoid hammering against cast extremities since they may break off. If this method fails, try using a wood wedge between the two components.

Caution: If the joint will not separate, double-check that you have removed all the fasteners.

7.1 If a pry point is provided, apply gentle pressure with a flat-bladed screwdriver

7.2 Tap around the joint with a soft-faced mallet if necessary - don't strike cooling fins

Removal of old gasket and sealant

● Paper gaskets will most likely come away complete, leaving only a few traces stuck

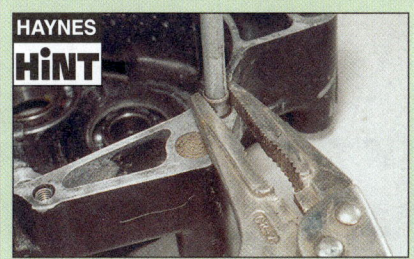

Most components have one or two hollow locating dowels between the two gasket faces. If a dowel cannot be removed, do not resort to gripping it with pliers - it will almost certainly be distorted. Install a close-fitting socket or Phillips screwdriver into the dowel and then grip the outer edge of the dowel to free it.

on the sealing faces of the components. It is imperative that all traces are removed to ensure correct sealing of the new gasket.
● Very carefully scrape all traces of gasket away making sure that the sealing surfaces are not gouged or scored by the scraper **(see illustrations 7.3, 7.4 and 7.5)**. Stubborn deposits can be removed by spraying with an aerosol gasket remover. Final preparation of

7.3 Paper gaskets can be scraped off with a gasket scraper tool . . .

7.4 . . . a knife blade . . .

7.5 . . . or a household scraper

Tools and Workshop Tips

7.6 Fine abrasive paper is wrapped around a flat file to clean up the gasket face

7.7 A kitchen scourer can be used on stubborn deposits

8.1 Tighten the chain breaker to push the pin out of the link . . .

8.2 . . . withdraw the pin, remove the tool . . .

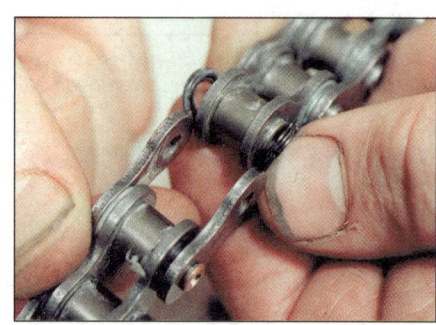

8.3 . . . and separate the chain link

8.4 Insert the new soft link, with O-rings, through the chain ends . . .

8.5 . . . install the O-rings over the pin ends . . .

8.6 . . . followed by the sideplate

8.7 Push the sideplate into position using a clamp

the gasket surface can be made with very fine abrasive paper or a plastic kitchen scourer **(see illustrations 7.6 and 7.7)**.

● Old sealant can be scraped or peeled off components, depending on the type originally used. Note that gasket removal compounds are available to avoid scraping the components clean; make sure the gasket remover suits the type of sealant used.

8 Chains

Breaking and joining final drive chains

● Drive chains for all but small bikes are continuous and do not have a clip-type connecting link. The chain must be broken using a chain breaker tool and the new chain securely riveted together using a new soft rivet-type link. Never use a clip-type connecting link instead of a rivet-type link, except in an emergency. Various chain breaking and riveting tools are available, either as separate tools or combined as illustrated in the accompanying photographs - read the instructions supplied with the tool carefully.

> **⚠ Warning:** The need to rivet the new link pins correctly cannot be overstressed - loss of control of the motorcycle is very likely to result if the chain breaks in use.

● Rotate the chain and look for the soft link. The soft link pins look like they have been deeply center-punched instead of peened over like all the other pins **(see illustration 8.9)** and its sideplate may be a different color. Position the soft link midway between the sprockets and assemble the chain breaker tool over one of the soft link pins **(see illustration 8.1)**. Operate the tool to push the pin out through the chain **(see illustration 8.2)**. On an O-ring chain, remove the O-rings **(see illustration 8.3)**. Carry out the same procedure on the other soft link pin.

> **Caution:** Certain soft link pins (particularly on the larger chains) may require their ends to be filed or ground off before they can be pressed out using the tool.

● Check that you have the correct size and strength (standard or heavy duty) new soft link - do not reuse the old link. Look for the size marking on the chain sideplates **(see illustration 8.10)**.

● Position the chain ends so that they are engaged over the rear sprocket. On an O-ring chain, install a new O-ring over each pin of the link and insert the link through the two chain ends **(see illustration 8.4)**. Install a new O-ring over the end of each pin, followed by the sideplate (with the chain manufacturer's marking facing outwards) **(see illustrations 8.5 and 8.6)**. On an unsealed chain, insert the link through the two chain ends, then install the sideplate with the chain manufacturer's marking facing outwards.

● Note that it may not be possible to install the sideplate using finger pressure alone. If using a joining tool, assemble it so that the plates of the tool clamp the link and press the sideplate over the pins **(see illustration 8.7)**. Otherwise, use two small sockets placed over

Tools and Workshop Tips

8.8 Assemble the chain riveting tool over one pin at a time and tighten it fully

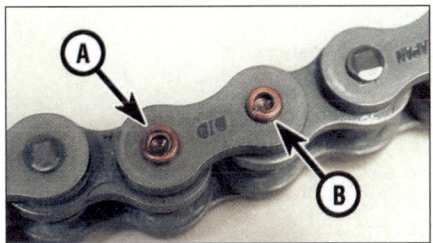

8.9 Pin end correctly riveted (A), pin end unriveted (B)

the rivet ends and two pieces of the wood between a C-clamp. Operate the clamp to press the sideplate over the pins.

 Assemble the joining tool over one pin (following the manufacturer's instructions) and tighten the tool down to spread the pin end securely **(see illustrations 8.8 and 8.9)**. Do the same on the other pin.

> **Warning: Check that the pin ends are secure and that there is no danger of the sideplate coming loose. If the pin ends are cracked the soft link must be replaced.**

Final drive chain sizing

● Chains are sized using a three digit number, followed by a suffix to denote the chain type **(see illustration 8.10)**. Chain type is either standard or heavy duty (thicker sideplates), and also unsealed or O-ring/X-ring type.

● The first digit of the number relates to the pitch of the chain, ie the distance from the center of one pin to the center of the next pin **(see illustration 8.11)**. Pitch is expressed in eighths of an inch, as follows:

8.10 Typical chain size and type marking

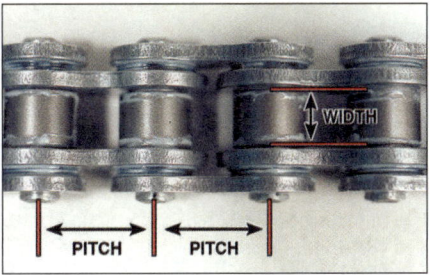

8.11 Chain dimensions

Sizes commencing with a 4 (for example 428) have a pitch of 1/2 inch (12.7 mm)

Sizes commencing with a 5 (for example 520) have a pitch of 5/8 inch (15.9 mm)

Sizes commencing with a 6 (for example 630) have a pitch of 3/4 inch (19.1 mm)

● The second and third digits of the chain size relate to the width of the rollers, for example the 525 shown has 5/16 inch (7.94 mm) rollers **(see illustration 8.11)**.

9 Hoses

Clamping to prevent flow

● Small-bore flexible hoses can be clamped to prevent fluid flow while a component is worked on. Whichever method is used, ensure that the hose material is not permanently distorted or damaged by the clamp.

a) A brake hose clamp available from auto parts stores **(see illustration 9.1)**.
b) A wingnut type hose clamp **(see illustration 9.2)**.

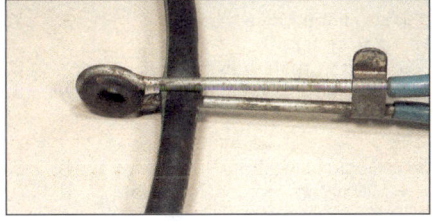

9.1 Hoses can be clamped with an automotive brake hose clamp . . .

9.2 . . . a wingnut type hose clamp . . .

c) Two sockets placed on each side of the hose and held with straight-jawed self-locking pliers **(see illustration 9.3)**.
d) Thick card stock on each side of the hose held between straight-jawed self-locking pliers **(see illustration 9.4)**.

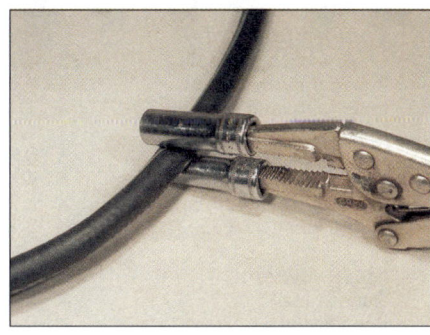

9.3 . . . two sockets and a pair of self-locking grips . . .

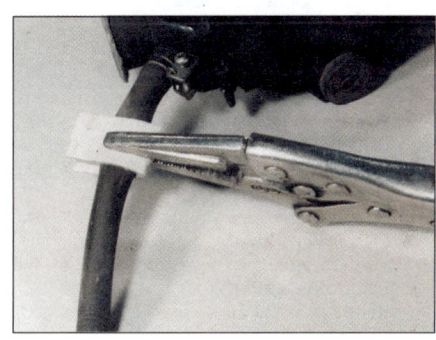

9.4 . . . or thick card and self-locking grips

Freeing and fitting hoses

● Always make sure the hose clamp is moved well clear of the hose end. Grip the hose with your hand and rotate it while pulling it off the union. If the hose has hardened due to age and will not move, slit it with a sharp knife and peel its ends off the union **(see illustration 9.5)**.

● Resist the temptation to use grease or soap on the unions to aid installation; although it helps the hose slip over the union it will equally aid the escape of fluid from the joint. It is preferable to soften the hose ends in hot water and wet the inside surface of the hose with water or a fluid which will evaporate.

9.5 Cutting a coolant hose free with a sharp knife

Conversion Factors

Length (distance)
Inches (in)	X 25.4	= Millimeters (mm)	X	0.0394	= Inches (in)
Feet (ft)	X 0.305	= Meters (m)	X	3.281	= Feet (ft)
Miles	X 1.609	= Kilometers (km)	X	0.621	= Miles

Volume (capacity)
Cubic inches (cu in; in^3)	X 16.387	= Cubic centimeters (cc; cm^3)	X	0.061	= Cubic inches (cu in; in^3)
Imperial pints (Imp pt)	X 0.568	= Liters (l)	X	1.76	= Imperial pints (Imp pt)
Imperial quarts (Imp qt)	X 1.137	= Liters (l)	X	0.88	= Imperial quarts (Imp qt)
Imperial quarts (Imp qt)	X 1.201	= US quarts (US qt)	X	0.833	= Imperial quarts (Imp qt)
US quarts (US qt)	X 0.946	= Liters (l)	X	1.057	= US quarts (US qt)
Imperial gallons (Imp gal)	X 4.546	= Liters (l)	X	0.22	= Imperial gallons (Imp gal)
Imperial gallons (Imp gal)	X 1.201	= US gallons (US gal)	X	0.833	= Imperial gallons (Imp gal)
US gallons (US gal)	X 3.785	= Liters (l)	X	0.264	= US gallons (US gal)

Mass (weight)
Ounces (oz)	X 28.35	= Grams (g)	X	0.035	= Ounces (oz)
Pounds (lb)	X 0.454	= Kilograms (kg)	X	2.205	= Pounds (lb)

Force
Ounces-force (ozf; oz)	X 0.278	= Newtons (N)	X	3.6	= Ounces-force (ozf; oz)
Pounds-force (lbf; lb)	X 4.448	= Newtons (N)	X	0.225	= Pounds-force (lbf; lb)
Newtons (N)	X 0.1	= Kilograms-force (kgf; kg)	X	9.81	= Newtons (N)

Pressure
Pounds-force per square inch (psi; lbf/in^2; lb/in^2)	X 0.070	= Kilograms-force per square centimeter (kgf/cm^2; kg/cm^2)	X	14.223	= Pounds-force per square inch (psi; lbf/in^2; lb/in^2)
Pounds-force per square inch (psi; lbf/in^2; lb/in^2)	X 0.068	= Atmospheres (atm)	X	14.696	= Pounds-force per square inch (psi; lbf/in^2; lb/in^2)
Pounds-force per square inch (psi; lbf/in^2; lb/in^2)	X 0.069	= Bars	X	14.5	= Pounds-force per square inch (psi; lbf/in^2; lb/in^2)
Pounds-force per square inch (psi; lbf/in^2; lb/in^2)	X 6.895	= Kilopascals (kPa)	X	0.145	= Pounds-force per square inch (psi; lbf/in^2; lb/in^2)
Kilopascals (kPa)	X 0.01	= Kilograms-force per square centimeter (kgf/cm^2; kg/cm^2)	X	98.1	= Kilopascals (kPa)

Torque (moment of force)
Pounds-force inches (lbf in; lb in)	X 1.152	= Kilograms-force centimeter (kgf cm; kg cm)	X	0.868	= Pounds-force inches (lbf in; lb in)
Pounds-force inches (lbf in; lb in)	X 0.113	= Newton meters (Nm)	X	8.85	= Pounds-force inches (lbf in; lb in)
Pounds-force inches (lbf in; lb in)	X 0.083	= Pounds-force feet (lbf ft; lb ft)	X	12	= Pounds-force inches (lbf in; lb in)
Pounds-force feet (lbf ft; lb ft)	X 0.138	= Kilograms-force meters (kgf m; kg m)	X	7.233	= Pounds-force feet (lbf ft; lb ft)
Pounds-force feet (lbf ft; lb ft)	X 1.356	= Newton meters (Nm)	X	0.738	= Pounds-force feet (lbf ft; lb ft)
Newton meters (Nm)	X 0.102	= Kilograms-force meters (kgf m; kg m)	X	9.804	= Newton meters (Nm)

Vacuum
Inches mercury (in. Hg)	X 3.377	= Kilopascals (kPa)	X	0.2961	= Inches mercury
Inches mercury (in. Hg)	X 25.4	= Millimeters mercury (mm Hg)	X	0.0394	= Inches mercury

Power
Horsepower (hp)	X 745.7	= Watts (W)	X	0.0013	= Horsepower (hp)

Velocity (speed)
Miles per hour (miles/hr; mph)	X 1.609	= Kilometers per hour (km/hr; kph)	X	0.621	= Miles per hour (miles/hr; mph)

Fuel consumption*
Miles per gallon, Imperial (mpg)	X 0.354	= Kilometers per liter (km/l)	X	2.825	= Miles per gallon, Imperial (mpg)
Miles per gallon, US (mpg)	X 0.425	= Kilometers per liter (km/l)	X	2.352	= Miles per gallon, US (mpg)

Temperature

Degrees Fahrenheit = (°C x 1.8) + 32   Degrees Celsius (Degrees Centigrade; °C) = (°F - 32) x 0.56

*It is common practice to convert from miles per gallon (mpg) to liters/100 kilometers (l/100km), where mpg (Imperial) x l/100 km = 282 and mpg (US) x l/100 km = 235

Fraction/decimal/millimeter equivalents REF•23

DECIMALS to MILLIMETERS

Decimal	mm	Decimal	mm
0.001	0.0254	0.500	12.7000
0.002	0.0508	0.510	12.9540
0.003	0.0762	0.520	13.2080
0.004	0.1016	0.530	13.4620
0.005	0.1270	0.540	13.7160
0.006	0.1524	0.550	13.9700
0.007	0.1778	0.560	14.2240
0.008	0.2032	0.570	14.4780
0.009	0.2286	0.580	14.7320
		0.590	14.9860
0.010	0.2540		
0.020	0.5080		
0.030	0.7620		
0.040	1.0160	0.600	15.2400
0.050	1.2700	0.610	15.4940
0.060	1.5240	0.620	15.7480
0.070	1.7780	0.630	16.0020
0.080	2.0320	0.640	16.2560
0.090	2.2860	0.650	16.5100
		0.660	16.7640
0.100	2.5400	0.670	17.0180
0.110	2.7940	0.680	17.2720
0.120	3.0480	0.690	17.5260
0.130	3.3020		
0.140	3.5560		
0.150	3.8100		
0.160	4.0640	0.700	17.7800
0.170	4.3180	0.710	18.0340
0.180	4.5720	0.720	18.2880
0.190	4.8260	0.730	18.5420
		0.740	18.7960
0.200	5.0800	0.750	19.0500
0.210	5.3340	0.760	19.3040
0.220	5.5880	0.770	19.5580
0.230	5.8420	0.780	19.8120
0.240	6.0960	0.790	20.0660
0.250	6.3500		
0.260	6.6040		
0.270	6.8580	0.800	20.3200
0.280	7.1120	0.810	20.5740
0.290	7.3660	0.820	21.8280
		0.830	21.0820
0.300	7.6200	0.840	21.3360
0.310	7.8740	0.850	21.5900
0.320	8.1280	0.860	21.8440
0.330	8.3820	0.870	22.0980
0.340	8.6360	0.880	22.3520
0.350	8.8900	0.890	22.6060
0.360	9.1440		
0.370	9.3980		
0.380	9.6520		
0.390	9.9060	0.900	22.8600
0.400	10.1600	0.910	23.1140
0.410	10.4140	0.920	23.3680
0.420	10.6680	0.930	23.6220
0.430	10.9220	0.940	23.8760
0.440	11.1760	0.950	24.1300
0.450	11.4300	0.960	24.3840
0.460	11.6840	0.970	24.6380
0.470	11.9380	0.980	24.8920
0.480	12.1920	0.990	25.1460
0.490	12.4460	1.000	25.4000

FRACTIONS to DECIMALS to MILLIMETERS

Fraction	Decimal	mm	Fraction	Decimal	mm
1/64	0.0156	0.3969	33/64	0.5156	13.0969
1/32	0.0312	0.7938	17/32	0.5312	13.4938
3/64	0.0469	1.1906	35/64	0.5469	13.8906
1/16	0.0625	1.5875	9/16	0.5625	14.2875
5/64	0.0781	1.9844	37/64	0.5781	14.6844
3/32	0.0938	2.3812	19/32	0.5938	15.0812
7/64	0.1094	2.7781	39/64	0.6094	15.4781
1/8	0.1250	3.1750	5/8	0.6250	15.8750
9/64	0.1406	3.5719	41/64	0.6406	16.2719
5/32	0.1562	3.9688	21/32	0.6562	16.6688
11/64	0.1719	4.3656	43/64	0.6719	17.0656
3/16	0.1875	4.7625	11/16	0.6875	17.4625
13/64	0.2031	5.1594	45/64	0.7031	17.8594
7/32	0.2188	5.5562	23/32	0.7188	18.2562
15/64	0.2344	5.9531	47/64	0.7344	18.6531
1/4	0.2500	6.3500	3/4	0.7500	19.0500
17/64	0.2656	6.7469	49/64	0.7656	19.4469
9/32	0.2812	7.1438	25/32	0.7812	19.8438
19/64	0.2969	7.5406	51/64	0.7969	20.2406
5/16	0.3125	7.9375	13/16	0.8125	20.6375
21/64	0.3281	8.3344	53/64	0.8281	21.0344
11/32	0.3438	8.7312	27/32	0.8438	21.4312
23/64	0.3594	9.1281	55/64	0.8594	21.8281
3/8	0.3750	9.5250	7/8	0.8750	22.2250
25/64	0.3906	9.9219	57/64	0.8906	22.6219
13/32	0.4062	10.3188	29/32	0.9062	23.0188
27/64	0.4219	10.7156	59/64	0.9219	23.4156
7/16	0.4375	11.1125	15/16	0.9375	23.8125
29/64	0.4531	11.5094	61/64	0.9531	24.2094
15/32	0.4688	11.9062	31/32	0.9688	24.6062
31/64	0.4844	12.3031	63/64	0.9844	25.0031
1/2	0.5000	12.7000	1	1.0000	25.4000

Storage

Preparing for storage

Before you start

If repairs or an overhaul is needed, see that this is carried out now rather than left until you want to ride the vehicle again.

Give the vehicle a good wash and scrub all dirt from its underside. Make sure the vehicle dries completely before preparing for storage.

Engine

● Remove the spark plug and lubricate the cylinder bore with approximately a teaspoon of motor oil using a spout-type oil can (**see illustration 1**). Reinstall the spark plug. Crank the engine over a couple of times to coat the piston rings and bores with oil. If the machine has a recoil starter, use this to turn the engine over. If not, flick the kill switch to the OFF position and crank the engine over on the starter (**see illustration 2**). If the nature of the ignition system prevents the starter operating with the kill switch in the OFF position, remove the spark plug and fit it back in its cap; ensure that the plug is grounded against the cylinder head when the starter is operated (**see illustration 3**).

> **Warning:** It is important that the plug is grounded away from the spark plug hole otherwise there is a risk of atomized fuel from the cylinder igniting.

> **HAYNES HiNT** On a single cylinder four-stroke engine, you can seal the combustion chamber completely by positioning the piston at TDC on the compression stroke.

● Drain the carburetor otherwise there is a risk of jets becoming blocked by gum deposits from the fuel (**see illustration 4**).

● If the machine is going into long-term storage, consider adding a fuel stabilizer to the fuel in the tank. If the tank is drained completely, and it's a metal tank, corrosion of its internal surfaces may occur if left unprotected for a long period. The tank can be treated with a rust preventative especially for this purpose. Alternatively, remove the tank and pour half a liter of motor oil into it, install the filler cap and shake the tank to coat its internals with oil before draining off the excess. The same effect can also be achieved by spraying WD40 or a similar water-dispersant around the inside of the tank via its flexible nozzle.

● Make sure the cooling system contains the correct mix of antifreeze. Antifreeze also contains important corrosion inhibitors.

● The air intakes and exhaust can be sealed off by covering or plugging the openings. Ensure that you do not seal in any condensation; run the engine until it is

Squirt a drop of motor oil into each cylinder

Flick the kill switch to OFF . . .

. . . and ensure that the metal bodies of the plugs (arrows) are grounded against the cylinder head

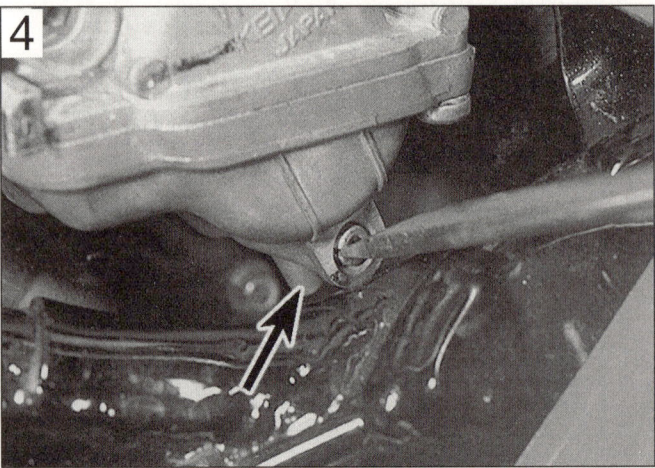
Connect a hose to the carburetor float chamber drain stub (arrow) and unscrew the drain screw

Storage REF•25

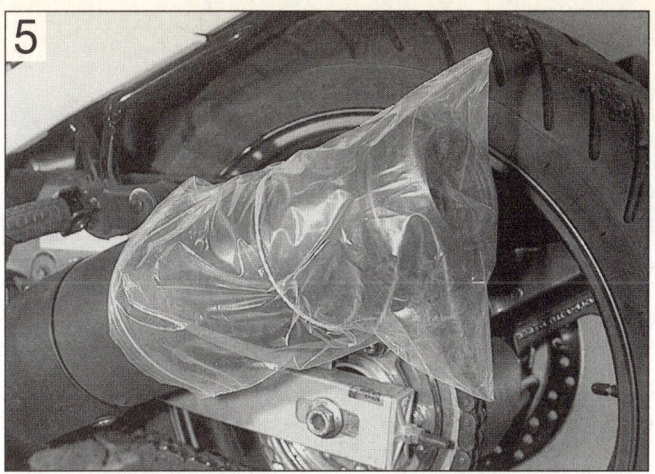

Exhausts can be sealed off with a plastic bag

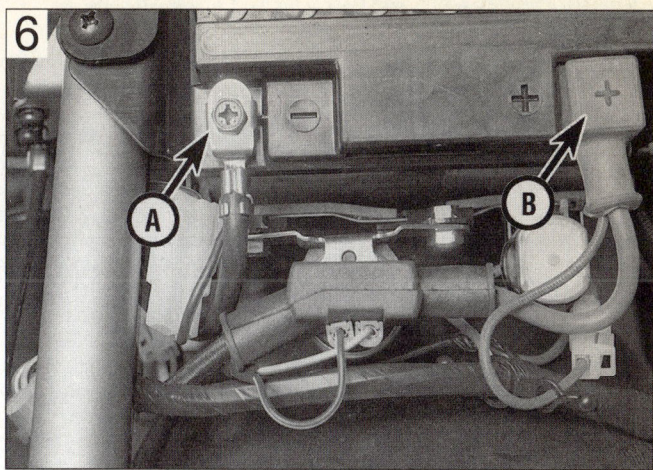

Disconnect the negative lead (A) first, followed by the positive lead (B)

hot, then switch off and allow to cool. Tape a piece of thick plastic over the silencer end **(see illustration 5)**. Note that some advocate pouring a tablespoon of motor oil into the silencer before sealing them off.

Battery

● Remove it from the machine - in extreme cases of cold the battery may freeze and crack its case **(see illustration 6)**.
● Check the electrolyte level and top up if necessary (conventional refillable batteries). Clean the terminals.
● Store the battery off the vehicle and away from any sources of fire. Position a wooden block under the battery if it is to sit on the ground.
● Give the battery a trickle charge for a few hours every month or keep it on a maintenance charger **(see illustration 7)**.

Tires

● Place the machine on jackstands; not only will this protect the tires, but will also ensure that no load is placed on the suspension bushings or wheel bearings.

Pivots and controls

● Lubricate all lever, pedal, stand and footrest pivot points. If grease nipples are fitted to the suspension components, apply lubricant to the pivots.
● Lubricate all control cables.

Other components

● Apply a wax protectant to all painted and plastic components. Wipe off any excess, but don't polish to a shine. Where fitted, clean the screen with soap and water.
● Coat metal parts with Vaseline (petroleum jelly).
● Apply a vinyl cleaner to the seat.

Storage conditions

● Aim to store the machine in a shed or garage which does not leak and is free from damp.

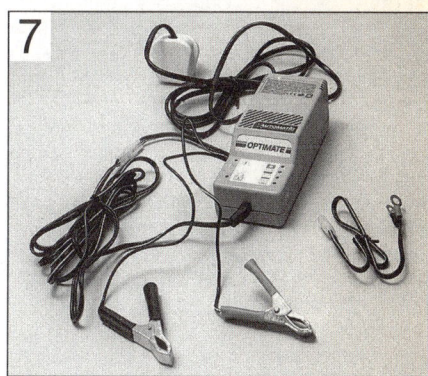

Use a suitable battery charger - this kit also assesses battery condition

● Drape an old blanket or bedspread over the vehicle to protect it from dust and direct contact with sunlight (which will fade paint).

Getting back on the road

Engine and transmission

● Change the oil and replace the oil filter. If this was done prior to storage, check that the oil hasn't emulsified - a thick whitish substance which occurs through condensation.
● Remove the spark plug. Using a spout-type oil can, squirt a few drops of oil into the cylinder. This will provide initial lubrication as the piston rings and bore come back into contact. Service the spark plug, or buy a new one, and install it in the engine.

● Check that the clutch isn't stuck on. The plates can stick together if left standing for some time, preventing clutch operation. Engage a gear and try rocking the machine back and forth with the clutch lever held against the handlebar. If this doesn't work on cable-operated clutches, hold the clutch lever back against the handlebar with a strong rubber band or cable tie for a couple of hours **(see illustration 8)**.
● If the air intakes or silencer end(s) were blocked off, remove the plug or cover used.

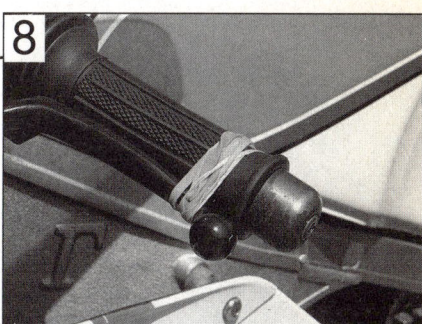

Hold the clutch lever back against the handlebar with rubber bands or a cable tie

Storage

● If the fuel tank was coated with a rust preventative, oil or a stabilizer added to the fuel, drain and flush the tank and dispose of the fuel sensibly. If no action was taken with the fuel tank prior to storage, it is advised that the old fuel is disposed of since it will go bad over a period of time. Refill the fuel tank with fresh fuel.

Frame and running gear

● Oil all pivot points and cables.
● Check the tire pressures.
● Lubricate the final drive chain (where applicable).
● Check that both brakes operate correctly. Apply each brake hard and check that it's not possible to move the vehicle forwards, then check that the brake frees off again once released. Brake caliper pistons can stick due to corrosion around the piston head, or on the sliding caliper types, due to corrosion of the slider pins. If the brake doesn't free after repeated operation, take the caliper off for examination. Similarly drum brakes can stick due to a seized operating cam, cable or rod linkage.
● If the vehicle has been in long-term storage, replace the brake fluid and clutch fluid (where applicable).
● Depending on where the vehicle has been stored, the wiring, cables and hoses may have been nibbled by rodents. Make a visual check and investigate disturbed wiring loom tape.

Battery

● If the battery has been previously removed and given top up charges it can simply be reconnected. Remember to connect the positive cable first and the negative cable last.
● On conventional refillable batteries, if the battery has not received any attention, remove it from the vehicle and check its electrolyte level. Top up if necessary then charge the battery. If the battery fails to hold a charge and a visual check show heavy white sulfation of the plates, the battery is probably defective and must be replaced. This is particularly likely if the battery is old. Confirm battery condition with a specific gravity check.
● On sealed (MF) batteries, if the battery has not received any attention, remove it from the machine and charge it according to the information on the battery case - if the battery fails to hold a charge it must be replaced.

Starting procedure

● If a recoil starter is fitted, turn the engine over a couple of times with the ignition OFF to distribute oil around the engine. If no recoil starter is fitted, flick the engine kill switch OFF and the ignition ON and crank the engine over a couple of times to work oil around the upper cylinder components. If the nature of the ignition system is such that the starter won't work with the kill switch OFF, remove the spark plug, fit it back into its cap and ground its body on the cylinder head. Reinstall the spark plug afterwards.

 Warning: It is important that the plug is grounded away from the spark plug hole otherwise there is a risk of atomized fuel from the cylinder igniting.

● Switch the kill switch to RUN, operate the choke and start the engine. If the engine won't start don't continue cranking the engine - not only will this flatten the battery, but the starter motor will overheat. Switch the ignition off and try again later. If the engine refuses to start, go through the troubleshooting procedures in this manual. **Note:** *If the machine has been in storage for a long time, old fuel or a carburetor blockage may be the problem. Gum deposits in carburetors can block jets - if a carburetor cleaner doesn't prove successful the carburetors must be dismantled for cleaning.*

● Once the engine has started, check that the lights and horn work properly.

● Treat the machine gently for the first ride and check all fluid levels on completion. Settle the machine back into the maintenance schedule.

Troubleshooting REF•27

This Section provides an easy reference-guide to the more common faults that are likely to afflict your machine. Obviously, the opportunities are almost limitless for faults to occur as a result of obscure failures, and to try and cover all eventualities would require a book. Indeed, a number have been written on the subject.

Successful troubleshooting is not a mysterious art but the application of a bit of knowledge combined with a systematic and logical approach to the problem. Approach any troubleshooting by first accurately identifying the symptom and then checking through the list of possible causes, starting with the simplest or most obvious and progressing in stages to the most complex. Take nothing for granted, but above all apply liberal quantities of common sense.

The main symptom of a fault is given in the text as a major heading below which are listed the various systems or areas which may contain the fault. Details of each possible cause for a fault and the remedial action to be taken are given. Further information should be sought in the relevant Chapter.

1 Engine doesn't start or is difficult to start
- [ ] Starter motor doesn't rotate
- [ ] Starter motor rotates but engine does not turn over
- [ ] Starter works but engine won't turn over (seized)
- [ ] No fuel flow
- [ ] Engine flooded
- [ ] No spark or weak spark
- [ ] Compression low
- [ ] Stalls after starting
- [ ] Rough idle

2 Poor running at low speed
- [ ] Spark weak
- [ ] Fuel/air mixture incorrect
- [ ] Compression low
- [ ] Poor acceleration

3 Poor running or no power at high speed
- [ ] Firing incorrect
- [ ] Fuel/air mixture incorrect
- [ ] Compression low
- [ ] Knocking or pinging
- [ ] Miscellaneous causes

4 Overheating
- [ ] Engine overheats
- [ ] Firing incorrect
- [ ] Fuel/air mixture incorrect
- [ ] Compression too high
- [ ] Engine load excessive
- [ ] Lubrication inadequate
- [ ] Miscellaneous causes

5 Clutch problems
- [ ] Clutch slipping
- [ ] Clutch not disengaging completely

6 Gear shifting problems
- [ ] Doesn't go into gear, or lever doesn't return
- [ ] Jumps out of gear
- [ ] Overshifts

7 Abnormal engine noise
- [ ] Knocking or pinging
- [ ] Piston slap or rattling
- [ ] Valve noise
- [ ] Other noise

8 Abnormal driveline noise
- [ ] Clutch noise
- [ ] Transmission noise
- [ ] Transfer case noise
- [ ] Final drive noise

9 Abnormal chassis noise
- [ ] Suspension noise
- [ ] Driveaxle noise (4WD models)
- [ ] Brake noise

10 Oil temperature indicator light comes on
- [ ] Engine lubrication system
- [ ] Electrical system

11 Excessive exhaust smoke
- [ ] White smoke
- [ ] Black smoke
- [ ] Brown smoke

12 Poor handling or stability
- [ ] Handlebar hard to turn
- [ ] Handlebar shakes or vibrates excessively
- [ ] Handlebar pulls to one side
- [ ] Poor shock absorbing qualities

13 Braking problems
- [ ] Front brakes are spongy, don't hold
- [ ] Brake lever pulsates
- [ ] Brakes drag

14 Electrical problems
- [ ] Battery dead or weak
- [ ] Battery overcharged

Troubleshooting

1 Engine doesn't start or is difficult to start

Starter motor does not rotate

- [ ] Engine kill switch Off.
- [ ] Fuse blown. Check fuse (Chapter 8).
- [ ] Battery voltage low. Check and recharge battery (Chapter 8).
- [ ] Starter motor defective. Make sure the wiring to the starter is secure. Test starter relay (Chapter 8). If the relay is good, then the fault is in the wiring or motor.
- [ ] Starter relay faulty. Check it according to the procedure in Chapter 8.
- [ ] Starter switch not contacting. The contacts could be wet, corroded or dirty. Disassemble and clean the switch (Chapter 8).
- [ ] Wiring open or shorted. Check all wiring connections and harnesses to make sure that they are dry, tight and not corroded. Also check for broken or frayed wires that can cause a short to ground (see Wiring Diagrams at the end of this manual).
- [ ] Ignition (main) switch defective. Check the switch according to the procedure in Chapter 8. Replace the switch with a new one if it is defective.
- [ ] Engine kill switch defective. Check for wet, dirty or corroded contacts. Clean or replace the switch as necessary (Chapter 8).
- [ ] Starting circuit cut-off relay, neutral relay, neutral switch, reverse switch or front brake switch defective. Check the switches according to the procedure in Chapter 8. Replace the switch with a new one if it is defective.

Starter motor rotates but engine does not turn over

- [ ] Starter motor clutch defective. Inspect and repair or replace (Chapter 8).
- [ ] Damaged starter idle or wheel gears. Inspect and replace the damaged parts (Chapter 8).

Starter works but engine won't turn over (seized)

- [ ] Seized engine caused by one or more internally damaged components. Failure due to wear, abuse or lack of lubrication. Damage can include seized valves, valve lifters, camshaft, piston, crankshaft, connecting rod bearings, or transmission gears or bearings. Refer to Chapter 2 for engine disassembly.

No fuel flow

- [ ] No fuel in tank.
- [ ] Tank cap air vent or breather hose obstructed. Usually caused by dirt or water. Remove it and clean the cap vent hole.
- [ ] Clogged strainer in fuel tap (carbureted models). Remove and clean the strainer (Chapter 1).
- [ ] Fuel line clogged. Disconnect the fuel line and carefully blow through it.
- [ ] Inlet needle valve clogged (carbureted models). A very bad batch of fuel with an unusual additive may have been used, or some other foreign material has entered the tank. Many times after a machine has been stored for many months without running, the fuel turns to a varnish-like liquid and forms deposits on the inlet needle valve and jets. The carburetor should be removed and overhauled if draining the float chamber doesn't solve the problem.
- [ ] Fuel pump or pressure regulator defective or fuel filter clogged (fuel injected models). See Chapter 4B.

Engine flooded

- [ ] Float level too high (carbureted models). Check as described in Chapter 3 and replace the float if necessary.
- [ ] Inlet needle valve worn or stuck open (carbureted models). A piece of dirt, rust or other debris can cause the inlet needle to seat improperly, causing excess fuel to be admitted to the float bowl. In this case, the float chamber should be cleaned and the needle and seat inspected. If the needle and seat are worn, then the leaking will persist and the parts should be replaced with new ones (Chapter 3).
- [ ] Starting technique incorrect (carbureted models). Under normal circumstances (i.e., if all the carburetor functions are sound) the machine should start with little or no throttle. When the engine is cold, the choke should be operated and the engine started without opening the throttle. When the engine is at operating temperature, only a very slight amount of throttle should be necessary. If the engine is flooded, turn the fuel tap off and hold the throttle open while cranking the engine. This will allow additional air to reach the cylinder. Remember to turn the fuel tap back on after the engine starts.
- [ ] Injector needle valve worn or stuck open (fuel injected models). A piece of dirt, rust or other debris can cause the needle to seat improperly, causing excess fuel to be admitted to the throttle body. If the engine is hard to start after sitting overnight, the injector may be slowly leaking fuel into the engine. The injector should be cleaned and the needle and seat inspected (see Chapter 4B). If the needle and seat are worn, the injector should be replaced.
- [ ] Starting technique incorrect (fuel injected models). Under normal circumstances (i.e., if all the components of the fuel injection system are good), the engine should start with the throttle closed.

Troubleshooting REF•29

1 Engine doesn't start or is difficult to start (continued)

No spark or weak spark

- [ ] Ignition switch Off.
- [ ] Engine kill switch turned to the Off position.
- [ ] Battery voltage low. Check and recharge battery as necessary (Chapter 8).
- [ ] Spark plug dirty, defective or worn out. Locate reason for fouled plug using spark plug condition chart and follow the plug maintenance procedures in Chapter 1.
- [ ] Spark plug cap (YFZ450R) or plug wire (all models) faulty. Check condition. Replace either or both components if cracks or deterioration are evident (see Chapter 5).
- [ ] Spark plug cap (YFZ450R) not making good contact. Make sure the cap is securely attached to the plug wire and fits securely over the top of the spark plug.
- [ ] CDI pulse generator (YFZ450) or crankshaft position sensor (YFZ450R) defective. Check the unit, referring to Chapter 5 (YFZ450) or Chapter 4B (YFZ450R).
- [ ] CDI unit (YFZ450) or ECU (YFZ450R) defective. Check the unit, referring to Chapter 5 (YFZ450) or Chapter 4B (YFZ450R).
- [ ] Ignition coil defective. Check the coil, referring to Chapter 5.
- [ ] Main key switch or kill switch shorted. This is usually caused by water, corrosion, damage or excessive wear. The kill switch can be disassembled and cleaned with electric contact cleaner. If cleaning doesn't help, replace the switches (see Chapter 5).
- [ ] Wiring shorted or broken between:
  a) *Main key switch or engine kill switch*
  b) *CDI unit (YFZ450) or ECU (YFZ450R) and engine kill switch*
  c) *CDI unit (YFZ450) or ECU (YFZ450R) and ignition coil*
  d) *Ignition coil and spark plug (YFZ450R)*
  e) *CDI unit and pulse generator (YFZ450) or crankshaft position sensor and ECU (YFZ450R)*

Compression low

- [ ] Spark plug loose. Remove the plug and inspect the threads. Reinstall and tighten to the specified torque (Chapter 1).
- [ ] Cylinder head not sufficiently tightened down. If the cylinder head is suspected of being loose, then there's a chance that the gasket or head is damaged if the problem has persisted for any length of time. The head nuts and bolts should be tightened to the proper torque in the correct sequence (Chapter 2).
- [ ] Improper valve clearance. This means that the valve is not closing completely and compression pressure is leaking past the valve. Check and adjust the valve clearances (Chapter 1).
- [ ] Cylinder and/or piston worn. Excessive wear will cause compression pressure to leak past the rings. This is usually accompanied by worn rings as well. A top end overhaul is necessary (Chapter 2).
- [ ] Piston rings worn, weak, broken, or sticking. Broken or sticking piston rings usually indicate a lubrication or carburetion problem that causes excess carbon deposits or seizures to form on the pistons and rings. Top end overhaul is necessary (Chapter 2).
- [ ] Piston ring-to-groove clearance excessive. This is caused by excessive wear of the piston ring lands. Piston replacement is necessary (Chapter 2).
- [ ] Cylinder head gasket damaged. If the head is allowed to become loose, or if excessive carbon build-up on a piston crown and combustion chamber causes extremely high compression, the head gasket may leak. Retorquing the head is not always sufficient to restore the seal, so gasket replacement is necessary (Chapter 2).
- [ ] Cylinder head warped. This is caused by overheating or improperly tightened head nuts and bolts. Machine shop resurfacing or head replacement is necessary (Chapter 2).
- [ ] Valve spring broken or weak. Caused by component failure or wear; the spring(s) must be replaced (Chapter 2).
- [ ] Valve not seating properly. This is caused by a bent valve (from over-revving or improper valve adjustment), burned valve or seat (improper carburetion) or an accumulation of carbon deposits on the seat (from carburetion or lubrication problems). The valves must be cleaned and/or replaced and the seats serviced if possible (Chapter 2).

Stalls after starting

- [ ] Improper choke action. Make sure the choke knob or lever is getting a full stroke and staying in the out position.
- [ ] Ignition malfunction. See Chapter 5.
- [ ] Carburetor malfunction (carbureted models). See Chapter 4A.
- [ ] Fuel contaminated. The fuel can be contaminated with either dirt or water, or can change chemically if the machine is allowed to sit for several months or more. Drain the tank and float bowl and refill with fresh fuel (Chapter 4).
- [ ] Intake air leak. Check for a loose joint between the carburetor or throttle body and intake manifold. On a YFZ450, check for a loose carburetor top. On a YFZ450R, check the intake air pressure sensor hose for cracks or a loose fit.
- [ ] Engine idle speed incorrect. On carbureted models, refer to Chapter 1 and adjust the idle speed. On fuel injected models, refer to Chapter 4B and check the idle speed control valve.

Rough idle

- [ ] Ignition malfunction. See Chapter 5.
- [ ] Idle speed incorrect. See Chapter 1.
- [ ] Carburetor or fuel injection system malfunction. See Chapter 4.
- [ ] Idle fuel/air mixture incorrect. See Chapter 3.
- [ ] Fuel contaminated. The fuel can be contaminated with either dirt or water, or can change chemically if the machine is allowed to sit for several months or more. Drain the tank and fuel system (Chapter 4).
- [ ] Intake air leak. Check for a loose joint between the carburetor or throttle body and intake manifold. On a YFZ450, check for a loose carburetor top. On a YFZ450R, check the intake air pressure sensor hose for cracks or a loose fit.
- [ ] Air cleaner clogged. Service or replace the air cleaner element (Chapter 1).

2 Poor running at low speed

Spark weak

- ☐ Battery voltage low. Check and recharge battery (Chapter 5).
- ☐ Spark plug fouled, defective or worn out. Refer to Chapter 1 for spark plug maintenance.
- ☐ Spark plug cap or secondary (HT) wiring defective. Refer to Chapters 1 and 5 for details on the ignition system.
- ☐ Spark plug cap not making contact.
- ☐ Incorrect spark plug. Wrong type, heat range or cap configuration. Check and install correct plug listed in Chapter 1. A cold plug or one with a recessed firing electrode will not operate at low speeds without fouling.
- ☐ CDI unit or ECU defective. See Chapter 4 or 5.
- ☐ CDI pulse generator or crankshaft position sensor defective. See Chapter 4 or 5.
- ☐ Ignition coil defective. See Chapter 5.

Fuel/air mixture incorrect

- ☐ Pilot screw out of adjustment (Chapter 4).
- ☐ Pilot jet or air passage clogged (carbureted models). Remove and overhaul the carburetor (Chapter 4).
- ☐ Air bleed holes clogged (carbureted models). Remove carburetor and blow out all passages (Chapter 4).
- ☐ Air cleaner clogged, poorly sealed or missing.
- ☐ Air cleaner-to-carburetor boot poorly sealed (carbureted models). Look for cracks, holes or loose clamps and replace or repair defective parts.
- ☐ Float level too high or too low (carbureted models). Check and replace the float if necessary (Chapter 4).
- ☐ Fuel tank air vent obstructed. Make sure that the air vent passage in the filler cap is open.
- ☐ Carburetor or throttle body intake joint loose. Check for cracks, breaks, tears or loose clamps or bolts. Repair or replace the rubber boot and its O-ring (if equipped).

Compression low

- ☐ Spark plug loose. Remove the plug and inspect the threads. Reinstall and tighten to the specified torque (Chapter 1).
- ☐ Cylinder head not sufficiently tightened down. If the cylinder head is suspected of being loose, then there's a chance that the gasket and head are damaged if the problem has persisted for any length of time. The head nuts and bolts should be tightened to the proper torque in the correct sequence (Chapter 2).
- ☐ Improper valve clearance. This means that the valve is not closing completely and compression pressure is leaking past the valve. Check and adjust the valve clearances (Chapter 1).
- ☐ Cylinder and/or piston worn. Excessive wear will cause compression pressure to leak past the rings. This is usually accompanied by worn rings as well. A top end overhaul is necessary (Chapter 2).
- ☐ Piston rings worn, weak, broken, or sticking. Broken or sticking piston rings usually indicate a lubrication or carburetion problem that causes excess carbon deposits or seizures to form on the pistons and rings. Top end overhaul is necessary (Chapter 2).
- ☐ Piston ring-to-groove clearance excessive. This is caused by excessive wear of the piston ring lands. Piston replacement is necessary (Chapter 2).
- ☐ Cylinder head gasket damaged. If the head is allowed to become loose, or if excessive carbon build-up on the piston crown and combustion chamber causes extremely high compression, the head gasket may leak. Retorquing the head is not always sufficient to restore the seal, so gasket replacement is necessary (Chapter 2).
- ☐ Cylinder head warped. This is caused by overheating or improperly tightened head nuts and bolts. Machine shop resurfacing or head replacement is necessary (Chapter 2).
- ☐ Valve spring broken or weak. Caused by component failure or wear; the spring(s) must be replaced (Chapter 2).
- ☐ Valve not seating properly. This is caused by a bent valve (from over-revving or improper valve adjustment), burned valve or seat (improper carburetion) or an accumulation of carbon deposits on the seat (from carburetion, lubrication problems). The valves must be cleaned and/or replaced and the seats serviced if possible (Chapter 2).

Poor acceleration

- ☐ Carburetor leaking or dirty (carbureted models). Overhaul the carburetor (Chapter 3).
- ☐ Timing not advancing. The CDI magneto or the CDI unit may be defective. If so, they must be replaced with new ones, as they can't be repaired.
- ☐ Engine oil viscosity too high. Using a heavier oil than that recommended in Chapter 1 can damage the oil pump or lubrication system and cause drag on the engine.
- ☐ Brakes dragging. Usually caused by debris which has entered the brake piston sealing boots, corroded wheel calipers or from a warped disc or bent axle. Repair as necessary (Chapter 7).
- ☐ Timing not advancing (fuel injected models). The crankshaft position sensor or ECU may be at fault (see Chapter 4B).

Troubleshooting REF•31

3 Poor running or no power at high speed

Firing incorrect
- [ ] Air cleaner restricted. Clean or replace element (Chapter 1).
- [ ] Spark plug fouled, defective or worn out. See Chapter 1 for spark plug maintenance.
- [ ] Spark plug cap or secondary (HT) wiring defective. See Chapters 1 and 5 for details of the ignition system.
- [ ] Spark plug cap not in good contact. See Chapter 5.
- [ ] Incorrect spark plug. Wrong type, heat range or cap configuration. Check and install correct plugs listed in Chapter 1. A cold plug or one with a recessed firing electrode will not operate at low speeds without fouling.
- [ ] CDI unit or CDI magneto defective. See Chapter 5.
- [ ] Ignition coil defective. See Chapter 5.

Fuel/air mixture incorrect (carbureted models)
- [ ] Pilot screw out of adjustment. See Chapter 4 for adjustment procedures.
- [ ] Main jet clogged. Dirt, water or other contaminants can clog the main jets. Clean the fuel tap strainer and in-tank strainer, the float bowl area, and the jets and carburetor orifices (Chapter 4).
- [ ] Main jet wrong size. The standard jetting is for sea level atmospheric pressure and oxygen content. See Chapter 4 for high altitude adjustments.
- [ ] Throttle shaft-to-carburetor body clearance excessive. Refer to Chapter 4 for inspection and part replacement procedures.
- [ ] Air bleed holes clogged. Remove and overhaul carburetor (Chapter 4).
- [ ] Air cleaner clogged, poorly sealed, or missing.
- [ ] Air cleaner-to-carburetor boot poorly sealed. Look for cracks, holes or loose clamps, and replace or repair defective parts.
- [ ] Float level too high or too low. Check float level and replace the float if necessary (Chapter 4).
- [ ] Fuel tank air vent obstructed. Make sure the air vent passage in the filler cap is open.
- [ ] Carburetor intake joint loose. Check for cracks, breaks, tears or loose clamps or bolts. Repair or replace the rubber boots (Chapter 4).
- [ ] Fuel tap clogged. Remove the tap and clean it (Chapter 1).
- [ ] Fuel line clogged. Pull the fuel line loose and carefully blow through it.

Fuel/air mixture incorrect (fuel injected models)
- [ ] Fuel tank vent hose or fitting obstructed.
- [ ] Fuel pump or pressure regulator faulty, or the fuel filter is blocked (see Chapter 4B).
- [ ] Fuel hose clogged. Remove the fuel hose (see Chapter 4B) and blow air through it.
- [ ] Fuel rail or injector clogged. Check the fuel pump. If the machine has been unused for several months, the fuel turns to a varnish-like liquid that can cause an injector needle to stick to its seat. Drain the tank and fuel system (see Chapter 4B).
- [ ] Intake air leak. Check for a loose connection between the throttle body and intake manifold, and check the intake air pressure sensor hose for leaks or a loose fit.
- [ ] Air filter clogged. Clean the air filter element or replace it with a new one (see Chapter 1).

Compression low
- [ ] Spark plug loose. Remove the plug and inspect the threads. Reinstall and tighten to the specified torque (Chapter 1).
- [ ] Cylinder head not sufficiently tightened down. If the cylinder head is suspected of being loose, then there's a chance that the gasket and head are damaged if the problem has persisted for any length of time. The head nuts and bolts should be tightened to the proper torque in the correct sequence (Chapter 2).
- [ ] Improper valve clearance. This means that the valve is not closing completely and compression pressure is leaking past the valve. Check and adjust the valve clearances (Chapter 1).
- [ ] Cylinder and/or piston worn. Excessive wear will cause compression pressure to leak past the rings. This is usually accompanied by worn rings as well. A top end overhaul is necessary (Chapter 2).
- [ ] Piston rings worn, weak, broken, or sticking. Broken or sticking piston rings usually indicate a lubrication or carburetion problem that causes excess carbon deposits or seizures to form on the pistons and rings. Top end overhaul is necessary (Chapter 2).
- [ ] Piston ring-to-groove clearance excessive. This is caused by excessive wear of the piston ring lands. Piston replacement is necessary (Chapter 2).
- [ ] Cylinder head gasket damaged. If a head is allowed to become loose, or if excessive carbon build-up on the piston crown and combustion chamber causes extremely high compression, the head gasket may leak. Retorquing the head is not always sufficient to restore the seal, so gasket replacement is necessary (Chapter 2).
- [ ] Cylinder head warped. This is caused by overheating or improperly tightened head nuts and bolts. Machine shop resurfacing or head replacement is necessary (Chapter 2).
- [ ] Valve spring broken or weak. Caused by component failure or wear; the spring(s) must be replaced (Chapter 2).
- [ ] Valve not seating properly. This is caused by a bent valve (from over-revving or improper valve adjustment), burned valve or seat (improper carburetion) or an accumulation of carbon deposits on the seat (from carburetion or lubrication problems). The valves must be cleaned and/or replaced and the seats serviced if possible (Chapter 2).

Knocking or pinging
- [ ] Carbon build-up in combustion chamber. Use of a fuel additive that will dissolve the adhesive bonding the carbon particles to the crown and chamber is the easiest way to remove the build-up. Otherwise, the cylinder head will have to be removed and decarbonized (Chapter 2).
- [ ] Incorrect or poor quality fuel. Old or improper grades of fuel can cause detonation. This causes the piston to rattle, thus the knocking or pinging sound. Drain old fuel and always use the recommended fuel grade.
- [ ] Spark plug heat range incorrect. Uncontrolled detonation indicates the plug heat range is too hot. The plug in effect becomes a glow plug, raising cylinder temperatures. Install the proper heat range plug (Chapter 1).
- [ ] Improper air/fuel mixture. This will cause the cylinder to run hot, which leads to detonation. Clogged jets or an air leak can cause this imbalance. See Chapter 4.

Miscellaneous causes
- [ ] Throttle valve doesn't open fully. Adjust the cable slack (Chapter 1).
- [ ] Clutch slipping. May be caused by improper adjustment or loose or worn clutch components. Refer to Chapter 1 for adjustment or Chapter 2 for clutch overhaul procedures.
- [ ] Timing not advancing.
- [ ] Engine oil viscosity too high. Using a heavier oil than the one recommended in Chapter 1 can damage the oil pump or lubrication system and cause drag on the engine.
- [ ] Brakes dragging. Usually caused by debris which has entered the brake piston sealing boot, or from a warped disc or bent axle. Repair as necessary.

4 Overheating

Engine overheats

☐ Coolant level low. Check and add coolant (see *Daily (pre-ride) checks* at the beginning of this manual)
☐ Leak in cooling system. Check cooling system hoses and radiator for leaks and other damage. Replace or repair parts as necessary (see Chapter 3).
☐ Defective thermostat. Check and replace if necessary (see Chapter 3).
☐ Bad radiator cap. Remove the cap and have it pressure tested.
☐ Coolant passages clogged. Drain, clean the passages and refill with fresh coolant (see Chapter 3).
☐ Water pump defective. Remove the pump and check the components (see Chapter 3).
☐ Clogged or damaged radiator fins (see Chapter 3).
☐ Faulty cooling fan, fan relay or fan switch (see Chapter 3).
☐ Engine oil level low. Check and add oil (Chapter 1).
☐ Wrong type of oil. If you're not sure what type of oil is in the engine, drain it and fill with the correct type (Chapter 1).
☐ Air leak at intake joint. Check and tighten or replace as necessary (Chapter 4).
☐ Fuel level low. Check and adjust if necessary (Chapter 4).
☐ Worn oil pump or clogged oil passages. Replace pump or clean passages as necessary.
☐ Clogged external oil line (YFZ450). Remove and check for foreign material (see Chapter 2).
☐ Carbon build-up in combustion chambers. Use of a fuel additive that will dissolve the adhesive bonding the carbon particles to the piston crown and chambers is the easiest way to remove the build-up. Otherwise, the cylinder head will have to be removed and decarbonized (Chapter 2).
☐ Operation in high ambient temperatures.

Firing incorrect

☐ Spark plug fouled, defective or worn out. See Chapter 1 for spark plug maintenance.
☐ Incorrect spark plug (see Chapter 1).
☐ Faulty ignition coil (Chapter 4).

Fuel/air mixture incorrect (carbureted models)

☐ Pilot screw out of adjustment (Chapter 3).
☐ Main jet clogged. Dirt, water and other contaminants can clog the main jet. Clean the fuel tap strainer, the float bowl area and the jets and carburetor orifices (Chapter 3).
☐ Main jet wrong size. The standard jetting is for sea level atmospheric pressure and oxygen content.
☐ Air cleaner poorly sealed or missing.
☐ Air cleaner-to-carburetor boot poorly sealed. Look for cracks, holes or loose clamps and replace or repair.
☐ Fuel level too low. Check fuel level and float level and adjust or replace the float if necessary (Chapter 3).
☐ Fuel tank air vent obstructed. Make sure that the air vent passage in the filler cap is open.
☐ Carburetor intake manifold loose. Check for cracks or loose clamps or bolts. Check the carburetor-to-manifold gasket and the manifold-to-cylinder head O-ring (Chapter 3).

Fuel/air mixture incorrect (fuel injected models)

☐ Fuel tank vent hose or fitting obstructed.
☐ Fuel pump or pressure regulator faulty, or the fuel filter is blocked (see Chapter 4B).
☐ Fuel hose clogged. Remove the fuel hose (see Chapter 4B) and blow air through it.
☐ Fuel rail or injector clogged. Check the fuel pump. If the machine has been unused for several months, the fuel turns to a varnish-like liquid that can cause an injector needle to stick to its seat. Drain the tank and fuel system (see Chapter 4B).
☐ Intake air leak. Check for a loose connection between the throttle body and intake manifold, and check the intake air pressure sensor hose for leaks or a loose fit.
☐ Air filter clogged. Clean the air filter element or replace it with a new one (see Chapter 1).

Compression too high

☐ Carbon build-up in combustion chamber. Use of a fuel additive that will dissolve the adhesive bonding the carbon particles to the piston crown and chamber is the easiest way to remove the build-up. Otherwise, the cylinder head will have to be removed and decarbonized (Chapter 2).
☐ Improperly machined head surface or installation of incorrect gasket during engine assembly.

Engine load excessive

☐ Clutch slipping. Can be caused by damaged, loose or worn clutch components. Refer to Chapter 2 for overhaul procedures.
☐ Engine oil level too high. The addition of too much oil will cause pressurization of the crankcase and inefficient engine operation. Check Specifications and drain to proper level (Chapter 1).
☐ Engine oil viscosity too high. Using a heavier oil than the one recommended in Chapter 1 can damage the oil pump or lubrication system as well as cause drag on the engine.
☐ Brakes dragging. Usually caused by debris which has entered the brake piston sealing boots (hydraulic front brakes), corroded wheel cylinders or calipers (hydraulic front brakes), sticking brake cam (mechanical front or all rear brakes) or from a warped drum, warped disc or bent axle. Repair as necessary (Chapter 6).

Lubrication inadequate

☐ Engine oil level too low. Friction caused by intermittent lack of lubrication or from oil that is overworked can cause overheating. The oil provides a definite cooling function in the engine. Check the oil level (Chapter 1).
☐ Poor quality engine oil or incorrect viscosity or type. Oil is rated not only according to viscosity but also according to type. Some oils are not rated high enough for use in this engine. Check the Specifications section and change to the correct oil (Chapter 1).
☐ Camshaft or journals worn. Excessive wear causing drop in oil pressure. Replace cam or cylinder head. Abnormal wear could be caused by oil starvation at high rpm from low oil level or improper viscosity or type of oil (Chapter 1).
☐ Crankshaft and/or bearings worn. Same problems as paragraph above. Check and replace crankshaft assembly if necessary (Chapter 2).

Miscellaneous causes

☐ Modification to exhaust system. Most aftermarket exhaust systems cause the engine to run leaner, which makes it run hotter. When installing an aftermarket exhaust system, always rejet the carburetor (if equipped).

Troubleshooting REF•33

5 Clutch problems

Clutch slipping

- [ ] Secondary clutch friction plates worn or warped. Overhaul the secondary clutch assembly (Chapter 2).
- [ ] Secondary clutch metal plates worn or warped (Chapter 2).
- [ ] Secondary clutch spring(s) broken or weak. Old or heat-damaged spring(s) (from slipping clutch) should be replaced with new ones (Chapter 2).
- [ ] Secondary clutch release mechanism defective. Replace any defective parts (Chapter 2).
- [ ] Secondary clutch boss or housing unevenly worn. This causes improper engagement of the plates. Replace the damaged or worn parts (Chapter 2).
- [ ] Primary (centrifugal) clutch weight linings or drum worn (Chapter 2).
- [ ] Wrong type of engine oil. The friction modifiers in automotive engine oils can sometimes caused the clutch to slip. Use oil that meets JASO standard MA.

Clutch not disengaging completely

- [ ] Secondary clutch improperly adjusted (see Chapter 1).
- [ ] Secondary clutch plates warped or damaged. This will cause clutch drag, which in turn will cause the machine to creep. Overhaul the clutch assembly (Chapter 2).
- [ ] Sagged or broken secondary clutch spring(s). Check and replace the spring(s) (Chapter 2).
- [ ] Engine oil deteriorated. Old, thin, worn out oil will not provide proper lubrication for the discs, causing the secondary clutch to drag. Replace the oil and filter (Chapter 1).
- [ ] Engine oil viscosity too high. Using a thicker oil than recommended in Chapter 1 can cause the secondary clutch plates to stick together, putting a drag on the engine. Change to the correct viscosity oil (Chapter 1).
- [ ] Secondary clutch housing seized on shaft. Lack of lubrication, severe wear or damage can cause the housing to seize on the shaft. Overhaul of the clutch, and perhaps transmission, may be necessary to repair the damage (Chapter 2).
- [ ] Secondary clutch release mechanism defective. Worn or damaged release mechanism parts can stick and fail to apply force to the pressure plate. Overhaul the release mechanism (Chapter 2).
- [ ] Loose secondary clutch center nut. Causes housing and center misalignment putting a drag on the engine. Engagement adjustment continually varies. Overhaul the clutch assembly (Chapter 2).
- [ ] Weak or broken primary clutch springs (Chapter 2).

6 Gear shifting problems

Doesn't go into gear or lever doesn't return

- [ ] Clutch not disengaging. See Section 5.
- [ ] Shift fork(s) bent or seized. May be caused by lack of lubrication. Overhaul the transmission (Chapter 2).
- [ ] Gear(s) stuck on shaft. Most often caused by a lack of lubrication or excessive wear in transmission bearings and bushings. Overhaul the transmission (Chapter 2).
- [ ] Shift drum binding. Caused by lubrication failure or excessive wear. Replace the drum and bearing (Chapter 2).
- [ ] Shift lever return spring weak or broken (Chapter 2).
- [ ] Shift lever broken. Splines stripped out of lever or shaft, caused by allowing the lever to get loose. Replace necessary parts (Chapter 2).
- [ ] Shift mechanism pawl broken or worn. Full engagement and rotary movement of shift drum results. Replace shaft assembly (Chapter 2).
- [ ] Pawl spring broken. Allows pawl to float, causing sporadic shift operation. Replace spring (Chapter 2).

Jumps out of gear

- [ ] Shift fork(s) worn. Overhaul the transmission (Chapter 2).
- [ ] Gear groove(s) worn. Overhaul the transmission (Chapter 2).
- [ ] Gear dogs or dog slots worn or damaged. The gears should be inspected and replaced. No attempt should be made to service the worn parts.

Overshifts

- [ ] Pawl spring weak or broken (Chapter 2).
- [ ] Shift cam stopper lever not functioning (Chapter 2).

Troubleshooting

7 Abnormal engine noise

Knocking or pinging

☐ Carbon build-up in combustion chamber. Use of a fuel additive that will dissolve the adhesive bonding the carbon particles to the piston crown and chamber is the easiest way to remove the build-up. Otherwise, the cylinder head will have to be removed and decarbonized (Chapter 2).
☐ Incorrect or poor quality fuel. Old or improper fuel can cause detonation. This causes the pistons to rattle, thus the knocking or pinging sound. Drain the old fuel (Chapter 4) and always use the recommended grade fuel (Chapter 1).
☐ Spark plug heat range incorrect. Uncontrolled detonation indicates that the plug heat range is too hot. The plug in effect becomes a glow plug, raising cylinder temperatures. Install the proper heat range plug (Chapter 1).
☐ Improper air/fuel mixture. This will cause the cylinder to run hot and lead to detonation. Clogged jets or an air leak can cause this imbalance. See Chapter 3.

Piston slap or rattling

☐ Cylinder-to-piston clearance excessive. Caused by improper assembly. Inspect and overhaul top end parts (Chapter 2).
☐ Connecting rod bent. Caused by over-revving, trying to start a badly flooded engine or from ingesting a foreign object into the combustion chamber. Replace the damaged parts (Chapter 2).
☐ Piston pin or piston pin bore worn or seized from wear or lack of lubrication. Replace damaged parts (Chapter 2).
☐ Piston ring(s) worn, broken or sticking. Overhaul the top end (Chapter 2).
☐ Piston seizure damage. Usually from lack of lubrication or overheating. Replace the pistons and bore the cylinder, as necessary (Chapter 2).

☐ Connecting rod upper or lower end clearance excessive. Caused by excessive wear or lack of lubrication. Replace worn parts.

Valve noise

☐ Incorrect valve clearances. Adjust the clearances by referring to Chapter 1.
☐ Valve spring broken or weak. Check and replace weak valve springs (Chapter 2).
☐ Camshaft or cylinder head worn or damaged. Lack of lubrication at high rpm is usually the cause of damage. Insufficient oil or failure to change the oil at the recommended intervals are the chief causes.

Other noise

☐ Cylinder head gasket leaking.
☐ Exhaust pipe leaking at cylinder head connection. Caused by improper fit of pipe, damaged gasket or loose exhaust flange. All exhaust fasteners should be tightened evenly and carefully. Failure to do this will lead to a leak.
☐ Crankshaft runout excessive. Caused by a bent crankshaft (from over-revving) or damage from an upper cylinder component failure.
☐ Engine mounting bolts or nuts loose. Tighten all engine mounting bolts and nuts to the specified torque (Chapter 2).
☐ Crankshaft bearings worn (Chapter 2).
☐ Camshaft chain tensioner defective. Replace according to the procedure in Chapter 2.
☐ Camshaft chain, sprockets or guides worn (Chapter 2).

8 Abnormal driveline noise

Clutch noise

☐ Secondary clutch housing/friction plate clearance excessive (Chapter 2).
☐ Loose or damaged secondary clutch pressure plate and/or bolts (Chapter 2).
☐ Broken primary clutch springs (Chapter 2).

Transmission noise

☐ Bearings worn. Also includes the possibility that the shafts are worn. Overhaul the transmission (Chapter 2).

☐ Gears worn or chipped (Chapter 2).
☐ Metal chips jammed in gear teeth. Probably pieces from a broken gear or shift mechanism that were picked up by the gears. This will cause early bearing failure (Chapter 2).
☐ Engine oil level too low. Causes a howl from transmission. Also affects engine power and clutch operation (Chapter 1).
☐ Chain not adjusted properly (see Chapter 1)
☐ Front or rear sprocket loose. Tighten fasteners (see Chapter 6).
☐ Sprockets and/or chain worn. Install new sprockets and chain (see Chapter 6).
☐ Rear sprocket warped. Install a new rear sprocket (see Chapter 6).

Troubleshooting REF•35

9 Abnormal chassis noise

Suspension noise
- [ ] Spring weak or broken. Makes a clicking or scraping sound.
- [ ] Steering shaft bearings worn or damaged. Clicks when braking. Check and replace as necessary (Chapter 6).
- [ ] Shock absorber fluid level incorrect. Indicates a leak caused by defective seal. Shock will be covered with oil. Replace shock (Chapter 6).
- [ ] Defective shock absorber with internal damage. This is in the body of the shock and can't be remedied. The shock must be replaced with a new one (Chapter 6).
- [ ] Bent or damaged shock body. Replace the shock with a new one (Chapter 6).

Brake noise
- [ ] Brake linings worn or contaminated. Can cause scraping or squealing. Replace the pads (Chapter 7).
- [ ] Brake linings warped or worn unevenly. Can cause chattering. Replace the linings (Chapter 7).
- [ ] Brake disc warped. Can cause chattering. Replace brake disc (Chapter 7).
- [ ] Loose or worn knuckle or rear axle bearings. Check and replace as needed (Chapter 6).

10 Coolant temperature indicator light comes on

Cooling system
- [ ] Coolant level low. Check and add coolant (see *Daily (pre-ride)* checks at the beginning of this manual)
- [ ] Leak in cooling system. Check cooling system hoses and radiator for leaks and other damage. Replace or repair parts as necessary (see Chapter 3).
- [ ] Defective thermostat. Check and replace if necessary (see Chapter 3).
- [ ] Bad radiator cap. Remove the cap and have it pressure tested.
- [ ] Coolant passages clogged. Drain, clean the passages and refill with fresh coolant (see Chapter 3).
- [ ] Water pump defective. Remove the pump and check the components (see Chapter 3).
- [ ] Clogged or damaged radiator fins (see Chapter 3).

Engine lubrication system
- [ ] High oil temperature due to operation in high ambient temperatures. Shut the engine off and let it cool.
- [ ] Engine oil level low. Inspect for leak or other problem causing low oil level and add recommended oil (Chapters 1 and 2).

Electrical system
- [ ] Coolant temperature sensor defective. Check the sensor according to the procedure in Chapter 5. Replace it if it's defective.
- [ ] Coolant temperature indicator light circuit defective. Check for pinched, shorted, disconnected or damaged wiring (Chapter 3).
- [ ] Cooling fan not working (Chapter 5).

11 Excessive exhaust smoke

White smoke
- [ ] Piston oil ring worn. The ring may be broken or damaged, causing oil from the crankcase to be pulled past the piston into the combustion chamber. Replace the rings with new ones (Chapter 2).
- [ ] Cylinders worn, cracked, or scored. Caused by overheating or oil starvation. If worn or scored, the cylinders will have to be rebored and new pistons installed. If cracked, the cylinder block will have to be replaced (see Chapter 2).
- [ ] Valve oil seal damaged or worn. Replace oil seals with new ones (Chapter 2).
- [ ] Valve guide worn. Perform a complete valve job (Chapter 2).
- [ ] Engine oil level too high, which causes the oil to be forced past the rings. Drain oil to the proper level (Chapter 1).
- [ ] Head gasket broken between oil return and cylinder. Causes oil to be pulled into the combustion chamber. Replace the head gasket and check the head for warpage (Chapter 2).
- [ ] Abnormal crankcase pressurization, which forces oil past the rings. Clogged breather or hoses usually the cause (Chapter 2).

Black smoke
- [ ] Air cleaner clogged. Clean or replace the element (Chapter 1).
- [ ] Main jet too large or loose. Compare the jet size to the Specifications (Chapter 3).
- [ ] Choke stuck (carbureted models), causing fuel to be pulled through choke circuit (Chapter 3).
- [ ] Fuel level too high (carbureted models). Check the fuel level and float level and adjust if necessary (Chapter 3).
- [ ] Inlet needle held off needle seat (carbureted models). Clean the float chamber and fuel line and replace the needle and seat if necessary (Chapter 3).
- [ ] Fuel injection system problem (YFZ450R). See Chapter 4B.

Brown smoke
- [ ] Main jet too small or clogged. Lean condition caused by wrong size main jet or by a restricted orifice. Clean float chamber and jets and compare jet size to Specifications (Chapter 3).
- [ ] Fuel flow insufficient. Fuel inlet needle valve stuck closed due to chemical reaction with old fuel. Float level incorrect; check and replace float if necessary. Restricted fuel line. Clean line and float chamber.
- [ ] Carburetor intake tube loose (Chapter 3).
- [ ] Air cleaner poorly sealed or not installed (Chapter 1).

12 Poor handling or stability

Handlebar hard to turn
- [ ] Steering shaft nut too tight (Chapter 6).
- [ ] Lower bearing or upper bushing damaged. Roughness can be felt as the bars are turned from side-to-side. Replace bearing and bushing (Chapter 6).
- [ ] Steering shaft bearing lubrication inadequate. Causes are grease getting hard from age or being washed out by high pressure car washes. Remove steering shaft and replace bearing (Chapter 6).
- [ ] Steering shaft bent. Caused by a collision, hitting a pothole or by rolling the machine. Replace damaged part. Don't try to straighten the steering shaft (Chapter 6).
- [ ] Front tire air pressure too low (Chapter 1).

Handlebar shakes or vibrates excessively
- [ ] Tires worn or out of balance (Chapter 1 or 7).
- [ ] Swingarm bearings worn. Replace worn bearings by referring to Chapter 6.
- [ ] Wheel rim(s) warped or damaged. Inspect wheels (Chapter 7).
- [ ] Wheel bearings worn. Worn front or rear wheel bearings can cause poor tracking. Worn front bearings will cause wobble (Chapter 7).
- [ ] Wheel hubs installed incorrectly (Chapter 6 or Chapter 7).
- [ ] Handlebar clamp bolts or bracket nuts loose (Chapter 6).
- [ ] Steering shaft nut or bolts loose. Tighten them to the specified torque (Chapter 6).
- [ ] Motor mount bolts loose. Will cause excessive vibration with increased engine rpm (Chapter 2).

Handlebar pulls to one side
- [ ] Uneven tire pressures (Chapter 1).
- [ ] Frame bent. Definitely suspect this if the machine has been rolled. May or may not be accompanied by cracking near the bend. Replace the frame (Chapter 8).
- [ ] Wheel out of alignment. Caused by incorrect toe-in adjustment (Chapter 1) or bent tie-rod (Chapter 6).
- [ ] Swingarm bent or twisted. Caused by age (metal fatigue) or impact damage. Replace the swingarm (Chapter 6).
- [ ] Steering shaft bent. Caused by impact damage or by rolling the vehicle. Replace the steering stem (Chapter 6).

Poor shock absorbing qualities
- [ ] Too hard:
    a) Shock internal damage.
    b) Tire pressure too high (Chapters 1 and 7).
    c) Shock setting too hard for conditions (see Chapter 6).
- [ ] Too soft:
    a) Shock oil insufficient and/or leaking (Chapter 6).
    b) Shock springs weak or broken (Chapter 6).

Troubleshooting REF•37

13 Braking problems

Front brakes are spongy, don't hold
- [ ] Air in brake line. Caused by inattention to master cylinder fluid level or by leakage. Locate problem and bleed brakes (Chapter 7)
- [ ] Linings worn (Chapters 1 and 7).
- [ ] Brake fluid leak. See first paragraph.
- [ ] Contaminated linings. Caused by contamination with oil, grease, brake fluid, etc. Clean or replace linings. Clean disc thoroughly with brake cleaner (Chapter 7).
- [ ] Brake fluid deteriorated. Fluid is old or contaminated. Drain system, replenish with new fluid and bleed the system (Chapter 7).
- [ ] Master cylinder internal parts worn or damaged causing fluid to bypass (Chapter 7).
- [ ] Master cylinder bore scratched by foreign material or broken spring. Repair or replace master cylinder (Chapter 7).
- [ ] Disc warped. Replace disc (Chapter 7).

Brake lever or pedal pulsates
- [ ] Axle bent. Replace axle (Chapter 6).
- [ ] Wheel warped or otherwise damaged (Chapter 7).
- [ ] Hub or axle bearings damaged or worn (Chapter 6).
- [ ] Brake disc warped. Replace brake disc (Chapter 7).

Brakes drag
- [ ] Master cylinder piston seized. Caused by wear or damage to piston or cylinder bore (Chapter 7).
- [ ] Lever balky or stuck. Check pivot and lubricate (Chapter 7).
- [ ] Wheel cylinder or caliper piston seized in bore. Caused by wear or ingestion of dirt past deteriorated seal (Chapter 7).
- [ ] Disc brake pads damaged. Lining material separated from pads. Usually caused by faulty manufacturing process or from contact with chemicals. Replace pads (Chapter 7).
- [ ] Pads improperly installed (Chapter 7).
- [ ] Rear brake pedal or lever free play insufficient (Chapter 1).

14 Electrical problems

Battery dead or weak
- [ ] Battery faulty. Caused by sulfated plates which are shorted through sedimentation or low electrolyte level. Also, broken battery terminal making only occasional contact (Chapter 5).
- [ ] Battery cables making poor contact (Chapter 5).
- [ ] Load excessive. Caused by addition of high wattage lights or other electrical accessories.
- [ ] Ignition switch defective. Switch either grounds internally or fails to shut off system. Replace the switch (Chapter 5).
- [ ] Regulator/rectifier defective (Chapter 5).
- [ ] Stator coil open or shorted (Chapter 5).
- [ ] Wiring faulty. Wiring grounded or connections loose in ignition, charging or lighting circuits (Chapter 5).

Battery overcharged
- [ ] Regulator/rectifier defective. Overcharging is noticed when battery gets excessively warm or boils over (Chapter 5).
- [ ] Battery defective. Replace battery with a new one (Chapter 5).
- [ ] Battery amperage too low, wrong type or size. Install manufacturer's specified amp-hour battery to handle charging load (Chapter 5).

REF•38 Troubleshooting Equipment

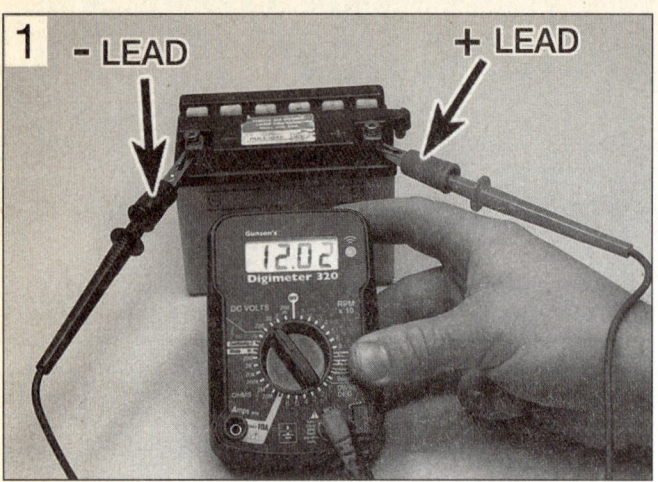

Measuring open-circuit battery voltage

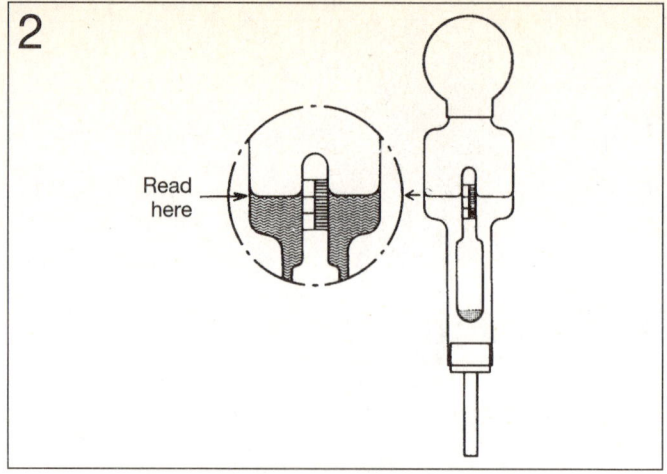

Float-type hydrometer for measuring battery specific gravity

Checking engine compression

- Low compression will result in exhaust smoke, heavy oil consumption, poor starting and poor performance. A compression test will provide useful information about an engine's condition and if performed regularly, can give warning of trouble before any other symptoms become apparent.
- A compression gauge will be required, along with an adapter to suit the spark plug hole thread size. Note that the screw-in type gauge/adapter set up is preferable to the rubber cone type.
- Compression testing procedures are described in Chapter 2.

Checking battery open-circuit voltage

 Warning: The gases produced by the battery are explosive - never smoke or create any sparks in the vicinity of the battery. Never allow the electrolyte to contact your skin or clothing - if it does, wash it off and seek immediate medical attention.

- Before any electrical fault is investigated the battery should be checked.
- You'll need a dc voltmeter or multimeter to check battery voltage. Check that the leads are inserted in the correct terminals on the meter, red lead to positive (+), black lead to negative (-). Incorrect connections can damage the meter.
- A sound, fully-charged 12 volt battery should produce between 12.3 and 12.6 volts across its terminals (12.8 volts for a maintenance-free battery). On machines with a 6 volt battery, voltage should be between 6.1 and 6.3 volts.

1 Set a multimeter to the 0 to 20 volts dc range and connect its probes across the battery terminals. Connect the meter's positive (+) probe, usually red, to the battery positive (+) terminal, followed by the meter's negative (-) probe, usually black, to the battery negative terminal (-) **(see illustration 1)**.

2 If battery voltage is low (below 10 volts on a 12 volt battery or below 4 volts on a six volt battery), charge the battery and test the voltage again. If the battery repeatedly goes flat, investigate the motorcycle's charging system.

Checking battery specific gravity (SG)

 Warning: The gases produced by the battery are explosive - never smoke or create any sparks in the vicinity of the battery. Never allow the electrolyte to contact your skin or clothing - if it does, wash it off and seek immediate medical attention.

- The specific gravity check gives an indication of a battery's state of charge.
- A hydrometer is used for measuring specific gravity. Make sure you purchase one which has a small enough hose to insert in the aperture of a motorcycle battery.
- Specific gravity is simply a measure of the electrolyte's density compared with that of water. Water has an SG of 1.000 and fully-charged battery electrolyte is about 26% heavier, at 1.260.
- Specific gravity checks are not possible on maintenance-free batteries. Testing the open-circuit voltage is the only means of determining their state of charge.

1 To measure SG, remove the battery from the motorcycle and remove the first cell cap. Draw some electrolyte into the hydrometer and note the reading **(see illustration 2)**. Return the electrolyte to the cell and install the cap.

2 The reading should be in the region of 1.260 to 1.280. If SG is below 1.200 the battery needs charging. Note that SG will vary with temperature; it should be measured at 20°C (68°F). Add 0.007 to the reading for every 10°C above 20°C, and subtract 0.007 from the reading for every 10°C below 20°C. Add 0.004 to the reading for every 10°F above 68°F, and subtract 0.004 from the reading for every 10°F below 68°F.

3 When the check is complete, rinse the hydrometer thoroughly with clean water.

Checking for continuity

- The term continuity describes the uninterrupted flow of electricity through an electrical circuit. A continuity check will determine whether an **open-circuit** situation exists.
- Continuity can be checked with an ohmmeter, multimeter, continuity tester or battery and bulb test circuit **(see illustrations 3, 4 and 5)**.
- All of these instruments are self-powered by a battery, therefore the checks are made with the ignition OFF.
- As a safety precaution, always disconnect the battery negative (-) lead before making checks, particularly if ignition switch checks are being made.
- If using a meter, select the appropriate

Troubleshooting Equipment REF•39

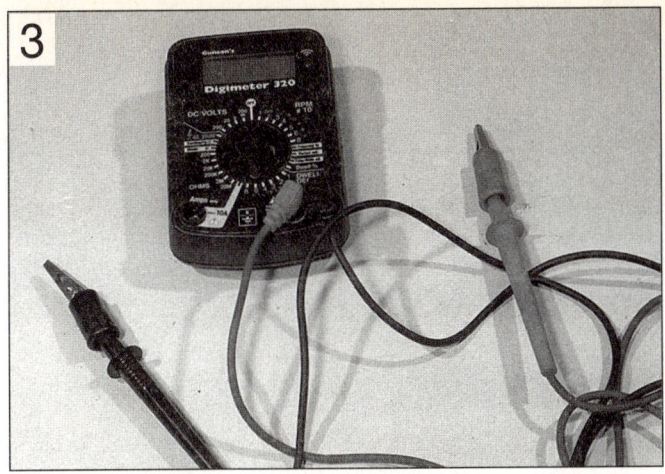
Digital multimeter can be used for all electrical tests

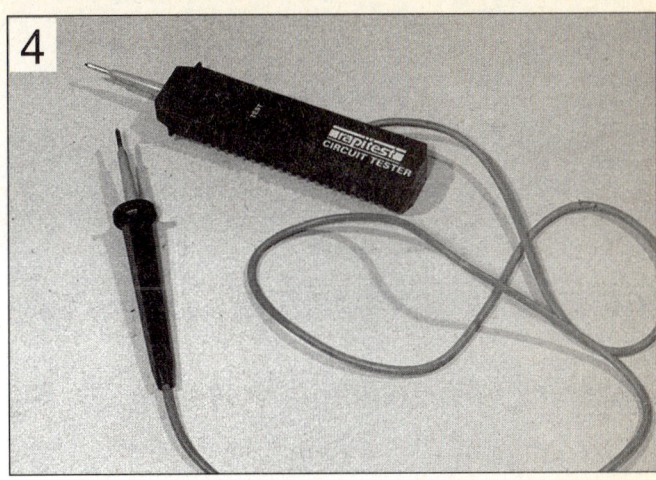
Battery-powered continuity tester

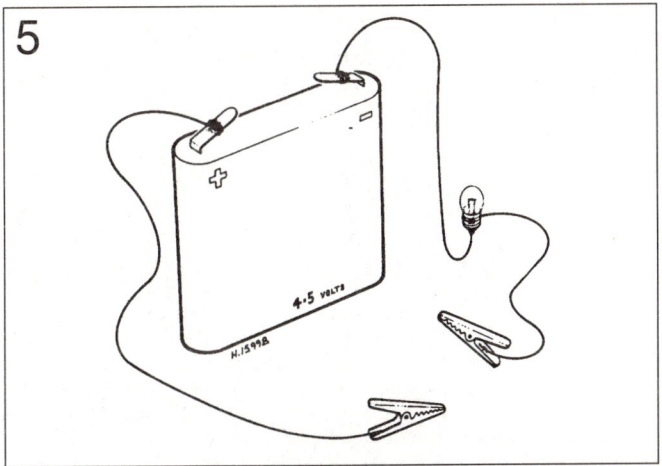
Battery and bulb test circuit

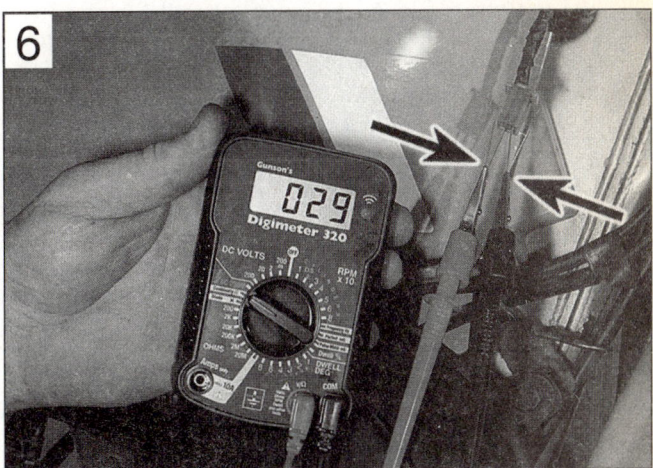
Continuity check of front brake light switch using a meter - note cotter pins used to access connector terminals

ohms scale and check that the meter reads infinity (∞). Touch the meter probes together and check that meter reads zero; where necessary adjust the meter so that it reads zero.
● After using a meter, always switch it OFF to conserve its battery.

Switch checks

1 If a switch is at fault, trace its wiring up to the wiring connectors. Separate the wire connectors and inspect them for security and condition. A build-up of dirt or corrosion here will most likely be the cause of the problem - clean up and apply a water dispersant such as WD40.
2 If using a test meter, set the meter to the ohms x 10 scale and connect its probes across the wires from the switch **(see illustration 6)**. Simple ON/OFF type switches, such as brake light switches, only have two wires whereas combination switches, like the ignition switch, have many internal links. Study the wiring diagram to ensure that you are connecting across the correct pair of wires. Continuity (low or no measurable resistance - 0 ohms) should be indicated with the switch ON and no continuity (high resistance) with it OFF.
3 Note that the polarity of the test probes doesn't matter for continuity checks, although care should be taken to follow specific test procedures if a diode or solid-state component is being checked.
4 A continuity tester or battery and bulb circuit can be used in the same way. Connect its probes as described above **(see illustration 7)**. The light should come on to indicate continuity in the ON switch position, but should extinguish in the OFF position.

Wiring checks

● Many electrical faults are caused by damaged wiring, often due to incorrect routing or chafing on frame components.
● Loose, wet or corroded wire connectors

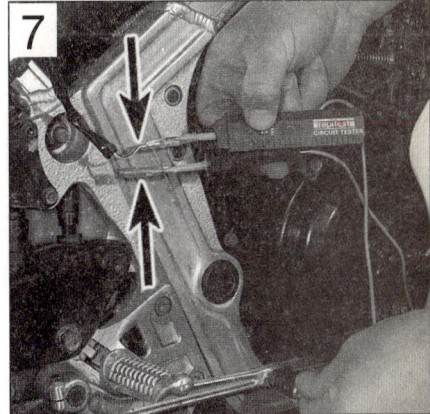
Continuity check of rear brake light switch using a continuity tester

REF•40 Troubleshooting Equipment

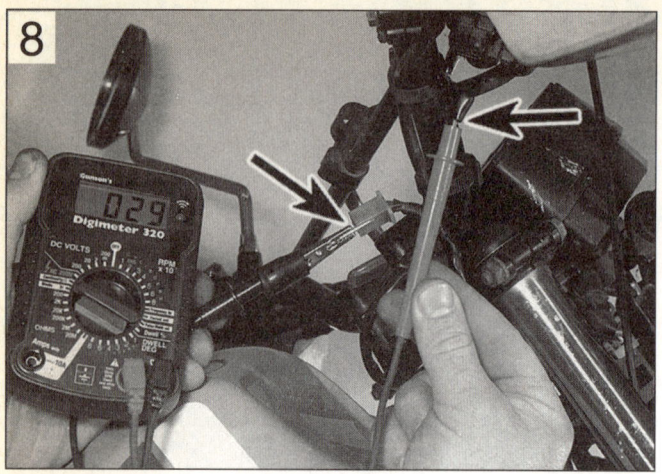
Continuity check of front brake light switch sub-harness

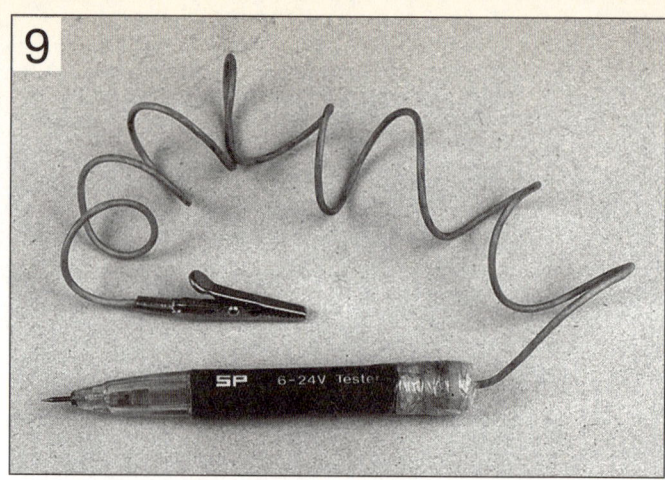
A simple test light can be used for voltage checks

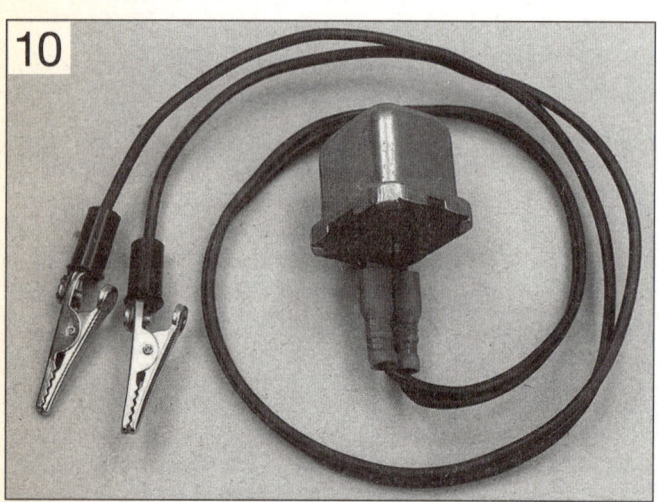
A buzzer is useful for voltage checks

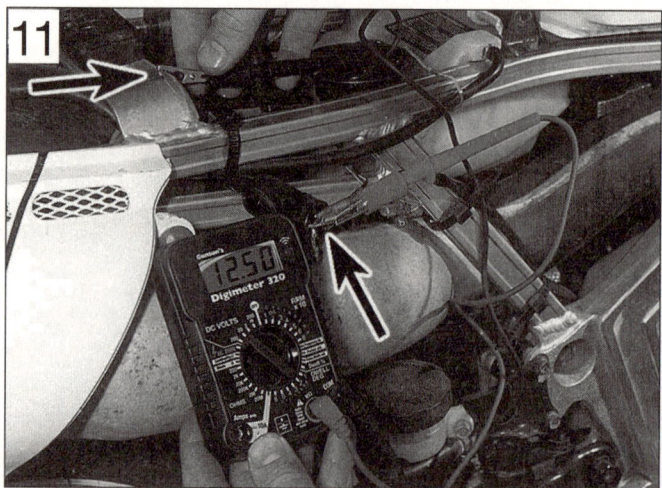
Checking for voltage at the rear brake light power supply wire using a meter . . .

can also be the cause of electrical problems, especially in exposed locations.

1 A continuity check can be made on a single length of wire by disconnecting it at each end and connecting a meter or continuity tester across both ends of the wire **(see illustration 8)**.

2 Continuity (low or no resistance - 0 ohms) should be indicated if the wire is good. If no continuity (high resistance) is shown, suspect a broken wire.

Checking for voltage

● A voltage check can determine whether current is reaching a component.
● Voltage can be checked with a dc voltmeter, multimeter set on the dc volts scale, test light or buzzer **(see illustrations 9 and 10)**. A meter has the advantage of being able to measure actual voltage.
● When using a meter, check that its leads are inserted in the correct terminals on the meter, red to positive (+), black to negative (-). Incorrect connections can damage the meter.
● A voltmeter (or multimeter set to the dc volts scale) should always be connected in parallel (across the load). Connecting it in series will destroy the meter.
● Voltage checks are made with the ignition ON.

1 First identify the relevant wiring circuit by referring to the wiring diagram at the end of this manual. If other electrical components share the same power supply (ie are fed from the same fuse), take note whether they are working correctly - this is useful information in deciding where to start checking the circuit.

2 If using a meter, check first that the meter leads are plugged into the correct terminals on the meter (see above). Set the meter to the dc volts function, at a range suitable for the battery voltage. Connect the meter red probe (+) to the power supply wire and the black probe to a good metal ground on the motor-cycle's frame or directly to the battery negative (-) terminal **(see illustration 11)**. Battery voltage should be shown on the meter with the ignition switched ON.

3 If using a test light or buzzer, connect its positive (+) probe to the power supply terminal and its negative (-) probe to a good ground on the motorcycle's frame or directly to the battery negative (-) terminal **(see illustration 12)**. With the ignition ON, the test light should illuminate or the buzzer sound.

4 If no voltage is indicated, work back towards the fuse continuing to check for voltage. When you reach a point where there is voltage, you know the problem lies between that point and your last check point.

Troubleshooting Equipment REF•41

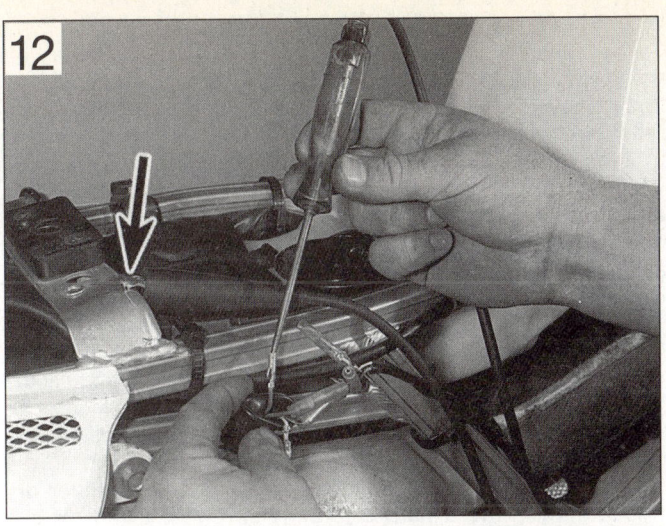

... or a test light - note the ground connection to the frame (arrow)

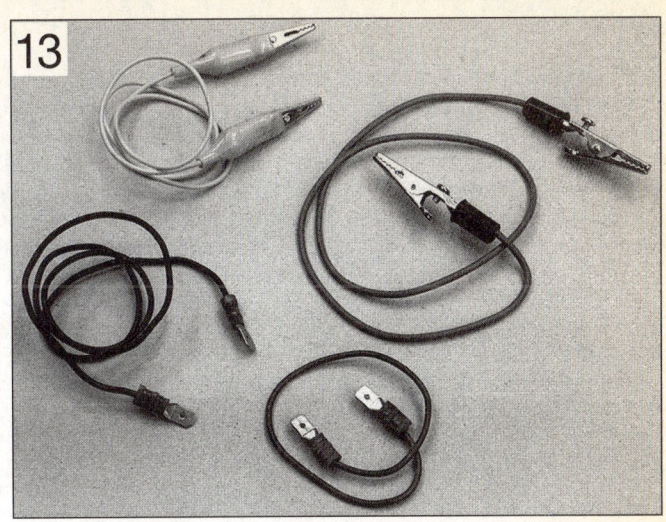

A selection of jumper wires for making ground checks

Checking the ground

● Ground connections are made either directly to the engine or frame (such as sensors, neutral switch etc. which only have a positive feed) or by a separate wire into the ground circuit of the wiring harness. Alternatively a short ground wire is sometimes run directly from the component to the motor-cycle's frame.
● Corrosion is often the cause of a poor ground connection.
● If total failure is experienced, check the security of the main ground lead from the negative (-) terminal of the battery and also the main ground point on the wiring harness. If corroded, dismantle the connection and clean all surfaces back to bare metal.
1 To check the ground on a component, use an insulated jumper wire to temporarily bypass its ground connection **(see illustration 13)**. Connect one end of the jumper wire between the ground terminal or metal body of the component and the other end to the motorcycle's frame.
2 If the circuit works with the jumper wire installed, the original ground circuit is faulty. Check the wiring for open-circuits or poor connections. Clean up direct ground connections, removing all traces of corrosion and remake the joint. Apply petroleum jelly to the joint to prevent future corrosion.

Tracing a short-circuit

● A short-circuit occurs where current shorts to ground bypassing the circuit components. This usually results in a blown fuse.

● A short-circuit is most likely to occur where the insulation has worn through due to wiring chafing on a component, allowing a direct path to ground on the frame.
1 Remove any body panels necessary to access the circuit wiring.
2 Check that all electrical switches in the circuit are OFF, then remove the circuit fuse and connect a test light, buzzer or voltmeter (set to the dc scale) across the fuse terminals. No voltage should be shown.
3 Move the wiring from side to side while observing the test light or meter. When the test light comes on, buzzer sounds or meter shows voltage, you have found the cause of the short. It will usually shown up as damaged or burned insulation.
4 Note that the same test can be performed on each component in the circuit, even the switch.

ATV Chemicals and Lubricants

A number of chemicals and lubricants are available for use in motorcycle maintenance and repair. They include a wide variety of products ranging from cleaning solvents and degreasers to lubricants and protective sprays for rubber, plastic and vinyl.

- **Contact point/spark plug cleaner** is a solvent used to clean oily film and dirt from points, grim from electrical connectors and oil deposits from spark plugs. It is oil free and leaves no residue. It can also be used to remove gum and varnish from carburetor jets and other orifices.

- **Carburetor cleaner** is similar to contact point/spark plug cleaner but it usually has a stronger solvent and may leave a slight oily residue. It is not recommended for cleaning electrical components or connections.

- **Brake system cleaner** is used to remove brake dust, grease and brake fluid from the brake system, where clean surfaces are absolutely necessary. It leaves no residue and often eliminates brake squeal caused by contaminants.

- **Silicone-based lubricants** are used to protect rubber parts such as hoses and grommets, and are used as lubricants for hinges and locks.

- **Multi-purpose grease** is an all purpose lubricant used wherever grease is more practical than a liquid lubricant such as oil. Some multi-purpose grease is colored white and specially formulated to be more resistant to water than ordinary grease.

- **Gear oil** (sometimes called gear lube) is a specially designed oil used in transmissions and final drive units, as well as other areas where high friction, high temperature lubrication is required. It is available in a number of viscosities (weights) for various applications.

- **Motor oil** is the lubricant formulated for use in engines. It normally contains a wide variety of additives to prevent corrosion and reduce foaming and wear. Motor oil comes in various weights (viscosity ratings) from 0 to 50. The recommended weight of the oil depends on the season, temperature and the demands on the engine. Light oil is used in cold climates and under light load conditions. Heavy oil is used in hot climates and where high loads are encountered. Multi-viscosity oils are designed to have characteristics of both light and heavy oils and are available in a number of weights from 0W-20 to 20W-50.

- **Gasoline additives** perform several functions, depending on their chemical makeup. They usually contain solvents that help dissolve gum and varnish that build up on carburetor and inlet parts. They also serve to break down carbon deposits that form on the inside surfaces of the combustion chambers. Some additives contain upper cylinder lubricants for valves and piston rings.

- **Brake and clutch fluid** is a specially formulated hydraulic fluid that can withstand the heat and pressure encountered in break/clutch systems. Care must be taken that this fluid does not come in contact with painted surfaces or plastics. An opened container should always be resealed to prevent contamination by water or dirt.

- **Chain lubricants** are formulated especially for use on motorcycle final drive chains. A good chain lube should adhere well and have good penetrating qualities to be effective as a lubricant inside the chain and on the side plates, pins and rollers. Most chain lubes are either the foaming type or quick drying type and are usually marketed as sprays. Take care to use a lubricant marked as being suitable for O-ring chains.

- **Degreasers** are heavy duty solvents used to remove grease and grime that may accumulate on the engine and frame components. They can be sprayed or brushed on and, depending on the type, are rinsed with either water or solvent.

- **Solvents** are used alone or in combination with degreasers to clean parts and assemblies during repair and overhaul. The home mechanic should use only solvents that are non-flammable and that do not produce irritating fumes.

- **Gasket sealing compounds** may be used in conjunction with gaskets, to improve their sealing capabilities, or alone, to seal metal-to-metal joints. Many gasket sealers can withstand extreme heat, some are impervious to gasoline and lubricants, while others are capable of filling and sealing large cavities. Depending on the intended use, gasket sealers either dry hard or stay relatively soft and pliable. They are usually applied by hand, with a brush or are sprayed on the gasket sealing surfaces.

- **Thread locking compound** is an adhesive locking compound that prevents threaded fasteners from loosening because of vibration. It is available in a variety of types for different applications.

- **Moisture dispersants** are usually sprays that can be used to dry out electrical components such as the fuse block and wiring connectors. Some types an also be used as treatment for rubber and as a lubricant for hinges, cables and locks.

- **Waxes and polishes** are used to help protect painted and plated surfaces from the weather. Different types of pain may require the use of different types of wax polish. Some polishes utilize a chemical or abrasive cleaner to help remove the top layer of oxidized (dull) paint on older vehicles. In recent years, many non-wax polishes (that contain a wide variety of chemicals such as polymers and silicones) have been introduced. These non-wax polishes are usually easier to apply and last longer than conventional waxes and polishes.

Technical Terms Explained

A

ABS (Anti-lock braking system) A system, usually electronically controlled, that senses incipient wheel lockup during braking and relieves hydraulic pressure at wheel which is about to skid.

Aftermarket Components suitable for the motorcycle, but not produced by the motorcycle manufacturer.

Allen key A hexagonal wrench which fits into a recessed hexagonal hole.

Alternating current (ac) Current produced by an alternator. Requires converting to direct current by a rectifier for charging purposes.

Alternator Converts mechanical energy from the engine into electrical energy to charge the battery and power the electrical system.

Ampere (amp) A unit of measurement for the flow of electrical current. Current = Volts ÷ Ohms.

Ampere-hour (Ah) Measure of battery capacity.

Angle-tightening A torque expressed in degrees. Often follows a conventional tightening torque for cylinder head or main bearing fasteners **(see illustration)**.

Angle-tightening cylinder head bolts

Antifreeze A substance (usually ethylene glycol) mixed with water, and added to the cooling system, to prevent freezing of the coolant in winter. Antifreeze also contains chemicals to inhibit corrosion and the formation of rust and other deposits that would tend to clog the radiator and coolant passages and reduce cooling efficiency.

Anti-dive System attached to the fork lower leg (slider) to prevent fork dive when braking hard.

Anti-seize compound A coating that reduces the risk of seizing on fasteners that are subjected to high temperatures, such as exhaust clamp bolts and nuts.

API American Petroleum Institute. A quality standard for 4-stroke motor oils.

Asbestos A natural fibrous mineral with great heat resistance, commonly used in the composition of brake friction materials. Asbestos is a health hazard and the dust created by brake systems should never be inhaled or ingested.

ATF Automatic Transmission Fluid. Often used in front forks.

ATU Automatic Timing Unit. Mechanical device for advancing the ignition timing on early engines.

ATV All Terrain Vehicle. Often called a Quad.

Axial play Side-to-side movement.

Axle A shaft on which a wheel revolves. Also known as a spindle.

B

Backlash The amount of movement between meshed components when one component is held still. Usually applies to gear teeth.

Ball bearing A bearing consisting of a hardened inner and outer race with hardened steel balls between the two races.

Bearings Used between two working surfaces to prevent wear of the components and a build-up of heat. Four types of bearing are commonly used on motorcycles: plain shell bearings, ball bearings, tapered roller bearings and needle roller bearings.

Bevel gears Used to turn the drive through 90°. Typical applications are shaft final drive and camshaft drive **(see illustration)**.

BHP Brake Horsepower. The British measurement for engine power output. Power output is now usually expressed in kilowatts (kW).

Bevel gears are used to turn the drive through 90°

Bias-belted tire Similar construction to radial tire, but with outer belt running at an angle to the wheel rim.

Big-end bearing The bearing in the end of the connecting rod that's attached to the crankshaft.

Bleeding The process of removing air from a hydraulic system via a bleed nipple or bleed screw.

Bottom-end A description of an engine's crankcase components and all components contained therein.

BTDC Before Top Dead Center in terms of piston position. Ignition timing is often expressed in terms of degrees or millimeters BTDC.

Bush A cylindrical metal or rubber component used between two moving parts.

Burr Rough edge left on a component after machining or as a result of excessive wear.

C

Cam chain The chain which takes drive from the crankshaft to the camshaft(s).

Canister The main component in an evaporative emission control system (California market only); contains activated charcoal granules to trap vapors from the fuel system rather than allowing them to vent to the atmosphere.

Castellated Resembling the parapets along the top of a castle wall. For example, a castellated wheel axle or spindle nut.

Catalytic converter A device in the exhaust system of some machines which

Technical Terms Explained

Cush drive rubber segments dampen out transmission shocks

converts certain pollutants in the exhaust gases into less harmful substances.

Charging system Description of the components which charge the battery, ie the alternator, rectifer and regulator.

Clearance The amount of space between two parts. For example, between a piston and a cylinder, between a bearing and a journal, etc.

Coil spring A spiral of elastic steel found in various sizes throughout a vehicle, for example as a springing medium in the suspension and in the valve train.

Compression Reduction in volume, and increase in pressure and temperature, of a gas, caused by squeezing it into a smaller space.

Compression damping Controls the speed the suspension compresses when hitting a bump.

Compression ratio The relationship between cylinder volume when the piston is at top dead center and cylinder volume when the piston is at bottom dead center.

Continuity The uninterrupted path in the flow of electricity. Little or no measurable resistance.

Continuity tester Self-powered bleeper or test light which indicates continuity.

Cp Candlepower. Bulb rating commonly found on US motorcycles.

Crossply tire Tire plies arranged in a criss-cross pattern. Usually four or six plies used, hence 4PR or 6PR in tire size codes.

Cush drive Rubber damper segments fitted between the rear wheel and final drive sprocket to absorb transmission shocks **(see illustration)**.

D

Degree disc Calibrated disc for measuring piston position. Expressed in degrees.

Dial gauge Clock-type gauge with adapters for measuring runout and piston position. Expressed in mm or inches.

Diaphragm The rubber membrane in a master cylinder or carburetor which seals the upper chamber.

Diaphragm spring A single sprung plate often used in clutches.

Direct current (dc) Current produced by a dc generator.

Decarbonization The process of removing carbon deposits - typically from the combustion chamber, valves and exhaust port/system.

Detonation Destructive and damaging explosion of fuel/air mixture in combustion chamber instead of controlled burning.

Diode An electrical valve which only allows current to flow in one direction. Commonly used in rectifiers and starter interlock systems.

Disc valve (or rotary valve) An induction system used on some two-stroke engines.

Double-overhead camshaft (DOHC) An engine that uses two overhead camshafts, one for the intake valves and one for the exhaust valves.

Drivebelt A toothed belt used to transmit drive to the rear wheel on some motorcycles. A drivebelt has also been used to drive the camshafts. Drivebelts are usually made of Kevlar.

Driveshaft Any shaft used to transmit motion. Commonly used when referring to the final driveshaft on shaft drive motorcycles.

E

ECU (Electronic Control Unit) A computer which controls (for instance) an ignition system, or an anti-lock braking system.

EGO Exhaust Gas Oxygen sensor. Sometimes called a Lambda sensor.

Electrolyte The fluid in a lead-acid battery.

EMS (Engine Management System) A computer controlled system which manages the fuel injection and the ignition systems in an integrated fashion.

Endfloat The amount of lengthways movement between two parts. As applied to a crankshaft, the distance that the crankshaft can move side-to-side in the crankcase.

Endless chain A chain having no joining link. Common use for cam chains and final drive chains.

EP (Extreme Pressure) Oil type used in locations where high loads are applied, such as between gear teeth.

Evaporative emission control system Describes a charcoal filled canister which stores fuel vapors from the tank rather than allowing them to vent to the atmosphere. Usually only fitted to California models and referred to as an EVAP system.

Expansion chamber Section of two-stroke engine exhaust system so designed to improve engine efficiency and boost power.

F

Feeler blade or gauge A thin strip or blade of hardened steel, ground to an exact thickness, used to check or measure clearances between parts.

Final drive Description of the drive from the transmission to the rear wheel. Usually by chain or shaft, but sometimes by belt.

Firing order The order in which the engine cylinders fire, or deliver their power strokes, beginning with the number one cylinder.

Flooding Term used to describe a high fuel level in the carburetor float chambers,

Technical Terms Explained

leading to fuel overflow. Also refers to excess fuel in the combustion chamber due to incorrect starting technique.

Free length The no-load state of a component when measured. Clutch, valve and fork spring lengths are measured at rest, without any preload.

Freeplay The amount of travel before any action takes place. The looseness in a linkage, or an assembly of parts, between the initial application of force and actual movement. For example, the distance the rear brake pedal moves before the rear brake is actuated.

Fuel injection The fuel/air mixture is metered electronically and directed into the engine intake ports (indirect injection) or into the cylinders (direct injection). Sensors supply information on engine speed and conditions.

Fuel/air mixture The charge of fuel and air going into the engine. See Stoichiometric ratio.

Fuse An electrical device which protects a circuit against accidental overload. The typical fuse contains a soft piece of metal which is calibrated to melt at a predetermined current flow (expressed as amps) and break the circuit.

G

Gap The distance the spark must travel in jumping from the center electrode to the side electrode in a spark plug. Also refers to the distance between the ignition rotor and the pickup coil in an electronic ignition system.

Gasket Any thin, soft material - usually cork, cardboard, asbestos or soft metal - installed between two metal surfaces to ensure a good seal. For instance, the cylinder head gasket seals the joint between the block and the cylinder head.

Gauge An instrument panel display used to monitor engine conditions. A gauge with a movable pointer on a dial or a fixed scale is an analog gauge. A gauge with a numerical readout is called a digital gauge.

Gear ratios The drive ratio of a pair of gears in a gearbox, calculated on their number of teeth.

Glaze-busting see Honing

Grinding Process for renovating the valve face and valve seat contact area in the cylinder head.

Ground return The return path of an electrical circuit, utilizing the motorcycle's frame.

Gudgeon pin The shaft which connects the connecting rod small-end with the piston. Often called a piston pin or wrist pin.

H

Helical gears Gear teeth are slightly curved and produce less gear noise that straight-cut gears. Often used for primary drives.

Helicoil A thread insert repair system. Commonly used as a repair for stripped spark plug threads **(see illustration)**.

Installing a Helicoil thread insert in a cylinder head

Honing A process used to break down the glaze on a cylinder bore (also called glaze-busting). Can also be carried out to roughen a rebored cylinder to aid ring bedding-in.

HT (High Tension) Description of the electrical circuit from the secondary winding of the ignition coil to the spark plug.

Hydraulic A liquid filled system used to transmit pressure from one component to another. Common uses on motorcycles are brakes and clutches.

Hydrometer An instrument for measuring the specific gravity of a lead-acid battery.

Hygroscopic Water absorbing. In motorcycle applications, braking efficiency will be reduced if DOT 3 or 4 hydraulic fluid absorbs water from the air - care must be taken to keep new brake fluid in tightly sealed containers.

I

lbf ft Pounds-force feet. A unit of torque. Sometimes written as ft-lbs.

lbf in Pound-force inch. A unit of torque, applied to components where a very low torque is required. Sometimes written as inch-lbs.

IC Abbreviation for Integrated Circuit.

Ignition advance Means of increasing the timing of the spark at higher engine speeds. Done by mechanical means (ATU) on early engines or electronically by the ignition control unit on later engines.

Ignition timing The moment at which the spark plug fires, expressed in the number of crankshaft degrees before the piston reaches the top of its stroke, or in the number of millimeters before the piston reaches the top of its stroke.

Infinity (∞) Description of an open-circuit electrical state, where no continuity exists.

Inverted forks (upside down forks) The sliders or lower legs are held in the yokes and the fork tubes or stanchions are connected to the wheel axle (spindle). Less unsprung weight and stiffer construction than conventional forks.

J

JASO Japan Automobile Standards Organization JASO MA is a standard for motorcycle oil equivalent to API SJ, but designed to prevent problems with wet-type motorcycle clutches.

Joule The unit of electrical energy.

Journal The bearing surface of a shaft.

K

Kickstart Mechanical means of turning the engine over for starting purposes.

REF•46 Technical Terms Explained

Only usually fitted to mopeds, small capacity motorcycles and off-road motorcycles.

Kill switch Handebar-mounted switch for emergency ignition cut-out. Cuts the ignition circuit on all models, and additionally prevent starter motor operation on others.

km Symbol for kilometer.

kmh Abbreviation for kilometers per hour.

L

Lambda sensor A sensor fitted in the exhaust system to measure the exhaust gas oxygen content (excess air factor). Also called oxygen sensor.

Lapping see **Grinding**.

LCD Abbreviation for Liquid Crystal Display.

LED Abbreviation for Light Emitting Diode.

Liner A steel cylinder liner inserted in an aluminum alloy cylinder block.

Locknut A nut used to lock an adjustment nut, or other threaded component, in place.

Lockstops The lugs on the lower triple clamp (yoke) which abut those on the frame, preventing handlebar-to-fuel tank contact.

Lockwasher A form of washer designed to prevent an attaching nut from working loose.

LT Low Tension Description of the electrical circuit from the power supply to the primary winding of the ignition coil.

M

Main bearings The bearings between the crankshaft and crankcase.

Maintenance-free (MF) battery A sealed battery which cannot be topped up.

Manometer Mercury-filled calibrated tubes used to measure intake tract vacuum. Used to synchronize carburetors on multi-cylinder engines.

Tappet shims are measured with a micrometer

Micrometer A precision measuring instrument that measures component outside diameters **(see illustration)**.

MON (Motor Octane Number) A measure of a fuel's resistance to knock.

Monograde oil An oil with a single viscosity, eg SAE80W.

Monoshock A single suspension unit linking the swingarm or suspension linkage to the frame.

mph Abbreviation for miles per hour.

Multigrade oil Having a wide viscosity range (eg 10W40). The W stands for Winter, thus the viscosity ranges from SAE10 when cold to SAE40 when hot.

Multimeter An electrical test instrument with the capability to measure voltage, current and resistance. Some meters also incorporate a continuity tester and buzzer.

N

Needle roller bearing Inner race of caged needle rollers and hardened outer race. Examples of uncaged needle rollers can be found on some engines. Commonly used in rear suspension applications and in two-stroke engines.

Nm Newton meters.

NOx Oxides of Nitrogen. A common toxic pollutant emitted by gasoline engines at higher temperatures.

O

Octane The measure of a fuel's resistance to knock.

OE (Original Equipment) Relates to components fitted to a motorcycle as standard or replacement parts supplied by the motorcycle manufacturer.

Ohm The unit of electrical resistance. Ohms = Volts ÷ Current.

Ohmmeter An instrument for measuring electrical resistance.

Oil cooler System for diverting engine oil outside of the engine to a radiator for cooling purposes.

Oil injection A system of two-stroke engine lubrication where oil is pump-fed to the engine in accordance with throttle position.

Open-circuit An electrical condition where there is a break in the flow of electricity - no continuity (high resistance).

O-ring A type of sealing ring made of a special rubber-like material; in use, the O-ring is compressed into a groove to provide the sealing action.

Oversize (OS) Term used for piston and ring size options fitted to a rebored cylinder.

Overhead cam (sohc) engine An engine with single camshaft located on top of the cylinder head.

Overhead valve (ohv) engine An engine with the valves located in the cylinder head, but with the camshaft located in the engine block or crankcase.

Oxygen sensor A device installed in the exhaust system which senses the oxygen content in the exhaust and converts this information into an electric current. Also called a Lambda sensor.

P

Plastigage A thin strip of plastic thread, available in different sizes, used for measuring clearances. For example, a strip of Plastigage is laid across a bearing journal. The parts are assembled and dismantled; the width of the crushed strip indicates the clearance between journal and bearing.

Polarity Either negative or positive ground, determined by which battery lead is connected to the frame (ground return). Modern motorcycles are usually negative ground.

Technical Terms Explained REF•47

Pre-ignition A situation where the fuel/air mixture ignites before the spark plug fires. Often due to a hot spot in the combustion chamber caused by carbon build-up. Engine has a tendency to 'run-on'.

Pre-load (suspension) The amount a spring is compressed when in the unloaded state. Preload can be applied by gas, spacer or mechanical adjuster.

Premix The method of engine lubrication on some gasoline two-stroke engines. Engine oil is mixed with the gasoline in the fuel tank in a specific ratio. The fuel/oil mix is sometimes referred to as "petrol".

Primary drive Description of the drive from the crankshaft to the clutch. Usually by gear or chain.

PS Pferdestärke - a German interpretation of BHP.

PSI Pounds-force per square inch. Imperial measurement of tire pressure and cylinder pressure measurement.

PTFE Polytetrafluroethylene. A low friction substance.

Pulse secondary air injection system A process of promoting the burning of excess fuel present in the exhaust gases by routing fresh air into the exhaust ports.

Q

Quartz halogen bulb Tungsten filament surrounded by a halogen gas. Typically used for the headlight (see illustration).

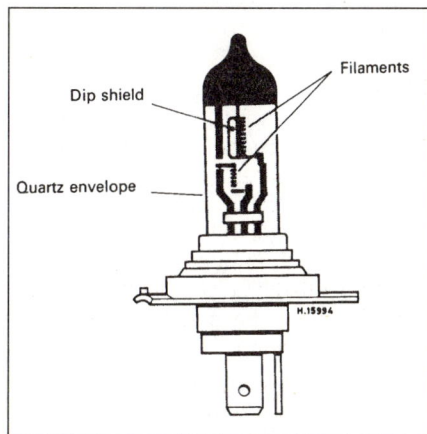

Quartz halogen headlight bulb construction

R

Rack-and-pinion A pinion gear on the end of a shaft that mates with a rack (think of a geared wheel opened up and laid flat). Sometimes used in clutch operating systems.

Radial play Up and down movement about a shaft.

Radial ply tires Tire plies run across the tire (from bead to bead) and around the circumference of the tire. Less resistant to tread distortion than other tire types.

Radiator A liquid-to-air heat transfer device designed to reduce the temperature of the coolant in a liquid cooled engine.

Rake A feature of steering geometry - the angle of the steering head in relation to the vertical (see illustration).

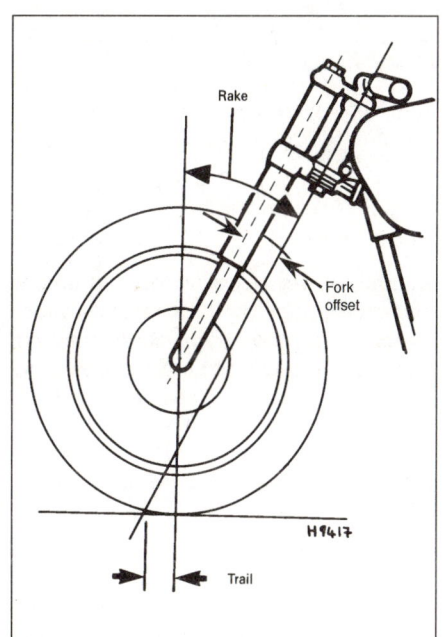

Steering geometry

Rebore Providing a new working surface to the cylinder bore by boring out the old surface. Necessitates the use of oversize piston and rings.

Rebound damping A means of controlling the oscillation of a suspension unit spring after it has been compressed. Resists the spring's natural tendency to bounce back after being compressed.

Rectifier Device for converting the ac output of an alternator into dc for battery charging.

Reed valve An induction system commonly used on two-stroke engines.

Regulator Device for maintaining the charging voltage from the generator or alternator within a specified range.

Relay A electrical device used to switch heavy current on and off by using a low current auxiliary circuit.

Resistance Measured in ohms. An electrical component's ability to pass electrical current.

RON (Research Octane Number) A measure of a fuel's resistance to knock.

rpm revolutions per minute.

Runout The amount of wobble (in-and-out movement) of a wheel or shaft as it's rotated. The amount a shaft rotates "out-of-true." The out-of-round condition of a rotating part.

S

SAE (Society of Automotive Engineers) A standard for the viscosity of a fluid.

Sealant A liquid or paste used to prevent leakage at a joint. Sometimes used in conjunction with a gasket.

Service limit Term for the point where a component is no longer useable and must be replaced.

Shaft drive A method of transmitting drive from the transmission to the rear wheel.

Shell bearings Plain bearings consisting of two shell halves. Most often used as big-end and main bearings in a four-stroke engine. Often called bearing inserts.

Shim Thin spacer, commonly used to adjust the clearance or relative positions between two parts. For example, shims inserted into or under tappets or followers to control valve clearances. Clearance is adjusted by changing the thickness of the shim.

Short-circuit An electrical condition where current shorts to ground bypassing the circuit components.

Technical Terms Explained

Skimming Process to correct warpage or repair a damaged surface, eg on brake discs or drums.

Slide-hammer A special puller that screws into or hooks onto a component such as a shaft or bearing; a heavy sliding handle on the shaft bottoms against the end of the shaft to knock the component free.

Small-end bearing The bearing in the upper end of the connecting rod at its joint with the gudgeon pin.

Snap-ring A ring-shaped clip used to prevent endwise movement of cylindrical parts and shafts. An internal snap-ring is installed in a groove in a housing; an external snap-ring fits into a groove on the outside of a cylindrical piece such as a shaft. Also known as a circlip.

Spalling Damage to camshaft lobes or bearing journals shown as pitting of the working surface.

Specific gravity (SG) The state of charge of the electrolyte in a lead-acid battery. A measure of the electrolyte's density compared with water.

Straight-cut gears Common type gear used on gearbox shafts and for oil pump and water pump drives.

Stanchion The inner sliding part of the front forks, held by the yokes. Often called a fork tube.

Stoichiometric ratio The optimum chemical air/fuel ratio for a gasoline engine, said to be 14.7 parts of air to 1 part of fuel.

Sulphuric acid The liquid (electrolyte) used in a lead-acid battery. Poisonous and extremely corrosive.

Surface grinding (lapping) Process to correct a warped gasket face, commonly used on cylinder heads.

T

Tapered-roller bearing Tapered inner race of caged needle rollers and separate tapered outer race. Examples of taper roller bearings can be found on steering heads.

Tappet A cylindrical component which transmits motion from the cam to the valve stem, either directly or via a pushrod and rocker arm. Also called a cam follower.

TCS Traction Control System. An electronically-controlled system which senses wheel spin and reduces engine speed accordingly.

TDC Top Dead Center denotes that the piston is at its highest point in the cylinder.

Thread-locking compound Solution applied to fastener threads to prevent loosening. Select type to suit application.

Thrust washer A washer positioned between two moving components on a shaft. For example, between gear pinions on gearshaft.

Timing chain See **Cam Chain**.

Timing light Stroboscopic lamp for carrying out ignition timing checks with the engine running.

Top-end A description of an engine's cylinder block, head and valve gear components.

Torque Turning or twisting force about a shaft.

Torque setting A prescribed tightness specified by the motorcycle manufacturer to ensure that the bolt or nut is secured correctly. Undertightening can result in the bolt or nut coming loose or a surface not being sealed. Overtightening can result in stripped threads, distortion or damage to the component being retained.

Torx key A six-point wrench.

Tracer A stripe of a second color applied to a wire insulator to distinguish that wire from another one with the same color insulator. For example, Br/W is often used to denote a brown insulator with a white tracer.

Trail A feature of steering geometry. Distance from the steering head axis to the tire's central contact point.

Triple clamps The cast components which extend from the steering head and support the fork stanchions or tubes. Often called fork yokes.

Turbocharger A centrifugal device, driven by exhaust gases, that pressurizes the intake air. Normally used to increase the power output from a given engine displacement.

TWI Abbreviation for Tire Wear Indicator. Indicates the location of the tread depth indicator bars on tires.

U

Universal joint or U-joint (UJ) A double-pivoted connection for transmitting power from a driving to a driven shaft through an angle. Typically found in shaft drive assemblies.

Unsprung weight Anything not supported by the bike's suspension (ie the wheel, tires, brakes, final drive and bottom (moving) part of the suspension).

V

Vacuum gauges Clock-type gauges for measuring intake tract vacuum. Used for carburetor synchronization on multi-cylinder engines.

Valve A device through which the flow of liquid, gas or vacuum may be stopped, started or regulated by a moveable part that opens, shuts or partially obstructs one or more ports or passageways. The intake and exhaust valves in the cylinder head are of the poppet type.

Valve clearance The clearance between the valve tip (the end of the valve stem) and the rocker arm or tappet/follower. The valve clearance is measured when the valve is closed. The correct clearance is important - if too small the valve won't close fully and will burn out, whereas if too large noisy operation will result.

Valve lift The amount a valve is lifted off its seat by the camshaft lobe.

Valve timing The exact setting for the opening and closing of the valves in relation to piston position.

Vernier caliper A precision measuring instrument that measures inside and outside dimensions. Not quite as accurate as a micrometer, but more convenient.

Technical Terms Explained REF•49

VIN Vehicle Identification Number. Term for the bike's engine and frame numbers.

Viscosity The thickness of a liquid or its resistance to flow.

Volt A unit for expressing electrical "pressure" in a circuit. Volts = current x ohms.

W

Water pump A mechanically-driven device for moving coolant around the engine.

Watt A unit for expressing electrical power. Watts = volts x current.

Wet liner arrangement

Wear limit see **Service limit**

Wet liner A liquid-cooled engine design where the pistons run in liners which are directly surrounded by coolant **(see illustration)**.

Wheelbase Distance from the center of the front wheel to the center of the rear wheel.

Wiring harness or loom Describes the electrical wires running the length of the motorcycle and enclosed in tape or plastic sheathing. Wiring coming off the main harness is usually referred to as a sub harness.

Woodruff key A key of semi-circular or square section used to locate a gear to a shaft. Often used to locate the alternator rotor on the crankshaft.

Wrist pin Another name for gudgeon or piston pin.

Reference

Trail rules

Just when you're ready to have some fun out in the dirt you get slapped with more rules. But by following these rules you'll ensure everyone's enjoyment, not just your own. It's important that all off-roaders follow these rules, as it will help to keep the trails open and keep us in good standing with other trail users. Really, these rules are no more than common sense and common courtesy.

• **Don't ride where you're not supposed to.** Stay off private property and obey all signs marking areas that are off limits to motorized vehicles. Also, as much fun as it might be, don't ride in State or Federal wilderness areas.

• **Leave the land as you found it.** When you've left the area, the only thing you should leave behind are your tire tracks. Stay on the trails, too. There are plenty of trails to ride on without blazing new ones. Be sure to carry out all litter that you create (and if you want to do a good deed, pick up any litter that you come across). Be sure to leave gates as you found them, or if the gate has a sign on it, comply with whatever the sign says (some people don't close gates after passing through them. Others may close gates when the landowner actually wants to keep them open).

• **Give other trail users the right-of-way.** There has been an ongoing dispute amongst trail users as to who belongs there and who doesn't. If the off-roading community shows respect and courtesy to hikers and equestrians, we stand a far better chance of being able to enjoy our sport in the years to come, and to keep the trails open for our children. When you ride up behind hikers or horses, give them plenty of room and pass slowly so as not to startle them. When you approach an equestrian from the opposite direction, stop your machine when the horse nears you so it won't get frightened and bolt.

• **Don't scare the animals!** Whether it be horses, cattle or wild animals like deer, rabbits or coyotes, leave them alone. Remember, you're visiting their home, so treat them with respect. Besides, startling animals can be dangerous. Loud noises or your sudden appearance can trigger an animal's defensive instinct, which could mean bad news for you.

• **Don't ride "over your head."** Sometimes the trails start to resemble ski runs, with a few irresponsible riders going so fast that they're barely able to maintain control of their bikes. They'd never be able to stop to avoid another trail user if they had to. Most collisions on the trail are caused by such individuals and the results are occasionally tragic. You should only ride fast in areas where you can clearly see a good distance ahead - never on trails with blind corners or rises high enough that prevent you from seeing what's on the other side.

• **Be prepared.** Carry everything you think you may need to make minor repairs should your machine break down. Know how to make basic repairs and keep your bike in good mechanical condition to minimize the chances of becoming stranded. Always let someone know where you're going, and ride with a friend whenever possible.

Index

Note: *References throughout this index are in the form, "Chapter number"•"Page number"*

A
About this manual, 0•7
Acknowledgements, 0•7
Air filter
　element and drain tube, cleaning, 1•11
　housing, removal and installation, 4B•8
Air/fuel mixture adjustment, 1•22
Alternator and regulator/rectifier, check and replacement, 5•7
ATV chemicals and lubricants, REF•42
Axle, rear
　hub and bearings, removal, inspection and installation, 7•15
　removal, inspection and installation, 6•9

B
Balljoints, removal, inspection and installation, 6•8
Battery
　charging, 5•4
　check, 1•19
　inspection and maintenance, 5•3
Brake
　fluid type, 1•2
　levers and pedal, check and adjustment, 1•6
　light switches, check, replacement and adjustment, 5•14
　system, general check, 1•6
Brake fluid level check, 0•13
Brakes
　caliper, removal, overhaul and installation
　　front, 7•5
　　rear, 7•8
　disc, inspection, removal and installation
　　front, 7•6
　　rear, 7•10
　hoses and lines, inspection and replacement, 7•14
　master cylinder, removal, overhaul and installation
　　front, 7•10
　　rear, 7•12
　pads, replacement
　　front, 7•4
　　rear, 7•7
　system bleeding, 7•15
Brakes, wheels and tires, 7•1
Bulb replacement, 5•12
Bumper, front, removal and installation, 9•2
Buying spare parts, 0•9

C
Caliper, brake, removal and installation
　front, 7•5
　rear, 7•8
Camshaft(s)
　and lifters, removal, inspection and installation, 2•11
　chain and guides, removal, inspection and installation, 2•30
　chain tensioner, removal, inspection and installation, 2•10
Carburetor
　disassembly, cleaning and inspection, 4A•4
　overhaul, general information, 4A•3
　pilot screw adjustment, 1•22
　reassembly, float check and accelerator pump check, 4A•7
　removal and installation, 4A•4
CDI unit (YFZ450), check, removal and installation, 5•6
Chain
　and sprockets, check, adjustment and lubrication, 1•8
　removal, cleaning, inspection and installation, 6•11
Chemicals and lubricants, REF•42
Choke (carbureted models), operation check, 1•19
Clutch
　lever freeplay, check and adjustment, 1•17
　primary drive gear and balancer, removal, inspection and installation, 2•31
　release mechanism, removal, inspection and installation, 2•26
　removal, inspection and installation, 2•26
Clutch switch, check and replacement, 5•13
Coil, ignition, check, removal and installation, 5•6
Conversion factors, REF•22
Coolant level check, 0•12
Coolant temperature sensor, check, removal and installation, 4B•15
Cooling system
　coolant reservoir, removal and installation, 3•2
　fan and circuit, check and switch replacement, 3•3
　hoses, removal and installation, 3•2
　inspection and coolant change, 1•16
　radiator and fan, removal and installation, 3•4
　radiator cap, check, 3•2
　water pump
　　removal, inspection and installation, 3•4
　　seals and bearing, replacement, 3•6
Crankcase
　components, inspection and servicing, 2•38
　covers, removal and installation, 2•24
　disassembly and reassembly, 2•37
Crankshaft and connecting rod, removal, inspection and installation, 2•41

Index

Crankshaft Position (CKP) sensor, check, removal and installation, 4B•14
Cylinder compression, check, 2•7
Cylinder head
 and valves, disassembly, inspection and reassembly, 2•16
 removal, inspection and installation, 2•15
Cylinder, removal, inspection and installation, 2•18

D

Daily (pre-ride) checks, 0•11
 brake fluid level check, 0•13
 coolant level check, 0•12
 engine/transmission oil level check, 0•11
 tire checks, 0•14
Diagnostic Trouble Codes (DTCs), accessing (YFZ450R), 4B•4
Dimensions and weights, REF•1
Disc, brake, inspection, removal and installation
 front, 7•6
 rear, 7•10
Drive chain
 and sprockets, check, adjustment and lubrication, 1•8
 removal, cleaning, inspection and installation, 6•11

E

Electrical troubleshooting, 5•3
Engine
 cam chain tensioner, removal, inspection and installation, 2•10
 camshaft chain and guides, removal, inspection and installation, 2•30
 camshafts and lifters, removal, inspection and installation, 2•11
 control module, removal and installation, 4B•15
 coolant temperature sensor, check, removal and installation, 4B•15
 crankcase
  components, inspection and servicing, 2•38
  covers, removal and installation, 2•24
  disassembly and reassembly, 2•37
 crankshaft and connecting rod, removal, inspection and installation, 2•41
 cylinder compression, check, 2•7

 cylinder head
  and valves, disassembly, inspection and reassembly, 2•16
  removal, inspection and installation, 2•15
 cylinder, removal, inspection and installation, 2•18
 disassembly and reassembly, general information, 2•9
 external oil tank and lines (YFZ450), removal and installation, 2•23
 initial start-up after overhaul, 2•42
 major repair, general note, 2•7
 oil pump, removal, inspection and installation, 2•33
 oil type and viscosity, 1•2
 operations possible with the engine in the frame, 2•7
 operations requiring engine removal, 2•7
 piston rings, installation, 2•21
 piston, removal, inspection and installation, 2•19
 recommended break-in procedure, 2•42
 removal and installation, 2•8
 valve cover, removal and installation, 2•10
 valves/valve seats/valve guides, servicing, 2•16
Engine coolant level check, 0•12
Engine oil and filter, change, 1•14
Engine, clutch and transmission, 2•1
Engine/transmission oil level check, 0•11
Exhaust system
 inspection, 1•21
 removal and installation
  YFZ450, 4A•8
  YFZ450R, 4B•15
External oil tank and lines (YFZ450), removal and installation, 2•23
External shift mechanism, removal, inspection and installation, 2•34

F

Fan and circuit, engine cooling system, check and switch replacement, 3•3
Fan, radiator, removal and installation, 3•4
Fasteners, check, 1•11
Fender, removal and installation
 front, 9•3
 rear, 9•4
Filter replacement
 air, 1•11
 engine oil, 1•14

Fluids and lubricants, recommended, 1•2
Footrests, removal and installation, 9•4
Fraction/decimal/millimeter equivalents, REF•23
Frame, general information, inspection and repair, 9•4
Front brake caliper, removal, overhaul and installation, 7•5
Front brake disc, inspection, removal and installation, 7•6
Front brake pads, replacement, 7•4
Front bumper, removal and installation, 9•2
Front wheel bearings, check, 1•10
Fuel system (YFZ450)
 carburetor
  disassembly, cleaning and inspection, 4A•4
  overhaul, general information, 4A•3
  reassembly, float check and accelerator pump check, 4A•7
  removal and installation, 4A•4
 fuel tank, removal and installation, 4A•3
 inspection, 1•12
 pilot screw adjustment, 1•22
 throttle cable, removal and installation, 4A•7
 throttle position sensor, check, removal and installation, 4A•9
Fuel system (YFZ450R)
 air filter housing, removal and installation, 4B•8
 Crankshaft Position (CKP) sensor, check, removal and installation, 4B•14
 engine control module, removal and installation, 4B•15
 engine coolant temperature sensor, check, removal and installation, 4B•15
 fuel injection system
  check, 4B•3
  general information, 4B•3
 fuel pressure relief procedure, 4B•5
 fuel pump, removal and installation, 4B•6
 fuel pump/fuel pressure, check, 4B•5
 fuel rail and injector, removal and installation, 4B•11
 Idle Speed Control (ISC) valve, check, 4B•9
 inspection, 1•12
 Intake Air Pressure (IAP) sensor, check and replacement, 4B•13
 Intake Air Temperature (IAT) sensor, check, removal and installation, 4B•13

Index

lean angle sensor, check and replacement, 4B•15
self-diagnosis system and trouble codes, 4B•4
tank, removal and installation, 4B•7
throttle body, removal and installation, 4B•9
throttle cable, removal and installation, 4B•11
throttle position sensor, check, adjustment and replacement, 4B•9
Vehicle Speed Sensor (VSS), check, removal and installation, 4B•14

Fuel tank
cover, removal and installation, 9•2
removal and installation
YFZ450, 4A•3
YFZ450R, 4B•7

Fuse, check and replacement, 5•4

H

Handlebar, removal and installation, 6•4
Headlight adjustment, 5•13
Hub, removal and installation
front, 7•3
rear, 7•9

I

Identification numbers, 0•8
Idle Speed Control (ISC) valve, check, 4B•9
Idle speed, check and adjustment, 1•18
Ignition and electrical systems, 5•1
alternator and regulator/rectifier, check and replacement, 5•7
battery
charging, 5•4
inspection and maintenance, 5•3
brake light switches, check, replacement and adjustment, 5•14
bulb replacement, 5•12
CDI unit (YFZ450), check, removal and installation, 5•6
clutch switch, check and replacement, 5•13
electrical troubleshooting, 5•3
fuse, check and replacement, 5•4
headlight adjustment, 5•13
ignition coil, check, removal and installation, 5•6
ignition system, check, 5•5
kill switch, check, removal and installation, 5•9

lighting circuit, check, 5•12
main key switch, check and replacement, 5•14
main relay check (YFZ450R), check and replacement, 5•14
neutral switch, check and replacement, 5•13
slipper clutch, removal, inspection and installation, 5•11
starter circuit, component check and replacement, 5•9
starter clutch, removal, inspection and installation, 5•11
starter motor, check and replacement, 5•10
starter reduction gears, removal and installation, 5•10

Ignition system
check, 5•5
coil, check, removal and installation, 5•6

Initial start-up after overhaul, 2•42
Intake Air Pressure (IAP) sensor, check and replacement, 4B•13
Intake Air Temperature (IAT) sensor, check, removal and installation, 4B•13
Introduction, 0•4
Introduction to tune-up and routine maintenance, 1•6

K

Kill switch, check, removal and installation, 5•9
Knuckles, steering, removal, inspection and installation, 6•8

L

Lean angle sensor, check and replacement, 4B•15
Lighting circuit, check, 5•12
Lubricants and chemicals, REF•42
Lubrication, general, 1•10

M

Main key switch, check and replacement, 5•14
Main relay check (YFZ450R), check and replacement, 5•14
Maintenance points, 1•4
Maintenance record, 0•15
Major engine repair, general note, 2•7

Master cylinder, brake, removal, overhaul and installation
front, 7•10
rear, 7•12
Mixture screw adjustment, 1•22

N

Neutral switch, check and replacement, 5•13

O

Oil level check, engine/transmission, 0•11
Oil pump, removal, inspection and installation, 2•33
Oil, engine, type and viscosity, 1•2
Operations possible with the engine in the frame, 2•7
Operations requiring engine removal, 2•7

P

Pads, brake, replacement
front, 7•4
rear, 7•7
Pilot screw adjustment, 1•22
Piston rings, installation, 2•21
Piston, removal, inspection and installation, 2•19
Primary drive gear and balancer, removal, inspection and installation, 2•31

R

Radiator and fan, removal and installation, 3•4
Radiator cap, check, 3•2
Rear axle
hub and bearings, removal, inspection and installation, 7•15
removal, inspection and installation, 6•9
Rear brake
caliper, removal, overhaul and installation, 7•8
disc, inspection, removal and installation, 7•10
pads, replacement, 7•7
Rear wheel hubs, removal and installation, 7•9
Recommended break-in procedure, 2•42

Index

Recommended lubricants and fluids, 1•2
Regulator/rectifier, voltage, check and replacement, 5•7
Reservoir, coolant, removal and installation, 3•2
Rotor, brake, inspection, removal and installation
  front, 7•6
  rear, 7•10
Routine maintenance, 1•1
Routine maintenance intervals, 1•3

S

Safety first!, 0•10
Seat, removal and installation, 9•2
Self-diagnosis system and trouble codes (YFZ450R), 4B•4
Service record, 0•15
Shock absorbers, removal, installation and adjustment, 6•5
Shock linkage and swingarm, removal and installation, 6•9
Side covers, removal and installation, 9•3
Skid plates
  check, 1•11
  removal and installation, 9•4
Slipper clutch, removal, inspection and installation, 5•11
Spark plug
  inspection, cleaning and gapping, 1•13
  type and gap, 1•1
Sprockets, check and replacement, 6•11
Starter
  circuit, component check and replacement, 5•9
  clutch, removal, inspection and installation, 5•11
  motor, check and replacement, 5•10
  reduction gears, removal and installation, 5•10
Steering
  knuckles, removal, inspection and installation, 6•8
  shaft, removal, inspection and installation, 6•4
  system, inspection and toe-in adjustment, 1•8
Storage, REF•24
Suspension, check, 1•8
Suspension arms and balljoints, removal, inspection and installation, 6•8
Swingarm
  and shock linkage, removal and installation, 6•9
  bearings
    check, 6•9
    replacement, 6•11

T

Technical terms explained, REF•43
Tensioner, cam chain, removal, inspection and installation, 2•10
Throttle body, removal and installation, 4B•9
Throttle cable and speed limiter, check and adjustment, 1•18
Throttle cable, removal and installation
  YFZ450, 4A•7
  YFZ450R, 4B•11
Throttle position sensor
  YFZ450, check, removal and installation, 4A•9
  YFZ450R, check, adjustment and replacement, 4B•9
Tie-rods, removal, inspection and installation, 6•7
Tire checks, 0•14
Tires
  general check, 1•10
  general information, 7•3
Tools and workshop tips, REF•4
Trail rules, REF•50
Transmission
  external shift mechanism, removal, inspection and installation, 2•34
  shafts and shift drums, removal, inspection and installation, 2•38
Trouble codes, accessing (YFZ450R), 4B•4
Troubleshooting, REF•27
Troubleshooting equipment, REF•38
Tune-up and routine maintenance, 1•1

V

Valve clearance specification, 1•1
Valve clearance, check and adjustment, 1•19
Valve cover, removal and installation, 2•10
Valves/valve seats/valve guides, servicing, 2•16
Vehicle Speed Sensor (VSS), check, removal and installation, 4B•14
Voltage regulator/rectifier, check and replacement, 5•7

W

Water pump
  removal, inspection and installation, 3•4
  seals and bearing, replacement, 3•6
Wheel(s)
  front hub and bearing, removal and installation, 7•3
  general check, 1•10
  inspection, removal and installation, 7•3
  rear hubs, removal and installation, 7•9
Winterizing, REF•24
Wiring diagram
  YFZ450, 9•1
  YFZ450R, 9•2
Workshop tips, REF•4